# The Figural Jew

**RELIGION AND POSTMODERNISM**
A Series Edited by Thomas A. Carlson

RECENT BOOKS IN THE SERIES

*Displacing Christian Origins: Philosophy, Secularity, and the New Testament*, by Ward Blanton (2007)

*After God*, by Mark C. Taylor (2007)

*The Indiscrete Image: Infinitude and Creation of the Human*, by Thomas A. Carlson (2008)

*Islam and the West: A Conversation with Jacques Derrida*, by Mustapha Chérif, translated by Teresa Lavender Fagan with a foreword by Giovanna Borradori (2008)

*The Gift of Death, Second Edition, and Literature in Secret*, by Jacques Derrida, translated by David Wills (2008)

# The Figural Jew

*Politics and Identity in*
*Postwar French Thought*

SARAH HAMMERSCHLAG

*The University of Chicago Press   Chicago and London*

PUBLICATION OF THIS BOOK HAS BEEN AIDED
BY A GRANT FROM THE BEVINGTON FUND.

SARAH HAMMERSCHLAG is assistant professor of Jewish
thought in the Department of Religion at Williams College.

The University of Chicago Press, Chicago 60637
The University of Chicago Press, Ltd., London
© 2010 by Sarah Hammerschlag
All rights reserved. Published 2010
Printed in the United States of America
19 18 17 16 15 14 13 12 11 10     1 2 3 4 5

ISBN-13: 978-0-226-31511-9 (cloth)
ISBN-13: 978-0-226-31512-6 (paper)
ISBN-10: 0-226-31511-8 (cloth)
ISBN-10: 0-226-31512-6 (paper)

Library of Congress Cataloging-in-Publication Data
Hammerschlag, Sarah.
    The figural Jew : politics and identity in postwar French thought /
Sarah Hammerschlag.
        p.    cm. — (Religion and postmodernism).
    Includes bibliographical references and index.
    ISBN-13: 978-0-226-31511-9 (hardcover : alk. paper)
    ISBN-13: 978-0-226-31512-6 (pbk. : alk. paper)
    ISBN-10: 0-226-31511-8 (hardcover : alk. paper)
    ISBN-10: 0-226-31512-6 (pbk. : alk. paper)
    1. Philosophy, Jewish—France—20th century.   2. Philosophy,
French—20th century.   3. Jews—Identity.   4. Blanchot, Maurice.
5. Derrida, Jacques.   6. Lévinas, Emmanuel.   7. Sartre, Jean-Paul,
1905–1980.   I. Title.   II. Series: Religion and postmodernism.
B2421.H25   2010
194—dc22                                              2009026828

*For Ryan, it is by the radiance of your mind and spirit that I light my days.*

*In memory of Gerson Tabor*

Men search for themselves in their unconditional foreignness.

EMMANUEL LEVINAS, *HUMANISM OF THE OTHER*

Denn der Jud, du weißts, was hat er schon, das ihm auch wirklich gehört, das nicht geborgt wär, ausgeliehen und nicht zurückgegeben. . . .

PAUL CELAN, *GESPRÄCH IM GEBIRG*

There remains the question of knowing what Judaism as a figure is. . . .

JACQUES DERRIDA, *QUESTIONING JUDAISM* (INTERVIEW WITH ELISABETH WEBER)

# Contents

# Acknowledgments

Over the course of the seven years it took to write, revise, rewrite, and edit this book, I have been, at times, a stubborn and persistent researcher, a frustrated and despondent writer, and a passionate and overzealous scholar. There have been a number of people who have not only had to bear the consequences of these states but also supported and encouraged me, reminding me that—in the words of David Tracy quoting Julian of Norwich—"all will be well, all manner of things will be well."

At the University of Chicago, my mentor, Françoise Meltzer, kept my sights set high. She read closely, edited deftly, and asked all the hardest questions. Paul Mendes-Flohr inspired the project on a fateful Saturday morning in Hutch Commons. Arnold Davidson's strategic savvy and improvisational skill have turned many an ill-formed thought of mine into an eloquent argument. The Martin Marty Center gave me financial support and also provided indispensable intellectual feedback.

I am indebted as well to the Erasmus Institute at the University of Notre Dame, to the National Foundation for Jewish Culture for the Maurice and Marilyn Cohen Doctoral Dissertation Fellowship in Jewish Studies, and to the University of Chicago Center in Paris for their support.

Williams College has provided the most hospitable environment imaginable for my scholarship and teaching. I am grateful to both chairs of the Religion Department at Williams, Bill Darrow and Denise Buell, for their generosity and encouragement. My colleagues in the Religion Department and the Jewish Studies Program were immensely helpful to me in myriad ways. Ali Garbarini has been a wonderful friend and a sage counselor. Edan Dekel has proved to be an unending font of knowledge and encouragement. Both Mark C. Taylor and Denise Buell generously read parts of the manuscript, provided outstanding feedback, and helped me navigate the field of academic publishing.

In preparing the manuscript for publication, I benefited from the wisdom of many. No one has been more instrumental in the editing process than Amy Hollywood, who read and commented on every word, offering her—as always—brilliant suggestions, and generously giving me huge chunks of her time, despite her commitments to so many others in the sandbox. I am additionally grateful to Wendy Lochner for her patience and encouragement. Alan Thomas and Randy Petilos at the University of Chicago Press were indispensable resources and guides throughout the process. Joseph Brown painstakingly combed the text for errors and improved it immensely by his work. Tom Carlson did much more for me than act as series editor. His influence goes back to 1998 when he discovered my interest in Edmond Jabès and encouraged me to read Emmanuel Levinas. I owe thanks as well to Leora Batnitzky, David Myers, Sam Moyn, Dana Hollander, Martin Kavka, and the anonymous readers of my manuscript, whose comments and criticism helped make this a better book.

Some material from chapter 3 and 4 appeared in "Reading May '68 through a Levinasian Lens: Alain Finkielkraut, Maurice Blanchot, and the Politics of Identity," *Jewish Quarterly Review* 98, no. 4 (2008): 522–51. Reprinted by permission of the University of Pennsylvania Press. Portions of chapter 5 appeared in "Another, Other Abraham: Derrida's Figuring of Levinas's Judaism," *Shofar* 26, no. 4 (Summer 2008): 74–96. Reprinted by permission of Purdue University Press. My thanks to these publishers for permission to reprint this material here.

I would never have been able to complete this project without the love and sustaining support of friends and family. My mother has (only half jestingly) referred to me as a philosopher since I was in preschool and inspired me to read thoughtfully and write carefully for as long as I can remember. My father gave me the bullheaded courage to scramble over many an obstacle, geologic and intellectual alike. Bonnie Hammerschlag and Del Persinger looked past my foibles and treated me as their own. Thanks are due as well to Sarabinh Levy-Brightman, Charles Stang, Jeff Israel, and Dina Berin for their friendship and advice. Finally, I owe gratitude above all to the man who became my roommate, fiancé, husband, and partner in parenthood all in the years that it took to write this book.

# Introduction

I am the last Jewish intellectual. You do not know anyone else like that. All the other Jewish intellectuals are masters from the suburbs. From Amos Oz to those who live here in America, so that I am the last one, the authentic follower of Adorno. I will articulate it like this: I am a Jewish Palestinian.

EDWARD SAID, "MY RIGHT OF RETURN"

## "Nous sommes tous des juifs allemands"

In November 1967, at a seemingly peripheral suburban outpost campus of the University of Paris, a handful of students calling themselves *les enragés*[1] initiated a university boycott over a series of government educational initiatives called the Fouchet Reforms.[2] What began as a squabble over required lab sessions and educational bureaucracy climaxed by May 1968 in a national uprising. At stake was not merely the structure of the university or anything as concrete as fair wages or work hours. Rather, the students aimed for a complete cultural transformation, the dismantling of structures of power, the elevation of freedom and creativity to the highest echelon of value. The walls of the Sorbonne were painted with demands: "It is forbidden to forbid," "All power to the imagination," "Answer exams with questions," "We want a world, new and original,"

---

Epigraph: Edward Said, "My Right of Return," reprinted in *Power, Politics and Culture: Interviews with Edward W. Said*, ed. Gauri Viswanathan (New York: Pantheon, 2001), 458.

1. A reference to one of the radical factions of the 1789 revolution.

2. For an analysis of why the protests began in Nanterre, see Alain Touraine, *The May Movement: Revolt and Reform*, trans. Leonard F. X. Mayhew (New York: Random House, 1971), 120–55.

"We refuse a world where the assurance of not dying from hunger is exchanged for the risk of dying from boredom."[3] At the center of this idealism was an unlikely French hero: the German Jew Daniel Cohn-Bendit. While refusing to claim for himself a role of leadership, resisting the very terms of authority, Cohn-Bendit was, nonetheless, both catalyst and symbol of the movement.[4] His status as foreigner and Jew made him a lightning rod, signaling as it did the radical nature of the students' demands, their dissociation from the old guard, and their rejection of French patriotism as an unquestionable value. At no moment was that clearer than on May 23, when the government announced that he would be blocked from reentering France.[5]

During the third week of May, tides had begun to turn against the student movement; spirits were low, and there was a lull in action. The Council of Ministers, sensing a return to order, issued the prohibition against Cohn-Bendit's reentry. This government decision reignited the students' fervor almost immediately.[6] Responding to the news broadcast over Paris radio, the crowds, without directive, organization, or planning, reassembled spontaneously. The same energy that many thought had finally been drained out of the protests animated the marchers and brought the protests to a head.[7] Pouring into the Place St. Michel, and heading en masse toward Montparnasse, thousands joined their voices in the streets, uniting under the cry: "Nous sommes tous des juifs allemands."[8] Under the banner of this cry, the students initiated a new wave

3. Andrew Feenberg and Jim Freedman, *When Poetry Ruled the Streets: The French May Events of 1968* (Albany: State University of New York Press, 2001), 38.

4. Cohn-Bendit first gained notoriety in 1966 when he faced expulsion from Nanterre for having disrupted the dedication of new campus athletic buildings, by publicly reproaching the minister of youth and sport for not having addressed the issue of sexuality in his white paper on youth. Touraine, *The May Movement*, 139.

5. Cohn-Bendit had made a brief trip to Germany and the Netherlands to help spread the student movement but was prohibited from returning. He nonetheless found his way back to Paris. According to his own account, he walked through the forest from Germany into France and "took a comfortable car to Paris." See Feenberg and Freedman, *When Poetry Ruled the Streets*, 62. See also Laurent Joffrin, *Mai 68: Histoire des événements* (Paris: Seuil, 1988), 212.

6. Feenberg and Freedman, *When Poetry Ruled the Streets*, 50.

7. On May 23, 1968, *Le monde* reported that with this decision the government had "once more failed to estimate the risks involved." One distinctive element of this moment is the fact that it marks a split between the students and the Communist Party and CGT (Confédération général du travail), which did not condemn the interdiction order against Cohn-Bendit and subsequently planned their own protests. See Joffrin, *Mai 68*, 213.

8. The chant was derived from posters made by the action committee at the École des beaux-arts that showed Cohn-Bendit's face. One poster read: "Nous sommes tous des juifs et des allemands." Another read: "Nous sommes tous 'indésirables.'" See Jonathan Judaken, *Jean-Paul Sartre and the Jewish Question: Anti-Antisemitism and the Politics of the French Intellectual* (Lincoln: University of Nebraska Press, 2006), 220.

of combat that lasted into the following day and culminated almost a week later in de Gaulle's May 29 dramatic departure from the capital.

On one level, the function of the slogan "We are all German Jews" was straightforward: it was a rallying cry, a statement of solidarity with the movement's leader and a response to the suspicion voiced in the Gaullist and Communist press that the ferment was being stirred up by foreign instigators.[9] Capitalizing on the historical resonances between the de Gaulle government's action and the Vichy government's anti-Jewish legislation of 1940 and 1941, which included provisions with restrictions on traveling Jews and authorizing the internment of those Jews who were foreign born, this slogan allowed for the easy (although obviously unfair) analogy between the de Gaulle government, Petain, and, by proxy, National Socialism.[10] Thus, the phrase underscored the position of the students as victims of an oppressive and authoritative regime. Simultaneously, it reenacted the ideal of *fraternité*, as illustrated by the students' insistence that nothing separated their status from that of their foreign-born Jewish leader.

Given this interpretation, the students' expression of solidarity may seem like a demonstration of the French republican spirit, one that recalls the position of the Dreyfusards some seventy years earlier. The intellectuals and politicians who defended Alfred Dreyfus, the Jewish French army captain accused of treason in 1894, were also fighting for the rights of an individual suspected of foreign sensibilities; they too rallied for justice in the name of a brotherhood that transcends the particularity of origins.[11] This parallel, however, does not take into account one remarkable difference: during the Dreyfus affair, those who rallied for Dreyfus's cause did so in the name of the Enlightenment ideal of humanity, an ideal uniting men above and beyond their differences.[12] They protested the suspicion directed at Dreyfus *as a Jew* and established their solidarity with him as a man and as a French citizen. As Émile Zola famously wrote to President Faure: "I have but one passion, that of the

9. Mark Poster, *Existential Marxism in Postwar France: From Sartre to Althusser* (Princeton, NJ: Princeton University Press, 1975), 392.

10. On the use of references to Nazi Germany in the May '68 revolt, see Patrick Seale and Maureen McConville, *Red Flag/Black Flag: French Revolution 1968* (New York: Putnam's, 1968), 29.

11. On the role of memory in May '68, see Raymond Aron, *La Révolution introuvable* (Paris: Fayard, 1968), translated by Gordon Clough as *The Elusive Revolution: Anatomy of a Student Revolt* (New York: Praeger, 1969). Aron describes the student revolt as a psychodrama, as the acting out or mimicking of revolution, where the participants referenced the heroes and scoundrels of past revolutions, role-playing according to their self-understood position in the conflict (33–34; 21–23).

12. This is, of course, something of an oversimplification. Chapter 1 complicates this narrative by considering the cases of Charles Péguy and Bernard Lazare.

Enlightenment, in the name of the humanity that has suffered so much and that has a right to happiness."[13] Dreyfus's Judaism was, for his supporters, almost beside the point.

The student protestors of May '68, in contrast, allied themselves with Cohn-Bendit by adopting his Jewish identity. They protested, not in the name of an idea of humanity, but in the name of "the Jew"; instead of claiming the status of the universal for Cohn-Bendit, they claimed the status of exception, of Jewish particularity, for themselves.[14]

From the very beginning, this statement sparked controversy. For some, it was a revolutionary moment in politics, marking a new form of political expression; for others, it was an occasion for skepticism and disgust. In *The Imaginary Jew*, Alain Finkielkraut, the child of two Jewish war refugees, describes his ambivalence over the slogan as a sincere sense of pride and victory that the identity of the Jew had developed a signification worthy of identification combined with a sense of infraction at the realization that with this identification the Jew lost the position of exception. He felt, he writes, as if he had been despoiled, the treasure of his identity "sullied [*galvaudait*]."[15] Out of this reaction, Finkielkraut develops a critique of the political impulse to identify with the outsider. Jews, he argues in his 2003 volume *Au nom de l'autre*, are the victims of this impulse, not its beneficiaries. For this desire to identify with the other marks a turn on the Left toward a "regime of equivalence" that is, he suggests, partially responsible for the newest form of anti-Semitism.[16] More recently, Finkielkraut noted with disgust the statement made by Edward Said, quoted by Tzvetan Todorov in a eulogy, that he was the last of the Jews. The claim to be the new Jews, "the ethical Jews," is for Finkielkraut the latest frontier, the latest battle to deprive "the ethnic Jews" of even their

13. "Je n'ai qu'une passion, celle de la lumière, au nom de l'humanité qui a tant souffert et qui a droit au bonheur" ("J'accuse," *L'aurore*, January 13, 1898).

14. On the Jewish element of May '68, see Judaken, *Jean-Paul Sartre and the Jewish Question*, chaps. 7–8. Jean-Michel Chaumont argues that one can date the moment that difference—Jewish difference—entered on the political scene as a positive value. He argues that the change occurred in 1967 and points to a conference held in New York on Jewish cultural values after the Holocaust by the journal *Judaism*. What emerges among the interlocutors (Emil Fackenheim, Elie Wiesel, George Steiner, and Richard H. Popkin), according to Chaumont, is that the language of Jewish election begins to infuse the historical understanding of the Holocaust, and, with it, the need arises to distinguish Jewish suffering as exemplary of human suffering and, thus, both unique and universally significant. See Jean-Michel Chaumont, *La concurrence des victimes: Génocide, identité, reconnaissance* (Paris, La découverte, 1997), 101–5. For the proceedings of the conference, see "Jewish Values in the Post-Holocaust Future: A Symposium," *Judaism*, no. 3 (1967): 266–99.

15. Alain Finkielkraut, *Le juif imaginaire* (Paris: Seuil, 1980), 26, translated by Kevin O'Neill and David Suchoff as *The Imaginary Jew* (Lincoln: University of Nebraska Press, 1994), 18.

16. Alain Finkielkraut, *Au nom de l'autre: Réflexions sur l'antisémitisme qui vient* (Paris: Gallimard, 2003).

identity.[17] For him, the potential for this slide has its origin in the slogan of 1968, in the use of Judaism as an emblem for victim and outsider, an emblem whose content is easily transferable.

Others have analyzed the slogan quite differently. In contrast with Finkielkraut, the novelist and literary critic Maurice Blanchot—who as a member of the Comité d'action étudiants-écrivains (Student Writers Action Committee) was deeply involved in the events—not only lauded the students' chant as one of the most powerful political acts in modern France, but also seemed to do so for the reason that Finkielkraut criticized the act: the students were taking up the position of the outsider, rather than defending their own Frenchness. For this very reason, Blanchot called it an "inaugural speech-event, opening and overturning borders." Recalling Walter Benjamin's analysis of revolution in the "Theses on the Philosophy of History," he went so far as to call the protestors' spontaneous initiation of the chant "messianic" in its dimensions.[18]

The philosopher Jacques Rancière in his frequent analyses of May '68 has exposed the complexity and political force behind what Finkielkraut dismisses as a usurpation of the position of the Jew. According to Rancière, the students' actions signaled quite the opposite. Rather than trying to possess the rightful position of an other, they were disavowing their own right to possess the legitimate identity of citizen. It was an incident of what he has termed *disidentification*. The students refused to identify with their own interest, their own social status, or their own nation-state.[19] Instead, they aligned themselves with a designation that could not, in fact, be assumed, one whose symbolic power derived from its inadmissibility. On the basis of this impossible association, they refused the terms of citizenship that defined them and resisted being counted among the French people. In making the term *German Jews* a "shared category," the students did not usurp the position of an other but formed an identity whose very significance arose from the fact that it was "no longer sociologically classifiable."[20]

According to Rancière's interpretation in *Aux bords du politique*, it is, in fact, the impropriety of the students' performance that makes it

17. Alain Finkielkraut, "Les juifs face à la religion de l'humanité," *Le débat* 131 (September–October 2004): 15.

18. Maurice Blanchot, "Les actions exemplaires," *Comité*, October 1, 1968, reprinted in Maurice Blanchot, *Écrits politiques, 1958–1993* (Paris: Lignes, 2003), 125, and Maurice Blanchot, *The Blanchot Reader*, trans. Christopher C. Stevens, ed. Michael Holland (Cambridge: Blackwell, 1995), 205.

19. Jacques Rancière, *La mésentente* (Paris: Galilée, 1995), 173, translated by Julie Rose as *Disagreement: Politics and Philosophy* (Minneapolis: University of Minnesota Press, 1999), 127.

20. See Kristin Ross, *May '68 and Its Afterlives* (Chicago: University of Chicago Press, 2002), 56; and Jacques Rancière, *Aux bords du politique* (Paris: La fabrique, 1998), 157.

effective and marks it as indicative of what he calls the entrance into the political sphere of "the cause of the Other." It is not an identification with the victim but a refusal to identify with a "certain self," the self that belongs to the nation. Thus, the chant does not mark the appearance of a new political subject; rather, it inverts "a stigmatized name in order to make it the principle of an open subjectivation of the uncounted, without confusing it with any representation of a socially identifiable group."[21] In an act of disidentification, the students aligned themselves with a name that could not be appropriated. In doing so, they marked the gap between their own position and that of the French nation as well as the gap between the French nation's account of the people and the people's own account of themselves.

Rancière's explanation effectively accounts for the political power of the chant and offers a powerful counternarrative to Finkielkraut's assumption that the students had appropriated the status of victim, seized the position of tragic hero.[22] It ignores, however, the specificity of their claim. Rancière, in his analysis of the event, is interested in the negative element of the students' gesture, the implication for those with whom the students chose *not* to identify. In that sense, *German Jews* functions as an empty signifier, one whose significance arises merely from its position as off-limits. It is clear that, in identifying with the German Jews, the students were identifying with those who had been made invisible, the annihilated. But is it not significant with whom the students did align themselves? To ignore the specificity of the students' gesture ignores the very powerful resonance that *Jewishness* had acquired in France by 1968 and, thus, misses the power of the trope.

In identifying with German Jews, the students made a gesture that was far more historic than either Finkielkraut or Rancière have allowed. For it does not mark just a moment in the history of the role of the outsider in politics; it marks a turning point in the history of the significance of the Jew as French cultural and political symbol. In order to be restored to its proper importance, this moment has to be considered within a history of the meaning of this symbol. By 1968, the statement "We are all German Jews" resonated as a gesture of resistance against the dominant mode of identification, not only because the students could not themselves properly identify as German Jews, but also because the idea of the Jew had developed its own significance as a symbol of the improper: what does not belong and to which nothing properly belongs. As Paul

---

21. Rancière, *Aux bords du politique*, 157.
22. Finkielkraut, *Le juif imaginaire*, 25–45, and *The Imaginary Jew*, 17–34.

Celan wrote in 1959: "The Jew, you know, what does he have that properly belongs to him, that wasn't borrowed, lent, and never returned."[23]


## Sans Racines

As a symbol, the figure of the Jew has been marked in French history by its unstable meaning. It shifted from signifying an entrenched particularism in the eighteenth century to functioning as a metonym for abstract universalism by the time of the French Revolution's centennial. Whatever the political ideal, the Jew was its antithesis. As a figure in the rhetoric of the 1789 revolution, it represented the negative image of the Enlightenment ideal. Prominent reformers described the Jew as a tribal remnant of an outmoded culture, a figure trenchantly attached to backward customs and superstition. The Jew was a symbol of particularism, which the Revolution was meant to overcome. One hundred years later, however, when the Catholic Right wanted to communicate its resistance to the Third Republic, its vocal leaders identified the cosmopolitan Jew as the secret victor of the 1789 revolution. Said to lack a relationship to French soil and, thus, to the natural world more generally, the cosmopolitan Jew, aligned with abstract reason rather than tradition, was seen as uprooted and in danger of corrupting the heritage of the true France.[24] The Jew was depicted as the wandering nomad, the foreigner who could claim no roots in France, or anywhere else for that matter.

As French ideals shifted, so too did the negative characteristics associated with the Jew. Out of the oscillation between these two poles emerges an ambivalent and paradoxical portrait of the Jew. Two seemingly opposed characteristics merge when the racialized stigma of the Jew comes to consist in the fact that the Jew is *sans racines* (without roots).

Before the Second World War, the valence of this characterization was clear. The values with which the Jew was associated were negative by definition. The rootless Jew was unable to shed the stigma of race, to claim the positive value of heritage and tradition. The Jew was quintessentially an outsider.

After the war, the figure of the Jew retained its symbolic status. Yet, in some moments, it gained a positive moral and political significance. Inadmissible in either of the dominant codes of constructing French identity—representing a resistance to an abstract humanism by its very

---

23. Paul Celan, "Gespräch im Gebirg," in *Gesammelte Werke*, 5 vols. (Frankfurt a.M.: Suhrkamp, 1983), 3:169–73.
24. See my discussions of Voltaire and Maurice Barrès in chapter 1.

exceptionality and the foil of foreignness to a French identity built on roots—it could be harnessed in its very negativity as a means to critique both political options. In identifying with the Jews, the students of May '68 announced their resistance to the available forms of political identity. In fact, they refused the very terms of identification. The position of outsider allocated to the Jew represented an alternative to the structures of allegiance put in place by both the universalist and the particularist models of French identity.[25] As a product of the racialized ideology of German and French fascism, the Jews came to represent "destabilization itself."[26]

Twenty years after the 1968 uprising, the effect of the students' gesture could still be felt in Jean-François Lyotard's more self-conscious move to coin the term *"the jews"* in his 1988 book *Heidegger and "the jews."* Lyotard, in the first paragraph of the book, clarifies that the term does not refer to any nation, ethnicity, or religious group but is, rather, a figure to describe "our lot . . . the lot of this nonpeople of survivors. Jews and non-jews . . . whose Being-together depends not on the authencity of any primary roots but on that singular debt of interminable anamnesis."[27] *Heidegger and "the jews"* was written in response to the 1987 publication in France of Victor Farias's controversial reexamination of Heidegger's role in the Nazi Party and was concerned to evaluate the relation between Heidegger's politics and his philosophy as well as the effect of this relation on French philosophy influenced by him.[28] More important, however, it made explicit the effects of the history of the representation of the Jew and mobilized this history toward the articulation of a concept that had been building since World War II. Like the slogan "Nous sommes tous des juifs allemands," Lyotard's *"juifs"* made *Jewishness* a category that was seemingly open to anyone and everyone

25. For a synopsis of the way in which these two forces animate French politics and continue to affect discussions of multiculturalism in France, see Jeremy Jennings, "Citizenship, Republicanism and Multiculturalism in Contemporary France," *British Journal of Political Science* 30 (2000): 575–98.

26. Philippe Lacoue-Labarthe, *La fiction du politique: Heidegger, l'art et la politique* (Paris: Christian Bourgois, 1987), 139, translated by Chris Turner as *Heidegger, Art and Politics: The Fiction of the Political* (London: Blackwell, 1990), 96.

27. Jean-François Lyotard, *Heidegger et "les juifs"* (Paris: Galilée, 1988), 152, translated by Andreas Michel and Mark Roberts as *Heidegger and "the jews"* (Minneapolis: University of Minnesota Press, 1990), 93.

28. Farias's work created an explosion of publicity in France because of its assertion that much of Heidegger's philosophical work bears the imprint of his sympathy with National Socialism. The very disclosure of this information does not, however, fully explain the vehemence of the reaction to Farias's book in France, which included newspaper articles, televised debates, and at least six book responses in the year or two following its publication. Much of the significant factual information about Heidegger's involvement in the party had already been disclosed in the posthumously published *Der Spiegel* interview and the reissue of the rectorate address in 1983, which coincided with the publication of Martin Heidegger, *Die Selbstbehauptung der deutschen Universität* (Frankfurt a.M.: Vittorio Klostermann, 1983).

to take up. Yet it in fact functioned in such a way that no one could take it up, for it was symbolic of the disappropriation of identity; it was a name for a "nonpeople." Insofar as the work thematized the figure of the Jew, it offered little that was not already familiar to a French readership. Lyotard was, rather, recycling a set of associations, associations that had developed as a consequence of anti-Semitism but had taken on a newly acquired positive value through the work of Jean-Paul Sartre and Emmanuel Levinas, then developed as a trope for disappropriation in the work of Maurice Blanchot and Jacques Derrida. While Lyotard himself offered little that was new to this narrative, his willingness, not only to articulate the fact that the Jew had become in France a symbol, but also to adopt *"the jews"* as a positively imbued label for political marginality placed him at the center of a critical backlash. He became the target of a number of American critics interested in exposing, if not the latent anti-Semitism of such a representation, then at least its reductive and essentializing tendencies. As such, he was perfectly positioned to become in the American context the exemplar of all that was wrong with postmodern French thought.[29] Lyotard's treatment of *"the jews"* subsequently reproduced on the American scene a reaction that recalls Finkielkraut's response to the May '68 slogan.

The critiques of Lyotard's book centered on two claims: first, that Lyotard offered an essentialized representation of Jewishness, one that in its philo-Semitism was no better than anti-Semitic reductions;[30] second, that the book's universalizing definition of *Jewishness* transformed the Jew into an allegorical figure, thus reproducing the supersession that first marked Christianity, consequently excluding "real Jews" from their position as proprietors of their own rightful identity. Daniel and Jonathan Boyarin were among the most outspoken critics of the work and clearly expressed the anxiety that Lyotard's work produced when they

29. There has been, of course, a significant French reaction to Lyotard's book as well. This is exemplified most recently by Élisabeth de Fontenay's *Une tout autre histoire: Questions à Jean-François Lyotard* (Paris: Fayard, 2006). In general, the French reaction to the postmodern appropriation of the figure of the Jew has been more sensitive to its history. Shmuel Trigano, e.g., sees how the appropriation grew out of a reading by Levinas and the other thinkers of what he terms *l'école de pensée juive de Paris* (a term coined by Levinas that refers to the other participants of the early Colloque des intellectuels juifs de langue française as well). He calls it a "caricature" of Levinas's and others' thinking. See Shmuel Trigano, "Qu'est-ce que l'école juive de Paris? Le judaïsme d'après la Shoa face à l'histoire," *Pardès: Revue européene d'études et de culture* 23 (1997): 27–44.

30. See Michael Weingrad, "Jews (in Theory): Representations of Judaism, Anti-Semitism, and the Holocaust in Postmodern French Thought," *Judaism* 45, no. 1 (Winter 1996): 82–84; Susan E. Shapiro, "'Écriture judaïque': Where Are the Jews in Western Discourse?" in *Displacements: Cultural Identities in Question*, ed. Angelika Bammer (Bloomington: Indiana University Press, 1994), 135; and Debra Bergoffen, "Interrupting Lyotard: Wither the We?" in *Lyotard: Philosophy, Politics, and the Sublime*, ed. Hugh J. Silverman (London: Routledge, 2002), 137.

wrote: "Although well intentioned, any such allegorization of the *Jew* is problematic in the extreme for the way that it deprives those who have historically grounded identities in those material signifiers of the power to speak for themselves and remain different."[31] Along with the book's other critics, the Boyarins thus argued that "real Jews" needed to speak for themselves and to take up the banner of a diasporic identity, which was finally being recognized as valuable and laudable.

In many ways, the reactions to Lyotard's book were more important than the book itself. Like Finkielkraut's response to the slogan "Nous sommes tous des juifs allemands," they expose the belief that there are only two options of identity expression available: one that is universal-ist and one that is particularist.[32] The Jew can either become an allegory and, thus, the object of a supersessionist move of some sort or vigilantly maintain the distinction of Jewish particularity by establishing a cipher that separates those who are authorized to speak for, about, or in the name of Jews from those who are not. This dichotomy excludes a third possibility that would function by drawing attention to the first two and the dangers inherent in taking up either position. This third possibility is, in fact, exactly what, because of its history, the trope of the Jew came to represent.

By tracing the history of the trope of the Jew in France leading up to Lyotard's restatement, I will reveal that what these critics refer to as *postmodern theory's Jew* or *écriture judaïque* arose, not because, as Susan Shapiro argues, Lyotard or any of his "postmodern" predecessors "for-got" the "historical construction of the Jew(s) in and by the West," but because they engaged with it critically.[33] It is my task to restore to the debates over the postmodern trope of the Jew its critical history, to reex-amine in light of that history whether and how the position of the Jew could subsequently become one with which anyone, even a non-Jew, might come to identify. Only in this way can we discern the contempo-rary political significance of the revalorization of this figure.

In the following chapters, I consider the development of the trope of the Jew as a figure for the uprooted, following its development in the thought of a number of France's most influential postwar think-ers: Jean-Paul Sartre, Emmanuel Levinas, Maurice Blanchot, and Jacques

31. Daniel Boyarin and Jonathan Boyarin, "Diaspora: Generation and the Ground of Jewish Iden-tity," *Critical Inquiry* 19, no. 4 (Summer 1993): 697.

32. The same assumption is operative in the recent championing of Pauline universalism (discussed in this work's conclusion), most evident in Alain Badiou's *Saint Paul: La foundation de l'universalisme* (Paris: Presses universitaires de France, 1997), translated by Ray Brassier as *Saint Paul: The Foundation of Universalism* (Stanford, CA: Stanford University Press, 2003).

33. Shapiro, "'Écriture judaïque,'" 191.

Derrida. My account traces a narrative between these thinkers, showing explicitly the influence of Sartre's account of Judaism on Levinas and of Levinas's account on Blanchot and Derrida.[34]

Maurice Barrès, whom I treat in the first chapter, acknowledges already in 1890 that the term *Jew* stands in for a series of associations: "*Juif* is only an adjective designating usurers, monopolizers, stockbrokers, all those that abuse money."[35] Yet he uses the term to differentiate, not between the roles of different people, but between their essences. Obviously, this type is an essentializing fabrication. For the figures I will discuss in the first three chapters, the function of this fiction is to provide a narrative that accounts for different modes of political identity. It reflects the marketplace of values in which it is produced and, thus, develops a currency of its own, a currency that can shift in value depending on the means of deployment. The political deployment of the term is meant, however, to mask its artificiality.

My purpose is to differentiate this *mythic* deployment of the idea of the Jew from a self-consciously *tropological* deployment. In the last two chapters, I argue that it is by redeploying the notion of the Jew in a self-consciously figurative manner that it gains its contemporary significance, that is to say, that it comes to function as a reminder of its own deception.

## Two Modes of Figuration: Myth versus Trope

I am using the term *myth* here in accordance with Jean-Luc Nancy and Philippe Lacoue-Labarthe's formulation. Myth is, they suggest, "a fiction, in the strong, active sense of 'fashioning' . . . whose role is to propose . . . types in imitation of which an individual, or a city, or an entire people,

---

34. My criteria for determining which thinkers to include in this study differ significantly from those of other scholars dealing with the figure of the Jew in twentieth-century French thought. The primary concern of other scholars on this subject has been to lambaste the troping of the Jew in French postmodern texts as anti-Semitism masquerading as philo-Semitism. Consequently, some have included thinkers I do not consider here, while none have considered the significance of Emmanuel Levinas. What these scholars have missed both in their treatment of the subject and in their choice of thinkers is the self-conscious engagement by a number of postwar French thinkers with the history of anti-Semitism as it has been manifested in modern philosophy and in fin de siècle and early modern European political texts. See, e.g., Elizabeth Bellamy, *Affective Genealogies: Psychoanalysis, Postmodernism, and the "Jewish Question" After Auschwitz* (Lincoln: University of Nebraska Press, 1997); Boyarin and Boyarin, "Diaspora"; Jonathan Judaken, "Mapping 'the New Jewish Cultural Studies,'" *History Workshop Journal* 51 (Spring 2001): 269–77; Shapiro, "'Écriture judaïque'"; Weingrad, "Jews (in Theory)"; and Seth Wolitz, "Imagining the Jew in France: From 1945 to the Present," *Yale French Studies* 85 (1994): 119–34.

35. Maurice Barrès, "La formule antijuive," *Le figaro*, February 22, 1890.

can grasp themselves and identify themselves."[36] Nancy and Lacoue-Labarthe construe myth as the dangerous mechanism whose conscious political deployment most clearly marks the movement from German romanticism to German totalitarianism. While myth might seem to be on the side of literature in a dichotomy that separates the literary from the philosophical, it is characterized, Nancy suggests, by the fact that it says nothing other than itself. Even as it participates in mimesis, it does not refer beyond itself but is, rather, as Nancy writes, borrowing a term from Schelling, *tautegorical*.[37] It represents a past for which the only reference is itself. In this sense, it is a form of incantation. It creates community by providing an origin narrative and installs the nexus for the political subject's identification with that community. Myth is, thus, the mechanism by which social fusion is created. It serves its function when it creates, as Nancy and Lacoue-Labarthe, write, "a total belief, an immediate, unreserved adhesion to the dreamed figure . . . it is both the model of identity *and* its present, effective *formed* reality."[38] For Nancy and Lacoue-Labarthe, myth represents the dangerous role that figuration serves when its function is reversed from imitation to formation, when formation produces, not re-presentation, but the model from which all copies must follow. As Lacoue-Labarthe writes: "The fascist haunting is, *de facto*, the haunting of figuration, of *Gestaltung*. It is a matter of simultaneously erecting a figure . . . and of producing, on the basis of this model, not a type of man, but the type of humanity—or an absolutely typical humanity."[39]

At the center of Nancy and Lacoue-Labarthe's account of myth is *The Myth of the Twentieth Century*, Alfred Rosenberg's tract of Nazi propaganda that itself constructs the German people as the mythic people par excellence.[40] According to the logic of the Nazi myth, the Jew is defined as "the rejection of myth."[41] Consequently, to speak of the "mythic Jew" is, in these terms, an oxymoron. The Jew was constructed in nineteenth- and twentieth-century European philosophical and political discourse as a figure for deracination, for a disruption of the structure of belonging. This idea of the Jew is, in fact, a by-product of the construction of European

36. Jean-Luc Nancy and Philippe Lacoue-Labarthe, *Le mythe Nazi* (Paris: L'aube, 1991), 34, translated by Brian Holmes as "The Nazi Myth," *Critical Inquiry* 16 (Winter 1990): 297.

37. Jean-Luc Nancy, *La communauté désoeuvrée* (Paris: Christain Bourgois, 1986), 131, translated by Peter Connor, Lisa Garbus, Michael Holland, and Simona Sawhney as *The Inoperative Community* (Minneapolis: University of Minnesota Press, 1991), 49.

38. Nancy and Lacoue-Labarthe, *Le mythe Nazi*, 56, and "The Nazi Myth," 306.

39. Philippe Lacoue-Labarthe, "The Spirit of National Socialism and Its Destiny," in *Retreating the Political*, by Philippe Lacoue-Labarthe and Jean-Luc Nancy, ed. Simon Sparks (London: Routledge, 1997), 151.

40. See Alfred Rosenberg, *The Myth of the Twentieth Century* (Torrance: Noontide, 1982).

41. Lacoue-Labarthe, *La fiction du politique*, 138, and *Heidegger, Art and Politics*, 96.

nationalist myths. The Jews are, thus, the "antimythic" people par excellence. Does that make the idea of the Jew mythically antimythic? Insofar as the idea of the Jew becomes either a site for designating the position of the other or a site for self-recognition and identification, the answer is yes. In the first three chapters, I will expose the way in which this mythic antimyth is constructed. I will argue, however, in the following two chapters for the possibility that the construction of the Jew as antimythic generates the possibility of an alternative deployment of the figure of the Jew, one that self-consciously harnesses the political potential of figurative language.

In the history of Western philosophy, there is a long tradition, stemming from Plato's critique of artistic representation, that treats figurative language as cognitively inferior to language that has a literal relation to its referent.[42] Figurative language, language that is defined by the fact that it is at a third remove from its proper referent, standing in for a word that is itself already a representation, is understood to be deceptive. As John Locke famously wrote: "All the artificial and figurative application of words eloquence has invented, are for nothing else but to insinuate wrong *ideas*, move passions, and thereby mislead the judgment, and so indeed are a perfect cheat."[43] A countertradition, most clearly articulated by Nietzsche, contends that *all* language is deceptive in its claim to represent reality. "Truths are illusions," Nietzsche argues, "whose illusionary nature has been forgotten, metaphors that have been used up and have lost their imprint and that now operate as mere metal, no longer as coins."[44]

Following Nietzsche, Lacoue-Labarthe and Nancy represent the operation of figuring as one that encompasses every operation of presentation and representation. It is, thus, tied acutely to the act of positing truth as something that can be presented as objective representation and is, thus, seen by them as an operation constitutive of the history of metaphysics.[45] Figuration would, thus, include, not only the language

42. The argument is made most famously, of course, in bks. 6 and 10 of the *Republic*. Certainly, it is a factor in much of Plato's (and, thus, philosophy's) general suspicion of rhetoric, evident also in the *Protagoras*, the *Gorgias*, and the *Phaedrus*. But, of course, this suspicion also reveals a certain dependence. As Paul Ricoeur writes: "Rhetoric is philosophy's oldest enemy and its oldest ally" (*La métaphore vive* [Paris: Seuil, 1975], 14, translated by Robert Czerny as *The Rule of Metaphor* [Toronto: University of Toronto Press, 1975], 10).

43. John Locke, *An Essay Concerning Human Understanding*, ed. Peter H. Nidditch (Oxford: Oxford University Press, 1975), 508.

44. Friedrich Nietzsche, "Über Wahrheit und Lüge im Aussermoralischen Sinn," in *Werke*, 15 vols. (Leipzig: C. G. Naumann, 1899–1905), 10:196, and "On Truth and Lies in an Extra-Moral Sense," in *The Portable Nietzsche*, ed. Walter Kaufmann (New York: Viking, 1959), 44.

45. See Philippe Lacoue-Labarthe and Jean-Luc Nancy, "Scene," *Nouvelle revue de psychanalyse* 17 (1992): 73–98. I am indebted here to Simon Spark's lucid introduction to Philippe Lacoue-Labarthe and Jean-Luc Nancy, *Retreating the Political*.

that is characteristically treated as figurative, but also, and more important, philosophical language that does not recognize its figural underpinnings. In his essay "Il faut," Lacoue-Labarthe introduces the notion of *défigurisation*, which he defines as the "retreat" of the figure. *Défigurisation* for Lacoue-Labarthe is an operation characteristic of poetic or literary language—language that "crosses the figure out or exposes it in the negative," that signals the failure of the figure to capture what it represents or marks the distinction between representation and the thing represented.[46] *Défigurisation* would, thus, mark the possibility of figural language calling attention to itself, calling itself into question as representation and truth source.

What differentiates such literary language from philosophical language is that, according to this Nietzschean model, philosophical language would be a language that, as Paul de Man puts it in "The Rhetoric of Tropes," "forgets its untruth."[47] As de Man asserts in his commentary on Nietzsche's project, such a view opens up an avenue for rethinking the relation between philosophy and literature. The self-conscious insertion of literature into philosophy can bring philosophy to reflect on its own forgetting. Figural language, which presents itself as such through the forms of metonymy and metaphor, marks itself as a substitution for some proper referent. It signals a relation of both proximity to and distance from its object, declares itself both to be and not to be what it represents.[48] This function is already evident in the very notion of a trope, whose origin lies in the Greek *tropos*, meaning "a turn." Poetic language, even as it would serve to represent an object, signals a turn away from that which is proper or fitting. Either as metaphor or as metonym, the literary figure appears as a bastard, imposing itself as what does not appropriately belong.[49]

Although Lacoue-Labarthe does not speak directly to the political potential of "defigurized" language, it is clear that poetic or literary language can serve a political purpose if it is harnessed as a mode of dis-

---

46. Philippe Lacoue-Labarthe, "Il faut," *Modern Language Notes* 107 (April 1992): 436.

47. Paul de Man, *Allegories of Reading: Figural Language in Rousseau, Nietzsche, Rilke, and Proust* (New Haven, CT: Yale University Press, 1979), 111.

48. As Paul Ricoeur writes of the metaphorical *is*, it "at once signifies both 'is not' and 'is like'" (Ricoeur, *La métaphore vive*, 11, and *The Rule of Metaphor*, 7).

49. In constructing this study, I have treated the notion of the trope interchangeably with that of the figure. In his *De institutione oratoria*, Quintillian (first century CE) acknowledges that *trope* and *figure* are often used interchangeably to refer to changes made in language for artful effect. However, he distinguishes between the two, designating the trope as a more particular kind of figurative language, as "an expression turned from its natural and principal signification to another, for the purpose of adorning style" (*The Institutio Oratoria*, 4 vols. [Cambridge, MA: Harvard University Press, 1921], 3:348–50 [bk. 9, chap. 1]).

course that interrupts myth. If, as Nancy and Lacoue-Labarthe claim, the function of myth is to provide a means for a people to grasp themselves, to find themselves in an identity that fuses them together as a group, the enactment of *défigurisation* within the public sphere would do the exact opposite, as is evidenced by the chant of "Nous sommes tous des juifs allemands." In this case, difference and separation are signaled rather than fusion. Not only does the literary figure here interrupt myth; it resists it by suggesting a new form of community utterance, one that mocks any mythic claim to fusion by expressing disjunction. It would, thus, be quintessentially the political mode opposed to totalitarian political expression.[50]

When the Jew is presented as a defigurized literary figure, the significance of this operation is doubled, for to add explicit attention to the process of figuration adds another layer of deracination to the notion of the Jew. This, I contend, is exactly the function of the trope of the Jew insofar as it is self-consciously developed by Maurice Blanchot and Jacques Derrida. Derrida in particular takes up the role of Judaism as figure. One of his larger aims is to further the Nietzschean project of troubling the distinction between literature and philosophy. He disputes claims to their clear distinction by exposing the way in which philosophy is itself a product of multiple literary effects, including metaphor and narrative voice, and by presenting his own thought in modes that are self-consciously literary.[51] Like Nietzsche, Derrida also exploits the capacity of literary language to disrupt the thetic act, to dislodge naive faith in the passage from sign to meaning or referent. His interest in the figure participates in both these moves. His concern with the notion of the figure is focused on the act of representation as such, on the way in which a particular entity—whether word, line, or symbol—can serve as an instantiation of a universal, and on the way in which the particularity of each representation, the language in which a word is spoken, the materiality of the symbol, disrupts its claim to universality. When one harnesses the ambivalence of language by calling attention to its turns, then the troubling particularity of representation becomes its literary

50. Nancy himself defines *literature* as the interruption of myth: "Literature interrupts itself: this is essentially what makes it literature (writing) and not myth. Or, better, what interrupts itself—discourse or song, gesture or voice, narrative or proof—*that* is literature (or writing). Precisely what interrupts or suspends its own *mythos*" (*La communauté desouvrée*, 179, and *The Inoperative Community*, 72). But Nancy is concerned not so much with the political function of figuration as with the way in which literature marks the separation between author and reader. Here, as will be made clear in the fourth chapter, he is clearly indebted to Blanchot.

51. See, e.g., Jacques Derrida, "La mythologie blanche," in *Marges de la philosophie* (Paris: Minuit, 1972), 247–324, translated by Alan Bass as "White Mythologies," in *Margins of Philosophy* (Chicago: University of Chicago Press, 1982), 207–71.

virtue. In an interview with Elisabeth Weber, Derrida remarks that, in thinking about Judaism, his own Judaism, he is always confronted with the problem of the figure, with a *"cas de figure."* The figure of the Jew is for him not merely one trope among others but, rather, an exemplar of the function of figurality as such. Derrida speaks of the way in which Judaism has a double valence as "an absolutely singular trait not shared by all men and all women, but represents itself, as Judaism, as the figure of the human universal."[52] When we consider the historical role that this figure of the Jew has played in French thought, then Derrida's claim is further nuanced and complicated, for the Jew appears as a figure of deracination, of the impossibility of any person to claim the status of Judaism as his or her own. In titling this study *The Figural Jew*, I want to signal, not only the philosophical and literary implications of treating the Jew as a trope, but also the history of representation that has imbued Jewishness with its particular meaning.

## Overview

In the first chapter, I begin the book by recounting the historical origins of the post–World War II figure of the rootless Jew. While the exact origins of the association between Jews and rootlessness can be traced back to the story of Abraham or even further to the expulsion from the Garden of Eden, my concern in this chapter is primarily to show how post-1945 French representations are inflected by the emphases on roots, race, and uprootedness that circulated heavily around the turn of the twentieth century in France. I begin my story thus with three key figures in the Dreyfus affair: Maurice Barrès, Bernard Lazare, and Charles Péguy. What all three of these thinkers share despite their differing position during and following the affair is a sense of the defining status of race in political life. By considering their representations of Jews and Judaism in conjunction and contrast with one another, we can discover how and why in the postwar context Jewish rootlessness was ripe for revalorization.

The second chapter argues for Sartre's significance in the history of the Jewish question in France. Although Sartre was clearly no expert on Judaism and wrote only occasionally on the topic, it is incontestable that his 1946 *Réflexions sur la question juive* had a profound impact on discourse about Jews and Jewish identity after the war. What emerges

---

52. Elisabeth Weber, *Questions au judaïsme* (Paris: Desclée de Brouwer, 1996), 75, translated by Rachel Bowlby as *Questioning Judaism* (Stanford, CA: Stanford University Press, 2004), 40.

from this book is an account of the way in which the representation of Judaism in France is tied to the nation's stuggle to determine political identity between the poles of universalism and particularism. The first part of the second chapter considers Sartre's investment in this debate and the role of the figure of the Jew in his treatment of the issue. It shows how the situation of the Jew comes to appear to Sartre as an intensification of the human situation and, thus, as a window into the stakes of existentialism. The second half of the chapter traces Sartre's engagement with Hegel and the role this played in his representation of Judaism. In particular, I argue that his late statements about Judaism recorded in *Hope Now*, the volume of interviews published by Benny Lévy soon after his death, can be explained and understood by means of his engagement with Hegelian philosophy of history.

The third chapter marks the turning point in the book. It considers Emmanuel Levinas's reconfiguration of the notion of deracination as a moral idea and the significance of this connection for his representation of Judaism. I show how Levinas expands the notion of uprooting so that it becomes one way of representing a moral subjectivity that is inaugurated in the response to the other who calls me to responsibility. His characterization of ethics as an uprooting of the self, I argue, not only facilitates the revalorization of Jewishness but also prepares the way for a theory of literary figuration as a function that uproots.

It is, thus, in the fourth chapter that, by considering Maurice Blanchot and Emmanuel Levinas in dialogue, a theory of the trope begins to emerge. I establish that Blanchot approaches Levinas's account both of ethics and of Judaism with a concern for the function of uprootedness in literature and politics. Despite Blanchot's consistent declarations of allegiance to Levinas and the rarity of his criticism of Levinas's philosophy, I argue that his conception of literature leads to a subtle critique of Levinas, one that results in radicalizing the notion of deracination and, thus, the figure of the Jew. Consequently, I argue, *being Jewish* comes to represent an exigency that calls into question allegiances of any sort.

In the final chapter, I show that it is in Jacques Derrida's own engagement with and ambivalent statements about his Jewish identity that we find both a theory and a practice of troping the Jew. This concern with the meaning of being Jewish follows from a set of concerns similar to Blanchot's, both in his treatment of literature and in his treatment of Judaism. With Derrida, however, the political implications of what it would mean to deploy the trope of the Jew politically are more fully developed. In this chapter, I examine Derrida's analysis of being Jewish from both the particularist and the universalist perspectives. Ultimately, I show that being

Jewish represents for Derrida an exemplary case of the very structure of exemplarity. This is the great asset and the great danger of its structure. The claim of being Jewish is the claim to exemplify the condition of uprootedness. Derrida uses the paradoxes inherent in this structure to argue that a just political and moral thinking can begin only with an aporia.

In tracing out the history of the postmodern trope of the Jew from its anti-Semitic origins to its tropological deployment in Blanchot and Derrida, I have three aims. The first is to offer a counternarrative to the one most often given to account for the philo-Semitism that marks post–World War II French thought. By reconstructing the history of the revalorization of the Jew, I am able to track its lineage back to the terms of French anti-Semitism and to reveal the process of resignification in the postwar era, showing how Sartre and Levinas mined the resources of anti-Semitism and exploited them in order to define an ideal that could be differentiated from both nostalgic nationalism and the rhetoric of universalizing humanism. What is generated in the process is a figural Jew, an archetype for a new kind of difference in particularity whose function is to suggest that there is a positive moral valence to resisting the discourse of belonging that dominates both the universalist and the particularist versions of political identity.

My second aim is to show that the portrait of the figural Jew must be self-critical if it is not, in fact, itself going to become a mythic antimyth and, thus, repeat the very dynamics of exclusivity and exemplarity that it would seem to oppose. As the postwar portrait of the deracinated Jew develops a moral valence, particularly in the thought of Emmanuel Levinas, we must question how the status of deracination can *in fact* retain an association with the Jew without developing a mythic function. Once deracination is imbued with an ethical content, it must become a source for critiquing the structure of allegiance that is at the heart, not only of any nationalistic discourse, but of any communitarian identity as well. While the trope of the Jew presents a means of critiquing communitarianism, it also runs the risk of facilitating it—if it is deployed as a means to characterize the Jewish community.

It is at this point that the *figural* element in the postwar French portrait of the Jew becomes crucial. My third and final aim in this project is to illustrate the way in which Blanchot's theory about the nature of literary language, articulated at the same time that he is developing a figural representation of the Jew, might provide resources for ensuring that the revalorization of the figure of the Jew always entails a self-critical operation. Making this claim involves three steps. The first is to show that the image of the Jew that is generated by post–World War II French thought is, in fact, a trope, that it is a metaphoric figure and, thus, functions as a literary representation with aspirations that distinguish it from the philosophical concept. The second step is to develop from Blanchot's and Derrida's writings a theory of the trope, or the literary "turn," that can be applied to figural representations of the Jew. The third step is to show how this literary operation can be deployed politically, as a demythologizing force, in the terms of Nancy and Lacoue-Labarthe.

It is with these considerations in mind that I return to the case of May '68. Was the students' identification with German Jews a blatant usurpation of the position of the victim that postwar Jews in Europe had been held to occupy? Or does an analysis of the figural Jew allow us to read such moments of identification differently? Might we read them as moments in which the ambivalence of metaphor is enacted, where the act of identification is thwarted by the impossibility of its expression, as acts of protest that express resistance to pledges of allegiance, through the performance of a claim to allegiance that fails by virtue of its own structure? What is the potential, finally, for this type of performance to serve as an effective mode of political action in our contemporary world?

## Political Implications

Although I do not work out a program or a system delineating how a performance of critical identification/disidentification might function in the face of our present-day ethnic and political conflicts, I have no doubt of the relevance of such an operation to current debates both in France and in the United States over multiculturalism and the politics of identity. Both Charles Taylor and Alain Finkielkraut have argued that the call for recognition that characterizes the debates over multiculturalism has its roots in Herder's theory that each *Volk* has a unique and distinct means of expressing its humanity.[53] It is questionable whether one can, in fact, prove Herder as a point of origin.[54] Nonetheless, it is fair

53. See Alain Finkielkraut, *La défaite de la pensée* (Paris: Gallimard, 1987), translated by Judith Friedlander as *The Defeat of the Mind* (New York: Columbia University Press, 1995); and Charles Taylor, "The Politics of Recognition," in *Multiculturalism and the Politics of Recognition* (Princeton, NJ: Princeton University Press, 1992), 30.

54. Robert Bernasconi rightly argues that Taylor and Finkielkraut are mistaken in locating the origins of multiculturalism in romanticism, given that the movement arises as a response to European hegemony. I would go a step further and argue that such claims seem to repeat the very logic that multiculturalism protests by locating Europe as the center and source and, thus, identifying "heretical" cultural forms as copies or perversions of Western movements. See Robert Bernasconi, "'Stuck inside of Mobile with the Memphis Blues Again': Interculturalism and the Conversion of Races," in *Theorizing Multiculturalism: A Guide to the Current Debate*, ed. Cynthia Willett (London: Blackwell, 1998), 282.

to say that the logic underpinning the multiculturalist position shares with Herder a suspicion of Enlightenment claims to unbiased universalism, validating instead the distinctiveness of cultures, and endorsing allegiance to one's culture, one's roots, one's shared past.[55]

Any comparison of debates over multiculturalism in France and the United States reveals that the links between multiculturalism and German romanticism have different historical resonances for each culture. The resistance to multiculturalism often associated with France has come to the world's attention with the debate over the Islamic head scarf (*hijab*) and the 2004 law prohibiting clothing or large symbols of religious affiliation in public schools. This resistance is often attributed to the strength of the republican tradition in France, to its adherence to a brand of universalism that resists difference in the name of equality.[56] Part of the resistance to "communitarianism," however, derives from the associations so easily drawn in France among political particularism, rootedness, and fascism. Finkielkraut makes this connection explicit in *The Defeat of the Mind* (*La défaite de la pensée*) and uses it to justify his own adherence to the classic republican model. His lament is, indeed, where have all the Dreyfusards gone?[57]

Certainly, Finkielkraut is not alone among postwar French philosophers in his concern over the return of tribalism or communitarianism in postmodernity.[58] Most notably, this position is evident in Alain Badiou's recent championing of Pauline universalism. His attack is against the proliferation of identities and the accompanying relativism,[59] which he associates with a fetishization of maintaining a "right to difference."[60] Like Finkielkraut, Badiou finds the warriors of difference on both the Right and the Left, among Jean-Marie Le Pen supporters and those fighting

55. See "Yet Another Philosophy of History," in which all the positions outlined above are clearly articulated. One might read this essay as predicting the movement of multiculturalism as an antidote to the consequences of Enlightenment rationalism: "Our age will soon open more eyes: before very long we will be impelled to seek spiritual springs to quench the thirst of the desert—we will learn to value the epochs we now despise—the sentiment of general humanity and happiness will be stimulated. . . . History of the world! The smallest empire and the largest, the smallest bird's nest, contribute to it" (J. G. Herder, *Auch eine Philosophie der Geschichte zur Bildung der Menschheit* [Frankfurt a.M.: Suhrkamp, 1967], 114, extract translated as "Yet Another Philosophy of History," in *J. G. Herder on Social and Political Culture*, ed. F. M. Barnard [Cambridge: Cambridge University Press, 1969], 218).

56. See John R. Bowen, *Why the French Don't Like Headscarves: Islam, the State and Public Space* (Princeton, NJ: Princeton University Press, 2007); and Jennings, "Citizenship, Republicanism and Multiculturalism."

57. The first subheading in Finkielkraut's chapter on multiculturalism in *The Defeat of the Mind* is "The Disappearance of the Dreyfusards."

58. See Zygmunt Bauman, *Intimations of Postmodernity* (London: Routledge, 1992), xxii.

59. Badiou, *Saint Paul* (French), 12, and *Saint Paul* (English), 12.

60. Alain Badiou, *L'éthique: Essai sur la conscience du mal* (Paris: Hatier, 1993), 21, translated by Peter Hallward as *Ethics: An Essay on the Understanding of Evil* (London: Verso, 2002), 20.

for minority recognition.[61] For Badiou, the target is explicitly the cult of difference that he associates with Levinasian ethics. Although he admits that those who politicize the other in the name of minority identity misread Levinas, it is nonetheless against Levinas that he champions Paul as the patriarch of universalism and a potential guide to us in our present moment. Paul, according to Badiou, preaches a universalism "indifferent to differences" and, thus, offers us a way out of the morass of identity politics.[62] Badiou's argument against Levinas is that the challenge of ethics is not to recognize difference, which confronts us everywhere and is undeniable, but rather to look past that difference in the name of a truth that can unite people in such a way that difference becomes irrelevant. The resonance is clear: Badiou is aligned with Paul and Levinas with the recalcitrant Jews in the epistles who hold tight to the law in the name of asserting and maintaining particularity. Badiou thus reproduces one of the age-old tropes of the Jew—as stubbornly attached to the dead letter. Once again, what we see in Badiou's position is the maintenance of a simple dichotomy that opposes particularism to universalism. Although Badiou would not align himself with Finkielkraut, he too is attempting to return to the rhetoric of universalism, a militant Marxist universalism rather than a Dreyfusard republicanism. What he fails to see in his work on Paul and his more explicit attack on contemporary Judaism in *Circonstances, 3* is that Levinas himself offers us the resources for overcoming identity politics.[63] It is, in fact, through Levinas's representation of the Jew that he does so. Levinas and a strand of his readers and commentators share with Badiou the concern to avoid a return to tribalism, yet they are equally suspicious of any facile return to universalism.

What we find in Derrida and Blanchot, as readers of Levinas, is the beginning of a new mode of thinking about political identity, one that commences from a critique of the very notion of belonging, one that suggests, not only that identity can be thought of as a performance, but also that the power of the performance might, in fact, be its failure. Such failures might help expose the ways in which the structures of belonging that seem so intrinsic to political thought are at the heart of what leads both a pure universalist republicanism and a politics of identity into exclusionary and discriminatory practices.

The United States is not immune from such problems, even if lacking in the historical associations between romantic valorizations of the

---

61. Badiou, *Saint Paul* (French), 9–10, and *Saint Paul* (English), 9–10.

62. Badiou, L'éthique, 27, and *Ethics*, 27.

63. Alain Badiou, *Circonstances, 3: Portées du mot "juif"* (Paris: Lignes, 2005). This work is treated at some length in my conclusion.

*Volksgeist* and the very racism that multiculturalism seems aimed at combating. Americans remain fascinated by and enamored of our roots, even as they tend to remind us of our distance from ancestral origins. Perhaps nothing illustrates this fascination more clearly then the recent spate of companies offering genetic analysis in order to determine "ancestral pedigrees."[64] In the belief that one can overcome the indeterminacy of the self by discovering one's genetic roots, we find ourselves again operating under the assumption that one's blood reveals one's essence. Yet this process of "self-discovery" is not treated in this country as the least bit politically or philosophically problematic. Nonetheless, we are beginning to reflect critically on the problems involved in a politics of identity. Increasingly, we are searching out ways to articulate difference without reifying race and gender identities.[65]

In the close of her essay "Wounded Attachments," Wendy Brown criticizes the modern tendency to reformulate "our historical exclusion as a matter of historically produced and politically rich *alterity*." This reappropriation of injury, she convincingly argues, follows from a reliance on ressentiment as a means of asserting power and leads to a guarding of suffering. One way out of the morass of identity politics, she suggests, is to begin rethinking political expression, "the language of 'I am'—with its defensive closure on identity, its insistence on the fixity of position, its equation of social with moral positioning." Her formulation of identity politics recalls the category of myth as it is formulated by Nancy and Lacoue-Labarthe and reminds us that this mode of political discourse can appear on both sides of the political spectrum. Brown proposes replacing this form of discourse with futural modes of expression focusing on desires, such as "wanting to be" or "wanting to have." Such formulations, she suggests, would "destabilize the formulation of identity as fixed position, as entrenchment by history."[66]

While I sympathize with Brown's aim to remove from political expression the need to protect attachments, particularly the attachment to certain wrongs as the defining cause of political identities, I would like

64. See Amy Harmon, "Seeking Ancestry in DNA Ties Uncovered by Tests," *New York Times*, April 16, 2006; and Steven Pinker, "Strangled by Roots: The Genealogy Craze in America," *New Republic*, August 6, 2007, 32–35.

65. For a summary of various liberal positions against identity politics and a defense of identity-based politics in the face of these critiques, see Courtney Jung, "Why Liberals Should Value Identity Politics," *Daedalus* 135, no. 4 (Fall 2006): 32–39. See also Seyla Benhabib, *The Claims of Culture: Equality and Diversity in the Global Era* (Princeton, NJ: Princeton University Press, 2002); and Nancy Fraser, "From Redistribution to Recognition? Dilemmas of Justice in a 'Post-Socialist' Age," in *Theorizing Multiculturalism*, ed. Cynthia Willett (Oxford: Blackwell, 1998), 19–50.

66. Wendy Brown, *States of Injury* (Princeton, NJ: Princeton University Press, 1995), 75.

to suggest that one must go further than saying "I want" rather than "I have" in order to disrupt the mythic operation of identity construction. We must ask first whether desires that focus on acquisition and ontology can, in fact, themselves be consistent with a moral positioning. To orient oneself toward a true futurity would, as both Derrida and Levinas have argued, require the renunciation of the assertion that such goals rightly *belong* to you.[67] This leaves political speech, however, in a conundrum. To renounce our political goals as our own would seem to amount to extreme quietism, to a final rejection of the political sphere. How can we cultivate activism without reasserting a politics of identity?

In sympathy with Brown, but in the hopes of further disarming the politics of identity, I propose that it is by way of figural modes of expression introducing comparison, performance, and irony into political speech that we can begin to destabilize the politics of identity without resorting to the nostalgia of a universalizing humanism. We can acknowledge the wrongs committed in the political sphere without returning to a politics of ethnic essentialism where morality is built on the morally pristine position of victimhood.

The history of the production of the trope of the Jew tells one story of how a proper label for an identity can become detached from its proper meaning and introduce performance back into politics. The very fact that we cannot help but identify something offensive in the reappropriation of certain political identities—in the declaration, for example, that the Palestinians are "the new Jews"—is part of the political power of the trope.

When Edward Said made his pronouncement in 2000 that he was "the last Jewish Intellectual," he no doubt perceived his own statement as provocative. He was himself, whether he knew it or not, repeating Jacques Derrida's claim in "Circumfession" (1993) that he was "the last of the Jews."[68] In his reference to Adorno, Said clearly means to use the term *Jew* as a metonym for *exile* in order to call attention to the irony that he himself had been uprooted by Jews. Nonetheless, the ironic function of

67. The idea that a true messianicity undoes any claims to possession is present throughout Derrida's later corpus. See, in particular, Jacques Derrida, *Spectres de Marx* (Paris: Galilée, 1993), translated by Peggy Kamuf as *Specters of Marx* (New York: Routledge, 1994), *Mal d'archive* (Paris: Galilée, 1995), translated by Eric Prenowitz as *Archive Fever* (Chicago: University of Chicago Press, 1998), *Adieu à Emmanuel Levinas* (Paris: Galilée, 1997), translated by Pascale-Anne Brault as *Adieu to Emmanuel Levinas* (Stanford, CA: Stanford University Press, 1997), and *Schibboleth pour Paul Celan* (Paris: Galilée, 1986), translated as "Shibboleth for Paul Celan," in Jacques Derrida, *Sovereignties in Question: The Poetics of Paul Celan*, ed. Thomas Dutoit and Outi Pasanen (New York: Fordham University Press, 2005).

68. Jacques Derrida, "Circonfession," in *Jacques Derrida*, by Geoffrey Bennington (Paris: Seuil, 1991), 178, translated as "Circumfession," in *Jacques Derrida*, by Geoffrey Bennington (Chicago: University of Chicago Press, 1993), 190.

the statement depends on the way in which he himself, through his identification with the Jews, is acting as an occupier, by usurping the "rightful" position of "real" Jews such as Amos Oz. It is exactly the political impact of such a statement of identification, in the way that it manages to valorize rootlessness and simultaneously to indicate the impossibility of staying true to this idea, that this book seeks to explore.

# ONE

# Roots, Rootlessness, and Fin de Siècle France

To be elsewhere: the great vice of this [the Jewish] race, its great secret virtue: the great vocation of this people. . . . They are always on camels' backs.

CHARLES PÉGUY, *NOTRE JEUNESSE*

## The Wandering Jew

A period postcard inspired by the Dreyfus affair depicts Alfred Dreyfus iconically, with pointy dark mustache and small spectacles. He is hunched and pulling a cart. The card, a pencil sketch with little embellishment, exposes the cart's contents spilling out the top: a patterned blanket, the top of a chair, the legs of a table. The title of the postcard is "Dreyfus as a Wandering Jew."[1]

The story of the Jew condemned to wander is so old it cannot be traced to a single origin. It is told in its most precise form in the medieval Christian tale of the Jew condemned by Christ to restlessness until the Second Coming. He is punished for his refusal to let Jesus, en route to Calvary, rest for a moment at his doorstep. This story is told and retold from the thirteenth century forward. By the end of the sixteenth century, the protagonist is conclusively named Ahasveras and becomes a symbol in folklore

---

Epigraph: Charles Péguy, *Notre jeunesse* (Paris: Gallimard, 1933), 109.

1. *The Dreyfus Affair through Postcards*, Modiya Project, Center for Religion and Media, http://modiya.nyu.edu/handle/1964/576.

across Europe of the sins of pride and revolt.[2] He is engraved in our cultural memory by Gustave Doré as a hoary old man in rags with a long beard and staff traveling through a somber landscape, haunted by the crucifixion.[3] The ubiquity of the legend—which appears in languages and regions across Europe, including Greece, Turkey, France, Italy, and the Slavic territories—helps cement the notion that the persistence of the exiled Jewish people in the Christian era serves as testimony to their error, testimony to the divinity of Christ. As the 1602 *Kurtze Beschreibung und Erzehlung von einem Juden mit Namen Ahasverus* records: "What God now intended to do with him, in leading him about so long in this wretched life, he could not explain otherwise than that perhaps he should be on judgment day a living witness of the Passion of Christ."[4]

Ahasveras continues to appear in the literature of the romantics. Representing both sin and freedom, punishment and rebellion, he shows up in five works by Shelley, in Schlegel and Brentano, in Wordsworth's "Song for the Wandering Jew," in Byron (as an allusion), and in Edgar Quinet's *Les tablettes du Juif errant* and *Ahasverus*, where the persistence of the Wandering Jew outlasts even the gods.[5] This romantic figure, also appearing in countless minor works of the period, is evidence of a larger cultural preoccupation with roots and rootlessness in eighteenth- and nineteenth-century Germany and France.[6]

Already in the eighteenth century, Herder argued that the uniqueness and authenticity of cultures is tied to the organic relationship that develops in a healthy community from its relationship to its own past, its traditions, its language, and its land. "Each form of human perfection then is, in a sense, national and time-bound and, considered most specifically, individual. Nothing develops, without being occasioned by time, climate, necessity, by world events or the accidents of fate," he

2. George K. Anderson, *The Legend of the Wandering Jew* (Providence, RI: Brown University Press, 1965), 10, 75.

3. Doré produced in the 1850s a series of twelve engravings on the theme of the wandering Jew that were published in a volume with verse by Pierre Dupont in 1856, with a second edition in 1862. See ibid., 260.

4. Quoted in ibid., 46.

5. See ibid., chaps. 8–9.

6. See Galit Hasan-Roken and Alan Dundes, eds., *The Wandering Jew: Essays in the Interpretation of a Christian Legend* (Bloomington: Indiana University Press, 1986). The legend is, as Jonathan Boyarin calls it, a quintessentially "non-Jewish story about the Other" (*Thinking in Jewish* [Chicago: University of Chicago Press, 1996], 147). In its many variations, it chronicles the Jew as seen by the gentile from the Middle Ages into modernity. It is not until the late nineteenth century that it is reappropriated by Jews. See Anderson, *The Legend of the Wandering Jew*, 292. Bernard Lazare, discussed later in the chapter, is one of the first to reappropriate the legend. He does not, however, attempt to retell the story in a way that redeems Ahasverus; rather, he repeats the Christian judgment.

writes in *Yet Another Philosophy of History* (1774). There is, thus, a contrast to be drawn between a culture that has attended to its own specificity, to its own history, a culture that has depth, and one that is superficial or rootless. Critiquing the eighteenth-century French philosophes, Herder laments their lack of concern for cultural specificity: "It could be that all these tired generalities are nothing but a foam which dissolves in the air of all times and peoples. How different this is from nourishing the veins and sinews of one's own people, from strengthening their hearts and refreshing them to their very marrow." He contrasts the efforts of the "philosophers of Paris," who claim to "civilize '*toute l'Europe*' and '*tout l'univers*,'" with the "vital culture" of the "medieval guilds and baronies," seeing the former as perpetuating nothing but a "haze of refinement," a mere "intellectual light," and the later as engendering "pride in the knights and craftsmen, self-confidence, steadfastness and manliness."[7] The contrast, which favors medieval provincialism over Enlightenment cosmopolitanism, emphasizes the value of tradition, hierarchy, and the cultivation of the warrior and the farmer over the freedom and illumination promised by rational thought.[8] One is clearly rooted, the other rootless.

Herder does not accuse the Jews of universalism, but he does fault them for not having their own roots, for having been, "almost from their beginning, parasitical plants on the trunks of other nations," for having "never been inspired with an ardent passion for their own honor, for a habitation, for a country, of their own."[9] Hegel faults the Jews similarly, most pointedly in his early theological writings. In *The Spirit of Christianity*, he speaks of them as an uprooted people, alienated from nature. Abraham, who clearly functions as a metonym for the Jews, is "a stranger on earth, a stranger to the soil and to men alike. Among men he always was and remained a foreigner." Snapping the bonds of communal life and love when he leaves his father's house, Abraham develops his people from the spirit of alienation. Nothing grounds the Jewish people; no ties of love bind them: "In this thoroughgoing passivity there remained to the Jews beyond the testification of their servitude, nothing save the sheer empty need of maintaining their physical existence and securing it against want." The Jews are consequently able

7. Herder, *Auch eine Philosophie der Geschichte zur Bildung der Menschheit*, 40, 83–84, and *J. G. Herder on Social and Political Culture*, 184, 203, 202.

8. Louis Dumont, *German Ideology: From France to Germany and Back* (Chicago: University of Chicago Press, 1994), 9–10.

9. J. G. Herder, *Ideen zur philosophie der Geschichte der Menschheit*, 4 vols. (Riga and Leipzig: J. F. Hartknoch, 1784–91), 3:98, translated as *Reflections on the Philosophy of the History of Mankind* (Chicago: University of Chicago Press, 1968), 144.

to relate to the earth only as an object of mastery and to God only as his subservient slave.[10]

Similar rhetoric surfaces in the French Enlightenment. Despite Voltaire's distrust of the Christian tradition that Herder and Hegel both defend, his vitriolic attacks on the Jews employ a set of tropes identical to theirs. The Hebrews, Voltaire writes in the *Dictionnaire philosophique*, "have ever been vagrants or robbers, or slaves, or seditious. They are still vagabonds upon the earth, and abhorred by men, yet affirming that heaven and earth and all mankind were created for them alone."[11] Unlike Herder's, however, Voltaire's barbs against the Jews do not aim to promote cultural specificity. Rather, they function as a means to expose the unreasonable and intolerant elements of all religion, all of which were to be abandoned in the enlightened age.[12]

What tends to characterize the French Enlightenment rhetoric about the Jews is the attempt to distinguish between that which is redeemable, insofar as the Jews are men, and that which is a product of their stunted and backward culture.[13] With the publication of his prize-winning *Essai sur la régénération physique, morale et politique des Juifs*, Abbé Grégoire became famous as the great defender of the Jews.[14] In this work, he argues for the complete melding of the Jews into the nation so that they too could become citizens in the fullest sense. This was advocated in the spirit of *régénération*, a process of which the Jews were apparently deeply

10. G. W. F. Hegel, "Der Geist des Christentums und sein Schicksal," in *Theologische Jugendschriften* (Tubingen: Mohr, 1907), 246 (first quote), 252 (second quote), 245–47, translated by T. M. Knox as "Spirit of Christianity and Its Fate," in *Early Theological Writings* (Philadelphia: University of Pennsylvania Press, 1971), 186, 194, 185–87.

11. Voltaire, *Dictionnaire philosophique* (Paris: Cluny, 1930), 278–79. The book was composed over the course of the 1750s and early 1760s. Its first edition was published in 1764, but it was further revised for the 1769 printing.

12. Peter Gay, "Voltaire's Anti-Semitism," in *The Party of Humanity: Essays in the French Enlightenment* (New York: Knopf, 1964). Gay has a tendency to play down the violence of Voltaire's attacks on the Jews. He went so far as to omit the entry "Les juifs," a sustained, thirty-page diatribe against the Jews, from his translation of the *Dictionnaire philosophique*, despite the fact that it is the longest entry in the text. For an alternate view, see Arthur Hertzberg, *The French Enlightenment and the Jews* (New York: Columbia University Press, 1968).

13. The question then on which the philosophes and, later, the revolutionaries were divided was what method of extraction was most suitable. The two most dominant voices in this dispute were Voltaire's and Montesquieu's. Behind one of these two figures the Enlighteners tended to line up: behind Montesquieu in defense of toleration, and, thus, in defense of the Jews, and behind Voltaire in an attack on Judaism as the most unreasonable of religions and on the Jews as its perpetrators. See Jay Berkovitz, *The Shaping of Jewish Identity in Nineteenth-Century France* (Detroit: Wayne State University Press, 1989); and Léon Poliakov, *Histoire de l'antisémitisme: De Voltaire à Wagner* (Paris: Calmann-Lévy, 1968), translated by Miriam Kochan as *The History of Antisemitism*, vol. 3, *From Voltaire to Wagner* (New York: Vanguard, 1975).

14. In the 1880s, Jews from across France donated money for a statue of him to be erected in Lunéville.

in need. For Grégoire, the Jews were essentially an obstacle on the road to universalism, one that could be surmounted through the amelioration of their circumstances with the ultimate goal of, first, complete assimilation and, finally, conversion.[15] Thus, for Grégoire, who was also deeply involved in efforts to eliminate regional dialects and identities in France, the Jew was a symbol of particularism, which the Revolution (compatible for Grégoire with a certain "republican Christianity") was meant to overcome.[16]

Even as the Jew was attacked in similar ways by both French and German political thinkers at the turn of the eighteenth century, the value of cultural particularity was not unambiguous in both cultures. For Herder, the French philosophes were themselves suffering from alienation. In theorizing humanity by abstracting from culture, they had lost touch with their unique past and traditions. Instead of nurturing their own culture, they were spouting ephemeral generalities as unsubstantial as vapor.

One hundred years later, after the discourse of nationalism had developed across Europe from its nascent beginnings in Herder, a faction of the French Right, dissatisfied with the consequences of republicanism in the Third Republic and disappointed by the results of the Franco-Prussian War, reemployed Herder's critique.[17] Of the French intellectual class, Maurice Barrès writes in 1902: "It tries to form our young Lorraines, Provencals, Bretons, Parisians of this year into an abstract man, ideal, identical everywhere with himself while what we need are men solidly rooted [racinés] in our soil, in our history, in our national conscience and adapted to the French necessities of this moment."[18] The rhetoric here is nearly identical to Herder's.[19] Barrès is fighting to save the French nation—from itself, but also from the enemy he thinks is attacking it from the inside, the rootless Jew.

The Jew in question is most explicitly Alfred Dreyfus, the Jewish army captain arrested for espionage in 1894 whose trial sparked what Pierre Birnbaum has called the climax of the war of the two Frances, between

15. Henri Grégoire, *Essai sur la régénération physique, morale et politique des juifs* (Paris: Flammarion, 1989), 131–32; Paula E. Hyman, *The Jews of Modern France* (Berkeley and Los Angeles: University of California Press, 1998), 21.

16. Pierre Vidal-Naquet, *Les juifs: La mémoire et present, II* (Paris: La découverte, 1991), 66, translated by David Ames Curtis as *The Jews* (New York: Columbia University Press, 1995), 69.

17. On further connections between German romanticism and the 1890s in France, see Zeev Sternhell, *Maurice Barrès et le nationalisme français* (Paris: Armand Colin, 1972), 9–11.

18. Maurice Barrès, *Scènes et doctrines du nationalisme* (Paris: Emile-Paul, 1902), 56.

19. In an ironic reversal, it is Kant, a German, whom Barrès holds responsible for the unmooring of French thought from its anchors. The sentence previous to the one quoted in the text cites Kantianism as the source of the intellectuals' error: "This Kantianism of our class tries to regulate universal man, abstract man, without taking account of individual differences" (ibid.).

the royalist Right and the republican Left.[20] Dreyfus's trial was the occasion for a dramatization of the antinomies animating the French conception of nationhood, and the figure of the Jew was center stage.

As will be clear in the coming chapters, the revalorization of the figure of the rootless Jew in post-1945 French philosophy has many sources. Hegel's brief comments in *The Spirit of Christianity* loom large in a number of postwar texts, as does the accompanying association of Kant with the Jews in nineteenth-century Germany.[21] That said, the rhetoric surrounding the figure of the Jew during the Dreyfus affair clearly supplies both material and motivation for the postwar revalorization. During this period, a notion of race circulates that is more cultural than it is biological.[22] Race is clearly linked to *les racines* (roots), while the discourse of rootedness becomes central to the ideology of nationalism and to the nascent movement of fascism. The Jews, as the instantiation of foreignness, are figured as the antithesis of a rooted French nationality, as the race without roots.

In this chapter, I will consider how turn-of-the-twentieth-century discussions of race and rootedness paved the way for the post-1945 revalorization of the Jew in France by analyzing the writings of three important voices in the Dreyfus affair: Maurice Barrès, Bernard Lazare, and Charles Péguy. The anti-Dreyfusard writer and political figure Maurice Barrès popularized the notion that France was suffering from the influence of *les deracinés*, a class of people including intellectuals, Jews, foreigners, and Protestants. Bernard Lazare, a literary figure of Jewish descent of the same generation as Barrès, is most famous for having written the pamphlet that first publicly defended Captain Dreyfus. His importance follows both from his having written the first systematic work on the origins of anti-Semitism and his influence as an early Zionist. Charles Péguy, also a Dreyfusard, was a great admirer and friend of Bernard Lazare's, casting him as a Hebrew prophet, as the positive antithesis to

20. Pierre Birnbaum, *La France imaginée: Déclin des rêves unitaires?* (Paris: Fayard, 1998), 169–70, translated by M. B. Debevoise as *The Idea of France* (New York: Hill & Wang, 2001), 125. Venita Datta's *Birth of a National Icon: The Literary Avant-Garde and the Origins of the Intellectual in France* (Albany: State University of New York Press, 1999) does much to disrupt this vision of the affair by exposing how intertwined the intellectuals on both sides of the affair were before they took sides. She shows not only their common roots as a generation of young men asserting the power of literature in the political sphere but also the shared assumptions that continued to operate in their public statements even as they defined each other as adversaries.

21. See Emil Fackenheim, *Encounters between Judaism and Modern Philosophy: A Preface to Future Jewish Thought* (New York: Basic, 1973); and Jürgen Habermas, "The German Idealism of the Jewish Philosophers," in *Philosophical-Political Profiles*, trans. Frederick G. Lawrence (Cambridge, MA: MIT Press, 1983), 21–43.

22. Sternhell, *Maurice Barrès et le nationalisme français*, 263.

the anti-Dreyfusard depiction of Captain Dreyfus. Péguy's ambivalent legacy is such that he is cited both as an important influence on such notorious French fascists as Drieu La Rochelle and Robert Brasillach and as an early theorist of cultural pluralism, able to recognize Jewish difference without denigrating it.[23]

These three thinkers demonstrate how the valorization of roots at the turn of the twentieth century contributes to a revalorization of rootlessness in the post-1945 era. With Barrès, the discourse of roots appears central to the development of right-wing French nationalism; the Jew is figured as the movement's nemesis. Despite the fact that Péguy and Bernard Lazare were Dreyfusards, they share with Barrès a belief in the defining status of race for political life. At the same time, they reject the depiction of the Jew as deracinated. While clearly engaged in positively resignifying the stereotypes of anti-Semitism, they see no way to do so without redefining Judaism as a particularism that is itself in tension with the universalism critiqued by anti-Dreyfusards and upheld by some Dreyfusards, most notably Émile Zola. These two figures serve as a hinge, then, between a philosophy of rootedness and the post-1945 revalorization of the rootless Jew.

## A Philosophy of Roots: Maurice Barrès

In France, the Dreyfus affair occupies a place of importance that, given only the concrete details of the event, might seem overblown. One man was accused of treason against the state. He was put on trial, wrongfully convicted, and sent to Devil's Island with a sentence of life imprisonment. After a retrial, a resentencing, and a presidential pardon, twelve years later he was finally exonerated. No international dispute followed. No armies were raised; no major death toll was tallied. Not even a shift in power ensued. The significance of the affair follows, not from the concrete details of Dreyfus's alleged crime and subsequent punishment, but from the public debate that the trial initiated. In this debate, the

23. For Péguy's influence on French fascists, see David Carroll, *French Literary Fascism: Nationalism, Anti-Semitism, and the Ideology of Culture* (Princeton, NJ: Princeton University Press, 1995), 42–70. On Péguy as an early theorist of cultural pluralism, see Annette Aronowicz, *Jews and Christians on Time and Eternity* (Stanford, CA: Stanford University Press, 1998), 10. This difference is most clearly present in the conflicting interpretations of Péguy by Bernard-Henri Lévy and Alain Finkielkraut. In *L'idéologie française* (Paris: Grasset, 1981), Lévy describes Péguy as a "prodigy of racism" (123), while, in *Le mécontemporain* (Paris: Gallimard, 1991), Finkielkraut describes him as one of the most maligned, misunderstood figures of the modern era, someone whose culturally pluralist humanism has been misread as nationalism (15).

republic itself was on trial. The meaning of citizenship was reanalyzed. Even the idea of the nation was questioned. It was a moment when the argument that reason is individual and, thus, unconditioned by history and culture was countered by the belief that reason is collective, constituted by a culture and, thus, dependent on history. "One rarely has such an occasion to make a clear-cut choice, at the threshold of life, between two fundamental ethics and to know immediately who one is," Julien Benda wrote of the affair.[24] As Zeev Sternhell has argued, the fact that this event raises in such a concrete manner the most essential questions of politics makes it unique in modern history.[25]

Maurice Barrès was instrumental in raising the stakes of the affair, in making it a platform for political and philosophical debate and self-consciously using anti-Semitism to popularize his philosophical and political agenda: "The Dreyfusards admit that this is not about a man but that the man is a symbol, either in the fight against anti-Semitism or in that against the military. The point is not to contest whether he is a symbol but to say that if he is a symbol, it is another affair, the Dreyfus affair. The triumph of the camp that supports Dreyfus would decidedly install in power those men who pursue the transformation of France according to their own spirit. And me, I want to conserve France."[26]

The facts of the case were not nearly as important to Barrès as the battle that began to take shape between those who fought for Dreyfus in the name of an abstract humanity and those who supported his conviction out of a desire to protect France and to unite it against its adversaries, both within and without: "*In abstracto*, one could support this thesis or that thesis; one could, according to one's heart, appreciate or depreciate the army, the military's jurisdiction, the battle of the races. But it is not a question of your heart; it is France that is at stake, and these questions must be treated according to the interest of France. . . . It is completely unnecessary to complain about the anti-Semitic movement at the instant that we're observing the enormous power of the Jewish nationality that threatens to overturn the French state."[27] According to Barrès, France was at stake because it was suffering from decadence and a lack of cohesion. The Dreyfus affair was merely an example of a larger crisis.[28] The nation was, he repeated again and again, "disassociated

24. Julien Benda, *La jeunnesse d'un clerc* (Paris: Gallimard, 1936), 204.
25. Sternhell, *Maurice Barrès et le nationalisme français*, 247.
26. Barrès, *Scènes et doctrines du nationalisme*, 33–34.
27. Ibid., 34.
28. Ibid., 29, 79. "The Dreyfus affair is only the tragic signal of a general state . . . under the accident, let us search out the deeper state" (80).

and leaderless" (*dissociée et décérébrée*):[29] "The decline of our birthrate, the exhaustion of our energy, since our most active compatriots were destroyed in wars and revolutions, has brought the invasion of foreign elements into our territory and our blood, elements that are working to subjugate us."[30]

Barrès's solution for resolving this crisis of strength was nationalism. "Nationalism means resolving every question from the perspective of France," he wrote. More specifically, nationalism meant for Barrès "the acceptance of determinism."[31] Barrès's determinism, which found its physiological and psychological basis in the work of the ardently anti-Semitic historian and theoretician of neuropsychology Jules Soury, was essentially a theory of rootedness.[32] This theory, which Barrès first explores in the *Culte du moi* trilogy of novels, is further developed and fully accepted in his 1897 novel *Les déracinés*,[33] from which he constructs his archetypal version of the intellectual, Paul Bouteiller.[34] Bouteiller, the lycée professor of Sturel, the novel's protagonist, is described as a deracinated Kantian, an orphan, "a son of reason, a stranger . . . totally abstract and truly suspended in the void." He "forms his dominating soul by deforming" the students' "Lorrainian souls." His goal? To deracinate his students, "to detach them from the soil and from their social group, to take them out of their prejudices," and to offer them only abstract reason in return.[35] The defense against such forces is recognition of one's roots. After Sturel attends Victor Hugo's funeral, an event that is an apotheosis

29. Ibid., 29, 36, 46, 71, 82, 95, etc. This phrase appears repeatedly throughout *Scènes et doctrines du nationalisme*. In addition, the title of chapter 9 of *Les déracinés* is "La France dissociée et décérébrée."

30. Barrès, *Scènes et doctrines du nationalisme*, 96.

31. Ibid., 81, 10.

32. Barrès attended Soury's courses at the Sorbonne from 1893 to 1897. See Maurice Barrès, *Mes cahiers*, 11 vols. (Paris: Plon, 1929–57), esp. 1:89–90 (but see vols. 1–2 generally). For an analysis of the influence, see Sternhell, *Maurice Barrès et le nationalisme français*, 254–66.

33. One of the central debates in Barrès scholarship is over the question of whether the *Culte du moi* trilogy prepared the way for Barrès's nationalism or whether his turn to nationalism involved a radical shift away from the cult of the self philosophy of *Sous l'oeil des barbares*, in which Barrès described a self that must batten down the hatches against all exterior influence, including that of one's own culture and one's contemporaries. Robert Soucy (*Fascism in France: The Case of Maurice Barrès* [Berkeley: University of California Press, 1972]) argues that the shift involved something of a conversion, while Sternhell (*Maurice Barrès et le nationalisme français*, 27–60) argues that Barrès's thought follows the same logic throughout. The logic of the *Culte du moi* is merely expanded to include the nation. In both cases, the goal is to protect what is interior from what is exterior. David Carroll argues similarly: "Barrès never in fact abandons his cult of the Self; rather, he pursues it all the more dogmatically when it is expressed as a nationalist-culturalist mythology and politics" (*French Literary Fascism*, 27). Barrès himself argues that he intended all along for the *Culte du moi* trilogy to lead toward nationalism (see *Scènes et doctrines du nationalisme*, 14).

34. Barrès refers to Bouteiller throughout *Mes cahiers* and in *Scènes et doctrines du nationalisme* as an archetype of the rootless intellectual.

35. Barrès, *Les déracinés*, 2 vols. (Paris: Plon, 1937), 1:22, 24, 21–22.

for Sturel and for the French nation, he recognizes his connection to the nation and to the collective, a connection that supersedes individual relationships and even the moral law.[36] This event marks a turning point for Sturel, a revelation. Both Hugo and the event are described in rapturous terms. Hugo is the prophet who "makes perceivable the innumerable secret threads that bind each one of us to the whole of nature," who awakens us to "the mystery of our ancestor"; he "dilates in us the faculty to feel the secrets of the past and the enigmas of the future." His funeral creates out of the masses a living, breathing, unified being:

In this barely conscious crowd, some seeing the glory trembled, others feeling death hastened to live, others still rubbing shoulders with their coreligionists wanted to fraternize. They did better than that; they were unified: this prodigious mix of enthusiasts and the debauched, thick-headed, simple, and good spirited, organized themselves into a single formidable being, camped at the feet of greatness. The face of the crowd, turned toward the casket, lit by funeral torches, was made of a hundred thousand gazes. Some were foul, others ecstatic, but none were without feeling. Its breathing was like the sound of the sea.[37]

Barrès does not shy away from religious language in his description of Hugo's funeral, employing terms such as *mystery, apotheosis,* and *sacrifice.*[38] As *Scènes et doctrines du nationalisme* illustrates, this is clearly not accidental. Despite his labeling those citizens of France who were not Catholic, namely, the Protestants and the Jews, as strangers to the French nation, nationalism, not Catholicism, served in the role of religion for Barrès. Going far beyond a mere politics, it represented a new metaphysics:

Catholics see in patriotism a prolongation of morals. It is on the commandments of the church that their idea of the homeland [*patrie*] is founded. But what if I am not a believer?

For a certain number of people the supernatural has been destroyed. Their piety, which wants an object, doesn't find it in the heavens. I gather my heavenly piety on the soil, on the soil of my dead.

The formula for this new metaphysics was *la terre et les morts*. According to Barrès, the unity of the fatherland arises from our acknowledging

36. Ibid., 2:222. By way of Hugo's funeral, Sturel realizes that his loyalty to his nation supersedes his attachment to his former lover, an "asiatic" foreigner, and, thus, he decides not to turn her murderers in to the police.
37. Ibid., 221, 219–20.
38. Ibid., 220.

our connection to the land out of which we were born and the blood of our forefathers, who speak in and through us: "There is, more profound than ourselves, a point of constancy, a nerve center; if one touches it, there is tremor of which I cannot be suspicious, it is the rumbling of my entire being. This is not merely the passing irritation of an ephemeral individual but what in awe I recognize as the looming of my entire race. . . . There is really no freedom of thought. I can live only in accordance with my ancestors. They and my soil order me toward a certain activity."[39] The recognition of this truth, which for Barrès is clearly foundational, gives rise to a religious experience, the land and the dead holding the position of deity.[40] They give rise in Barrès to an experience that recalls Otto's description of the *mysterium tremendum*.[41] The feeling is one of awe and terror, a feeling that demands submission: "Terrified of my dependence, powerless to create myself, I want at least to contemplate face-to-face the powers that govern me. I want to live with these masters and to devote to them a reflective service, to participate fully in their force. Everything else falls apart with analysis; it is by this dependence that I am put back together and connect to my truth."[42] This comment, which appears in the opening pages of *Scènes et doctrines du nationalisme*, seems to refer to Barrès's own "conversion to rootedness." It also describes France's disease and its remedy. France itself is falling apart because it is suffering from deracination, from forces that impose on it cosmopolitanism and abstraction. Barrès's claim is that overemphasis on the intellect has weakened the ability of the French to act according to their instincts, to be true to what they are: a nation that arises out of its past, from its dead, on its particular soil.[43] Barrès's biological and psychological determinism amounts to the claim that the only freedom we have is to recognize our rootedness: "Between all the caprices of fortune, there is a place for our free will. Freely we submit ourselves to that for which we were born."[44]

39. Barrès, *Scènes et doctrines du nationalisme*, 10.

40. Zeev Sternhell makes this point in *Maurice Barrès et le nationalisme français*: "Barresian nationalism constitutes a complete vision of the man and of the collectivity. He replaces revealed religion; his objective is to create a world with fixed criteria, free of doubt, purified of all foreign imports; his goal is to give to the French their authenticity and, in making them hear the voice of the blood, to reestablish the compromised unity of the nation" (24).

41. Rudolph Otto, *Das Heilige: Über des Irrationale in der Idee des Göttlichen und sein Verhältnis zum Rationalen* (Gotha: F. A. Perthes, 1924), translated by John W. Harvey as *The Idea of the Holy* (London: Oxford University Press, 1924).

42. Barrès, *Scènes et doctrines du nationalisme*, 12.

43. On Nietzsche's influence on Barrès, see Sternhell, *Maurice Barrès et le nationalisme français*, 16–18.

44. Barrès, *Mes cahiers*, 3:284.

In sum, Barrès's philosophy of rootedness is a thoroughgoing particularist ideology whose central claim is that there is, in fact, no way
to surmount one's circumstances.[45] We are what we are born into—our
strength, our identity, our loyalties, even our reason, all thus arise out of
these circumstances. The claim that there is some universal reason that
transcends our circumstances and, thus, some universal morality is merely
the consequence of disconnection, deracination from one's instincts.

Morally, this position amounts to relativism, a term that Barrès openly
owns and espouses. "There is no absolute truth, only relatives," he writes
in his notebooks.[46] He seems not to recognize the obvious contradiction
in this claim, given his insistence on determinism as an ultimate value.
It is the combination of these two potentially contradictory factors that
give his thinking its violent and xenophobic thrust. Relativism might
appear to offer a foundation for a philosophy of tolerance; instead,
for Barrès such a thinking leads to a philosophy of absolute aggression
toward all who do not belong to the "we" that absorbs the "I."[47]

Barrès's aim during the Dreyfus affair was to harness the event as a
means to unify the nation by expelling the deracinated forces that had
besieged it. Anti-Semitism proved to be in the 1880s and 1890s one of
the most successful methods of national unification. By identifying Jews
with capital, social anti-Semitism was able to direct the resentment of
the lower classes and the petit bourgeois away from class conflict and
toward the Jew. Barrès was himself well aware of the effectiveness of this
tactic. As he wrote in *Le figaro* in 1890: "The crowd always needs a word
of war to rally itself; it wants some cry of passion that makes abstract
ideas tangible. Never has this truth been more evident than at the present hour when the disinherited are weary of programs and even discussions. . . . *Juif* is only an adjective designating usurers, monopolizers,
stockbrokers, all those that abuse money."[48] Nothing showed the power
of this strategy more clearly than the astonishing success of Édouard
Drumont's vituperative *La France juive*, which sold more than 100,000
copies in its first year and was reprinted two hundred times.[49] Barrès was

45. I am borrowing this phrase from Soucy's *Fascism in France*.
46. Barrès, *Mes cahiers*, 2:163.
47. Barrès, *Les déracinés*, 1:260.
48. Barrès, "La formule antijuive."
49. Édouard Drumont, *La France juive*, 200th ed., 2 vols. (Paris: Flammarion, ca. 1880s), 1:d. Drumont attributed the success of *La France juive*, perhaps rightly, to the fact that he was voicing the
"pensée secrète" that many could scarcely admit to themselves but nonetheless believed. He cast
himself, moreover, as a prophet predicting a great battle between the Jewish forces, represented by
the Alliance israélite universelle and depicted as the vehicle of the international Jewish conspiracy
seeking to master the world, and the Alliance antisémite universelle, which, according to Drumont,

a great admirer of Drumont's, and his own anti-Semitic rhetoric often seems to echo the infamous editor of *La libre parole*, particularly in allying rationalism, modernization, and Judaism. For Barrès, however, anti-Semitism was one piece of a larger ideology, not the core of his message, as was the case for Drumont. Rather, anti-Semitism fit quite neatly with Barrès's larger philosophy of rootedness.

The danger of the Jews for Barrès was not merely that they were strangers, a fact that he emphasized insistently.[50] What made the Jews particularly dangerous, what made them suspicious from the beginning, was their rootlessness:

The Jews don't have a fatherland in the sense that we understand. For us, the fatherland is the soil and our ancestors; it is the land and the dead. For them, it is the place where they find their greatest interest. Their "intellectuals" arrive thus at their famous definition: the fatherland, it is an idea. But what idea? That which is most useful to them, for example, the idea that all men are brothers, that nationalism is a prejudice to destroy, that military honor reeks of blood, that it is necessary to disarm (and leave no other force but money).[51]

Here, Barrès is able to include a number of the anti-Semitic tropes that were currently circulating and to attribute all these traits to Jewish rootlessness. He proposes that "their intellectuals" are the authors of the idea that all men are brothers. This could mean either that the eighteenth-century Enlightenment thinkers were somehow Jewish or that the Jews are themselves credited as the authors of the notion of fraternity. Either way, the sentiment recalls the claim made by Drumont, Maurras, and others at the centenary of the 1789 revolution—that the Jews were its true beneficiaries, perhaps even its architects.[52] The association between the Jews and republicanism and between the Jews and capital derives

would ultimately prevail in a fight that would take place on the backs of the Jews (139). The strategy of his argument was to show that the Jews had been the greatest beneficiaries of the Revolution and, thus, were to blame for the corrosion of the values of *la vieille France*: "The only one who profits from the Revolution is the Jew. All of it comes from the Jew; all of it returns to the Jew" (i). Drumont was not isolated in his views. In the 1880s, the great majority of popular newspapers were anti-Semitic. See Zeev Sternhell, *La droite révolutionnaire, 1885–1914* (Paris: Seuil, 1978), 217.

50. "Is it necessary to call them 'dirty Jews' or 'first aristocrats of the world'? You can think whatever you want according to your temperament and according to circumstances. That is not at all interesting. But you cannot deny that the Jew is a different being" (Barrès, *Scènes et doctrines du nationalisme*, 64).

51. Ibid., 63–64.

52. Drumont, e.g., wrote: "The centenary of '89 is their centenary, the centenary of those foreigners who have chased the brave native Frenchmen from their homes, Frenchmen born on [French] soil.... They have money and honors.... The centenary of 1789 is the centenary of the Jew" (quoted in Birnbaum, *La France imaginée*, 156, and *The Idea of France*, 114).

from Barrès's claim that the Jews do not understand what it means to be tied to a homeland. They are not merely out of touch with their roots; they have none.

From this claim, which clearly has the status of fact for him, Barrès is easily able to deduce Dreyfus's guilt. The *real* facts of the case are irrelevant:

> This deracinated [Jew], who feels ill at ease in one of the squares of our old French Gardens, must naturally admit that it is in another milieu that he has found his happiness. . . . [R]ancor incited him . . . because he has no roots. . . . I don't need anyone to tell me why Dreyfus betrayed. Psychologically, it suffices for me to know that he betrayed. The interval is filled in. That Dreyfus is capable of betraying, I conclude from his race. . . . As for those who say that Dreyfus is not a traitor . . . So be it! They are quite right: Dreyfus doesn't belong to our nation, so how could he betray it?[53]

Barrès's logic can be boiled down to the following: to be a Jew is to lack roots in France; to lack French roots is to lack loyalty to France; to lack loyalty to France is to be the enemy. This logic makes the Jew, who has no land in which to be rooted, universally suspect.

That said, Barrès is able to extend similar "reasoning" to anyone who lines up with the Dreyfusards. To side with Dreyfus is to display a lack of loyalty to France. If one lacks loyalty to France, one must not, in fact, be truly French. Why, then, does Émile Zola defend Dreyfus? Because Zola is not *truly* French. Barrès does not go so far as to accuse Zola of being Jewish. Rather, he claims that Zola's Italian background "predestined [him] for Dreyfusism. He obeyed a profound interior necessity. . . . [T]here is a frontier between you and me. What frontier, the Alps. . . . Émile Zola thinks naturally as a deracinated Venetian."[54]

Insofar as Zola is deracinated, he belongs to that tribe that Barrès famously defined in *Scènes et doctrines du nationalisme: les intellectuels*. One of Barrès's lasting legacies is his baptism of the notion of the intellectual,[55] a nomination that many accepted with pride throughout the rest

---

53. Barrès, *Scènes et doctrines du nationalisme*, 152–53.

54. Zola was born in France, but his father was an Italian engineer who acquired French citizenship. See ibid., 40–41.

55. Pascal Ory and Jean-François Sirinelli date the origin of the modern category of the intellectual to its first usage by Clemenceau on January 23, 1898, in *L'aurore*, but they credit Barrès with popularizing and politicizing the category in a column written for *Le journal* one week later under the headline "La protestation des intellectuels!" (*Les intellectuels en France: De l'affaire Dreyfus à nos jours* [Paris: Armand Colin, 1986], 6). The affair deeply affects the future conception of the intellectual in France by defining him in terms of his action and communication rather than his mere thinking: "He is not a man 'who thinks' . . . but the man who communicates a thought" (ibid., 9).

of the twentieth century.[56] In *Scènes et doctrines*, Barrès offers the following definition: "Intellectual: an individual who is persuaded that society must be founded on logic and who fails to recognize that it rests in fact on anterior necessities and may be at odds with individual reason."[57]

Not only does Barrès want to distinguish himself from those he terms *intellectuals*—"We prefer to be intelligent rather than intellectual," he writes—but he wants also to establish distance between the intellectuals and the people of France: "A demi-culture [*les intellectuals*] destroys its instinct without substituting a conscience. All these aristocrats of thought show that they don't think like the vile crowd. One sees that too well. They no longer feel spontaneously in accord with their natural group."[58]

One effect of Barrès and other right-wing literary figures distinguishing themselves from *les intellectuels* was to establish the intellectual as a quintessentially antifascist figure.[59] Both the Dreyfusards and the literary figures of the Left from later generations happily owned the traits for which they were being denigrated. Barrès himself quotes Anatole France:

In calling us intellectuals . . . one mocks men capable of understanding. One defames them. . . . Are there then objects on which the faculty of comprehension ought not be exercised? I am sorry for our contradictors, but there is not an object that intelligence is unable to look at in the face. Everything is its domain. The men who have consecrated their life to the research of scientific truths, the men dedicated to the work of laboratories and libraries are better suited than the vulgar to discern true from false in

56. On the origins of the intellectual in France, see ibid.; and Datta, *Birth of a National Icon*. On the legacy of this category, see Jeremy Jennings, ed., *Intellectuals in Twentieth-Century France: Mandarins and Samurais* (New York: St. Martin's, 1993). Tony Judt's *Past Imperfect: French Intellectuals, 1944–1956* (Berkeley and Los Angeles: University of California Press, 1992) argues—following a trajectory begun by Julien Benda's *La trahison des clercs* (Paris: Bernard Grasset, 1927)—that the notion of the politically committed intellectual was dangerous and led to the misguided commitment to communism in the post-1945 era on the part of a number of French intellectuals (most famously Sartre), a commitment that disregarded the atrocities of totalitarianism. For a compelling rejoinder, see Jeremy Jennings, "Of Treason, Blindness and Silence: Dilemmas of the Intellectual in Modern France," in *Intellectuals in Politics: From the Dreyfus Affair to Salman Rushdie*, ed. Jeremy Jennings and Anthony Kemp-Welch (New York: Routledge, 1997), 64–85.

57. Barrès, *Scènes et doctrines du nationalisme*, 44. In 1965, when Jean-Paul Sartre was himself defining the mission of the intellectual, he traced the origins of the term back to the Dreyfus affair and, implicitly, Barrès. See Jean-Paul Sartre, *Plaidoyer pour les intellectuels* (Paris: Gallimard, 1972), 12, translated by John Mathews as "A Plea for Intellectuals," in Jean-Paul Sartre, *Between Existentialism and Marxism* (New York: Morrow Quill, 1979), 232.

58. Barrès, *Scènes et doctrines du nationalisme*, 45, 46.

59. See Jennings, "Of Treason, Blindness and Silence," 69–71; and Judt, *Past Imperfect*, 242. Although Barrès's main work predates the rise of fascism as a political movement in France, the "literary fascists" of the 1930s considered him to be the intellectual father of this movement. See Carroll, *French Literary Fascism*, 20.

the general order of affairs and in the issues that are of public interest. As they can be useful there, their duty is to employ themselves with these concerns.[60]

In claiming the legacy of eighteenth-century humanism, in claiming to be men of abstract reason, the Dreyfusards could easily accept the barbs directed their way. When Julien Benda reflected back on the affair in his 1927 *La trahison des clercs*, he reoriented Barrès's critique by arguing that it was Barrès and those who had followed him into nationalism that had been the traitors: "The 'clerks' who indulged in this fanaticism betrayed their duty, which is precisely to set up a corporation whose sole cult is that of justice and truth, in opposition to the peoples and the injustice to which they are condemned by their religions of this earth." Benda cast Zola as a hero for exactly the reason that Barrès condemns him: he behaved as an "officiant of abstract justice . . . sullied with no passion for a worldly object."[61] And it is as a hero, of course, that Zola is remembered.[62]

A secondary effect of Barrès's strategy was that it associated the intellectual with the Jew. Both were enemies of the people. If the Jew and the intellectual were not synonymous, then they at least were held to suffer from the same delusion: that all men are brothers. The association between intellectual and Jew was further compounded by the fact that, in the 1890s, Jewish intellectuals such as Émile Durkheim and Henri Bergson were themselves gaining prominence. As Pierre Birnbaum has shown, the centenary of the Revolution coincided with the rise of the class of "state Jews," intellectuals and bureaucrats who identified closely with the ideals of the republic and who held high positions both in government and in the academy.[63]

Consequently, while the Jew might never be cast as national hero in France, there is also a sense in which Barrès's association of the Jew, not only with republican values, but also with the very identity of the intellectual made possible the revalorization of the notion of the Jew.[64]

60. Barrès, *Scènes et doctrines du nationalisme*, 44.

61. Benda, *La trahison des clercs*, 70–71, 63, translated by Richard Aldington as *The Treason of Intellectuals* (New York: William Morrow, 1928), 57, 51.

62. In 1908, Zola's remains were buried in the Pantheon, where, ironically, he shares a crypt with Victor Hugo, the heroic mascot of French nationhood in Barrès's *Les déracinés*.

63. See Pierre Birnbaum, *Les fous de la République* (Paris: Fayard, 1992).

64. In "La formule antijuive," which appeared in *Le figaro* in 1890, Barrès described the way in which anti-Jewish sentiment provided a rallying point around which to unify the crowd: "The crowd always needs a word of war to rally itself, it wants some cry of passion that makes abstract ideas tangible. Never has this truth been more evident than at the present hour when the disinherited are weary of programs and even discussions. . . . *Juif* is only an adjective designating usurers, monopolizers, stockbrokers, all those that abuse money" (quoted in Phillip Ouston, *The Imagination of Maurice Barrès* [Toronto: University of Toronto Press, 1974], 127).

Just as the intellectual developed a positive and emblematic sense as a consequence of the concept's reclamation by those defending Dreyfus, so the concept of the Jew gained by virtue of the affair the possibility of attaining an emblematic status linked to that of the intellectual as the antithesis of the nationalist.

In fact, Barrès's clear-cut constructive agenda to form a nationalist vision of the French race through a determinist account of the relationship of France's native sons to *la terre et les morts* might help explain why the Jew became such an important figure for revalorization. After 1945, in the wake of fascism, when the values that he advocated so strongly—such as the authenticity of the self, rootedness, and struggle—take on the shadings of evil, the fact that Barrès consistently shaped his image of the French race in his literary texts through the contrasting depiction of the barbarian or the foreigner, who was for him best exemplified by the Jew, gives the very values with which he associated the Jew a certain glint of goodness. These qualities include intellective reflection, rootlessness, anxiety, and a certain dis-ease in one's environment. These are, indeed, the very terms Barrès uses to describe Dreyfus and to explain his certainty of Dreyfus's guilt.[65]

As we will see in the next chapter, the resonances of these associations were clearly evident fifty years later in Sartre's depictions of Judaism and anti-Semitism. But, even before Sartre, even during the affair, in the writings of some of Dreyfus's staunchest supporters, there is evidence of an acceptance—accompanied by a reorientation—of the racialist essentializations put forth by anti-Semites. In the texts of Bernard Lazare and Charles Péguy, we find a rejection of the universalizing language of human nature that had been the primary tool of defense for the Jews up until this moment and, with that, an acceptance of racial terminology.

## The Roots of Revalorization: Bernard Lazare

In October 1908, five years after Bernard Lazare's death, a statue of his likeness was erected in honor of Nîmes's native son. On the following Bastille Day, a ritual of destruction commenced. The royalist faction, the Camelots du roi, gathered to desecrate the monument in an act of protest against the republic, of which—despite his philosophy of social anarchism—this Jewish defender of Alfred Dreyfus had become a symbol. In the first year, the group succeeded in breaking off the statue's nose. For

---

65. See Barrès, *Scènes et doctrines du nationalisme*, 152–53.

the next thirty-one years, the same group gathered each July 14 to ritual-ize their destruction, attacking what was left of the effigy, lobbing ink bot-tles at it, presumably a symbol of Lazare's weapon of choice: the written word. By 1940, they had achieved their goal: the statue—along with the Third Republic—was destroyed. It was not until 1966, on the centenary of Bernard Lazare's birth, that the statue was replaced, under the auspices of the Ligue des droits de l'homme, with a plaque commemorating its former existence or, more precisely, its absence. The plaque bears the fol-lowing inscription: "Ici était dressée une effigie de Bernard-Lazare qui en des jours difficiles défendit la vérité, la justice et les droits de l'homme, méconnus et foulés aux pied dans la personne de Dreyfus."[66]

In its most absurd details, this story encapsulates the ironies of the his-tory of the Jewish question in France. First, there is the nose, destroyed in an act that reminds us that the statue had become a symbol of the Jew, for which the nose itself served as a metonym. The Jew, in turn, was a target of the royalist Right because of the association between the Jew and the republic after the Dreyfus affair. Ironically, it was exactly the republican way of thinking that Lazare spent the last ten years of his life fighting, for it is the universalism of the republic that calls for the Jew to sacrifice allegiances to Judaism for the sake of the universal idea of man.[67] Lazare, in contrast, formulated an ideology of racialized Jewish nationalism against the ideal of assimilation, a way of thinking for which the notorious anti-Semite Édouard Drumont would ultimately praise him.[68] The story climaxes with the destruction of the statue at the very moment that France put in place its Statut des Juifs, which began the process of stripping Jews of their rights as citizens. At this moment, in 1940, the destruction of the statue was able to symbolize the eradica-tion of both the republic and the Jew. In 1966, the statue was, not resur-rected, but replaced by a plaque that indicated that a statue of Bernard Lazare had *once* stood there. The significance of the plaque, then, was in its signaling of absence, an absence that would seem to evoke the failure

66. "Here there had stood an effigy of Bernard-Lazare who in difficult days defended truth, justice, and the rights of man, which went unrecognized and were trampled on in the person of Dreyfus" (quoted in Nelly Wilson, *Bernard-Lazare* [Cambridge: Cambridge University Press, 1978], 273–75 [my translation]).

67. As Wilson notes, J. S. McClelland uses the term *ideogram* to describe the way in which the Jew served "as a shorthand" for all that Barrès and Maurras detested about the Third Republic. See ibid., 273, referencing J. S. McClelland, *The French Right: From De Maistre to Maurras* (New York: Harper & Row, 1970), 30–31.

68. In the obituary for Bernard Lazare in *La libre parole*, Drumont's anti-Semitic newspaper, on September 5, 1903, Drumont wrote of him: "We can only hope one thing, that Christians embue the greatness and the duties of the Christian name, with the same grandeur and duty that Bernard-Lazare bestowed on the name of the Jew" (quoted in Wilson, *Bernard-Lazare*, 270).

of France to protect its Jews. But the inscription elides this meaning. Both Lazare and the Dreyfus affair are described in universalizing terms. Lazare had defended "the rights of man." Both Lazare's mission as Jewish activist and the anti-Semitism that exploded in France in conjunction with the Dreyfus affair go unmentioned. It is not the Jew who was trampled on, according to the plaque, but "the rights of Man . . . in the person of Dreyfus." Thus, even the plaque participates in the republican rhetoric that Bernard Lazare spent the last years of his life battling, a rhetoric that refuses to acknowledge difference even when it clearly does not go unseen.[69]

Bernard Lazare is a pivotal figure in our narrative of the revalorization of the figure of the rootless Jew because of the way in which he absorbed and transformed the anti-Semitic stereotype, accepting the discourse of race that was being perpetrated by anti-Semites, and rereading it as the basis for Jewish nationalism. Bernard Lazare's vision of the Jew is not, however, monolithic. Just as the story of his Nîmes monument manages to encapsulate the shifts, reversals, and ironies of the history of the Jewish question in France, so, indeed, does his own shifting perspective on the Jews uncannily mirror its multiple stages. In his earliest writings on Jewishness, Bernard Lazare echoes the tropes of medieval Jew hatred in his retellings of Christianity's classic anti-Jewish legends. In his history of anti-Semitism, he mirrors the rhetoric of the Revolution, calling for the dissolution of Jewish allegiances. In his late works following the affair, the works for which he is now seen as a pioneer for the cause of Jewish identity, he mirrors the critique that Jews are deracinated and calls for a revalorization of Jewishness along racial lines.

Bernard Lazare was himself an assimilated Jew. Born Lazare Manassé Bernard, he became a journalist, critic, favorite of the symbolist literary community, and self-professed anarchist. He is best known for his public defense of Dreyfus written at the behest of the Dreyfus family. His work on the Jewish question, however, began a few years previous to the affair. In the pre-Dreyfus texts, his views seem anything but philo-Semitic.

Following study of the history of religions at the École practique des hautes études between 1890 and 1892, Lazare wrote a collection of stories published under the title *Le miroir des légendes* (1892), in which he displayed a fascination with and an acceptance of the medi-

---

69. The same rhetoric is evident in the inscription on the Mémorial des martyrs de la déportation on the Île de la Cité dedicated to the 200,000 French martyrs who lost their lives in the war, thus avoiding reference to the fact that the vast majority of those 200,000 were Jews.

eval depiction of the Jew as traitor to Christ.[70] In this text, he offers his own twist on the legend of the Wandering Jew, describing an encounter between the eternal wanderer Ahasverus and an apparition of Jesus Christ. Between the 1840s and the 1890s, portrayals of the Wandering Jew in popular literature proliferated. Most famous was Eugene Sue's *Le Juif errant*, which appeared first as a serial in the Paris *Constitutionnel*. Though Ahasverus plays only a small role in the novel, the vast popularity of the serial, reprinted over forty times in France and translated into every language of modern Europe, no doubt created the conditions for an almost ubiquitous familiarity with the figure in the second half of the century in France.[71] In Sue's novel, the Wandering Jew and Jewess (the latter something of an innovation on Sue's part) are defenders of the working class. They appear at strategic moments, temporarily thwarting a Jesuit plot to underhandedly accumulate millions from the Huguenot family Rennepont.[72] In other texts of the period, the Wandering Jew spans the spectrum from romantic hero to satiric target, appearing to rescue a pair of lovers from danger in one text, as a merely cantankerous and ungrateful shoemaker in another, and as modern doctor thwarted by anti-Semitism in a third.[73] It is striking, then, that Bernard Lazare's version of the story stays very close to the legend's theological heart, bringing the folktale back to the issue of Ahasverus's betrayal of Christ. In Lazare's version, Ahasverus, standing outside the walls of the city of Jerusalem, meets a leper who sympathizes with his punishment for an unconscious crime. The Wandering Jew replies that the crime was, indeed, unconscious, adding that he did not know that it was God that he beat and chastised. The leper asks him whether he desires to end his wandering and to be put to rest in death. Ahasverus admits his envy for the sleep of the dead. The leper is transformed into Christ on the cross. He then offers to grant the Jew his wish if he agrees to beat Christ again after having admitted that he recognizes that he is God. The Jew refuses, crying out: "No, I do not want to die. I will not commit blasphemy, for Christ is God."[74] Laughter then resounds through the air, along with

70. Michael R. Marrus, *The Politics of Assimilation: A Study of the French Jewish Community at the Time of the Dreyfus Affair* (Oxford: Clarendon, 1971), 172.

71. Anderson, *The Legend of the Wandering Jew*, 238.

72. Anderson reports two earlier appearances of the Wandering Jewess, one in an eighteenth-century narrative by Frau Krüger and Edgar Quinet's companion for the Wandering Jew, Rachel. See ibid., 414.

73. See, respectively, Adolph H. Povinelli's *Ahasverus in Tyrol* (Vienna and Leipzig, 1890), Christian Hostrup's *Gjenboerne* (Copenhagen, 1847), and Fritz Mauthner's *Der Neue Ahasver* (Leipzig and Dresden, 1882), cited in Anderson, *The Legend of the Wandering Jew*, 279, 267, and 277–78.

74. Bernard Lazare, *Le miroir des légendes* (Paris: A. Lemerre, 1892), 134.

the noise of flight, and the cross is reabsorbed into the sky. Accepting the righteousness of his punishment, the Jew continues his wandering. Confirming once again the medieval Christian fantasy that the suffering of the Jews testifies to the truth of Christianity, Ahasverus receives redemption only by admitting that the punishment he has received is not heavy enough. A Coptic priest later witnesses him being taken up into the sky in a chariot surrounded by angels. In this version of the story, then, not only is Jewish guilt confirmed, but also forgiveness is granted only when the Jew himself accepts his guilt and recognizes his role in history as its consequence.

At the time that he wrote these tales, Bernard Lazare was himself a confirmed atheist, surely not on the verge of a conversion to Christianity. Thus, we cannot read the stories as theological meditations on Jewish history. We can recognize, nonetheless, the way in which his own understanding of Jewishness was tied inextricably to Christian anti-Judaic renderings of its symbolic value. The Jew is already a pariah for him, but the route to redemption is not through self-affirmation—as it will be later—but through self-flagellation and, ultimately, conversion.

Only in one story of the collection does Lazare take up in a style closer to realism the political and theological position of the Jews. In this story, "Les incarnations," he narrates a first-person encounter between a Western Jew and one of those far-flung descendants of the tribe in China who calls himself a "schismatic Jew." After acknowledging their hereditary connection to the Jewish people, the two proceed to exchange reasons for their independence from the tradition. Both find the Jews to have the basest preoccupations, but the first-person narrator argues that this is not their worst fault, for this is a fault to be found among all peoples. What the Jews are to be held accountable for is their harsh rejection of the actualization of ideas that have been their guide since the beginning of time. In other words, they are to be held accountable for their refusal to accept a redeemer.[75] While this sounds once again like a classically Christian anti-Judaic response to the misery of the Jews, in the mouth of the atheist Bernard Lazare (who suggests that any redeemer would do, including Sabbatai Zvi) it is probably more accurately interpreted as a criticism of the insistence of the Jews on setting themselves apart.

75. Ibid., 222. I am here making explicit the interpretation of Michael Marrus, who reads this comment purely politically and ignores the theological content. "His [Lazare's] principle objection to the Jews . . . lay in the fact that they so resolutely remained apart, throughout history from the societies in which they lived," writes Marrus, citing the page of *Miroir* where the narrator describes his chief objection to the Jews as their refusal to accept any candidate that has arisen in history as their redeemer, something the narrator sees as a manifest contradiction of the Jews' stated beliefs. See Marrus, *The Politics of Assimilation*, 172.

Bernard Lazare made this critique explicit, in fact, in the following year in his historical examination of the sources of anti-Semitism.

Between 1891 and 1893, he examined the Jewish question more self-consciously. *L'antisémitisme: Son histoire et ses causes*, the first systematic consideration of the problem, defines Jewishness—and to some extent defends it—in response to anti-Semitism. Lazare begins from the perspective of the anti-Semite, asking what is it about the Jews themselves that incites hatred: "Inasmuch as the enemies of the Jews belong to diverse races, as they dwelled far apart from one another, were ruled by different laws and governed by opposite principles; as they had not the same customs and differed in spirit from one another, so that they could not possibly judge alike of any subject, it must needs be that the general causes of anti-Semitism have always resided in Israel itself, and not in those who antagonized it."[76]

Bernard Lazare affirms the traits of the Jews that were assigned to them by the eighteenth-century Enlightenment thinkers arguing for Jewish emancipation and identifies the teachings of the Talmud as the cause of Jewish degeneracy. Like Abbé Gregoire, who had called for Jewish regeneration in the eighteenth century, Bernard Lazare argues that the doctors of the Talmud had worked to isolate the Jewish people, making of Israel "a sullen recluse, a rebel against all laws, foreign to all feeling of fraternity, closed to all beautiful, noble and generous ideas."[77] In an earlier essay, "Juifs et israélites," Lazare suggests that those French Jews, or "les israélites," who had in fact assimilated in France should not be grouped in with Eastern "juifs" who still lived in exclusive communities bound by their antiquated laws and acted as money changers.[78] *Les israélites* were at least on their way to full dispersal into the nation. Full assimilation, Lazare wrote as late as 1893, was the only solution to anti-Semitism.[79] Lazare envisioned anti-Semitism as a phenomenon destined to disappear. For the only thing that maintained the distinctiveness of the Jews, according to Lazare, was their exclusivism.

At least that is what Lazare says in some places.[80] In other places, there are inklings of the racialist/nationalist definition of Jewishness

76. Bernard Lazare, *L'antisémitisme: Son histoire et ses causes* (Paris: Albin Michel, 1982), 11, translated as *Antisemitism: Its History and Causes*, with an introduction by Robert S. Wistrich (Lincoln: University of Nebraska Press, 1995), 9.

77. Ibid., 16–17; 14.

78. Bernard Lazare, "Juifs et israélites," in *Entretiens politiques et littéraires*, quoted in Marrus, *The Politics of Assimilation*, 170.

79. Bernard Lazare, "La nationalité et les juifs français," quoted in ibid., 171.

80. The book was written between 1889 and 1994, a period when Lazare's relation to Judaism was clearly in flux; thus, the diversity in positions recorded in the text can probably be attributed to a changing attitude toward his subject.

that pervade his later essays. For example, he refers to the Jews' inherited spirit of revolution, claiming the baptized Marx as a clear representative of this tendency, and describes the Jews as ably equipped for modernity, having developed certain qualities through centuries of engagement in commerce. The Jew, he wrote, "is cold and calculating, supple and energetic, persevering and patient, clear and exact, qualities which he has inherited all from his ancestors, the money changers and traders of medieval times."[81]

Despite this apparent racial determinism, Bernard Lazare's goal was nonetheless to identify the causes of anti-Semitism in order to point to a solution. At the time that he was composing L'antisémitisme, he undoubtedly still thought that the solution would arise as the distinction between Jew and gentile disappeared and as the forces of conservatism were replaced by a growing sense of solidarity among the nations. Presumably, then, Lazare thought that he was sending out a message of hope to the Jews of France when he concluded his book in a messianic tone: "In every way I am led to believe that it [anti-Semitism] must ultimately perish . . . above all, because anti-Semitism is one of the last, though most long lived, manifestations of that old spirit of reaction and narrow conservatism, which is vainly attempting to arrest the onward movement of Revolution."[82]

Lazare's socialist vision of the future was bright, but it depended on the disappearance of Judaism, not its acceptance. It is not surprising, then, that his book was not greeted warmly by les israélites, who saw their modern religious life as consistent with republican values and felt that anti-Semitism was an aberration that, if ignored, would have little or no consequence for their lives. Ironically, Lazare's warmest reception came from the anti-Semites, who identified the work as "the only book on the subject by a Jew . . . worth reading."[83] Édouard Drumont praised the book for its impartiality, adding: "In reality, he [Lazare] says what we say everyday, only he says it differently from us."[84]

Surely it was not Bernard Lazare's intention to mirror the rhetoric of anti-Semitism. Nonetheless, that is what the book had done. By this time in France, any discussion of the Jew was dominated by the terms set for it by anti-Semitism. Lazare himself identified this phenomenon at a later date when he had already rejected his earlier views. "The Jews,"

81. Lazare, L'antisémitisme, 182, and Antisemitism, 167.

82. Ibid., 199; 183.

83. Robert S. Wistrich, introduction to Lazare, Antisemitism, xv.

84. Édouard Drumont in La libre parole, January 10, 1895, quoted in Marrus, The Politics of Assimilation, 174.

he wrote, "look upon themselves always in relation to Christians and never as themselves."[85] Although, as a Zionist, Lazare continued to be deeply influenced by the tenets of nationalism, any perceived agreement between him and Drumont vanished soon after the publication of *L'antisémitisme*, as did Lazare's messianic hope about the future unity of humanity.

As Lazare became more active in the Dreyfus affair, trading barbs with Drumont in the public forum, he also developed a new relationship to the Jewish community.[86] In *L'antisémitisme*, Lazare's tone had been self-consciously objective. He had insistently referred to "the Jews" using the third-person plural, not once identifying himself with either their history or their destiny. During the Dreyfus affair, that changed. As the defender of Dreyfus, Lazare also became the defender of the Jews and, consequently, identified himself vehemently as a member of the Jewish nation: "I have overcome the pride of being a Jew; I know why I am one, and that binds me to the past of my own people, links me to their present, obliges me to serve them, allows me to cry out for all their rights as men."[87] Presumably, Lazare's change of heart came from witnessing the growing anti-Semitism in France. He had clearly already identified the racial nature of Jew hatred in his anti-Semitism book but, nonetheless, had believed that the Jews' refusal to assimilate was its cause. The Dreyfus affair convinced him otherwise. "We made a mistake," he wrote, "and the accusation brought against Captain Dreyfus suffices to show us the evidence of our error."[88] Though many Jews refused even to see the affair as a Jewish matter, Lazare saw it as a sign that a "moral ghetto" had been created in Paris, one that was latent and unavowed but nonetheless included all Jews, assimilated and unassimilated alike, within its walls. The only way to fight the ghetto was to make it visible. "Henceforth," he wrote, "I am a pariah."[89]

For Lazare, identifying himself as a pariah involved divesting himself of assimilationist ambitions in order to fight for the Jews as a Jew, giving

85. Bernard Lazare, *Le fumier de Job* (Paris: Circé, 1990), 77, translated by Harry Lorin Binsse as *Job's Dungheap: Essays on Jewish Nationalism and Social Revolution* (New York: Schocken, 1948), 43. The English edition includes only excerpts from the French original. However, it also includes essays that were not published in the French, such as "Nationalism and Jewish Emancipation," cited below.

86. As Marrus (*The Politics of Assimilation*, 182) reports, in 1896 the men actually engaged in a duel, though neither was injured. Throughout their correspondence, which was quite extensive, they treated one another like worthy adversaries. In fact, the duel was a consequence of Lazare's participation on the jury of *La libre parole*'s contest for solutions to the Jewish question. For a record of this correspondence, see the letters printed in Philippe Oriol, ed., *Bernard Lazare: Anarchiste et nationaliste juif* (Paris: Honoré Champion, 1999).

87. Lazare, *Le fumier de Job*, 76, and *Job's Dungheap*, 45.

88. Bernard Lazare, "Le nouveau ghetto," *La justice*, November 17, 1894.

89. Lazare, *Le fumier de Job*, 25, and *Job's Dungheap*, 45.

up the illusion that *les israélites* had succeeded through assimilation in achieving equality. This meant recognizing that what separated the Jew from the Israelite was, not that one was enslaved and the other free, but rather that the Israelite had merely exchanged the miseries of the ghetto "for a new source of miseries." The assimilated Jew, or the Western Jew, was now a slave to the opinions of those who had emancipated him. The assimilated Jew had to show himself worthy of the great gift of emancipation, which meant accepting the assessment of the Christian and then trying to overcome that judgment through self-transformation. The Jew "looked upon himself from the point of view of Christian anti-Semitism, for which the Jew can only be tolerated in the Christian state."[90] In accepting the Christian judgment of the Jews, the assimilated Jew had to prove that the judgment of the Christian no longer applied to him. He denied his relation to his own past and tried to "forget the miserable ancestor from whom he had sprung." But the Christian would never let him forget. He was, thus, plagued by the duplicity of the dominant culture, which first condemned him for his past and then condemned him for trying to avoid it—for being cosmopolitan, for having no roots. "Whereas most people go out of the way to find themselves ancestors, he [the Jew] wants to forget that he ever had one," wrote Lazare.[91]

In this new phase of Lazare's thinking, the dichotomy is no longer between Jew and Israelite. Rather, it is, as Hannah Arendt shows, between "pariah" and "parvenu." To claim the role of pariah as positive, the Jew, like Anatole France's intellectual, defines himself in relation to his accusers but dignifies the accusation by deploying it politically as a form of resistance. As Arendt describes this position, it was a form of engagement, of activism, a way to resist oppression:

In other words he [Lazare] wanted him [the Jew] to feel that he was himself responsible for what society had done to him. He wanted him to stop seeking release in an attitude of superior indifference or in lofty and rarefied cogitation about the nature of man *per se*. However much the Jewish pariah might be, from the historical viewpoint, the product of an unjust dispensation ("look what you have made of the people, ye Christians and ye princes of Jews"), politically speaking every pariah who refused to be a rebel was partly responsible for his own position and therewith for the blot on mankind which it represented.[92]

90. Bernard Lazare, "Nationalism and Jewish Emancipation" (in French), *L'echo zioniste*, March and April 1901, reprinted in *Job's Dungheap*, 94.

91. Bernard Lazare, "Le nationalisme juif," first given as a lecture at the Association des étudiants israélites russes, March 6, 1897, and reprinted in *Le fumier de Job*, 93, and *Job's Dungheap*, 57.

92. Hannah Arendt, "The Jew as Pariah: A Hidden Tradition," *Jewish Social Studies* 4 (April 1944): 109.

Ultimately, Lazare's position amounted to a rejection of the emancipa-
tory bargain and all that it implied. It amounted to a refusal to give up
being a Jew in order to be a man. "We stand up and we say to them,"
Lazare wrote, "We are ever the ancient stiff-necked people, the unruly
and rebel nation; we want to be ourselves, and we shall know well
how to conquer the right which is ours, not only to be men but also
to be Jews."[93]

But what did this mean, to be men *and* also to be Jews? It did not
mean a return to the ghetto or a return to religious practice. Lazare was
a confirmed atheist until the end of his days and did not lose his disdain
for Jewish religious life even as he accepted his role as a Jew. Ironically,
it did mean accepting the accusations leveled at the Jews, owning them
and investing them with power, declaring, in other words, "We are a
rebel nation." On the one hand, Lazare was developing a compelling
strategy for political resistance. On the other hand, his formula illustrates the fact that he had absorbed the criticisms of the anti-Semites,
absorbed their ideology of nationalism, and absorbed their claim that
the Jew could never be French. Sounding very much like Maurice Barrès,
he wrote: "He [the Jew] was able to absorb into himself, like a school-
boy, the history, philosophy, literature and art of the countries of which
he became a citizen, but that art, that literature, that philosophy, that
history could not belong to his very fiber, or make his being deeply
vibrate; and it is true that in Christian societies the Jew can only be an
assimilator; he will be a creator only on the day when he comes again
to draw on Jewish sources, those wellsprings into which a Heine could
dive so deep."[94]

Lazare wanted to combat the anti-Semitic element of French nationalism, not by fighting against its premises, like Zola, but by advocating
Jewish nationalism. He explained his strategy this way: "Do not insist
upon entering a house where you will be insulted, on sitting at a table
whence you will be driven away. Learn how to build your own house, a
house where you will welcome all men."[95] Lazare clearly distinguished
his welcoming brand of nationalism from the exclusive brand of French
nationalism and wanted to use his nationalism to help regenerate Jewish

93. Lazare, "Nationalism and Jewish Emancipation," 87.
94. Ibid., 95. It was, indeed, probably no surprise that Lazare sounds something like the later Barrès as Barrès's notion of the *culte du moi* had deep influences beyond the circle of traditionalism with
which it was, ultimately, associated. The young Léon Blum, who in the 1930s would become the first
Jewish prime minister of France, described Barrès's influence in the 1880s and 1890s on the generation
of writers coming of age at that time: "He was for me and most of my friends not only the *maître* but
the guide" (Blum quoted in Marrus, *The Politics of Assimilation*, 173).
95. Lazare, *Job's Dungheap*, 100.

pride so that Jews would no longer feel that their dignity depended on aping the gentile. Ironically, however, the very premises of his nationalism were deeply dependent on some of the basic notions underlying French nationalism. Even the ideal image of the Jew that his new way of thinking promoted was just as much a reaction to the charges of modern anti-Semitism as the patriotic image of Judaism that arose after the Revolution was a reaction to the critical image of the Jew promoted by the Enlightenment.

One of the first points of contact between Lazare's new way of thinking and modern anti-Semitism is his redefinition of Jewishness along national and racial lines, an affinity with the anti-Semites that Lazare himself acknowledged, writing: "People told me that by affirming the permanence and the reality of a Jewish nation, I made myself an ally of the anti-Semites. I have reflected a great deal upon this grave complaint, and I insist upon remaining, on this point, in alliance with the anti-Semites." There are, indeed, "Jewish types," he affirmed, insisting on some racial affinity among Jews where even Ernest Renan resisted.[96] What the Jews share more profoundly, he argued, is nationhood and all that it implies in terms of common history and a common fount of tradition. The ideas that arose out of this history "belong" to the Jews, are theirs exclusively.[97] This is true of the Jewish nation just as it is of the French nation and the German nation, Lazare claimed.

But, unlike the German nation and the French nation, the Jewish nation formed its fundamental characteristics through its subjection to oppression:

During the long years of bondage it was the consolation and the strength of Israel, whom the peoples struck as a hammer strikes the anvil. Jewish brotherhood and solidarity were strengthened in tears and blood. Today tears and blood can still cause their rebirth in the souls of those among the rich who are not yet gangrenous. Sorrow, that great reconciler of souls, accomplished what joy and triumph could not have done. It taught those who languished under contempt and under blows, those whose faces were covered with spittle and whose backs were flogged, that nothing

96. Lazare, *Le fumier de Job*, 95, 91–92, and *Job's Dungheap*, 60, 56. Ernest Renan played an ambiguous role in the history of French anti-Semitism. It was his description of the Semite in his writings on religious history and Semitic languages that provided much of the ammunition for Drumont and Barrès, among others. He, however, distinguished the modern Jew from the ancient Semite, rejected a racial definition of Judaism, and proposed a concept of the nation that was clearly pluralistic, if not in intention, then at least in consequence. See his "Le judaïsme comme race et comme religion" and his classic 1882 lecture opposing racialist and religious definitions of the nation, "What Is a Nation?" both in Ernest Renan, *Discours et conferences* (Paris: C. Levy, 1887).

97. Lazare, *Le fumier de Job*, 95, and *Job's Dungheap*, 59.

is as dear to a groaning heart as the breast, itself lacerated, of the brother in suffering and despair.[98]

The fundamental characteristics of the Jewish nation, according to Lazare, were those that grew out of a life of hardship; they included the prophet's demand for justice and the compassion and solidarity that came from suffering under the same whip. Lazare envisioned the Jews forming a nationalist movement and fighting for freedom and the right to self-determination.

Bernard Lazare's goal was clearly noble, and the vision of the Jew as an emblem for the downtrodden and the oppressed was a powerful one that invested the Jewish condition with moral significance. It provided for the first time the possibility for revalorization, a revalorization that seemingly would not necessitate an abnegation of Jewish history and Jewish values. It did, however, involve siding with the anti-Semites by rejecting one of the dominant Jewish stereotypes of the moment and, in that sense, still seemed determined by the anti-Semitic portrait of the Jew. The target of anti-Semitism was not the *shtetl* Jew with sidelocks and dark clothing, even if he was often its victim. The target was the assimilated Jew, the rich Jew, the Jew involved in trade and government—the parvenu. Lazare was almost as unrelenting on these Jews as were the anti-Semites. Unlike the anti-Semites, however, he described the parvenu, not as the epitome of the Jew, but rather as the "de-Judaized." In a reversal of the anti-Semitic claim that the Jew was a corrupting force, he claimed that the assimilated Jew had "became corrupt upon contact with Christian society . . . lost his own virtues and acquired only the vices of those who surrounded him." These Jews were now aligned with the oppressor, the enemy. "The best of anti-Semitic agents," Lazare called them, speaking particularly of the French Jews. "Well do I know them, and I know of what they are capable; they did not limit themselves to rejecting all solidarity with foreign Jews, they even wanted to hold them [foreign Jews] responsible for evils which their own cowardice alone begot." But *les israélites* were no longer his concern. They were suffering the consequences of their actions, and the downtrodden Jews "should become indifferent toward them." The assimilated were, indeed, the Jews worthy of the name Judas, Lazare implied, once again echoing the rhetoric of Christian anti-Semitism: "In spite of their begging, their reasoning, their purely scientific argument, men will always look upon them as individuals set apart. . . . [W]e know of course that they are

98. Lazare, *Job's Dungheap*, 90.

ready for every betrayal, for every abjectness, in order to prove to the hilt that they have abandoned everything which binds them to the past and everything which joins them to their brothers in this world. . . . This Jewish bourgeoisie, rich and not Jewish, is our garbage, our rubbish; we must rid ourselves of it."[99] Much of the formulaic anti-Semitic rhetoric is evident in this passage. Those described were the Jews of the republic who clutched the humanistic rhetoric of the French Revolution in the hopes that it would raise them out of abjection. They were rootless, both figuratively and literally, having broken ties with their true brothers, their fellow Jews.

Lazare took the tropes of anti-Semitism and, without invalidating them, tried to build a notion of the downtrodden Jew that would allow him to extract "Jewishness" from anti-Semitic accusations. In order to do this, he had to rebut the charge that the Jews have always been pre-occupied with money, always involved in usury, and always traitors. He thus returned to the biblical and rabbinic sources in order to revive a Jewish agrarian ethic. He drew on the talmudic prohibition against usury to show that the Christian prohibition against the practice was derived from the Jews. If there were usurers among the Jews, it was only among those who participated in the Christian world, those who were, in fact, corrupted by this contact.[100]

This renegotiation of the ideology surrounding the Jew was a master-ful strategy that responded to anti-Semitic charges by turning to Jewish sources. In the process, Lazare helped revive these sources as a national literature whose purpose was, not to guide daily life, but to serve as a cultural treasury, a national heritage. He was, however, fighting back, but not by resisting the values that undergirded turn-of-the-century nation-alism. Rather, like the nineteenth-century French Jews who wanted to prove that the Revolution was the fulfillment of *Jewish* values, he argued that, with their centuries-old solidarity and strong national identity, Jews embodied the values of nationalism long before nationalism existed. They embodied these accusations, however, not because they were strong but because as a people they were weak. This is where Lazare was at his most radical. By combining the rhetoric of Marxism with the rhetoric of Jewish nationalism, he helped create a form of cultural Zionism that merged the principles of nationalism with those of revolutionary socialism.

Bernard Lazare was one of the founding figures of modern Zionism and, in line with Ahad Ha-Am, tried to conceptualize "cultural Zionism,"

99. Ibid., 93, 97, 99.
100. Ibid., 122–23.

a movement that saw Jewish nationalism as being as much about renewing solidarity among the Jews, reclaiming their nationhood, as it was about solving a political problem: "For a Jew, the word nationalism should mean freedom. A Jew who today may declare, 'I am a nationalist,' will not be saying in any special precise, or clear cut way, 'I am a man who seeks to rebuild a Jewish state in Palestine and who dreams of conquering Jerusalem.' He will be saying, 'I want to be a man fully free, I want to enjoy the sunshine, I want to escape the oppression, to escape the outrage, to escape the scorn with which men overwhelm me.'"[101]

Lazare's impact on Zionism was not significant, partly because he died young, and partly because, as a consequence of ideological differences with Herzl, he resigned from the Zionist Central Committee less than three years after it was founded. His lasting legacy is, thus, as a defender of both Dreyfus and the principles of the republic, a role for which he was honored by the statue in Nîmes. It is, nonetheless, fitting that the drama that played out over this statue managed to demonstrate the pitfalls of the French republican model. Lazare, I imagine, would have felt confirmed, at least, in his views.

### Roots without Soil: Charles Péguy on the Jews

The legacy of Charles Péguy, unlike that of Bernard Lazare, transcends his role in the Dreyfus affair. He is, perhaps, remembered less as a champion of the rights of a Jew than as an architect of French nationalism.[102] What sets him apart from the nationalists of his generation is his vision of Judaism. Not only was he a Dreyfusard committed to fighting anti-Semitism in France; he also celebrated in the Jews the very traits that others denigrated. For Péguy, it was the Jews' errancy that defined their worldly mission. In *Notre jeunesse*, he offers a new chapter to the legend of the Wandering Jew. Bernard Lazare, who became for him a symbol of the Jews, was his very own modern-day Ahasverus.[103]

Lazare died of cancer in 1903 at the age of thirty-eight. Péguy subsequently made it his mission to propagate Lazare's memory and his portrait of the Jew as representative of the downtrodden. In the process,

---

101. Lazare, *Le fumier de Job*, 104, and *Job's Dungheap*, 73.

102. This has led to the accusation, moreover, that Péguy is "one of those . . . who precipitated the European catastrophe" (Finkielkraut, *Le mécontemporain*, 17). Bernard-Henri Lévy (*L'idéologie française* [Paris: Grasset, 1981]) is one of the most vocal accusers of Péguy's, while Finkielkraut is one of his most vocal defenders.

103. For Péguy, there was no reversal involved in his movement from Dreyfusard to nationalist. He insists throughout *Notre jeunesse* on the continuity between these positions.

he transformed Lazare's vision of the Jewish nation into a theological trope. His portrait of the Jew relies, like Herder's, Hegel's, and Barrès's, on the depiction of the Jew as fundamentally alienated. Péguy reverses the negative associations with this stereotype and is able to produce a philo-Semitic version of the same portrait. In *Notre jeunesse*, his retrospective account of the Dreyfus affair, this transformation is performed by overlaying the modern image of the Jew beset by anti-Semitism with biblical and theological accounts of both the early Jewish prophets and the Christians.[104] All the while, Péguy, like the later Lazare, maintains a racialist logic. While his view of race was quite different from the biological discourse of race that circulated in the 1930s and helped lend a scientific air to anti-Semitism, it was, nonetheless, deterministic. What was true of the biblical Jews is, for Péguy, true of contemporary Jews. Modern Jews share the same character with early nomads because they come from the same roots, because theirs is a blood lineage that can be traced back to those early portraits. The common essence asserted between the ancient Jews and their modern predecessors Péguy holds to be a consequence of a racial essence, bred and transmitted from generation to generation.

Péguy and Lazare met through their active engagement in the Dreyfus affair, circumstances that deeply shaped Péguy's impressions of Lazare. At the time of their meeting, Péguy was himself an active socialist and an avowed atheist.[105] Ironically, it may have been his involvement in the affair and, potentially, even his friendship with the atheist Jew Lazare that helped turn him back toward the Christian faith. He developed, as a consequence of socialist involvement with the anti-Dreyfusard cause, a deep distrust of the socialist movement, which, he claimed, had committed an error in judgment by conflating the categories of Jew and capitalist.[106] The clarity of this differentiation for Péguy was undoubtedly a consequence of Lazare's influence. The distinction that Lazare made in his own writings between the minority of rich Jewish parvenus, who incited anti-Semitism, and the poor Jewish majority, who suffered

104. The work was written in part, Péguy suggests, as a counternarrative to Daniel Halevy's "Apologie pour notre passé," *Cahiers de la quinzaine*, ser. 40, no. 10 (1910). In response to Halevy's critique of the Dreyfusards, Péguy insists on the righteousness of his position and actions during the affair: "Not only is there not a comma that we would disavow; there is not a comma that we would not glory in" (Charles Péguy, *Notre jeunesse* [Paris: Gallimard, 1933], 57–58).

105. Lazare Prajs, *Péguy et Israël* (Paris: Nizet, 1970), 79. The extent to which Péguy was an atheist even at the beginning of the affair is a point of contestation among scholars. Jules Isaac suggests that, despite his own contestations, he never underwent a conversion back to Christianity because he never *really* left the faith to begin with. See Jules Isaac, *Expériences de ma vie, Péguy* (Paris: Calmann-Lévy, 1959).

106. Prajs, *Péguy et Israël*, 82.

from it, allowed for a realignment of associations. To be a true socialist, and, finally, for Péguy, to be a true Christian, one had to recognize the Jews as representing the wretched of the earth.

In his early essays on the affair, Péguy was highly critical of the role the church played in condemning Dreyfus. He denounced the church for attributing theological significance to the alleged crime, for imbuing the accompanying events with an air of the sacred, and for employing religious language and categories in order to take stock of the gravity of the crime. In 1899, Péguy wrote in *La revue blanche*: "That the culpability of Dreyfus was feigned, imagined, cultivated by the Jesuits and by an immense majority of Catholics is an obvious fact. . . . Dreyfus had become an anathema. Whoever defended him would be an anathema with him. The arrest of the Council of War was an article of faith. These words 'the honor of the army' became a sacred formula, ready for the Latin of the next litanies."[107] Eleven years later, however, in *Notre jeunesse*, Péguy himself describes the affair as having religious significance: "Our Dreyfusism was a religion, I use this word in its most literal sense, a religious upsurge, a religious crisis, and I would even suggest to whomever wants to study, consider, be acquainted with a religious movement in modern times . . . to seize on this unique example." What lent the affair this religious quality, which Péguy refers to as *mystique*, was the devotion it elicited: "[Dreyfus] did not die for himself; but many died for him. Many sacrificed their careers for him, their bread, their life . . . their children. Many were thrown into an inexpiable misery. It is this that makes, this that consecrates, this that sanctions *mystique*."[108]

Throughout *Notre jeunesse*, Péguy divides people and events into those that participated in *la mystique* and those that degenerated into *la politique*. These categories do not split the affair in such a way that the Dreyfusards achieve *la mystique* while the anti-Dreyfusards are mired in *la politique*. Rather, all sides in this conflict had their mystical moments and their political moments: "The degradation of the mystical into the political—is that not a common law? . . . Everything begins *en mystique* and finishes *en politique*."[109] The differentiation between these two categories has less to do with what one believed and more to do with the character of one's participation. *La mystique* is for Péguy marked by passion and self-sacrifice, investment in something that supersedes the self. *La politique* is for him the absence of the mystical. It predominantly

---

107. Charles Péguy, *Notes politiques et sociales* (Paris: Cahiers de l'amitié Charles Péguy, 1957), 63.
108. Péguy, *Notre jeunesse*, 55, 113, 66.
109. Ibid., 27.

characterizes the modern world, which for him is a place dominated by the demands of money, self-interest, and personal ambition.

The distinction between *la mystique* and *la politique* allows Péguy to rescue the legacy of the affair from those he felt allowed it to degrade into a political battle. Primary among those was Jean Jaurès: "He among others . . . was a politician like the others, worse than the others." Péguy accused Jaurès of creating the illusion that the anti-Dreyfusards were anti-French and anti-Christian by aligning with the anticlerical Émile Combes.[110] In his critiques of Jaurès and other Dreyfusard "politicians," his rhetoric is very close to Barrès's. He too harangues against intellectuals, aligns himself with tradition and against the modern world, and sees the Dreyfus affair as religious in spirit. Péguy himself acknowledged the commonality between his own position and that of his opposition.[111] But his fight was to resist the dichotomy that placed the anti-Dreyfusards on the side of patriotism, tradition, and religion. He argued that it was, in fact, the true Dreyfusards who best represented these values. For Péguy, the true Christian, the true patriot, was one who would not allow a "single injustice, a single crime, a single illegality," one who fought for the moral purity of the nation, not out of allegiance to some universal law that transcends the nation, but for the sake of the honor of the nation. To be a Dreyfusard thus meant for him to be the truer Christian. Where the anti-Dreyfusards had battled for the nation's temporal salvation, Péguy had battled for its eternal salvation.[112]

By aligning his true republicanism with Christianity, Péguy thus reappropriated the territory that had formerly belonged to the anti-Dreyfusards: "The movement of derepublicanization of France is profoundly the same movement as France's de-Christianization. Together they are the same, a single profound movement of demystification."[113] Like the right-wing Catholics of the moment, Péguy opposed *la mystique*

110. Ibid., 123 (quote), 121. Péguy's relationship with Jaurès began in great admiration. Péguy referred to him as late as 1898 as a teacher and a friend. By 1899, however, the relationship began to degenerate in a series of small incidents. By 1900, Péguy was denouncing Jaurès's "evolution" toward atheism and materialism. For a full account of the relationship, see Henri Guillemin, *Charles Péguy* (Paris: Seuil, 1981), 63–103.

111. "Monsieur Barrès has noted many times that the Dreyfus movement was a religious movement. He even wrote a long time ago that it is to be regretted that this religious force was lost. On this point at least we are in time to reassure him" (Péguy, *Notre jeunesse*, 66). When Péguy published *Le mystère de la charité de Jeanne d'Arc* in 1910, Barrès was largely responsible for the public attention the play garnered, having written two articles on it a month after its January publication. See Guillemin, *Charles Péguy*, 96.

112. Péguy, *Notre jeunesse*, 205–6.

113. Ibid., 16.

*chrétienne* to the values of the modern world, but he did so by aligning the Dreyfusard movement and the republic with *la mystique.*

When Péguy takes up theological language in *Notre jeunesse,* he is not reversing his opinion on the role of the Catholic Church in the affair. Rather, he uses the *mystique/politique* dichotomy to argue that the church's anti-Dreyfusard position was the true betrayal, a betrayal that repeated the pattern in the church of turning against the mystical out of political interests: "The political forces of the church are always against *la mystique.* Notably against *la mystique chrétienne.* This is the most eminent application of this general rule that there ever was." Péguy maintained throughout his years as a Dreyfusard that the church's support of the anti-Dreyfusard cause was a case that recalled the Spanish Inquisition. As such, the truly heroic act, the truly Christian act, was to try to save the church and the nation from committing "a mortal sin."[114]

Not surprisingly, Péguy's theological reading of the affair affected his interpretation of the Jewish community and infused his feelings for and interpretations of Lazare. In *Notre jeunesse,* Péguy paints a portrait of Lazare as the indefatigable prophet, calling for justice in the face of scorn: "The prophet in the great crisis of Israel and of the world was Bernard Lazare. Because a man wears spectacles, because he wears eyeglasses athwart a fold on his nose, in front of two big eyes, modern man believes him to be modern. Modern man is incapable of seeing, does not see, does not know how to recognize the ancientness of the prophetic look." He mythologizes Lazare and his work by dehistoricizing his descriptions of Lazare's deeds. He thus creates out of the Dreyfus affair a parable of Israel modeled clearly on the Hebrew Bible's prophetic narratives. "Israel passes the Just Man by and scorns him. Israel passes the prophet by, follows him, and does not see him. Israel's unawareness of the prophets and yet Israel's guidance by the prophets—that is the whole history of Israel," he writes, comparing the Jewish community during the affair with the ancient Israelites.[115]

Inevitably, once the affair was a parable, it was a Christian parable. Thus, while Péguy is fairly consistent in *Notre jeunesse* in his use of Judaic metaphors, he occasionally refers to Lazare as a saint. The story even has Christian resonances that make Lazare almost Christ-like. Péguy describes the prophet/saint's death and burial with great flourish, pointing out that, although he died of cancer, the true cause was the toll that his relentless fight for Dreyfus took on him: "He lived and died for them

114. Ibid., 115, 207.
115. Ibid., 100, 75.

as a martyr. . . . People above all held it against him, the Jews above all held it against him." He continues: "Israel once again . . . was pursuing its temporally eternal destiny." Only a tiny flock attended his burial, "a handful of people, the same madmen, the same fanatics, Jews and Christians. . . . For all those wretched, for all those persecuted folk, he was still a flash of lightning, a rekindling of the torch that through all eternity will never be quenched. Temporally through all eternity."[116]

*Notre jeunesse* tells the story of a man who was, or should have been, a hero for his race. In telling that story, Péguy lapses into the medieval stereotype of the Jews as traitors. In not rallying behind Lazare, in letting him die poor and alone, the Jews once again had not recognized their messiah. The behavior of the French Jewish population during the affair, their resistance to getting involved in the scandal, to publicly offering their support to Dreyfus, merely confirmed for Péguy a pattern that was archetypal. By reading Lazare as Christ-like, he inevitably recasts the historical events of the affair into a parable that makes most of the Jews appear blind, cowardly, and stubborn.[117]

Péguy furthermore repeats the supersessionist move of subsuming a Jewish narrative into a Christian typology. "You could even say that Israel's unawareness of the prophets is a *figure* of the sinners' unawareness of the saints," he writes.[118] The function for Péguy of the Jewish narrative is to illuminate the Christian narrative. On one level, this return to the medieval image of the Jew seems profoundly disturbing in its double-layered act of mythologizing. Péguy makes of Lazare the prophet who goes unrecognized and then makes that the paradigm for the Christian to reflect on his own status as sinner. On another level, it suggests something quite subversive. According to Péguy's logic, hatred of the Jews arises out of self-recognition. The Christian sees in the Jews' sin his own weakness. If the inability of the Jews to recognize their prophet reminds Christians of their own inability to see correctly, then the Jew hater in this scenario persecutes the Jew so as not to have to face himself in the mirror as a sinner.

It seems that Péguy manages in his portrait of Lazare to repeat anti-Semitic stereotypes unreflexively. At the same time, he also manages to alter them by shifting their connotation and, thus, reorients their effect. As was evident in the case of Barrès, it was clear to many on both

116. Ibid., 35. According to police estimates, some two to four hundred mourners were present at the funeral. See Wilson, *Bernard-Lazare*, 270.

117. For more on the actual behavior of the French Jewish community during the affair, see Marrus, *The Politics of Assimilation*.

118. Péguy, *Notre jeunesse*, 76.

sides during the Dreyfus affair that anti-Semitism was a tool to unite the masses, that the anger directed against the Jew had little to do with Jews in actuality and far more to do with the role they played as symbols of republicanism and capitalism. Lazare himself did not alter this paradigm. Rather, he exposed the discrepancy between this portrayal and the state of *most* of France's Jews, who were just as much victims of the monopolizer as the rest of the French working class. It is only Péguy who alters the symbolism by infusing it with theological undertones.

Péguy engages the anti-Semitic trope that Jews were the architects of modernity in order to reorient it. Repeating the rhetoric of the anti-Semite, he writes: "It is a regime that they [the Jews] made with their hands, that they imposed upon us, through which they govern us, tyrannize us, in which they are perfectly happy, and we are made perfectly miserable." He then argues that to think this way is not only to misunderstand the state of the Jews but also to misunderstand the malady that is modernity. The Jews are not just the victims of modernity, like everyone else; they are, in fact, more its victims than anyone else. In their state of persecution, they *exemplify* the modern experience: "In this temporal hell of the modern world, I see them [the Jews] as us, more than us, slaving away like us, tested like us, exhausted like us, overworked like us. In sickness, in fatigue, in neurasthenia, in all the exhaustion, in this temporal hell . . . I see thousands who, with just as much difficulty, more difficulty, more horribly than us, earn miserably their miserable life."[119] Péguy's description of the state of the Jews is meant here—as are so many of Lazare's descriptions—to oppose the notion of the Jewish capitalists to a portrait of *les pauvres juifs*, a community in Paris consisting predominantly of immigrants who came from the East in the 1890s and suffered from the antipathy of both the anti-Semites and those Jews who did not themselves want to be associated with this "Oriental" culture. However, unlike Lazare's descriptions, which were firmly rooted in contemporary life, Péguy's portrait points toward a theological archetype. Péguy sees the Jews as playing the role of the suffering servant within history. For him, the Jews have a peculiar destiny to which they must be faithful and a privileged genealogy that determines their prophetic mission and their character. It is for him more a matter of destiny than of moral choice: "It is a singular fact, unique in the history of the world, that there was a single prophet who came from another race, that of the prophets, that it is the race that is the only one that provided the prophets, that was the race of the prophets, that it is the race of this people that since then

119. Ibid., 180, 185.

has luckily come to dwell among us."[120] The importance of the Jews is not only that they represent the family of Christ but also that they have been in the past and continue to be the unique source of prophecy.[121] Their role in history has been and continues to be prophetic. Their restlessness is tied to this role, as is their misfortune.

It is clear from the passage just quoted and from many others on the subject of the Jews that Péguy sees a clear dichotomy between the Christian and the Jew. He speaks consistently of "us," meaning the Christians, and "them," meaning the Jews. The significance of this prophetic race is clearly determined by its relationship to Christians and Christianity. This means that the significance of the Jews for Péguy is not in the humanity they share with Christians. He does not praise the Jews because they are at the same time both men and Jews, more men than Jews, to echo Christian Wilhelm von Dohm.[122] Rather, he praises them because they are *them* and not *us*. As Annette Aronowicz points out, this is one of the factors that leads Jewish commentators to praise him.[123] Gershom Scholem, the historian of Jewish mysticism, wrote of Péguy: "Nothing in German literature corresponds to those unforgettable pages in which Charles Péguy, the French Catholic, portrayed the Jewish anarchist Bernard Lazare as a true prophet of Israel, and this at a time when French Jews themselves— out of embarrassment or malice, out of rancor or stupidity—knew no better than to treat one of their greatest men with deadly silence."[124]

120. Charles Péguy, *Un poète l'a dit* (Paris: Gallimard, 1953), 151.

121. For commentators such as Bernard-Henri Lévy, Péguy's uncritical appropriation of racial terminology taints his work in such a way that, despite his praise of the Jews in so much of his work and his idealistic socialism, the work and the man remain too immersed in the history of French nationalism and anti-Semitism to be recuperable. "And I ask myself," Lévy writes in *L'idéologie française*, "how it could be that a man so well regarded, that an apostle of the values of justice, that a defender of the 'humble and the small,' could have participated with his epoch in the most ignoble language, in a history always reduced to the never-ending war of the races" (115). Further on, he describes Péguy as a "prodigy of a racism without racism, a racism of roots, of a racism that without killing, without noise or din, excludes that which simply does not belong to the collective lineage. The greatest marvel of all is that this real French racism that has become so banal, so habitually ingrained in our countryside, our *terroirs*, that it has become a philosophy of the world, a philosophy of society, an entire architecture for the cities of Pétain of the past and maybe of the future" (123). Although it seems important to recognize the proximity of Péguy's use of the notion of race and his contemporaries' anti-Semitic usage, Lévy errs in not acknowledging here the difference between Péguy's genealogical concept of race and the biological notion.

122. In the 1781 essay "Concerning the Amelioration of the Civil Status of the Jews," Von Dohm famously said that the "Jew is even more man than Jew" (from *Ueber die Buergerliche Verbesserung der Juden* [Berlin, 1781], extracted in *The Jew in the Modern World: A Documentary History*, ed. Paul Mendes Flohr and Judah Reinharz [New York: Oxford University Press, 1980], 27). Christian Wilhelm Dohm, an economist, was hired by Cerf Berr, the leader of Alsatian Jewry in the period surrounding the Revolution, to write a defense of the Jews.

123. Aronowicz, *Jews and Christians on Time and Eternity*, 10.

124. Gershom Scholem, *On Jews and Judaism in Crisis*, ed. Werner A. Danhauser (New York: Schocken, 1976), 87.

Such an approach to Lazare and to Judaism suggests that Jewish differ-ence is itself praiseworthy. Péguy seemed to offer a way forward for Jews in modernity that did not demand assimilation. As Alain Finkielkraut argues, this fact profoundly differentiates him from the other Drey-fusards, who were proudly and avowedly *les lumières* at heart. For them, Judaism was a relic, a fossil, something to be overcome through rea-son.[125] Péguy offered a depiction of Judaism that managed to acknowl-edge the Jewishness of the Jew without dishonoring the tradition itself. He not only valorizes Jewish differences; he also grants an archetypal significance to that difference.

Picking up on the familiar representation of the Jew as alienated and restless, this archetype recalls the now-familiar notion of the Jew as nomad. In portraying these traits positively, Péguy foreshadows the postwar thinkers examined in the coming chapters. He muses on the relation of the Jews to exile and erring, suggesting that such a relation to land is somehow laudable:

> *To be elsewhere*: the great vice of this race, its great secret virtue; the great vocation of this people. A lineage of fifty centuries made it so that no train trip could differ from a caravan of fifty centuries ago. Every crossing is for them a crossing of the desert. The most comfortable homes, the most established, masses of stone as large as the columns of the temple . . . , are never more to them than tents in the desert. . . . What importance have these masses of stone larger than the columns of the temple? They are always on camels' backs. A remarkable people . . . for whom the most propertied homes will never be more than tents. . . . A people for whom the stone of houses will always be the canvas of tents. And for us, on the contrary, it is the canvas of tents that already was, that always will be the stone of our houses.

It is the Jews' "secret virtue" to be wanderers, Péguy writes, tying their relationship to the land to the quality of *inquietude* that Péguy sees as constitutive of the Jewish people and their relation to prophecy. Once again, however, this virtue is measured in terms of contrast with an "us" that is Christian. If the Jews make every permanent dwelling into a tent, the Christian makes every tent into a permanent dwelling. The role of the Jew seems to be to agitate the Christian. The agitation of the Jews gains its value from its *effect* on the Christian. Additionally, it is evident in this passage that Péguy derives his interpretation of the Jews by over-laying a biblical and archetypal interpretation on an interpretation of his contemporary observations. Further on in the passage, he applies his

125. Finkielkraut, *Le mécontemporain*, 40.

interpretation to Lazare, about whom he recounts that, unlike "us," who are ill at ease with the metro *"because it transports us too fast,"* he had a special affection for the metro as a consequence of his fundamental restlessness: *"You see Péguy . . . I only begin to feel I am at home when I arrive at a hotel,"* Péguy reports him as having said.[126] And this serves as evidence for Péguy that, for the Jews, a state of wandering is the only state in which the Jews are at home. Fundamentally, they are a people still wandering in the desert, a tribe of nomads perpetually "on camels' backs."

The trope of choice for Péguy concerning the Jews is undoubtedly that of the prophet. He does not speak of the talmudic sage who makes his homeland the book rather than territory; he does, however, depict the Jews as fundamentally a *literary* people, a people for whom the acts of reading and writing are undeniably central:

In the social category to which he belongs, the Jew can go back generation upon generation, and he can go back for centuries: he will always find someone who knows how to read. Whether he were to trace himself back to some seller of matches . . . or to some Bedouin in the desert, the Jew is of a race in which one always finds someone who knows how to read. And, not only that, but to read is to read the Book. It is to read the Book and the Law. To read is to read the word of God, the very inscriptions of God on the tablets and in the Book. In this immense sacred apparatus, the most ancient of all, reading is the sacred performance as it is the originary performance. All Jews are readers. All Jews are reciters. It is because of this that all Jews are visual and visionary. And that they see everything instantaneously. And at a single glance they instantaneously run over, cover surfaces. . . . Seeing this the Catholic looks to his own case. No matter which way he goes back, he is illiterate beyond the second generation.[127]

It seems at first that Péguy is elevating the Jew over the Christian by virtue of what he recognizes as a Jewish tradition of literacy. He seems to be equating the Catholic with the peasant, with humble origins, probably his own.[128] As inaccurate as the claim is, it points toward an association between the peasant culture of France and *la mystique chrétienne* that Péguy emphasizes in some of his more avowedly Christian writings, such as *Le mystère de la charité de Jeanne d'Arc*, the literary work for which he is probably best known. It is also this association that explains the

126. Péguy, *Notre jeunesse*, 127, 126.

127. Péguy, "Note conjointe sur M. Descartes et la philosophie cartésienne," in *Oeuvres en prose, 1909–1914* (Paris: Pleiade, 1957), 1318–19.

128. Born in 1873, Péguy's father was a carpenter who died when Péguy was very young. Péguy's mother and grandmother supported him by mending chairs.

right-wing appropriation of his work.[129] Through this alliance, Péguy is able to associate Christianity with the land, with the nation. Insofar as *la mystique chrétienne* is for him tied to the simplicity of peasant faith and this simplicity is starkly opposed to modernity and technology, forces against which he was consistently opposed, peasant illiteracy would, in fact, appear to be superior to Jewish literacy. There are inklings in the passage quoted above that suggest that the nomadic nature of the Jew aligns him with modernity even if it also aligns him with prophecy. Péguy associates Lazare's pride in the Paris subway system, for example, with his restlessness. The practice of reading itself he aligns with speed and with surfaces rather than depths. Even as Péguy seems to resist associating the Jew with the detrimental forces of modernity, he nonetheless manages to fall back on the stereotype of the deracinated Jew.

Alain Finkielkraut argues, to the contrary, that Péguy uniquely "recognizes and affirms the positive sense of exile at the same time that he denounces the modern world as the epoch of deracination."[130] While Finkielkraut seems to be overlooking some of the negative connotations of Péguy's depiction of Judaism, there is a sense in which he is right, for Péguy's depiction of the Jew as nomad does not amount to the claim that Jews lack roots. The Jews have roots, according to Péguy; they are just not in the soil.[131] The Jews are clearly a race, and, as a race, they must clearly have *les racines*.

In a manner that recalls the medieval Jewish philosopher Judah Ha-Levi, Péguy accounts for what he sees as consistent and persistent characteristics of the Jews through their shared genealogy.[132] He compares the Jewish people to a tree that produces a fruit that is particularly rare. It is their very particularism, their exclusivity, that accounts for their ability to produce such a fruit, the fruit of prophecy: "Stem that is a race, plant stem, organic stem . . . stem of the race of the people of Israel. The prophets are nothing other than the nodes of this stem."[133] Once again,

129. The publication of *Le mystère de la charité de Jeanne d'Arc* prompted many of his former adversaries to claim that Péguy had finally come over to the other side. "Voilà le vrai mouvement, le veritable patriotisme français," wrote Georges Valois in *L'action française* (quoted in Finkielkraut, *Le mécontemporain*, 25–27).

130. Finkielkraut, *Le mécontemporain*, 47.

131. Rosenzweig famously makes a similar claim in *The Star of Redemption*. See Franz Rosenzweig, *Der Stern der Erlösung* (Frankfurt: Suhrkamp, 1993), translated by William W. Hallow as *The Star of Redemption* (Notre Dame: University of Notre Dame Press, 1985). Annette Aronowicz pursues the parallel in *Jews and Christians on Time and Eternity*.

132. Ha-Levi was a twelfth-century Jewish philosopher who attributed Jewish greatness to genealogy, claiming that the book of Genesis illustrates the way in which God separated the wheat from the chaff. See Judah Ha-Levi, *Kuzari*, trans. Henry Slonimsky (New York: Schocken, 1964), 64–67.

133. Péguy, *Un poète l'a dit*, 159–62.

the endorsement of racial politics also evident in Lazare's writings can be read as a reorientation, but it can also be read as an acceptance of the rhetoric of race that was so central to Barrès's anti-Semitic discourse. In Péguy's work, the claims that united the anti-Jewish tirades of Voltaire, Abbé Grégoire, Drumont, and even Lazare in his early writings—that the Jew is stiff-necked, backward, narrow-minded, and exclusive—become the very claims that illustrate the faithfulness of this people to their historic mission: to be the people of prophecy with all the hardship and punishment that that entails.

Péguy's definition of Jewishness resists the charge that the Jews are fundamentally uprooted. To be Jewish for Péguy is to be true to the roots of the Jewish people. Jewish identity is material, organic, genealogical, and racial. For Péguy, the Jew may be wandering, but he is not deracinated. It is the racial connection of the Jews to their ancestors that allows Péguy to make claims about the Jews that are dehistoricized. Lazare may be an atheist who wears spectacles on his too-thick nose, but he is nonetheless a prophet. If for Barrès the Jews represent universalism, abstraction, and rootlessness, for Péguy, on the contrary, they are the instantiation of particularism—not because they have *terroir*, but because they are a race, because they are riveted to their roots by the blood in their veins.

The flip side of Péguy's valorization of Jewish distinctiveness is a criticism of Jewish attempts to escape that identity. If Jews are defined by their mission and their destiny, they are also defined by the attempt to escape that destiny. In Péguy, as in Lazare, along with a valorization of Jewish particularity arises a critique of those Jews who attempt to shirk the fate that particularity implies:

They know what it costs to be the carnal voice and the temporal body. They know what it costs to bear God and his agents the prophets. His prophets, the prophets. Thus, vaguely they would prefer it not to start again. They are afraid of blows. . . . Camping among the modern peoples, they would very much like to find themselves doing well. Israel's entire *politique* is not to make noise in the world (there has been enough), to buy peace through a prudent silence. Except for a few pretentious scatterbrains, whom everyone denounces, Israel wants to let itself be forgotten. So many of its wounds are still bleeding. But the whole *mystique* of Israel is to pursue its resounding and painful mission in the world. From this arises the incredible rifts, the most painful internal antagonisms that there have perhaps ever been between a *mystique* and a *politique*. A people of merchants. The same people, a people of prophets. The one group knows for the other about calamity.[134]

134. Péguy, *Notre jeunesse*, 71.

Péguy's rhetoric here recalls the German-Jewish philosopher Hermann Cohen. Like Cohen, Péguy suggests that the Jews' role in history, their mission, their *mystique*, is to pass up the happiness that is the lot of other nations.[135] To try and do otherwise is a betrayal. Lazare too argues that the Jews who had chosen to assimilate, who wanted to shirk their allegiances, are guilty. The difference between Lazare and Péguy on this score is the significance with which the critique is imbued. For Lazare, this critique was part of a larger campaign to find a new method of responding to modernity, a new way forward. For Péguy, its function is to reveal an archetypal pattern. Péguy's aims are not, ultimately, political. They are theological, and in that sense they transcend their historical moment.

Péguy reimbues the classic archetypes that fueled medieval Jew hatred with a meaning that validates Jewish existence. If the Jews betrayed Christ, this was the historic role tied to their prophetic mission. If they are intolerant and particularistic, it is out of faithful adherence to their own destiny, as miserable as the consequences of such adherence may be. If they represent a race distinct from the French, "we" are blessed to have them among us. If they are wandering and restless, that is their secret virtue.

Undoubtedly, one of the key factors that allowed Péguy to reorient these stereotypes was his Christian theological interpretation of Jewish history. At the same time, he never seems to transcend the notion that the Jews are valuable *for* Christians. He is, furthermore, unable to endorse difference without imbuing it with the rhetoric of race. He thus provides a portrait of the Jew that shares Barrès's vision of the French nation and, thus, portrays the Jews as a people without a land. But he shares as well Lazare's later reappropriation of a Jewish racial distinction while adding a layer of theology. The result is a philo-Semitic vision of the Jew that is deeply influenced by the fin de siècle discourse about roots and race yet seems at the same time to abstract from history in order to make claims that transcend the current moment. While his positions may be derived from his contemporary political landscape, his presentation of his position resists being confined to his moment.

As will be made clear in the next chapter, one could say of Jean-Paul Sartre as well that his vision of the Jew is inaccurate because it is

---

135. "And since this national existence [of the Jewish people] is not inhibited by a state of one's own, it is protected against the fate of a materialization of its nationalistic idea. The national peculiarity in its stateless isolation is the symbol for the unity of the confederation of mankind, as the ultimate value of world history" (Hermann Cohen, *Die Religion der Vernunft aus den Quellen des Judentums* [Leipzig: Gustav Fock, 1919], 298, translated by Simon Kaplan as *Religion of Reason Out of the Sources of Judaism* [Atlanta: Scholars, 1995], 254).

dehistoricized. Unlike Sartre, however, Péguy never acknowledges that the traits he attributes to the Jew are themselves a projection of the Christian. Rather, they are assumed to be racial. As such, a mere shift in connotation lends them the tint of anti-Semitism. While the same can be said of a number of thinkers considered in this study, the difference between Péguy and others, such as Sartre and Blanchot, is his validation of *race* as a category. While the Jew is clearly a figure of exile in his work, an emphasis on Jewish rootedness is instrumental to Péguy's attempt to redeem the anti-Semitic portrait of the Jew.

Péguy thus remains at the beginning of our narrative, even as he allows us to witness the way in which the terms of Jewish denigration could become the terms for a revalorization. Indeed, all three thinkers considered in this chapter set the stage for the post-1945 recuperation of the rootless Jew by illustrating the way in which the Jew figured as a key symbol in a national debate over the political value of discourses of particularism and universalism. Neither a symbol of nationalist particularism nor fully absorbable into a homogeneous republican vision, the rootless Jew emerges in the first decades of the twentieth century as a symbol of difference. Almost four decades after Péguy's *Notre jeunesse*, it is Jean-Paul Sartre who is able to diagnose the Jewish situation as such, and, thus, it is Sartre who first valorizes Jewish rootlessness precisely because it calls into question the value of roots.

# TWO

# Stranger and Self: Sartre's Jew

Between Sartre and the Jew in person, the Jew as idea, the phantasm of the Jew intervened.

BENNY LÉVY, "SARTRE ET JUDÉITÉ"

## I. Anti-Semite and Jew

On returning from a visit to Jerusalem in 1978, Jean-Paul Sartre commented to his assistant and interlocutor Benny Lévy that in *Réflexions sur la question juive* (his 1946 phenomenological essay on the anti-Semite and the Jew): "It is me that I was describing when I thought I was describing the Jew, a type who has nothing, no land, an intellectual."[1] Did he picture himself a new incarnation of the Wandering Jew, pipe in hand, pushing a wheelbarrow full of his meager belongings? It is, indeed, hard to imagine. Such an image, of course, belies his circumstances. Yet, as inaccurate, even ridiculous as it was, the comment is, nonetheless, revealing. It illustrates the enduring effect of the portrait of the Jew that developed out of the Dreyfus affair. The image of the Jew that Sartre offers—an uprooted intellectual—could be lifted directly from Barrès. The

---

*Epigraph*: Benny Lévy, "Sartre et judéité," *Études sartriennes* 2–3 (1986): 142.

1. Sartre quoted in Benny Lévy, "Sartre et judéité," *Études sartriennes* 2–3 (1986): 141. I refer to *Réflexions sur la question juive* by its French title throughout this chapter in order to maintain the integrity of the original, for its English translation, *Anti-Semite and Jew*, carries a different resonance. I will, however, refer to the title in English when quoting English sources that use the translation.

description remains the same; only the value has changed. Additionally, Sartre's statement exposes the Jewish "type" as a projection not only of the anti-Semite but also of the avowed defenders of the Jews. Sartre claimed in 1946 that the figure of the Jew was "created" by the anti-Semites as a means of solidifying their identity with France. In 1978, he suggests that his portrait was actually his own fantasy projected onto an other.

For the many critics who have argued that *Réflexions sur la question juive* suffers from Sartre's lack of knowledge of Jewish history and religion, his statement could be read as a long-awaited admission of failure. Finally, Sartre had admitted to the book's inaccuracy; he had realized the consequences of his lackadaisical method, a method that seemed to consist in relating casual observations and anecdotes from personal experience. With this admission, the book, which by 1978 seemed outdated to many and problematic to most, could finally be put to rest.

Despite its laudable intentions and its timely appearance—Sartre was the first to address the problem of anti-Semitism following World War II—*Réflexions sur la question juive* has served over the years as a testament to Sartre's ignorance of the Jewish tradition. For, in the text, he makes statements such as: "[The Jews] cannot take pride in any collective work that is specifically Jewish, or in a civilization properly Jewish or in a common mysticism."[2] While the work was intended to expose the fraudulence of anti-Semitism, critics argued that Sartre's ignorance seemed to lead only to a recapitulation of anti-Semitic stereotypes. As Pierre Birnbaum has written:

Hurriedly formulated on the basis of more than dubious empirical material and drafted, as Sartre himself admitted in his last interview with Benny Lévy, without any research into the existing body of scholarly works, except for the anti-Semitic writings of his time, *Anti-Semite and Jew* can only wound, despite the praiseworthy intention. . . . *Anti-Semite and Jew*, taking as its starting point the French case, disconcerts with its banal images and clichés, and we are struck by Sartre's ignorance concerning French Jews. It is this ignorance that leads Sartre to statements that belong to anti-Semitic propaganda—and this even after Vichy.[3]

Sartre's own commentary in his conversations with Lévy served for Birnbaum and many others as the final nail in the book's coffin.

2. Jean-Paul Sartre, *Réflexions sur la question juive* (Paris: Paul Morihien, 1946), 110, translated by George J. Becker as *Anti-Semite and Jew* (New York: Schocken, 1995), 85.
3. Pierre Birnbaum, "Sorry Afterthoughts on *Anti-Semite and Jew*," trans. Carol Marks, *October*, no. 87 (Winter 1999): 94.

However, Sartre's admission that the book was a projection may also give us reason to exhume the text. For if, on the one hand, this admission helps explain what, in a 1979 consideration of the volume, Menachem Brinker registers as "a certain measure of incomprehension in a conception which ignores the common culture possessed by the Jews as a collective and attributes to their common historical memory only memories of persecutions and pogroms,"[4] on the other hand it also creates a puzzle. How is it possible to square Sartre's claim that he *identified* with the portrait of the Jew that his text generates with the fact that this portrait draws heavily on anti-Semitic stereotypes?[5]

We could respond to this puzzle in numerous ways. We could, of course, dismiss Benny Lévy's report. After all, Simone de Beauvoir accused Lévy of manipulating the aged and blind Sartre. "Victor [i.e., Lévy] did not express any of his own opinions directly," she argued. "He made Sartre assume them while he, by virtue of who knows what revealed truth, played the part of district attorney."[6] Yet Sartre's sense of identification with the Jew is documented elsewhere and by others, in his memoirs as well as in anecdotes from friends and relatives.[7] In *Les mots* (*The Words*), discussing his bookish ways as a child, he comments: "[When I] heard anti-Semites reproach Jews any number of times with not knowing the lessons and silence of nature; I would answer: 'In that case, I'm more Jewish than they.'"[8]

4. Menahem Brinker, "Sartre on the Jewish Question: Thirty Years Later," *Jerusalem Quarterly* 10 (Winter 1979): 130. Other critics who have made similar comments include Arnold Mandel, who in 1962 remarked that the book failed miserably in its "categorical refusal to consider the nevertheless real dimension" of Judaism (Mandel quoted in Michel Rybalka, "Publication and Reception of *Anti-Semite and Jew*," *October*, no. 87 (Winter 1999): 176.

5. Elaine Marks goes as far as arguing: "Sartre is transformed in the third part of his essay into the antisemite against whom he rails in the first part" (Elaine Marks, "The Limits of Ideology and Sensibility: J-P Sartre's *Réflexions sur la question juive* and E. M. Cioran's *Une peuple de solitaires*," *French Review* 45, no. 4 [March 1972]: 784).

6. Simone de Beauvoir, *La cérémonie des adieux* (Paris: Gallimard, 1981), 150, translated by Patrick O'Brian as *Adieux: A Farewell to Sartre* (New York: Pantheon, 1984), 119. On Lévy's pseudonym—Pierre Victor—see n. 11 below.

The debate over the character of Lévy's relationship with Sartre is extensive, with de Beauvoir claiming that Benny Lévy had bullied Sartre, taken advantage of an old, frail man, and forced him to say things he did not mean. Others such as Bernard-Henri Lévy argue that Sartre's late collaboration with Benny Lévy shows the way in which his thought had finally come to approach Levinas's. For an elaboration of this claim, see the epilogue to Bernard-Henri Lévy, *Le siècle de Sartre* (Paris: Grasset, 2000), translated by Andrew Brown as *Sartre: The Philosopher of the Twentieth Century* (Cambridge: Polity, 2003). For a summary of the debate, see Ronald Aronson, introduction to *Hope Now: The 1980 Interviews*, trans. Adrian can den Hoven (Chicago: University of Chicago Press, 1996).

7. See Stuart Charmé, "Sartre's Jewish Daughter: An Interview with Arlette Elkaim-Sartre," *Midstream* 32, no. 8 (October 1986): 24–28.

8. Jean-Paul Sartre, *Les mots* (Paris: Gallimard, 1964), 37, translated by Bernard Frechtman as *The Words* (New York: Vintage, 1964), 49.

Another way out of this puzzle would be to assume with Susan Suleiman that, though clearly insidious, the anti-Semitism inscribed in *Réflexions* is not a consequence of intention but a fact of Sartre's being "a man of his time." In other words, Sartre had unknowingly "'soaked it up' without being aware of it."[9] However, as Suleiman and Birnbaum note, in Sartre's late interviews with Benny Lévy he seemed fully aware of the fact that the source of his description derived from the discourse of anti-Semitism. When asked what his sources were for *Réflexions*, what it was "taking off from," Sartre replied: "Taking off from nothing, taking off from anti-Semitism, which I wanted to combat."[10]

The solution that I propose does not dismiss Sartre's contradictory statements about the Jews or his relationship to them. Rather, it attempts to bridge these contradictions, without attempting to recuperate his thought. Although *Réflexions* did, in its moment, have an electrifyingly positive effect, there is no doubt that the text now strikes the contemporary reader (and even Sartre in his later years) as outdated, anachronistic, and blatant in its reliance on clichés and stereotypes. Nonetheless, the contradictions, tensions, and stereotypes in the text may be the key to the book's importance, if not as a living text on anti-Semitism and Jewish identity, then as a crucial juncture in the history of the figure of the Jew. They disclose how this text contributed to the revalorization of the very notions that anti-Semitism denigrated, ideas that, through anti-Semitic discourse, became affixed to the figure of the Jew.

In many ways, the casual remark to Benny Lévy encapsulates the role that the Jew played for Sartre throughout his life. The Jew is primarily defined negatively, circumscribed by the notions the concept resists: ownership, an ethic of rootedness, hegemony. Indeed, these are the values that Sartre identified with bourgeois life, values that he consistently battles in all aspects of his work, in his literature, his phenomenological treatises, his Marxist essays, and even his collaborative work with Benny Lévy.

Two years before his death, Sartre seemed to have recognized that, as a category of resistance, the Jew, as he had described him, was an imaginary construct produced by the position of Jews on the margins of French culture. When Benny Lévy said himself that Sartre's vision of the Jew was a fantasy, he undoubtedly meant this as both an explanation and a critique.[11]

9. Susan Suleiman, "Sartre's *Réflexions sur la question juive*," in *The Jew in the Text*, ed. Linda Nochlin and Tamar Garb (London: Thames & Hudson, 1995), 216.
10. Jean-Paul Sartre, *L'espoir maintenant: Les entretiens de 1980* (Paris: Verdier, 1991), 72, translated as *Hope Now*, 104.
11. For Lévy's remarks, see the epigraph to this chapter. Lévy had himself shifted his allegiance from Maoism to Judaism, in the process giving up the pseudonym that he had used in France up to this point—Pierre Victor—and returning to his given name.

But it is exactly the fact that the idea of the Jew was for Sartre constructed from an amalgamation of anti-Semitic portraits that makes *Réflexions sur la question juive* important for my argument. As the moment when the denigrated characteristics associated with the Jew take on a positive value, that text represents a turning point in the history of the Jewish question in France. Given his mode of description in *Réflexions*, compounded with his own later admission that the portrait was a projection, Sartre made it possible to disentangle the idea of the Jew from real Jews, allowing for the idea to function as a metaphor for the outsider and, thus, for Sartre as an ideal. Ironically, by describing the Jew as society's other, Sartre in fact facilitated a description of the Jew that made this figure worthy of emulation.

There is much written on the effect that *Réflexions* had on young Jews at the time, men like Claude Lanzmann, Albert Memmi, Pierre Vidal-Naquet, and Robert Misrahi, who saw it as a call to reinvigorate Jewish life, to live authentically, and, ultimately, to prove to Sartre himself that Judaism was far more than the product of the anti-Semitic gaze, that it was a vital faith with a rich cultural heritage.[12] With the exception of Jonathan Judaken's *Jean-Paul Sartre and the Jewish Question* (2006), which focuses on the inter-relation between Sartre's development of the notion of the intellectual and the figure of the Jew, little has been written on what it is about Sartre's text that allows for the positive revalorization of the idea of the Jew, what it is that makes this imaginary construct, culled from anti-Semitic texts of the late nineteenth century and the early twentieth, a potentially positive model.[13] *Réflexions* does not itself explicitly develop the idea of the Jew as a positive ideal. However, on considering the continuities between the depiction in *Réflexions* and that in *Hope Now*, Sartre's collaborative dialogue with Benny Lévy composed over a period that includes Sartre's 1978 trip to Israel and published after his death almost thirty-five years later, it becomes evident that the earlier text already established the basis for an idealization of the Jew's position in society.

12. Claude Lanzmann said that his very way of walking was transformed by reading the book (Lanzmann cited in Pierre Vidal Naquet, "Remembrances of a 1946 Reader," *October*, no. 87 [Winter 1999]: 7). Pierre Vidal-Naquet, whose parents died in the camps, responded: "In a single word, then: when I read the *Anti-Semite and Jew*, I felt myself avenged indeed" (ibid., 9). Robert Misrahi, a student of Sartre's from 1943 into the 1970s, wrote: "Jews were very affected by these words and full of admiration for the writer. We were also astonished, even stunned, for what we [Jews] were used to was hatred and contempt" ("Sartre and the Jews: A Felicitous Misunderstanding," *October*, no. 87 [Winter 1999]: 64).

13. Even Judaken, however, assumes too quickly that Sartre himself is unaware of the fact that he is dealing with a trope, and, similiarly, I think, like most American critics of this phenomenon, he over-simplifies the symbolic usage of the Jew in postwar French thought. Two critics who err on the overly enthusiastic side in interpreting Sartre's interest in the Jew are Stuart Charmé (*Vulgarity and Authenticity: Dimensions of Otherness in the World of Jean-Paul Sartre* [Amherst: University of Massachusetts Press, 1991]) and Bernard Henry-Lévy (*Le siècle de Sartre*).

The shift in value that Sartre's depiction of the Jew inaugurates is not isolated to these two texts. We must consider the associations that Sartre makes throughout his work between the Jew and other key philosophical categories. This requires consideration, not only of *Réflexions sur la question juive*, but also of the depictions of Judaism and anti-Semitism in the early fiction, the phenomenology, and in the controversial late interviews with Benny Lévy. It will be revealed, thus, how Sartre's concern with rootlessness, with cultural and subjective alienation, and, finally, with a form of nonutopian hope transforms the Jew in his final reflections into a positive emblem with political and moral implications.

There are two persistent threads in Sartre's work for which the figure of the Jew serves as a touchstone: the first is his construction of human subjectivity outside the particularist-versus-universalist dichotomy that dominated nineteenth-century philosophical and political discourse; the second is his ongoing fixation with Hegel's thought, both on the level of the subject and on the level of history. Although his repeated encounters with Hegel's thought rarely note the position of the figure of the Jew in Hegel's texts, his focus on the modality of unhappy consciousness and his concern with articulating a philosophy of history, from which the Jews, according to Hegel, would be omitted, lead Sartre to bump up against the representation of Judaism in Hegel's thought more than perhaps he is even aware. Taken together, these two strands aptly reflect the two sources—political and philosophical—from which a revalorization of the figure of the rootless Jew in post-1945 France arises. By considering these two themes as they appear in Sartre's fiction, philosophy, and political writings, I will expose the way in which a revalorized representation of the Jew is generated as a *by-product* of his fixation on political identity and the dialectics of Marxian/Hegelian history.[14]

*Between Essentialist and Universalist*

In the last chapter, I argued that Bernard Lazare's and Charles Péguy's depictions of the Jew borrow from racialist thinking to develop a positive portrait of the Jewish race. Lazare uses this strategy to oppose the revolutionary bargain, which was founded on a rhetoric of universalism

14. In the essay "Between Existentialism and Zionism," Paul Mendes-Flohr shows that there is an intrinsic link between Sartre's argument that the Jew is torn between universalism and particularism and the association of the Jew with "unhappy consciousness" in Sartre's thought. The former is merely the social expression of the latter. See Paul Mendes-Flohr, *Divided Passions: Jewish Intellectuals and the Experience of Modernity* (Detroit: Wayne State University Press, 1991), 427.

and culminated in the creation of what Lazare calls "the assimilator," the "Jewish bourgeoisie, rich and not Jewish . . . our garbage, our rubbish."[15] This approach is then echoed by Péguy in his treatment of the Jew and the Christian as archetypes. The essentialist overtones to their depictions, however, lend to their portraits a moral ambivalence that derives from their acceptance of the underlying logic of racism. Both Péguy and Lazare endorse the notion that nature defines the character of a people, its traits, its essence. Thus, their work reflects a certain racial determinism and leads to the claim on both their parts that attempting to overcome one's racial nature amounts to duplicity, insincerity, and cultural alienation. Jews who attempt to reject their culture thus injure Judaism, deaden its creativity, and transform their people into cowards.

There are those commentators who have seen in Sartre's own critique of the democrat and his depiction of the inauthentic Jew in the second and third sections of *Réflexions* an echo of such racialist thinking, despite the strongly worded attack in the first section of the book against the feverish hatred of the anti-Semite.[16] It seems clear, however, that, if there is one continuity in Sartre's work, it is a distrust of and an antagonism toward any doctrine of essences, a militancy even, that is, in fact, responsible for the other highly criticized claim in *Réflexions*, that the Jew has *no* essence, that "the Jew is [merely] one whom other men take for a Jew."[17]

In a 1938 interview, Sartre stated his position this way: "Jews have undoubtedly their distinguishing characteristics. But we are unable to establish them, since it is impossible to determine to what extent they are attributable to the times, the living conditions, or the ethnic origin. And every attempt to isolate and define these characteristics is a concession to anti-Semitism. Among the Jews I have the opportunity to know, I cannot find any common features. If we find any, it is because we put them there ourselves."[18] Despite the concession that we find Jews conforming to stereotypes, the attribution of those characteristics to the environment rather than race or lineage distances Sartre from the

15. Lazare, *Job's Dungheap*, 99.

16. Naomi Schor has a sophisticated take on Sartre's own position in relation to democratic universalism and fascist particularism but nonetheless comes to the following conclusion: "Sartre's adoption of the doxa of anti-democracy and anti-universalism is the trace of his barely visible yet troubling complicity with fascist ideology, the sign that they draw from the same polluted European fascist source" (Naomi Schor, "Anti-Semitism, Jews and the Universal," *October*, no. 87 [Winter 1999]: 115).

17. Sartre, *Réflexions sur la question juive*, 88, and *Anti-Semite and Jew*, 69 (translation slightly altered).

18. From a 1939 interview with Arnold Mandel, printed in the June–July 1947 issue of *La revue juive de Genève*, quoted in Rybalka, "Publication and Reception of *Anti-Semite and Jew*," 173.

position of Péguy and Bernard Lazare.[19] Unlike Lazare and Péguy, he sees any attempt to identify the *nature* of the Jew as a concession to anti-Semitism. This critique of racial essentialism would seem to place him in the camp of those universalists who defended the ideals of the Revolution against the growing tide of French fascism, from the Dreyfus affair through to the inauguration of the Pétain government. But his own critique of the democrat in *Réflexions* is founded on the claim that the democrat does not acknowledge the factor of human difference, the particularities of peoples and groups. This raises the question of the source of such differences. Given his critique of democratic universalism, where can we situate Sartre in relation to the two poles of universalism and particularism, the antitheses that seemed to dominate the discourse surrounding the Jewish question from the Enlightenment forward? The answer to this question lies in Sartre's existentialism and its accompanying notion of existential limits or conditions. It is his notion of condition that constitutes an attempt to overcome the very terms of the universalism-particularism polarity.

## Against Barrès

A preoccupation with the politics of identity is already evident in Sartre's prewar fiction, particularly in the story "L'enfance d'un chef" ("Childhood of a Leader"), which foreshadows many of his convictions about anti-Semitism as he expressed them nearly ten years later, after a devastating war.[20] Written in 1938, "L'enfance d'un chef" describes the childhood and adolescence of Lucien Fleurier, who discovers his sense of self, for which he searches throughout the story, by taking up the stance of the anti-Semite and joining Action française. One of the key elements of the text, which has gone unrecognized by critics, is the way in which it responds to Maurice Barrès's cult of the self and particularly to his novel *Les déracinés*.

The story recounts how Lucien's childhood and adolescence are dominated by the recurring sense that he does not exist. This feels at one and the same time like a terrifying abyss and a powerful secret. In possession of this secret, he tries out various remedies for his own "pathology":

19. Sartre seems to be simultaneously granting the possibility that the Jews have distinguishing characteristics and claiming that whatever distinguishing characteristics we perceive in the Jew are the product of the onlooker. As we will see, this makes sense when one considers the category of "Being-for-others" that he develops in *Being and Nothingness*.

20. I came to see the significance of this story to Sartre's presentation of Judaism and his construction of the intellectual thanks to Judaken, *Jean-Paul Sartre and the Jewish Question*, 23–48.

psychoanalysis, surrealism, and homosexuality. The first of these is under the guidance of a friend, Berliac, who, we discover later, is a quarter Jewish. Coming out of these explorations, and returning home to his provincial birthplace from Paris, Lucien is overwhelmed once again by a sense of instability, by the feeling that he is nothing, that he lacks a self. When a schoolmate, who is already a member of Action française, lends him Barrès's novel, Lucien finds a diagnosis for his own condition—he is himself *déraciné*. In response to this discovery, he cultivates his sense of belonging to the land and its people, joins Action française, and becomes, after contemplating the role of his Jewish friend in his earlier pathological behaviors, a rabid anti-Semite: "Lucien threw out several biting reflections about the Jews and spoke of Berliac who was so miserly: 'I always asked myself: why is he so cheap. Then one day I understood: he was one of the tribe.' Everybody began to laugh and a sort of exaltation came over Lucien: he felt truly furious about the Jews and the memory of Berliac was deeply unpleasant to him. Lemordant looked him in the eyes and said, 'You're a pure one, you are.'" The sense of identity that Lucien receives from Lemordant's comment, the feeling of power that comes from being told that he *is*, in fact, something, a pure Jew hater in this case, gives him what he has been looking for all along—the feeling that he is a rock, solid, immovable, and grounded. The story ends, however, with Lucien glimpsing himself in the mirror and having a sense of the disparity between his own desired self-image, that of a man, "un chef parmi les Français," and what he sees before himself, "a small, pretty, stubborn face which was not yet fearsome enough." He is, nonetheless, undaunted by the discovery of this disparity, for at least now he knows what it means to be a man. Thus, the story concludes: "'I will grow a moustache' he decided."[21]

Sartre's use of Barrès in the story is key for two reasons. Barrès is, on one level, functioning merely as a representative of the nationalist literature of the far Right and as a figure associated with the anti-Dreyfusard movement. Additionally, it is keenly relevant here that he played a role in resignifying the definition of the intellectual in France. As discussed in the previous chapter, it was through a reclamation of his notion of the intellectual, a revalorization of the idea, that the figure of the twentieth-century French intellectual gained its particular overtone. Sartre, of course, was its icon.[22] Thus, in "L'enfance d'un chef," the path of the intellectual, explored only through Lucien's friendship with the Jew Ber-

21. Jean-Paul Sartre, *Le mur* (Paris: Gallimard, 1939), 206, 270, translated by Lloyd Alexander as *The Wall* (New York: New Directions, 1948), 252, 219.
22. See Judt, *Past Imperfect*, 141–43, 242–43.

liac, functions as the path not taken. It is the path rejected because of its instability, because it represents deracination.

Barrès's significance to the story is further underscored when we take into account his early development of the notion of *le culte du moi* in the trilogy of novels given this collective title. The first of these novels, *Sous l'oeil des barbares* (1892), describes the self "in its plenitude" and encourages the cultivation of self as that which must be pruned and developed, purified of all that is foreign to it.[23] This way of thinking leads Barrès to his traditionalism when he discovers that, at the bottom, what founds the self is the collectivity, one's predecessors, one's culture.[24] "Je suis eux-mêmes" becomes Barrès's slogan with this discovery. "And this consciousness, what consequences it will have! What acceptance! You glimpse it. It is a vertigo in which the individual founders, only to rediscover himself in family, race, and nation."[25]

Sartre's story, perhaps self-consciously, plays out the very movement of the journey that Barrès describes in the preface to *Scènes et doctrines du nationalisme*, the sense of vertigo that is resolved by the discovery of the foundation of *la terre, la famille, la race, la nation*. Barrès describes the search as a sinking into quicksand, without resistance, until the discovery of what, in fact, lies at the bottom.[26] What appears, however, as the solution to this dilemma for Barrès is, ultimately, described by Sartre as a form of bad faith.

Although Sartre does not develop bad faith as a phenomenological category until *Being and Nothingness*, it is evident, nonetheless, that he is already working out the dynamics of the category in "L'enfance d'un chef." As he describes the mode of bad faith in *Being and Nothingness*, it arises with the self's fleeing from its own groundlessness, fleeing from the fact that it has no foundation, no essence, that it *is* a nothingness and is, thus, radically free. Undoubtedly, this description applies to Lucien in his discovery of Barrès's philosophy, his joining Action française, and his taking on the identity of the anti-Semite. It is best captured by the final action of the story—Lucien's decision to grow a moustache. This is the perfect image of self-deception, the choice to become more oneself by literally hiding behind a sign of masculinity.

"L'enfance d'un chef" illustrates that, from early on, Sartre associated territorial and racial identity with self-deception. Given the pivotal role that Maurice Barrès plays in this early story, it follows that Sartre's own

23. Maurice Barrès, *Sous l'oeil des barbares* (Paris: Plotin, 1952), 20–22.
24. Barrès, *Scènes et doctrines du nationalisme*, 17.
25. Ibid., 18.
26. Ibid., 17.

philosophy develops in part as a reaction to Barrès's categories. There is a subtle value dichotomy functioning in the story that reappears in much of Sartre's later work. On one side, we have all the notions that arise with Barrès's "solution" to the problem of the self: determinism, nationalism, anti-Semitism. Sartre will add to this list bad faith or self-deception. On the other side of the dichotomy are located the Jew and the intellectual, linked by their status as the uprooted. These figures share the associations of groundlessness, abstraction, and universalism—and, ultimately for Sartre, freedom.

## Being and Nothingness

In Sartre's later work, Maurice Barrès's name appears only in passing, but the theme of rootlessness remains prominent.[27] The very structure of consciousness is for Sartre conceptualized around this metaphor. In *Being and Nothingness*, he describes consciousness as constituted by negativity, structured by a lack of coincidence. This lack of coincidence is what defines consciousness as consciousness. If the self were pure identity, it would not be consciousness; it would have the form of what Sartre calls the *en-soi*, or the "in-itself," and would, thus, be static; it would have the structure of "it-is-what-it-is," or identity. Consciousness, rather, which is always already self-consciousness for Sartre, does not have the structure of the *en-soi*; it is not a thing. It is the destruction of identity. It has the structure of "not-being-what-it-is":

Presence to self . . . supposes that an impalpable fissure has slipped into being. If being is present to itself, it is because it is not wholly itself. Presence is an immediate deterioration of coincidence, for it supposes separation. . . . Thus the for-itself must be its own nothingness. The being of consciousness qua consciousness is to exist *at a distance from itself* as a presence to itself, and this empty distance which being carries in its being is Nothingness. Thus in order for the *self* to exist, it is necessary that the unity of this being include its own nothingness as the nihilation of identity.[28]

27. While most references to Barrès in Sartre's later work are merely casual, in *What Is Literature?* he does associate him again with the ethic of the bourgeois "proprietor": "Barrès was the first to invent it; the bourgeois is one with his property. If he remains in his province and on his estate, something passes into him from the gentle foot-hills of his region, from the silvery trembling of the poplars, from the mysterious and slow fecundity of the soil, from the rapid and capricious changes of mood in the skies, in assimilating the world, he assimilates its depth; henceforth his soul has substrata, mines, gold-lodes, veins, underground sheets of oil. Henceforth the *rallié* writer has his path cut out for him, to save himself he will save the bourgeoisie depthwise" (Jean-Paul Sartre, *Qu'est-ce que la littérature?* [Paris: Gallimard, 1948], 176, translated as *What Is Literature? and Other Essays* [Cambridge, MA: Harvard University Press, 1988], 147).

28. Jean-Paul Sartre, *L'être et le néant* (Paris: Gallimard, 1943), 120, translated by Hazel E. Barnes as *Being and Nothingness* (New York: Washington Square, 1992), 124–25.

This negativity at the heart of consciousness, which, in fact, *is* consciousness, is also the very structure of freedom. Freedom is the possibility of negation, of withdrawal, the ability of consciousness to distance itself from what is before it. "Every psychic process of nihilation implies a cleavage between the immediate psychic past and the present. This cleavage," Sartre writes, "is precisely nothing." Freedom is the fact that consciousness is not determined. The nature of human consciousness is pure contingency—groundlessness. It is the severing of the past from the present. Consciousness as the possibility of negation is defined by its being undetermined: "The for-itself, as the foundation of itself, is the upsurge of the negation. The for-itself founds itself insofar as it denies *in relation to itself* a certain being or mode of being. What it denies or nihilates, as we know, is being-in-itself. But no matter *what* being-in-itself: human reality is before all else its own nothingness." Only by negating the structure of the object, by nihilating the very structure of identity, does consciousness come into being. Consciousness is in its very nature deracinated. Sartre goes so far as to call the structure of consciousness "diasporetic": "In the ancient world the profound cohesion and dispersion of the Jewish people was designated by the term 'Diaspora.' It is this word which will serve to designate the mode of being of the For-itself; it is diasporetic." Here the trope of rootlessness applied to the Jews becomes the defining characteristic of consciousness in that consciousness comes into being, becomes what it is, "holds to itself by a single thread," in the very act of cutting itself off from the stability of determination.[29]

One element of bad faith, by contrast, is the denial of this contingency and its accompanying freedom. Bad faith arises from anguish. Anguish is the consciousness of my own freedom; otherwise stated, it is "precisely my consciousness of being my own future in the mode of not-being."[30] Sartre's definition of *anguish* may seem related to Heidegger's notion of angst. But there are some key differences. Heidegger defines *angst* as the collapse of the significance of the structures of worldliness and as a retreat from the world as such, with the result that the fact that "it [*Dasein*] is nothing and nowhere" becomes manifest.[31] Sartre's description of anguish is a description of possibility. This is probably best encapsulated by his description of vertigo. While one might imagine that Sartre's conception of vertigo would follow from Heidegger's portrayal of angst, as the very experience of groundlessness, this

29. Ibid., 131–32, 182; 138, 195.

30. Ibid., 69; 68.

31. Martin Heidegger, *Sein und Zeit*, 11th ed. (Tübingen: Max Niemeyer, 1967), 186, translated by John Macquarrie and Edward Robinson as *Being and Time* (New York: Harper & Row, 1962), 231.

Heideggerian modality, while relevant to Sartre's own description, does not fully exhaust it.[32] "Vertigo," Sartre writes, "is anguish to the extent that I am afraid not of falling over the precipice but of throwing myself over." He distinguishes between fear and anguish, not by whether one is reacting to an object, but by whether "we envision the situation as acting on the man or the man acting on the situation."[33] For it is the indeterminacy of the self, the fact that *nothing* of the self's past can act as a guarantor for its future, that creates anguish; at each and every moment I must decide again who I am and how I will act.

As a response to anguish, bad faith is a mode of the self in which I assume a determination. Because of the nature of the self, this constitutes a form of self-deception. Ironically, then, Sartre's notion of self-deception does not depend on a denial of my nature; rather, it is an attempt to determine my nature as such. Thus, for Sartre, sincerity is already a species of bad faith. To illustrate this principle, Sartre gives us the example of two men: one denies that his sleeping with men makes him a "homosexual," and the other, a critic of the first, or the "champion of sincerity," urges the homosexual to admit to what he is. Sartre then asks which of these two are in bad faith. If we conceive of bad faith as a form of self-deception, Sartre's basic definition, it may seem that the homosexual is in bad faith, for he cannot admit to the consequences of his actions. Insofar as his denial is replacing one form of being-in-itself with another, as in the statement, "I am a heterosexual, not a homosexual," he is, indeed, in bad faith. If, however, he understands that in denying that he is a homosexual he means that human reality cannot ultimately be defined by patterns of conduct, he is not in bad faith. It might seem, further, that the champion of sincerity is trying to convince the homosexual out of a state of self-deception and, thus, cannot himself be in bad faith. But, insofar as bad faith is a consequence of assuming that one can determine the nature of the self, sincerity and bad faith

32. The influence of *Being and Time* on Sartre's *Being and Nothingness* is well documented. After having discovered phenomenology through Levinas's early translations of and commentaries on Husserl, Sartre traveled to Berlin in 1933 in order to study phenomenology and attend Husserl's lectures. Nonetheless, it is often contended that he never gained a solid grasp of the thought of either Heidegger or Husserl. As Derrida famously said: "What must a society like ours be if a man who, in his own way, rejected or imperfectly understood so many theoretical and literary events of his time . . . who multiplied and broadcast incredible misunderstandings of Heidegger, sometimes of Husserl, came to dominate the cultural scene to the extent of becoming a great popular figure" (Jacques Derrida in *Le nouvel observateur*, September 9, 1983, translated as "An Interview with Derrida" in *Derrida and Différance*, ed. David Wood and Robert Bernasconi [Evanston, IL: Northwestern University Press, 1988], 75). Thus, in comparing Sartre's phenomenological categories of existence to Heidegger's, we can choose to read them either as willful divergences or as misunderstandings.

33. Sartre, *L'être et le néant*, 66, and *Being and Nothingness*, 65, 66.

are essentially one and the same—attempts to escape anguish, or the consciousness of freedom.

Given the reasoning outlined above, it is not difficult to see how Barrèsian anti-Semitism, based on the acceptance of essences, constitutes a form of bad faith. It would seem to represent the farthest extreme of bad faith, for it secures the self against the feeling of groundlessness. Self-deception itself is a condition that is unavoidable, as it is built into the structure of consciousness not to be what it is and to be what it is not. The only way out of bad faith is authenticity, a mode that Sartre describes in *Being and Nothingness* only in a note: "It is indifferent whether one is in good faith or in bad faith, because bad faith re-apprehends good faith and slides to the very origin of the project of good faith; that does not mean that we cannot radically escape bad faith. But this supposes a self-recovery of being which was previously corrupted. This self-recovery we shall call authenticity, the description of which has no place here."[34] The mode of authenticity is elaborated in *Réflexions sur la question juive* when the anti-Semite is treated for the first time as an object of phenomenological analysis.

### Anti-Semite and Jew: Two Forms of Flight

When *Réflexions* is read in light of *Being and Nothingness*, it becomes evident that Sartre characterizes the anti-Semite and the Jew in a manner that reflects his particular construction of phenomenology. While this fact does not excuse him from the easy stereotyping in which he engages, it does reveal that his attributions of certain qualities to the Jew and the anti-Semite are not generated on the level of nature or essence. Rather, they emerge for him through his consideration of the conditions according to which each type arises and the motives behind certain beliefs and behaviors.

Speaking in language that manages to unify both the literary metaphors of "L'enfance d'un chef" and the technical language of *Being and Nothingness*, Sartre describes the anti-Semite in *Réflexions* this way: "Now the anti-Semite flees responsibility as he flees his own consciousness, and choosing for his own personality the permanence of rock, he chooses for his morality a scale of petrified values. . . . We begin to perceive the meaning of the anti-Semite's choice of himself. He chooses the irremediable out of fear of being free; he chooses mediocrity out of fear of being alone, and out of pride he makes of his irremediable mediocrity a rigid

34. Ibid., 111; 116.

aristocracy. To this end he finds the existence of the Jew absolutely nec-essary."[35] Echoing the analysis of bad faith in *Being and Nothingness*, he describes the anti-Semite as fleeing his own freedom. In response to the groundlessness of his own consciousness, he seeks "the permanence of rock" and "petrified values." He projects the Jew as a symbol of deracina-tion in order to be able to raise his own materiality, his own link to the land, his own status as proprietor, to the level of moral value.

Repeating the dichotomy that is nascent in "L'enfance d'un chef," the anti-Semite, Sartre writes, is opposed to the Jew, "just as sentiment is to intelligence, the particular to the universal, the past to the present, the concrete to the abstract, the owner of real property to the possessor of negotiable securities." Here, implicitly following Barrès, he groups together the attributes of the intellectual, as Barrès has described him, and the Jew. They seem, in fact, to inhabit one and the same territory, that of the abstract and the universal. Elsewhere, Sartre describes the Jew as exhibiting "a passion for the universal."[36] His own association with this category is already evident in *The Words*, his 1963 memoir, in which he claims to be more Jewish than the Jews by virtue of his read-ing habits.[37] Yet, if he places himself (even as a child) in the category of the intellectual/Jew and, thus, associates himself with the abstract and universal, how do we account for the critique of universalism that is one of the primary arguments in *Réflexions*?

In *Réflexions*, this critique takes place on two fronts: it is conducted as an attack on the position of the democrat and as an attack on the "inau-thentic Jew." In his critique of the democrat, Sartre's argument has the same target as Bernard Lazare's and foreshadows the arguments made by Jewish thinkers from the late 1960s forward in their rejection of a "revolutionary bargain" that grants everything to the Jew as citizen and nothing to the Jews as a people.[38] The democrat, Sartre argues, purports to be the friend of the Jew by claiming that all men have equal rights. At the same time, he refuses to see the distinctions of the individual case:

The democrat, like the scientist, fails to see the singular; to him the individual is only a sum of universal traits. It follows that his defense of the Jew saves the latter as man and annihilates him as Jew. . . . For a Jew conscious and proud of being Jewish, assert-

35. Sartre, *Réflexions sur la question juive*, 33–34, and *Anti-Semite and Jew*, 27–28.
36. Ibid., 30, 144; 25, 111.
37. See Sartre, *Les mots*, 37, and *The Words*, 49.
38. For an example, see Shmuel Trigano, "From Individual to Collectivity: The Rebirth of the 'Jewish Nation' in France," in *The Jews in Modern France*, ed. Frances Malino and Bernard Wasserstein (Hanover, NH: University Press of New England, for Brandeis University Press, 1985).

ing his claim to be a member of the Jewish community . . . , there may not be so much difference between the anti-Semite and the democrat. The former wishes to destroy him as a man and leave nothing in him but the Jew, the pariah, the untouchable; the latter wishes to destroy him as a Jew and leave nothing in him but the man, the abstract and universal subject of the rights of man and the rights of the citizen.[39]

The argument that Sartre critiques here is essentially the argument of the Dreyfusards, as exemplified by Zola's *J'accuse*. It was against this model of assimilation that both Lazare and Péguy constructed their depictions of the Jew in his particularity. Yet, as we have seen, Sartre's own critique of the doctrine of race precludes him from following the same path. Nonetheless, there are marked similarities between Sartre's analysis of the inauthentic and authentic Jew and Lazare's own distinction between the Jew as parvenu and the Jew as pariah.[40]

Like Bernard Lazare, Sartre points out that the revolutionary promise that the Jew can enter society as a Frenchman only if he discards his particular traits is itself a false promise. First, it is built on a false conception of the universal. What is the definition of the human that the Jew is expected to fulfill if not the definition of the Christian? "We have seen that the latter have the art and the audacity to pretend before the Jew that they are not *another race*, but purely and simply *men*; if the Jew is fascinated by Christians, it is not because of their virtues, which he values little, but because they represent humanity without race." Sartre argues here that it is only the Jew who is being asked to discard his particularity, for the very notion of the universal has been defined in the French state on the model of the Christian. It is as though one were to suggest that to be white is to be without race or to be a man is to be without gender. As a consequence, the very ideal of the universal is unattainable. "The principle behind this drive toward assimilation is an excellent one," he continues. "The Jew is claiming his rights as a Frenchman. Unfortunately, the realization of this enterprise rests on an inadequate foundation. He wants people to receive him as 'a man,' but even in the circles which he has been able to enter, he is received as a Jew." Here, once again, Sartre sounds similar to Lazare, who during the Dreyfus affair pointed out that emancipation did not break down the ghetto

39. Sartre, *Réflexions sur la question juive*, 71–72, and *Anti-Semite and Jew*, 56–57.
40. These terms are not Lazare's. I have borrowed them from Hannah Arendt, who uses particularly the latter to describe Lazare's rethinking of the social role of the Jew after the Dreyfus affair. The former she gleans, not from Lazare's work, but rather from her own analysis of nineteenth-century French Jews, applying it most evocatively to the character of Swann from Proust's *In Search of Lost Time*. Nonetheless, her description of the parvenu matches up very neatly with Lazare's description of the bourgeois Jews of Paris. See Arendt, "The Jew as Pariah," 109.

walls; it merely made those walls invisible. Unfortunately, the only one who seemed to think the walls themselves were gone was the Jew, who was reproached for this very assumption. For both Sartre and Lazare, the Jew's refusal to recognize his situation constitutes a betrayal of his Jewish identity. For Sartre, the inauthentic Jew, like the anti-Semite, is in a state of flight. He does not use the term *bad faith* to describe the inauthentic Jew; rather, he replaces it with the dichotomy between authenticity and inauthenticity: "In a word, the inauthentic Jews are men who other men take for Jews and who have decided to run away from this unbearable situation. The result is that they display various types of behavior not all of which are present at the same time in the same person but each of which may be characterized as an *avenue of flight*."[41]

In *Being and Nothingness*, Sartre introduces the category of authenticity as the possibility of a recovery from bad faith. In *Réflexions*, he defines it: "Authenticity . . . consists in having a true and lucid consciousness of the situation, in assuming the responsibilities and the risks it involves, in accepting it in pride or humiliation, sometimes in horror and hate."[42] What is similar about bad faith and inauthenticity is that they are both forms of flight. The primary object of flight, however, seems to have shifted between the two texts. For, in *Being and Nothingness*, where the focus is on freedom, it seems that it is by accepting a determination of identity that one is deceiving oneself and, thus, in flight.[43] In *Réflexions*, the focus is on another form of self-deception: the refusal to recognize the determinations that others have imposed on you. To be authentic, one would have to maintain a particular relation to those determinations, a relation that recognizes them (where the anti-Semite, who assumes them as essence and, thus, uses them to deny freedom, does not) in such a way that one's freedom is dependent on an awareness of the way in which one is seen by others. Freedom here is married to ownership of one's situation.

We have, then, in *Réflexions* a portrait of two types of flight, the characterization of which situates the Jew and the anti-Semite at opposite ends of our particularism-universalism spectrum. The Jew takes flight toward the ideal of the universal, whereas the anti-Semite takes flight toward racialized particularism. Besides the obvious sociological and historical factors that explain this typology, it is important in terms of Sartre's phenomenology to see that the flight of the Jew is a flight, not

---

41. Sartre, *Réflexions sur la question juive*, 127, 127–28, 120, and *Anti-Semite and Jew*, 98, 98–99, 93.

42. Ibid., 116; 90 (translation slightly altered).

43. This is something of an oversimplification, as in later sections of the work where Sartre thematizes bad faith as an attempt to escape from being-for-others.

*from* freedom, but is the flight toward the freedom that the rhetoric of Enlightenment reason seems to promise: "If reason exists, then there is no French truth or German truth; there is no Negro truth or Jewish truth. There is only one truth, and he is best who wins it. In the face of universal and eternal laws, man himself is universal."[44] This ideal, Sartre argues, itself veils an essentialist assumption; in this case, it is an assumption about the essence of human nature.

Sartre opposes a rationalist, universalist definition of humanity with his concept of situation, and it is the concept of situation, along with the accompanying notion of condition, that provide the key to working out how he will simultaneously oppose any language of essence yet claim that authenticity involves accepting a characterization of one's self that is designated by others. These concepts are essential to seeing how Sartre could seem interested both in breaking down stereotypes and in retaining them: "For us, man is defined first of all as a being 'in a situation.' That means that he forms a synthetic whole with his situation—biological, economic, political, cultural, etc. . . . What men have in common is not a 'nature' but a condition, that is, an ensemble of limits and constraints: the necessity of dying, of working for a living, of existing in a world already inhabited by other men."[45]

Thus, one cannot consider man apart from his material and social circumstances. Although these contingencies do not determine the nature of the human being, they do provide us with the parameters to determine where his limits will arise. This notion of situation becomes more and more central to Sartre's thinking as his writings take on a Marxist bent. It arises as a central concept only in 1946 with the publication of both *Réflexions* and "Existentialism Is a Humanism." Its roots, however, already lie in *Being and Nothingness*.

Sartre's definition of situation as fundamentally limiting may seem in tension with the description of consciousness in *Being and Nothingness* as radically free and defined by its indeterminacy. Indeed it is, but that tension is essentially what constitutes the experience of human subjectivity. The limits on human freedom arise in Sartre's analysis of consciousness the moment that the subject must account for the existence of the other. For Sartre, the other is essentially the one who looks at me. In apprehending the other, I apprehend that I am the object of his gaze. By being an object seen by the other, I receive for the first time a sense of the self, myself, as an object in the world. My being as pure *for-itself*

44. Sartre, *Réflexions sur la question juive*, 144, and *Anti-Semite and Jew*, 111.
45. Ibid., 76; 59–60 (translation altered).

is no longer boundless transcendence: "This means that all of a sudden I am conscious of myself as escaping myself, not in that I am the foundation for my own nothingness but in that I have a foundation outside of myself. I am for myself only as I am a pure reference for the Other." At this moment I experience shame. Shame is the apprehension of myself "as a nature although that very nature escapes me and is unknowable as such."[46] The experience of being the object of the other's gaze is the experience of my transcendence transcended.

To illustrate this experience, Sartre gives the example of peering through a keyhole in a moment of jealousy, curiosity, or vice. At this moment, "I am pure consciousness of things." My attention is absorbed by the spectacle on the other side of the door. I do not consider what it means to be listening at doors; I do not apprehend the moral connotations of my action; my experience is of the object on which I am intent. Until, that is, I hear footsteps. Suddenly, at this moment, I apprehend myself in the hallway, down on my knees. Whether or not someone is there, I am now no longer merely acting; I am now acted on. Thus, my identity is given to me in the context of being seen: "My beauty or my ugliness or the insignificance of my features are apprehended by the Other in their full concreteness which the Other's speech will indicate to me; it is toward this that I shall emptily direct myself. Therefore we are not dealing with an abstraction but with an ensemble of structures, of which certain are abstract but whose totality is an absolute concrete, an ensemble which simply is indicated to me as on principle escaping me. This ensemble is in fact what I am." Already in *Being and Nothingness* the experience of receiving a definition of myself as it is constituted by the other's gaze is cast in the terms of the anti-Semite's relation to the Jew. In describing how the other's gaze determines the limits to my existential freedom, Sartre comes back to Jewishness as one of the characteristics, like beauty or ugliness, that is bestowed on me by the other.[47]

For Sartre, it is Kafka who most clearly expresses the phenomenological state of being-for-others, both for the Jew in particular and for humanity more generally.[48] Kafka's novels illustrate the way in which the gaze of the other saps me of the role of master of my own actions:

46. Sartre, *L'être et le néant*, 318, 319, and *Being and Nothingness*, 349, 352.
47. Ibid., 317 (first quote), 610 (second quote), 605–12; 347, 675, 670–78.
48. As will be clear in coming chapters, there is a persistent association between Kafka and the figure of the Jew, particularly as the Jew is figured as denaturalized. This connection is dealt with tangentially in Gilles Deleuze and Félix Guattari, *Kafka: Pour une littérature mineure* (Paris: Minuit, 1975), translated by Dana Polan as *Kafka: Toward a Minor Literature* (Minneapolis: University of Minnesota Press, 1986).

It is this unpredictability which Kafka's art attempts to describe in *The Trial* and *The Castle*. In one sense everything which K. and the Surveyor are doing belongs strictly to them in their own right, and insofar as they act upon the world the results conform strictly to anticipations; they are successful acts. But at the same time the *truth* of these acts constantly escapes them; the acts have on principle a meaning which is their *true meaning* and which neither K. nor the Surveyor will ever know. Without doubt Kafka is trying here to express the transcendence of the divine; it is for the divine that the human act is constituted in truth. But God here is only the concept of the Other pushed to the limit.[49]

Sartre does not mention Kafka's Judaism in this passage but, rather, accepts a theological reading of *The Castle*. In reading God as "the concept of the Other pushed to the limit," he nonetheless follows the same schema that he uses to designate the state of the Jew. The Jew is one whose state of being is overdetermined by the gaze of the other. This passage appears in *Being and Nothingness* and is among a number in which Kafka's novels and stories are analyzed as examples of the limits of the subject's freedom as such.[50] In *Réflexions sur la question juive*, Sartre provides a similar description of Kafka's *The Trial*, although there the novel is analyzed as an expression of *Jewish* subjectivity:

This is perhaps one of the meanings of *The Trial* by the Jew [*l'israélite*] Kafka. Like the hero of the novel, the Jew is engaged in a long trial. He does not know his judges, scarcely even his lawyers; he does not know what he is charged with, yet he knows that he is considered guilty; judgment is continually put off—for a week, two weeks— he takes advantage of these delays to improve his position in a thousand ways, but every precaution taken at random pushes him a little deeper into guilt. His external situation may appear brilliant, but the interminable trial invisibly wastes him away, and it happens sometimes, as in the novel, that men seize him, carry him off on the pretense that he has lost his case, and murder him in some vacant lot of the suburbs.[51]

Here, the experience of Kafka's hero is described in terms of guilt; nevertheless, the notion persists that the meaning of the hero's existence is determined by the other, who renders K's freedom useless by refusing him access to the structure of meaning by which his actions are judged.

What becomes evident in the juxtaposition of these two passages is the way in which Jewishness is conceived by Sartre according to the

---

49. Sartre, *L'être et le néant*, 324, and *Being and Nothingness*, 356.
50. See, e.g., ibid., 583, 635; 644, 703.
51. Sartre, *Réflexions sur la question juive*, 113–14, and *Anti-Semite and Jew*, 88.

model of being-for-others. This is significant first because it situates his highly controversial thesis that the Jew is created by the anti-Semite in a phenomenological context. As such, we can recognize that the Jew's creation by the anti-Semite is not unique to the Jew; rather, the relationship described by this statement is identical for all subjects insofar as Sartre conceives of the self as given by the gaze of the other.[52] This is as true of the Aryan as of the Jew: "Here I am—Jew or Aryan, handsome or ugly, one-armed, *etc*. All this I am *for the Other* with no hope of apprehending this meaning which I have *outside* and, still more important, with no hope of changing it."[53] In defining the Jew, then, as created by the anti-Semite, Sartre is restating the contention that my identity is given to me by the other.

We can easily argue that the very failure of this definition to account for cultural specificity, as illustrated by *Réflexions*, points to its inadequacy. What is relevant for our purposes, however, is that, for Sartre, being Jewish represents an intensification of the experience of *being human*. Just as Kafka's novels throw into relief the condition of being-for-others by the sheer overabundance of signification, so too does the category of the Jew in Sartre's own thinking fulfill this emphatic and crucial function:

We shall see later on that the root of Jewish disquietude is the necessity imposed upon the Jew of subjecting himself to endless self-examination and finally of assuming a phantom personality, at once strange and familiar, that haunts him and is no one other than himself, himself such as he is for the Other. You may say that this is the lot of all, that each of us has a character familiar to those close to us and which escapes us. No doubt: this is the expression of our fundamental relation to the Other. But the Jew has a personality like the rest of us, and on top of that he is Jewish. It amounts in a sense to a doubling of the fundamental relationship with the Other. *The Jew is over-determined*.[54]

---

52. This should be qualified by the acknowledgment that Sartre makes statements in *Réflexions* that indicate that this thesis is not *merely* phenomenological. For he does, indeed, seem to think that the Jewish people have neither a cultural heritage nor a collective history.

53. Sartre, *L'être et le néant*, 610, and *Being and Nothingness*, 671. The inadequacy of this category for understanding forms of cultural identity is evidenced by nearly every page of *Réflexions*, and, though his conception of existential situation ought to have given him a greater appreciation for history, it is an inadequacy that Sartre did not himself become aware of until years later, when he admitted, in 1966, that, if he had the book to do over again, he would base it historically in works such as Leon Poliakov's *History of Antisemitism* and would, thus, "try to deepen it" through historical and economic analysis (Sartre in *Cahiers Bernard Lazare* 4 [April 1966]: 8, quoted in Rybalka, "Publication and Reception of *Anti-Semite and Jew*," 169).

54. Sartre, *Réflexions sur la question juive*, 101–2, and *Anti-Semite and Jew*, 79 (translation altered; emphasis added).

While this state sets the Jew apart, it also makes of Sartre's description of the Jewish situation and of the possibility for living authentically in the face of these conditions an exemplum for the possibility of authenticity as such.

In *Réflexions sur la question juive*, Sartre offers two possibilities for thinking through political identity, each presented as a perspective on the Jewish question. The first is the perspective of the anti-Semite, a determinist vision of the human in which social legitimacy is conceived as a product of nature, of essence, of race. The second is the perspective of the democrat or the universalist. In the later, reason is conceived as the power by which all human beings transcend the conditions of tribal existence. The definition of man is homogeneous. The Jew is defined by Sartre as the man who is caught by these two discourses, defined as the necessary other for particularism and annihilated in the very process of abstraction by the latter.

The possibility of authenticity arises for Sartre as a refusal of either of these paths. Each and every person is faced with both paths of flight; each and every person must choose to live authentically by refusing flight, accepting freedom and the conditions of one's circumstances. Nonetheless, by existing in an intensified state of being-for-others, there is a sense in which the Jewish condition serves as a privileged example, revealing the possibility for authenticity. In *Réflexions sur la question juive*, Sartre writes that, if the Jew did not exist, the anti-Semite would invent him.[55] As Stuart Charmé has pointed out, we could say the same for Sartre.[56]

In the process of working out the notion of engaged literature, the figure of the Jew becomes a locus around which Sartre can develop a notion of authenticity that is in conversation with the universalist and particularist/determinist models of human subjectivity but conceived in contrast with them. In the *présentation* to the first issue of *Les temps modernes*, published on October 1, 1945, after he had composed much of *Réflexions* but before its publication, Sartre first elaborates on the model of literature *engagé*. While this is not the first time that he has described his project as a literature of involvement, it is probably the closest he comes to producing its manifesto.[57]

55. Ibid., 15; 13.
56. Stuart Charmé, *Vulgarity and Authenticity*, 141.
57. According to Jonathan Judaken, Sartre's "New Writing in France," published in *Vogue* in July 1945, is his first introduction to the notion of a literature of *involvement* (this is the term used in the English *Vogue* article and may have been *engagement* in French). In the *Vogue* article, Sartre does not advocate *engagement* as a mission but speaks of the "literature of involvement" as the future of French letters, arising out of the experience of the Resistance. See Jean-Paul Sartre, "New Writing in France: The Resistance 'taught that literature is no fancy activity independent of politics,'" *Vogue*, July 1945, 84–85; and Judaken, *Jean-Paul Sartre and the Jewish Question*, 151.

The literature of engagement is a refusal of the model of the bourgeois writer who takes a position of impartiality in relation to politics, who situates himself above or outside social and political dilemmas. In contrast, Sartre writes: "For us the writer is neither a Vestal or Ariel, he is in the fray . . . our intention is to contribute to the production of certain changes in the society by which we are surrounded."[58] What is crucial in this description is the sense of the writer being embedded in his society. With that arises a conception of thought that can be situated, determined, only by the circumstances of its production. This means a revision of the classic Enlightenment (or bourgeois) conception of reason and of man where the essence of man is understood to be independent of his conditions. This does not, however, entail a form of determinism. Along with a notion of abstract freedom, Sartre rejects both a strictly Marxist determinism and a racial determinism. He recognizes these options as the antinomy by which his own culture seems to be torn and responds: "We do not permit ourselves to separate the thesis and the antithesis."[59]

The way out of the opposition between abstract freedom and determinism is the notion of situation, which allows for a common understanding of humanity without assigning it some kind of essence and accounts further for the particularities that separate the Jew from the Christian, man from woman, American from Frenchman:

For us, that which men have in common is not a nature, it is a metaphysical condition: and by that we understand the ensemble of constraints which limit men *a priori*, the necessity of being born and dying, that of being finite and of existing in the world among other men. As for the rest, they constitute totalities which cannot be broken down, of which the ideas, the moods, and the acts are secondary and dependent structures, and of which the essential character is to be situated and they differ among one another as their situations differ among them.

The conception of the human situation that Sartre proposes in *Les temps modernes* is crucial to his notion of the engaged writer. While he recognizes certain precursors in French letters to his model of the French intellectual, most notably Émile Zola, his model is, ultimately, a departure from the classic image of the Dreyfusard intellectual, that is, the one who defended Dreyfus "in the name of justice" as a human being, not as a Jew. If the project of the intellectual was until this point conceived along the lines of the Dreyfus affair—as a fight for the republican notion

58. Jean-Paul Sartre, "Présentation," *Les temps modernes*, October 1, 1945, 2.
59. Ibid., 17.

of man—Sartre has shifted this notion to take account of the way in which the contingencies of man's situation shape his character. Thus, the intellectual, like the Jew, must give up on the inauthenticity of the Dreyfusard notion and accept his responsibility to affect society; to be in it, not above it; to fight the battles of his *époque*, to love it passionately, and to accept that he will perish with it.[60]

Concretely, the task of the engaged intellectual is not only to expose his culture's injustices but also to take part in a specific anthropological project: to describe the human being in his conditions, to describe the way those conditions form him. This shall be done, Sartre declares, not merely with the aim of "contributing to the progress of pure knowledge; the further aim upon which we fix is *liberation*. Because man is a total-ity, it does not suffice, in effect, to accord him the right to vote without touching on the other factors that constitute him: it is necessary that he be completely delivered."[61]

In December 1945, two months after publishing this manifesto for the launch of his magazine, Sartre published his first piece in the magazine following the dictates of the manifesto—the "Portrait de l'antisémite," which in the following year would become the first half of *Réflexions sur la question juive*. In this text, the situation of the Jew provides him with the perfect example by which he can make concrete the very distinctions that were first elaborated in the *présentation* to *Les temps modernes*.[62]

There are, of course, obvious reasons why Sartre would choose the Jew as his subject at the moment he did. Knowledge of the death camps was beginning to surface at the time of the book's composition, and the horrific consequences of anti-Semitism, which had, in fact, had a certain mainstream appeal in France as a species of anticapitalism and antimod-ernism, had become widely and horrifically evident even to many who had once situated themselves in the camp of Action française.[63] Yet, as

60. Ibid., 13 (quote), 7.

61. Ibid., 14. In Sartre's more Marxist moments in this text, *Réflexions*, and *What Is Literature?* there seems to be some tension between his vision of a future in which distinctions of class, race, etc. disap-pear and his call for social and cultural pluralism.

62. Further support for the notion that the figure of the Jew serves as the prime exemplar for Sar-tre's working out of the category of being-for-others can be found in his treatment of *Réflexions* in *What Is Literature?* Here, Sartre refers to his own treatment of the Jew as an example of committed lit-erature and defends his definition of the Jew as "'a man whom other men consider as a Jew and who is obliged to choose himself on the basis of the situation which is made for him,'" with the explanation: "There are qualities which come to us solely by means of the judgment of others" (Sartre, *Qu'est-ce que la littérature?* 84, and *What Is Literature?* 77).

63. For more on the attraction of fascism for French intellectuals in the 1920s and 1930s, see Jef-frey Mehlman, *Legacies of Anti-Semitism in France* (Minneapolis: University of Minnesota Press, 1983); and Alice Yaeger Kaplan, *Reproductions of Banality, Fascism, Literature and French Intellectual Life* (Min-neapolis: University of Minnesota Press, 1986).

many critics have noted, the treatment of anti-Semitism and the Jew in *Réflexions* draws very little from the rhetoric of Nazism. The phenomena Sartre describes under the name of anti-Semitism conform to the model of Drumont's and Barrès's anti-Semitism; it is the anti-Semitism of the Dreyfus affair and the decades immediately following.[64] While critics are often puzzled by this choice, the timeliness of the text—the fact that it was approaching the issue of anti-Semitism when no one else yet dared, the fact that it was one of the first important texts on the Jewish question after the war—allows readers to pass over its anachronistic aspects. When we consider it, however, not merely as a timely meditation on an important issue, but as the instantiation of a larger project, Sartre's topic and his approach to the topic develop a new logic.

In the anti-Dreyfusard discourse of the anti-Semite and the Dreyfusard rhetoric of the democrat, Sartre has the perfect instantiation of the antinomy that he describes in *Les temps modernes*. The ramifications of both these discourses are, for Sartre, most evident in their production of the figure of the Jew. The anti-Semite annihilates the Jew as a man and recognizes him only as a Jew, but the democrat annihilates him as a Jew and permits him to be only a man. Both the rhetoric of particularist determinism and that of abstract universalism are imposed on the Jew; what they create, according to Sartre, is, in fact, the Jewish situation—the situation of being overdetermined: "Thus the Jew remains the stranger, the intruder, the unassimilated at the very heart of our society. Everything is accessible to him, yet he possesses nothing." The authentic Jew accepts these terms as his situation:

Jewish authenticity consists in choosing oneself *as Jew*—that is, in realizing one's Jewish condition. The authentic Jew abandons the myth of the universal man; he knows himself and wills himself into history as a historic and damned creature; he ceases to run away from himself and to be ashamed of his own kind. He understands that society is bad; for the naïve monism of the inauthentic Jew he substitutes a social pluralism. He knows that he is one who stands apart, untouchable, scorned, proscribed—and it is *as such* that he asserts his being. At once he gives up his rationalistic optimism; he sees the world is fragmented by irrational divisions, and in accepting this fragmentation—at least in what concerns him—in proclaiming himself a Jew, he makes some of these values and these divisions his. . . . He stakes everything on human grandeur, for he accepts the obligation to live in a situation that is defined precisely by the fact that it is unlivable; he derives his pride from his humiliation.[65]

64. See Nicholas Hewitt, "'Portrait de l'antisémite' dans son contexte: Antisémitisme et judéocide," *Études sartriennes* 1 (0000): 111–22.

65. Sartre, *Réflexions sur la question juive*, 178–79, and *Anti-Semite and Jew*, 136–37.

What we have here once again is the notion of the pariah as hero. We encountered this idea in Bernard Lazare as a version of Jewish national-ism, although, for Lazare, it was uniquely an option for the Jew because of his race, his past, and his history. It is not so much that the notion of the pariah as hero has been shaped for Sartre by the Jewish situation as that his notion of the Jewish situation has been shaped by his philo-sophical system. Jewishness is, here, described as an intensification of the existentialist's choice. The Jew is rootless; he is a stranger; he is defined and determined by the gaze of the other. The existentialist hero embraces his circumstances and the freedom and responsibility that exist therein. He does not flee; he chooses and engages. The Jew, as the stranger, as "a type who has nothing, no homeland," has a function like Kafka's hero: the insupportable weight of his situation allows us to see our own.

## II. Dialectical History, Unhappy Consciousness, and the Messiah

I have been arguing that, as a response to the political dialectic between universalism and particularism, Sartre's prescription for authenticity in *Réflexions* seems to advocate a nonnaturalized pluralism, a respect for difference founded on historical and cultural context that does not at the same time reinscribe the language of nature and essence, a posi-tion that Sartre referred to as *concrete liberalism*. As a thinker advocating respect for difference, Sartre has been read as both anticipating and even helping to initiate the politics of pluralism that developed in France in the late 1960s and the 1970s, as marginalized groups in France grew sus-picious of the revolutionary rhetoric that recognized them as men but not as Jews, Arabs, or Bretons.[66] This understanding of his work must, however, also be squared with the following passages:

It is with his character, his customs, his tastes, his religion if he has one, his name and his physical traits that we *must* accept him. And if that acceptance is total and sincere, the result will be, first, to facilitate the Jew's choice of authenticity, *and then, bit by bit, to make possible, without violence and by the very course of history, that assimilation to which some would like to drive him by force.*

Anti-Semitism manifests the *separation* of men and their isolation in the midst of the community, the conflict of interests and the crosscurrents of passions: it can exist only in a society where a rather loose solidarity unites strongly structured pluralities; it is

66. See, e.g., Misrahi, "Sartre and the Jews"; and Lévy, *Le siècle de Sartre.*

a phenomenon of social pluralism. In a society whose members feel mutual bonds of solidarity, because they are all engaged in the same enterprise, there would be no place for it. . . . The Jew of today is in full war. What is there to say except that *the socialist revolution is necessary and sufficient for the suppression of the anti-Semite? It is for the Jews also that we shall make the revolution.*[67]

In these two passages, Sartre advocates a tolerance for difference with an aim toward ultimately dissolving it. The goal, he suggests, is the dissolution of difference in a classless society. In such a society, there would be no anti-Semitism and, thus, by consequence, no Jew; certainly, there would be no marginalized other, no perpetual stranger. The mechanism proposed for dissolving this difference is history in the first passage and revolution in the second. Is concrete liberalism, then, merely a stage on the way toward the Marxist state? Is difference asserted merely so that it can be dissolved in the dialectic of history?

The answer to these questions depends on the way in which we interpret the role of Hegel and, subsequently, Marx in Sartre's thinking. His position on Marx and Hegel, their role in the shaping of his own thought, is something that Sartre himself struggled with and renegotiated continually throughout his career. While the Jew is in no way central to his negotiation with Hegel and Marx, his representation of Jewishness is, nonetheless, generated by way of his reading of Hegel. What might seem a sign of the irrelevance of Judaism—the Jew's position outside the dialectics of history—becomes the source for Jewish significance in his late writing.

As Levinas wrote in his 1980 eulogy for Sartre: "A philosopher settling his views on Hegel is like a weaver installing a loom—a necessary preliminary task to all subsequent work."[68] We must, then, retrace the steps Sartre took in forming that loom to understand how he came in the end of his life to make this statement: "For me, messianism is an important thing that Jews have conceived of alone, but that could be used by non-Jews for other purposes."[69]

## Hegel and the Jews

In his final interviews with Benny Lévy, Sartre returns to the Jewish question. The texts from these interviews can be read as a sequel to *Réflexions*

67. Sartre, *Réflexions sur la question juive*, 190, 194–95, and *Anti-Semite and Jew*, 147 (translation slightly altered; emphasis added), 149–50 (emphasis added).

68. Emmanuel Levinas, *Les imprévus de l'histoire* (Paris: Fata Morgana, 1994), 131–32, translated by Nidra Poller as *Unforeseen History* (Urbana: University of Illinois Press, 2004), 94–95.

69. Sartre, *L'espoir maintenant*, 78, and *Hope Now*, 107.

*sur la question juive*. In Levinas's words: "They contain a final witness of sympathy for Jewishness, for the distance traveled since *Anti-Semite and Jew* appeared a third of a century ago. There we find something else as well: the reconsideration by a great philosopher of his attitude toward Hegel."[70] As Levinas suggests here, Sartre's expression of sympathy for the Jews in this final text is linked to his reconsideration of Hegel's philosophy of history. We must ask how Sartre's relation to Hegel's philosophy of history shifts over the intervening years and, furthermore, how this journey produces, from the perspective of Sartre's Jewish readers, what Levinas referenced in the title of his 1980 eulogy for Sartre—namely, "a language familiar to us"?[71]

The interviews themselves are the consequence of a collaborative project between Benny Lévy and Sartre, an attempt, in Sartre's words, to think "plural thoughts."[72] Lévy acted as Sartre's secretary for the last seven years of Sartre's life after Sartre had gone blind. As previously mentioned, the controversy surrounding the interviews rests primarily on Simone de Beauvoir's contention that the interviews do not, in fact, represent Sartre's thinking but are, rather, the consequence of his "abduction" by Lévy, who, by 1978, had himself discovered Levinas's work and been inspired by it to read the Talmud, reassert his Jewish identity, and, ultimately, live life as an Orthodox Jew. There is little in the interviews, however, to warrant this reading, for they are marked by Sartre's strong disagreement with Lévy, even when Lévy comes close to badgering Sartre. It is important also to separate Lévy's commentary on the interviews from the interviews themselves, for, at times, Lévy seems to want to push what Sartre says about the metaphoric importance of Jewishness to a more literal level. Finally, as they are clearly the consequence of a collaborative project, the interviews represent an encounter between Lévy's own Levinas-infused messianic Judaism and Sartre's concern to turn away from political theory and toward ethics.[73]

70. Levinas, *Les imprévus de l'histoire*, 131, and *Unforeseen History*, 94.
71. As mentioned above, these interviews have been viewed as controversial by many of Sartre's readers, both because they seem to represent a radical departure from many of Sartre's earlier positions and because of doubt cast on the legitimacy of the circumstances surrounding their composition. As the weight of my argument is on illustrating the way in which Sartre's thought functions to produce a trope of the Jew, I do not think that these debates contaminate my argument. For the eulogy, see ibid., 128–33; 92–95.
72. Sartre, *L'espoir maintenant*, 42, and *Hope Now*, 74.
73. At the close of *Being and Nothingness*, Sartre suggests that his next project will be an ethics founded on the principles of *Being and Nothingness*. This project was then continually suspended, showing up only obliquely in notebooks and through works such as his Flaubert biography, *L'idiot de la famille: Gustave Flaubert de 1821–1857*, 3 vols. (Paris: Gallimard, 1971–72), translated by Carol Cosman as *The Family Idiot: Gustave Flaubert, 1821–1857*, 5 vols. (Chicago: University of Chicago

The discussion of the Jew/Judaism makes up the most substantive section of the published material and functions as its conclusion. This section begins with Sartre's admission that he knew little to nothing about Judaism when he wrote *Réflexions*. As I have indicated, this has often been read as an important acknowledgment of the book's weakness. It is important to note, however, that, while Sartre admits that "the reality of the Jew is lacking in the book," he also defends the project as an outgrowth of the dichotomy of consciousness that he works out in *Being and Nothingness*: "There was a consciousness of self that I stripped of all individual characteristics that might have come from within and that I then made it rediscover from the outside. Once the Jew was deprived of metaphysical and subjective characteristics, he could not exist in my philosophy."[74] As much as this sounds like a self-criticism, it is also an affirmation of the book as a self-conscious attempt to sketch out the idea of the Jew produced by anti-Semitism. One product of *Réflexions* is a vision of the Jew as having no history or being outside history. It is here that the figure of Hegel looms large. Sartre writes:

A concrete historical community is basically *national* and *religious*; but the Jewish community, which once was both, has been deprived bit by bit of both these characteristics. We may call it an abstract historical community. Its dispersion implies the breaking up of common traditions, and it was remarked above that its twenty centuries of dispersion and political impotence forbid it having a *historic past*. If it is true as Hegel says, that a community is historical to the degree that it remembers its history, then the Jewish community is the least historical of all, for it keeps a memory of nothing but a long martyrdom, that is, of a long passivity.[75]

In this passage from 1946, Sartre repeats Hegel's explicit judgment of the Jews as passive and slavish, a dehistoricized, fossilized people who "aborted" their own mission, a people who are ahistorical because they are never truly political.[76] Whether or not Sartre has in mind those passages in which Hegel explicitly addressed Judaism or the Jewish people,

---

Press, 1981–1993). The interviews were supposed to have been a preparatory exercise for a work finally addressing this theme. See Sartre, *L'espoir maintenant*, 27, and *Hope Now*, 59.

74. Sartre, *L'espoir maintenant*, 73, and *Hope Now*, 102.

75. Sartre, *Réflexions sur la question juive*, 85, and *Anti-Semite and Jew*, 66.

76. On the Jews as passive and slavish, see Hegel, "Der Geist des Christentums und sein Schicksal," 243–60, and "Spirit of Christianity and Its Fate," 182–204. On the Jews as a fossilized people, see Yirmiyahu Yovel, *Dark Riddle: Hegel, Nietzsche, and the Jews* (Cambridge: Polity, 1998), 55. On the Jews as ahistorical, see G. W. F. Hegel, *Vorlesungen über die Philosophie der Geschichte*, vol. 12 of *Werke*, 20 vols. (Suhrkamp: Frankfurt, 1969–72), 273, translated by J. Sibree as *Lectures on the Philosophy of History* (New York: Dover, 1956), 197.

what he affirms is that, by the very *logic* of Hegelian thinking, the Jews must stand outside history.[77]

In the context of *Réflexions*, there is little to suggest that Sartre himself saw this description of the Jewish people as necessarily positive; rather, he saw it as a justification for his own interpretation of Jewishness as a category imposed on the Jew by the gaze of the other. Given his loyalty to a method of historical dialectics that shows itself already in *Réflexions* and is articulated further in "Materialism and Revolution," published the same year, we can assume that, if the claim that Jews have no history is not necessarily negative, it is certainly not positive. Sartre at this earlier stage sees the dialectics of history as necessary to bringing about social justice. Thus, to assign the Jews a position outside history is, at the very least, to make them irrelevant to the mechanisms of justice.

In the interviews, the issue of Jewish historicity is revisited. Lévy asks Sartre whether he would have written that the Jews had no history if by then he had read Salo Baron's history of Israel, which at that point he had just recently finished.[78] Sartre responds that he does not imagine it would have altered his judgment on that point:

Because at the time that I said that there was no Jewish history, I was thinking of history in a certain well-defined sense—the history of France, the history of Germany, the history of America, of the United States. In any case the history of a sovereign political entity that has its own territory and relations with other states like itself. Whereas one would have had to conceive of history differently if one wanted to say that there is a Jewish history not only as the history of the Jews' dispersion throughout the world but also as the unity of this Diaspora, the unity of the dispersed Jews.

[Lévy]: In his profoundest reality, then, the Jew can permit us to give up on the philosophy of history.

[Sartre]: Exactly. The philosophy of history isn't the same if there's a Jewish history or if there isn't. But obviously there is a Jewish history.

[Lévy]: In other words, the history that Hegel introduced into our intellectual landscape sought to get rid of the Jew, and it's the Jew who will make it possible to get away from the view of history Hegel wanted to impose on us.[79]

---

77. G. W. F. Hegel, *Phänomenologie des Geistes* (Banberg and Würzburg, 1807), 198, translated by A. V. Miller as *Phenomenology of Spirit* (Oxford: Oxford University Press, 1977), 206.

78. Lévy provides no bibliographic information, but we can assume that he is referring to Salo Baron, *A Social and Religious History of the Jews* (New York: Columbia University Press, 1937).

79. This is one of the places where we can see the indirect influence of Levinas on Sartre. For Lévy's comment here mirrors the comment to the same effect that Levinas makes in "Hegel and the Jews" when he asks "whether we should leave the System, even if we do so by moving backwards, through

[Sartre]: Absolutely, because this proves there is a real unity of Jews in historical time, and that real unity is due not to their being gathered together on a historical territory but to actions and writings and bonds that don't derive from the idea of a homeland, except for the last few years.[80]

In this interlocution, Sartre and Lévy explicitly rehabilitate the previous negative designation of the Jews. The very fact that Hegel excluded the Jew from the dialectic and defined him by his resistance to history becomes the means by which Hegel himself can be critiqued. Thus, the Jew can serve as a positive political emblem of a mode of being that is, by Hegel's definition, apolitical. The Jew's rootlessness takes on a positive valence.

Now, the dynamics of the conversation disallow us from attributing this move purely to Sartre, for it is Lévy who asserts the thesis that the position of the Jew becomes a source for resisting a Hegelian philosophy of history, but it is by means of Sartre's reassertion in *Réflexions* of the Hegelian thesis that this shift takes place. Moreover, in the course of their conversation, it is evident that the Jew is functioning as an emblem. Sartre at first seems to resist this language. He refers to "Jews" and to "Jewish history," while Lévy refers to "the Jew." But then Sartre too begins to speak of "the Jew's" metaphysical nature and "the Jew's" relation to God. Sartre and Lévy shift here from the question of whether Hegel's or Sartre's descriptions are accurate to the issue of how the figure produced by Hegel's/Sartre's depictions can function when the aim is to resist the dialectics of history. Though neither thinker references Rosenzweig or Hermann Cohen, for any reader of modern Jewish thought the resonance is clear. Both thinkers figure the Jew as outside history but reclaim this position from Hegel as *the* positive moral and political fact of Judaism. For Rosenzweig, in *The Star of Redemption*, the position of Jews as outside history is indicative of their already existing in a messianic time, where Christians are still "on the way." For Lévy, this resonance is already evident in Sartre's statements in *Réflexions*, although he acknowledges that Sartre's own thinking is too close to Hegel's at the time of the text's composition for Sartre himself to recognize the powerful potential of his own words. In his interpretation of the interviews, published four years after Sartre's death, Lévy writes:

---

the very door by which Hegel thinks we enter it" (Emmanuel Levinas, *Difficile liberté* [Paris: Albin Michel, 1963], 333, translated by Sean Hand as *Difficult Freedom* [Baltimore: Johns Hopkins University Press, 1990], 238).

80. Sartre, *L'espoir maintenant*, 74–75, and *Hope Now*, 103–4.

But this desire for a pure sociality without *"inconscient agreste"* to which the Jew is condemned, does this not place the Jew outside of the game of universal history? It seems so, first: the Jew, in *Réflexions* has no history. From this unbearable constant, Sartre could go two ways: One possibility is that the Jew departs from universal history. But then Sartre cannot ask, where is the Jew? And he is so close to hearing Franz Rosenzweig: "to condemn history and its tendencies, we have only to signal from time to time the pacifist and deaf fact of our existence."[81]

If Sartre cannot take up the possibility suggested by his words in 1946, it is because his own view of history at the point of his writing—and for at least fifteen more years—is devoted to attempting to synthesize his own thought with the Marxism of his day, which he refers to as "an unsurpassable horizon."[82]

Yet it is impossible to say that Sartre's turn to what some will consider "Judaic" thinking in these final essays is unanticipated by his earlier work.[83] I have already shown the manner in which the Jew resurfaces periodically in Sartre's texts both as an image for his own subjectivity and as a privileged example illustrating the difficult straits of the human condition. Sartre's lifelong engagement with the Hegelian dialectic reveals another, if more oblique, avenue of preparation for his supposed turn to "Jewish" thinking.

*Sartre and Hegel*

According to Benny Lévy, Sartre admitted to having come to study Hegel seriously only after the war, with the publication of Hyppolite's translation and commentary. Yet, in *Being and Nothingness*, he is already grappling with what he sees as the problematic movement in Hegel's thought to absolve difference.[84]

Sartre's theory of consciousness is from the very beginning engaged with a Hegelian conception of the relation between Being and Knowing. Sartre adopts a view of consciousness that functions by means of

---

81. Benny Lévy, *Le nom de l'homme* (Paris: Verdier, 1984), 159.

82. Jean-Paul Sartre, *Questions de méthode* (Paris: Gallimard, 1960), 188, translated by Hazel E. Barnes as *The Problem of Method* (London: Methuen, 1961), 136.

83. The very terms by which this so-called turn is enacted need to be called into question. In the conclusion to the chapter, I return to this issue.

84. As Michael Surya notes, although Sartre was markedly absent from Alexandre Kojève's 1933–39 lectures on *The Phenomenology of Spirit*, one must assume that he was indirectly influenced by Kojève's interpretation given the profound impact the lectures had on the French philosophical and psycho-analytic scene. See Michael Surya, *Georges Bataille: An Intellectual Biography*, trans. Krysztof Fijalkowski and Michael Richardson (London: Verso, 2002), 187.

negation and transcendence. The relation of the for-itself (consciousness) to the in-itself (objects in the world) is perpetually one defined by
the for-itself conducting an operation of nihilation in order to surpass
itself. Sartre distinguishes his own model from what he sees as the totalizing movement of Hegelian thought wherein nihilation is perpetually
productive, providing by its operation the possibility of consciousness's
satisfaction. Reflective consciousness is "not a unity which contains
a duality, not a synthesis which transcends and raises up the abstract
moments of thesis and antithesis, but a duality which is unity," Sartre
writes. In other words, consciousness is constituted by its difference,
a difference that is fundamental to its structure and, thus, not in the
process of being overcome. On one level, for Sartre, activity is always in
vain, for it relates to a goal that it cannot achieve: "Thus human reality
arises as such in the presence of its own totality or self as a lack of that
totality. And this totality can not be given by nature since it combines in
itself the incompatible characteristics of the in-itself and the for-itself."
The very structure of the for-itself, constituted as it is by lack, prohibits
the possibility that it can fulfill its desire to achieve completeness, to
which it relates as an ideal; to do so would by definition be to lose itself
by becoming the in-itself. Thus, for Sartre, Hegel's stage of unhappy consciousness is not merely a stage in the process of self-consciousness; it is
the very structure of consciousness: "The being of human reality is suffering because it rises in being as perpetually haunted by a totality which
it is without being able to be it, precisely because it could not attain the
in-itself without losing itself as for-itself. Human reality therefore is by
nature an unhappy consciousness with no possibility of surpassing its
unhappy state."[85]

Quintessentially alienated from his own powers, Hegel's Jew is often
understood as the iconic figure for the stage of unhappy consciousness,
despite the fact that Hegel does not explicitly make this association in the
*Phenomenology of Spirit*.[86] What allows for Sartre's assignation of the category of unhappy consciousness to consciousness as such is what he sees

85. Sartre, *L'être et le néant*, 118, 133, 134, and *Being and Nothingness*, 123, 140. In *Subjects of Desire:
Hegelian Reflections in Twentieth Century France* (New York: Columbia University Press, 1987), Judith
Butler emphasizes the lack of coincidence within identity as characteristic of the Hegelian subject as
well, offering a reading that might seem to put Sartre closer to Hegel than Sartre assumes himself to be
(9). She distinguishes Sartre's view of mediation, however, as one in which the relation to the world
is marked by the disparity between self and world, where the Hegelian subject "is lucky enough to
discover the world as internal to its own consciousness" (129).

86. "The Jewish Consciousness is indeed the unhappy consciousness" (Jacques Derrida, *L'écriture
et la différence* [Paris: Seuil, 1967], 104, translated by Alan Bass as *Writing and Difference* [Chicago: University of Chicago Press, 1978], 68). See also Yovel, *Dark Riddle*, 56; and George Steiner, "Our Homeland, the Text," in *No Passion Spent* (London: Faber & Faber, 1996), 307.

as the inability of consciousness to overcome the distance between itself and the ideal of a totality—an idealized image of itself as totality. This is, according to Hegel, exactly what characterizes Jewish alienation. The Jewish sensibility is unable to overcome the distance between the transcendent God, to which it has attributed all things good, and itself, which has, thus, been constituted as lack.[87] Sartre gives no indication that he is aware of the connection, at least not at the time that he was composing *Being and Nothingness*. In later years, however, when he returns to the category of unhappy consciousness in his characterization of the intellectual in "A Plea for Intellectuals," he could not have been unaware of the association, for he had by then read (and to a great extent depended on) Hyppolite's commentary on *The Phenomenology of Spirit*, in which it is argued that Hegel's section on unhappy consciousness, which explicitly refers to Catholicism, is also an implicit reference to Judaism.[88]

To return to *Being and Nothingness*, Sartre's process of differentiating his own thinking from Hegel's takes place both on the level of consciousness and on the level of intersubjective relations. The difference Sartre asserts in relation to consciousness will markedly affect his attempt to work out a dialectical model of history. What he contests in Hegel's model of intersubjectivity is the assumption that particularity is overcome through the act of recognition. On the level of the encounter, he argues for the impossibility of simultaneous and mutual recognition: "The Other is not a *for-itself* as he appears to me; I do not appear to myself as I am *for the Other*. I am incapable of apprehending on the basis of the *Other-as-object* which appears to me, what the Other is for himself." Here, we see an intensification of Sartre's critique of the structure of consciousness in Hegel. The fact that the structure of consciousness cannot be identity, the fact that there is a fundamental split between the for-itself and the in-itself in Sartre's model of consciousness, prohibits the possibility of a mutual recognition between subjects. The other can appear to me as in-itself (as an object), or it can appear to me as that which judges me as an object, but this does not give me access to the interiority of the other. Rather, what I relate to is the experience of being seen, and, thus, the other's gaze becomes one more object on which I pass judgment. Sartre accuses Hegel of a form of "epistemological optimism" for assuming that universal knowledge "can be derived from the

87. See Hegel, "Der Geist des Christentums und sein Schicksal," 243–60, and "Spirit of Christianity and Its Fate," 182–204.

88. Jean Hyppolite, *Genèse et structure de La phénoménologie de l'esprit* (Paris: Aubier, 1946), 185, translated by Samuel Cherniak and John Heckman as *Genesis and Structure of Hegel's Phenomenology of Spirit* (Evanston, IL: Northwestern University Press, 1974), 196.

relation of consciousness."[89] For Sartre, a fundamental ontological separation makes this move impossible.

Sartre's attribution to Hegel of "optimism" reveals his own orientation. The goals of transparency, unity, and even totality are not at issue here. They remain an ideal for Sartre as they did for Hegel. This becomes especially apparent in the critique of what Sartre refers to as Hegel's "vantage point of truth." The only solution to the irreconcilability between two conscious subjects is the possibility of a vantage point outside consciousness. This is what Hegel has granted to himself, Sartre argues, through the positing of the Absolute:

> When Hegel writes that every consciousness, since it is identical with itself, is other than the Other, he has established himself in the whole outside consciousnesses, and he considers them from the point of view of the Absolute. For individual consciousnesses are moments in the whole, moments which by themselves are *Unselbständig*, and the whole is a mediator between consciousnesses. Hence is derived an ontological optimism parallel to the epistemological optimism: plurality can and must be surpassed toward the totality. But if Hegel can assert the reality of this surpassing, it is because he has already given it to himself at the outset.[90]

The absolute is the means for accomplishing totality. From the perspective of the Absolute, all consciousnesses are equivalent. But, as my own interiority is itself impossible to transcend, I cannot, according to Sartre, enter into a relationship of reciprocity with another consciousness, so it is impossible that I could, in fact, see my being as equivalent to that of the other and accede to the position of absolute knowledge.

This view does not imply that Sartre rejects a Hegelian view of truth as equivalent to an absolute knowledge that takes its shape through the becoming of history. Rather, it means that the achievement of that truth will be perpetually suspended, undone by the very plurality of consciousnesses, which cannot be synthesized into a totality.

Sartre turns to the philosophy of history in his *Critique of Dialectical Reason*. Ze'ev Levy argues that it was, in fact, Sartre's attempt in *Réflexions sur la question juive* to apply the philosophy of *Being and Nothingness* to a social group that led him more thoroughly to work out a notion of situation and to consider the force of history as a determiner of social action. What he realized, Levy argues, was that a philosophy of freedom could not take into account the Jewish situation, a sociohistorical situa-

---

89. Sartre, *L'être et le néant*, 298, 299, and *Being and Nothingness*, 327, 328.
90. Ibid., 299; 328.

tion from which there is no means of opting out.[91] As conjectural as this argument may be, it is the case that, soon after the publication of *Réflexions*, Sartre published the essay "Materialism and Revolution," in which he develops more thoroughly a model of situated freedom and begins the decades-long process of thinking through the relation between his own thinking and Marxism.[92] In "Materialism and Revolution," he has already transitioned from theorizing freedom as a psychological fact to conceiving of it as a practical possibility. He writes: "The possibility of rising above [*décoller*] a situation in order to get a perspective on it (a perspective which is not pure knowledge, but an indissoluble linking of understanding and action) is precisely that which we call freedom."[93] Freedom, then, in this new definition is still defined by the ability of the subject to create a space between material forces and his own action; it is still the power of nihilation, but now that capacity is understood in relation to the forces of materiality that press in on the subject. Where Sartre sees contemporary Marxists pushing for a purely determinist vision of history, he wants to propose a "situated freedom."

By 1960, with the publication of the *Critique of Dialectical Reason*, Sartre has begun to argue that existentialism must itself take the position of handmaiden to Marxism, providing Marxism with an anthropology founded on an analysis of existence. Existentialism must provide Marxism with the analysis that it has lacked as a consequence of its focus on clarifying "social and political *praxis*." This role is itself conceived as temporary: "From the day that Marxist thought will have taken on the human dimension (that is, the existential project) as the foundation of anthropological Knowledge, existentialism will no longer have any reason for being."[94] Existentialism will then be absorbed into Marxism.

In terms of the philosophy of history, for Sartre Marx is a corrective to Hegel. Marx shares with Kierkegaard the conviction that the real cannot be absorbed into knowledge, that experience is incommensurable with

91. Ze'ev Levy, *Spinoza's Interpretation of Judaism: A Concept and Its Influence on Jewish Thought* (in Hebrew) (Tel-Aviv: Safreet Poalim, 1972), 121–50.

92. Steven Schwarzschild contests Levy's reading because of the exemplary position Judaism is already given in *Being and Nothingness* as representative of the notion of situation. See Steven Schwarzschild, *The Pursuit of the Ideal*, ed. Menachem Kellner (Albany: State University of New York Press, 1990), 173.

93. While this may already sound like an adoption of a Hegelian perspective, Sartre is referring to the personal process of disengaging from the material world in order to evaluate one's actions and, thus, act; he is not referring to the attainment of a position of objectivity that abstracts oneself out of the picture altogether. See Jean-Paul Sartre, "Matérialisme et révolution," *Les temps modernes* (1946), republished in *Situations III: Lendemains de guerre* (Paris: Gallimard, 1947), 194, translated by Annette Michaelson as "Materialism and Revolution," in *Literary and Philosophical Essays* (New York: Criterion, 1955), 220.

94. Sartre, *Questions de méthode*, 245, 250–51, and *The Problem of Method*, 177, 181.

reason. But, like Hegel, Marx situates the problem of humanity within a larger objective framework: "He too asserts that the human fact is irreducible to knowing, that it must *be lived* and *produced*; but he is not going to confuse it with the empty subjectivity of a puritanical and mystified petite bourgeoisie. He makes of it the immediate theme of the philosophical totalization."[95]

Thus, for Sartre, Marx's advance over Hegel and Kierkegaard is his ability to retain the dialectic as a movement that is in the process of becoming without positing Absolute Spirit. But, for Sartre, the only Marxist philosophy that is acceptable is one that makes room for an anthropology that is not purely materialist and, thus, retains a theory of subjectivity wherein the subject is not defined *by* his condition but exists in relation to it. The question then becomes, How does one determine the meaning of history as it is developing if one claims neither a determinist vision of its workings nor a perspective that allows one to rise above it? Working out the conditions for the possibility of such a thinking and its necessary structures is, thus, the task of the *Critique of Dialectical Reason*.

In relation to *Being and Nothingness*, one of Sartre's concerns in the *Critique* is to overcome the obstacle that he claimed that Hegel himself could not overcome: that of being able to theorize the truth of history without taking a perspective outside history. In accepting the dialectical method, Sartre accepts this mission and the Hegelian presuppositions that come with it. Speaking in *The Problem of Method* of his own existentialism, which he now defines as an ideology—that is, a philosophy engaged in the world and in the activity of transforming the world—Sartre is explicit about these presuppositions: "From Marxism which gave it a new birth, the ideology of existence inherited two requirements which Marxism itself derives from Hegelianism: if such a thing as a Truth can exist in anthropology, it must be a truth that has *become*, and it must make itself a *totalization*. It goes without saying that this double requirement defines that movement of being and of knowing (or of comprehension) which since Hegel is called dialectic."[96] Within this dynamic, the thinker is clearly a participant in history and in the development of change. Dialectic is revealed to the thinker as the experience of his own freedom acting on what Sartre calls the *Practico-inerte*, those material forces that resist my action and transform them. In this interaction—fueled for Sartre by scarcity on the one side and need on the other—

95. Ibid., 22; 14.
96. Ibid., xxxiv (English).

the investigator recognizes the dialectical movement of history, not as a determined process governed by its own incontrovertible laws, but as the product of human freedom acting and reacting in a world that resists its powers. Yet, on this level, what is it that the investigator can claim to discover? It seems that the investigator's goals would, by virtue of his perspective, have to be modest: "We must give notice that the investigation we are undertaking, though in itself historical, like any other undertaking, does not attempt to discover the movement of History, the evolution of labor or of the relations of production, or class conflicts. Its goal is simply to reveal and establish dialectical rationality, that is to say the complex play of *praxis* and totalisation." But this, of course, amounts to an admission that his method cannot itself achieve the *Truth*, the definition of which existentialism has inherited from Hegel. Sartre promises, however, to provide in the second volume a reconstruction of the "schema of intelligibility proper to the totalisation."[97]

In both the first and the second (unfinished and posthumously published) volume of the *Critique*, Sartre struggles with a concern to comprehend history according to a unifying end. He speaks in *The Problem of Method*, moreover, of a time when the struggle between need and scarcity will be overcome: "As soon as there will exist *for everyone* a margin of *real* freedom beyond the production of life, Marxism will have lived out its span. A philosophy of freedom will take its place. But we have no means, no intellectual instrument, no concrete experience which allows us to conceive of this freedom or of this philosophy."[98]

Sartre conceives of the philosophy of history as a struggle over resources and even seems to predict a future beyond that struggle while at the same time refusing to project himself into a transcendent point of view. A fluctuation is evident throughout the work between claims that would seem to assume a unified meaning and unified ends to history and an acknowledgment that the aims of historical actors are constantly in conflict and, thus, ungraspable as a totality.[99]

This fluctuation is indicative of a fundamental tension in Sartre's thinking between a drive to protect the particularity and freedom of individual agents and the drive to articulate a philosophy/ideology that orients itself toward the future, toward the making of an ideal society.

97. Jean-Paul Sartre, *Critique de la raison dialectique* (Paris: Gallimard, 1960), 134, translated by Alan Sheridan-Smith as vol. 1 of *Critique of Dialectical Reason* (London: Verso, 2004), 39.
98. Sartre, *Questions de méthode*, 50, and *The Problem of Method*, 34.
99. Sartre, *Critique de la raison dialectique*, 667, and *Critique of Dialectical Reason*, 708. For a more involved discussion of this tension, see Bruce Baugh, "The Unhappy Consciousness in Sartre's Philosophy," in *French Hegel* (New York: Routledge, 2003).

Until the final years of his life, Sartre could not see the movement toward social justice in anything but Marxist terms. By those final years, he came to view his entanglement with Marxism, with its parties and its problems, as a failure, but he did not give up on what he still maintained was the guiding motivations of his involvement with Marxism: a thinking of hope and a thinking of sociality. In the Lévy interviews, he revisits both these themes.

*Hope Now*

The interviews were published in three installments, on March 10, 17, and 24, 1980, only weeks before Sartre's death on April 15, 1980. While those close to Sartre, including his adopted daughter, Arlette el-Kaim Sartre, and Simone de Beauvoir, admit that Sartre himself approved the version of the interviews that was published, there was, nonetheless, the sense among his compatriots from *Les temps modernes* that they did not reflect Sartre's thought. This may have been because the interviews themselves construct a narrative in which Sartre's interest in, sympathy with, and even advocacy of Judaic thinking seems to follow directly from the earlier work. By illustrating that his interest in a Hegelian/Marxist philosophy of history grew out of a drive to find a method of grounding a philosophy of social change in a theory of sociality, the interviews present his interest in Jewish messianism as a philosophical response to the tension between that drive and his concern to maintain a thinking of particularity. The first two-thirds of the interviews revisit the earlier work, focusing particularly on *Being and Nothingness* and the *Critique of Dialectical Reason*, while the last third discusses the role of Judaism in Sartre's thinking.

Lévy opens the interview with a question about the interrelation between hope and failure in Sartre's work. Hope, Sartre responds, is fundamental to any philosophy of human action: "I think hope is part of man. Human action is transcendent—it always aims at a future object from the present in which we conceive of the action and try to realize it. It situates its end, its realization, in the future, and hope is in the way man acts, in the very positing an end as having to be realized." Lévy points out that *Being and Nothingness* disallows the possibility of the subject attaining its goals and then follows up with a question suggesting that the turn to Marxism arose out of a desire to escape the dialectics of bad faith in *Being and Nothingness*. "You believed one might get around the impasse that *Being and Nothingness* led to if the meaning of history were what Hegel and Marxism defined it as," he argues. Sartre agrees but suggests that he was always uneasy with the movement: "It was a question of finding a future for society. Society had to stop being the shitty mess it is everywhere today. I didn't think I could change the world all by myself and on the strength of my own ideas, but I did discern social forces that were trying to move forward and I believed my place as among them." A theory of the social group and the concept of fraternity become the avenue through which change is considered: "Yes, I need men who are united, because one unit alone or even several separate units will not be able to shake the social body and make it collapse. One must imagine a body of people who struggle as one." Yet, given Sartre's own concession to difference, he agrees that, in the *Critique of Dialectical Reason*, his pursuit of fraternity was not successful, for "every time one expects to encounter fraternity, one bumps into terror."[100]

It is in the context of these themes that the possibility of Judaism as a thinking opposed to Hegel's arises. The Jews, conceived as a people whose past does not fit into the Hegelian/Sartrean vision of world history, appear now as the antidote to Hegel and Marx. They represent the possibility of "a real unity . . . due not to their being gathered together on a historical territory but to actions and writings and bonds that don't derive from the idea of a homeland."[101] Jewish messianism appeals to Sartre because it represents a position in relation to the future that is opposed to historically progressivist Marxism.[102] "It is not," he writes,

100. Sartre, *L'espoir maintenant*, 21, 29, 33, 34, 35, and *Hope Now*, 53, 60, 65, 66.
101. Ibid., 75; 104.
102. Sartre treats Jewish messianism here as an easily circumscribable notion and assumes something like a unified understanding of what Gerschom Scholem has shown us is, in fact, a complex of ideas that range from regressive to progressive, from apocalyptic to merely political. See Gershom Scholem, *The Messianic Idea in Judaism*, trans. Michael Meyer (New York: Schocken, 1971). In terms of its content, what Sartre seems to be referring to here is closer to what Paul Mendes-Flohr in "'To Brush History against the Grain': The Eschatology of the Frankfurt School and Ernst Bloch" refers to as "the eschatology of the Frankfurt School." What the thinkers of the Frankfurt school share with the later Sartre is a vision of the messianic as a conception of the future as radically other, a conception that would counter a purely progressive view of history and break with a Hegelian totalizing vision. It is clear that, in the writings of Benjamin, as in those of Horkheimer and Adorno, insofar as they are using a religiously imbued notion of the future as radically other, they are clearly detheologizing it, as, I speculate, Sartre would have, had he had the opportunity to fully work out the significance of this notion of Jewish messianism for his own thought. The history of the depersonalization, and, ultimately the detheologizing of the Messiah and messianism can clearly be traced back at least to Hermann Cohen's vision of messianism in *Religion of Reason* and then through Rosenzweig, who, as Mendes-Flohr argues, clearly had a profound impact on the Frankfurt school by way of Walter Benjamin. Probably this strand of messianic thought also has its roots in Kant's *Religion within the Limits of Reason Alone*. Along the way, particularly as a consequence of Rosenzweig, the depersonalized notion of the Messiah is transformed from an idea consistent with a progressive vision of history to one whose value lies in its vision of a future that would contest progressive thinking. See Mendes-Flohr, *Divided Passions*, 370–83. Mendes-Flohr's reading of Ernst Bloch also leads me to believe that Sartre may have been influenced by Bloch's conception of hope in *Das Prinzip Hoffnung*. Another excellent text on the development of messianism in nineteenth- and early-twentieth-century

"an end that is defined in terms of the present situation and then projected into the future, one that will be attained by stages through the development of certain facts today." It suggests a futurity that escapes the dialectical movement of history: "The Jewish religion implies that this world will end, and, at the same moment, another world will appear." This new world represents for Sartre an ethical kingdom in which the gap between the *is* and the *ought* is overcome. Of course, the very possibility of such an end is dependent on the action of a transcendent and divine lawgiver the existence of which, we can assume, given his atheism, Sartre is not willing to admit. When Lévy reminds him of this fact, Sartre responds by suggesting that this element of Judaism—the idea that the overcoming of law is from God and not from humans—is exactly what makes Judaism important for non-Jews: "That's why for me, messianism is an important thing that Jews have conceived of alone but that could be used by non-Jews for other purposes."[103]

For Sartre, the crux of messianism is respect for the unsurpassable gap between the *is* and the *ought*, between the de facto society and the de jure. It is the distance between the two that revolutionaries forget. Messianism reminds us that the de jure society is beyond the political, that it is, in fact, an ideal. What messianism seems to teach, according to Sartre, is that despair and hope are intertwined, that they are necessary counterpoints to one another. Working in tandem, they demonstrate that social justice does not amount to a mere redistribution of resources yet hope nonetheless demands that we live and fight in relation to an ideal.

It is in this vein that Sartre's final published words can be understood:

In any event, the world seems ugly, evil and hopeless. Such is the calm despair of an old man who will die in that despair. But the point is, I'm resisting, and I know I shall die in hope.

We must try to explain why the world of today, which is horrible, is only one moment in a long historical development, that hope has always been one of the dominant forces of revolutions and insurrections, and how I still feel that hope is my conception of the future.[104]

---

Central European Jewish thought is Michael Löwy's *Redemption and Utopia: Jewish Libertarian Thought in Central Europe* (London: Athlone, 1992). In his conclusion, Löwy summarizes the trend this way: "Historical messianism, or the romantic/millenarian conception of history, constitutes a break with the philosophy of progress and with the positivist worship of scientific and technological development. It brings a qualitative, non-evolutionary perception of historical time, in which the detour through the past becomes the necessary point of departure for the leap towards the future, as opposed to the linear, unidimensional and purely quantitative vision of temporality as cumulative progress" (204).

103. Ibid., 77, 76–77, 78; 106, 105, 107.

104. Ibid., 81; 110.

By way of messianism, Sartre sought a position that could hold together moral judgment of history's crimes without forgoing historical meaning or purpose. At the end of his life, it was Judaism that seemed to represent that possibility.

Walter Benjamin famously came to a similar conclusion when, at the end of his life, Marxism seemed compromised. For Benjamin, the messianic vision of the Jews was clearly one that managed to make room for redemption without giving in to optimism or the progressive determinism of crass materialism.[105] What Benjamin and Sartre share is the recuperation of what they both considered to be Jewish temporality without an acceptance of Jewish metaphysics. Is it possible to say that this recuperation makes either of their thinking in some way Jewish? Scores of monographs and articles have considered this question in Benjamin's case.[106] Fewer have in Sartre's. More interesting than the answer to this question are the visions of *judéité* (Jewishness) that such a query produces.

*Sartre as Jew; or, The Creation of a Trope*

In what follows, I will consider three essays that treat Sartre's *judéité* in light of his final statements about Jewish messianism in *Hope Now*: Steven Schwarzschild's "Sartre as Jew," Emmanuel Levinas's "A Language Familiar to Us," and Bernard-Henri Lévy's "Jewish Like Sartre." While each of these essays attempts on some level to argue for a reading of Sartre *as* a Jew, I contend, rather, that what a reading of these essays illustrates is the way in which Sartre's wranglings with Hegel produce his particular articulation of the figurative Jew.

About six months after Sartre's death, Steven Schwarzschild, a scholar of modern Jewish thought, a Reform and Conservative rabbi and disciple of Hermann Cohen's, delivered a lecture with the title "Jean-Paul Sartre as Jew." Given Sartre's avowed atheism and his insistence throughout the

105. Walter Benjamin, "Über den Begriff der Geschichte," in *Illuminationen: Ausgewählte Schriften 1* (Frankfurt: Suhrkamp, 1977), 261, translated by Harry Zohn as "Theses on the Philosophy of History," in *Illuminations* (New York: Schocken, 1968), 264.

106. On this question in Benjamin, see Robert Alter, *Necessary Angels: Tradition and Modernity in Kafka, Benjamin and Scholem* (Cambridge, MA: Harvard University Press, 1991); Robert Alter, *Walter Benjamin and the Bible* (New York: Continuum, 1996); Susan A. Handelman, *Fragments of Redemption: Jewish Thought and Literary Theory in Benjamin, Scholem and Levinas* (Bloomington: Indiana University Press, 1991); Margarete Kohlenbach, *Walter Benjamin: Self-Reference and Religiosity* (Basingstoke: Palgrave, 2002); Stéphane Mosès, *L'ange de l'histoire: Rosenzweig, Benjamin, Scholem* (Paris: Seuil, 1992); Gershom Scholem, *The Correspondence of Walter Benjamin and Gershom Scholem, 1932–1940*, trans. Gary Smith and Andre Lefevre (Cambridge, MA: Harvard University Press, 1992); Scholem, *On Jews and Judaism in Crisis*; and Irving Wohlfarth, "On Some Jewish Motifs in Benjamin," in *The Problems of Modernity: Adorno and Benjamin* (London: Routledge, 1989).

interviews that his interest in Jewish ideas was the interest of a "non-Jew" (he claimed until the end that he had no access to the interiority of Jewish experience), it would seem to be a challenge to prove anything about Sartre's Jewishness beyond his own claim that he identified with the Jew as stranger. For Schwarzschild, the reading of Sartre *as* a Jew depends on the conclusion that Sartre came at the end of his life to accept what Schwarzchild identifies as the *true* Jewish vision of history: "Jewish messianism is often misunderstood, even by Jews, as some sort of metaphysical, even fatuous, optimism—that things always get better and are bound in the end to lead to success, whereas what Sartre is here proposing is that one pursue the good the more the invariable triumph of evil—thus, out of despair, because of one's realistic expectation of failure."[107] According to Schwarzschild, in coming to this view, in which hope and despair are closely aligned, Sartre arrives at a vision that is *authentically* Jewish.[108] For Schwarzschild, this authenticity amounts to having a philosophy remarkably similar to the German philosopher Hermann Cohen's. Schwarzschild makes the argument that there is an affinity between the two thinkers' philosophies, an argument based on essentially four points.[109]

The first point is a shared project of socialism, which for Cohen is underpinned by a vision of the unity of all humanity, a vision of the world in which nationalism and class division would be transcended. For Cohen, it is the Jews' mission in Diaspora to be a people without a nation who in their suffering attest to the possibility of a unification of humanity. This, according to Schwarzschild, is also the vision of Judaism that Sartre has himself arrived at in the final interviews: "Sartre now stipulates that Jewish, autonomous culture, which has existed and been activated all along, breaks up the totalization of Hegelian/Marxist historiography and of his own existentialist-phenomenological metaphysics by possessing, from the outset and continuously, its own inherent ethico-cultural, indeed 'metaphysical' substance. In other words Judaism is the only entity which (if one is to take the last interview at its word) is not originally the creature of its environment. It alone seems not to be 'thrown' but to be created *ex-nihilo*—to be *ab initio* completely 'authentic.'"[110] Surely, this interpretation does more than take Sartre at his word. According to Schwarzschild, Judaism has transitioned from

107. Schwarzschild, *The Pursuit of the Ideal*, 164.
108. I reuse this Sartrean term here to signal the problematic way in which Schwarzschild's text assumes a definition of Jewishness that is itself dehistoricized.
109. Given the high probability that Sartre was not even familiar with Cohen, we must assume that Schwarzschild is making his argument on the basis of the similarity that he reads each thinker as having to Kant and Hegel.
110. Schwarzschild, *The Pursuit of the Ideal*, 177.

being *the* privileged example of being-for-others in Sartre's thought to becoming the *only* example of an entity immune to the factors of situation. This reading would suppose, of course, a complete reversal from Sartre's position in *Réflexions*. That said, it is by means of this interpretation that Schwarzschild is able to produce a reading of Sartre that posits him as close to Cohen.

As Schwarzschild attempts to harmonize this reading with Sartre's philosophy, he arrives at a second affinity between Sartre and Cohen. "If this is a correct reading of Sartre's last statement," Schwarzschild continues,

then his final apostrophe to Judaism is, indeed, extraordinary. But it might also, unless explicated with extreme caution, be taken to undermine at its foundation everything that Sartre ever said before throughout his life. Where would that Jewish substance come from—God? Hardly as far as Sartre is concerned. The Jew, i.e. Jewish man, monadically self-made outside the networks of worldly, human and social, relations in which every man starts out by finding himself? If so, all of Sartre's earlier epistemology and anthropology would be belied. I can and want to think of only one possible answer: Sartre now holds that the Jew, Jewry, is—as he put it—the only historic entity that "projected" a Messianic goal of autonomous human beings in a true human community not by sublimating, "surpassing," its externally given conditions but out of autonomous reason alone.[111]

The question here is how to understand what it is that would allow Sartre to locate the Jews outside the forces of history given his philosophy of situated freedom and, moreover, given his previous descriptions of the Jews. Sartre says that it is the Jews' relationship to God that allows for that possibility. Given that we cannot take seriously the possibility that Sartre was willing to grant the existence of God, we must assume, Schwarzschild suggests, that Sartre meant something else. Here he appeals to Cohen's conception of God as a concept of pure reason in order to read Sartre's own statement as following the same logic: "It thus turns out that what Sartre is really saying when he proclaims his atheism is what for two-hundred years Kant and H. Cohen's neo-Kantianism had said all along—except that they regard this as religious faith: belief in God is not a cognitive or pseudo-cognitive act (indeed, pseudo-cognitive belief in God is idolatry) but an ethical, 'practical,' regulative one. God 'is' not, even as the human self 'is' not; he ought to be (pro-jected) as man has to pro-ject himself in order to come to be, and all ought's

111. Ibid., 177–78.

(ought to) flow from this."[112] Schwarzschild thus finds another affinity between the two thinkers and is able to create a narrative of Sartre's work that illustrates the following: by coming to the conclusion that the Jews are guided by a principle of pure reason, thus undetermined by historical forces, Sartre's work has finally been "purified" of its dialecticism and, in effect, become neo-Kantian, which for Schwarzschild seems to amount to saying that it is authentically Jewish.

But this brings me to the third and most important perceived affinity between the two thinkers, the affinity that grounds Schwarzschild's entire argument. Cohen and Sartre (with the help of Benny Lévy) share a concept of Judaism that defines it as that which calls Hegel's philosophy of history into question. For what is it that ultimately allows Schwarzschild to read Sartre as coming "to consummate his life and its work in . . . [a] notion of hope," a Kantian/Jewish hope? It is the assumption that the Jew provides Sartre with an exit ramp from the Hegelian vision of history, thus opening up the possibility of a nontotalizing approach to the future. As Schwarzschild himself puts it, Judaism is defined in these interviews as that which "breaks up the totalization of Hegelian/Marxist historiography." The affinity between Cohen and Sartre here is a product of *that* similarity. For Cohen, the Jewish mission is to persist outside the history of states.[113] Schwarzschild uses this similarity to argue for a neo-Kantian Sartre. What he fails to see is that Sartre's vision of Judaism displays, in fact, a distinct loyalty to the Hegelian reading of Judaism. Sartre has not altered that reading; he has merely shifted the value. For Sartre, like Hegel, describes the Jew as "ruled by his relationship with God. And the whole history of the Jews consists precisely of this primary relationship."[114] For Hegel, this is exactly what causes Jewish alienation. It is not necessary, then, to assume that, like Cohen, Sartre had come to think of God as a concept of practical reason; rather, he had come to think of the Jews conceptually. At issue for him was, not what it means to be a Jew, but how the Jews open up a new relation to history. What might it mean, Sartre asks, for non-Jews to relate to the future messianically or to take up the position of Hegel's Jews in relation to a dialectical view of history?

For Schwarzschild to read Sartre *as* a Jew amounts to reading Sartre as though he were Hermann Cohen, but that affinity is essentially a product of conceptualizing Judaism as that which breaks up the totality of the Hegelian/Marxist vision of history. What Schwarzschild produces by the very claim that we can read Sartre *as* a Jew is a definition of Juda-

112. 182.
113. Cohen, *Religion der Vernunft*, chap. 13.
114. Sartre, *L'espoir maintenant*, 76, and *Hope Now*, 104.

ism as "resistance to Hegel." For Schwarzschild, this seems to amount to an authentically Jewish mode of being, and Schwarzschild opposes this understanding of the Jew to that produced by Sartre in *Réflexions sur la question juive*, in which the definition of the Jew is a product of an anti-Semitic reading of Jewishness.

Yet are these two understandings really so different? If we grant that Sartre's "new" understanding of Judaism gains, not only its value, but also, to some extent, its content from Hegel and, thus, functions in opposition to Hegel, are we not dealing in both cases with a process of revalorizing a negative judgment?

Bernard-Henri Lévy and Levinas also take up the possibility of reading Sartre as a Jew, but they do so only to reject the option. Nonetheless, what is relevant about these two arguments is that, in each, a definition of Judaism conceived according to its relation to Hegelian history remains intact. For Levinas and Bernard-Henri Lévy, the importance of Sartre's last interviews is not in showing that Sartre had himself come to think as a Jew; it is the fact that Jewish thinking had come to do essential work in Sartre. Paraphrasing the interviews, Levinas writes:

If there is a Jewish history, Hegel is wrong, but the fact is that there is a Jewish history. Thus in humanity there is a dimension of meaning other than that provided by universal history. There is another history. This though is not the result of a meditation on Moses and the prophets, but it is rather a consequence of reading an American historian [Baron].

It is not metaphysics that imposes such a conclusion, but rather sociology, and all the world does not have to call this other history "sacred history" under one name or another. Is it not, however, an essential dimension of the sensible? Is it not reasonable from now on for a statesman, when questioning himself on the nature of decisions that he is making, to ask not only whether the decisions are in agreement with the other history?[115]

What is fascinating about this passage, which comes nearly at the end of Levinas's short eulogy for Sartre, is that, like Schwarzschild, Levinas focuses on the fact that the meaning of a Jewish history lies in its opposition to Hegelian history. Thus, the importance of the Jews arises from this relation to Hegel's dismissal of them. But it is Sartre who teaches us something further. When Schwarzschild comes to the impasse of Sartre's atheism, he substitutes a concept of pure reason for God in order to read Sartre as himself taking up the position of the Jew. When Levinas comes

---

115. Levinas, *Les imprévus de l'histoire*, 154, and *Unforeseen History*, 95.

to this junction, he suggests that it is in his acceptance of Jewish history and messianism *without* the metaphysical framework that accompanies it that Sartre has something important to say. "One does not have to call this other history 'sacred history' under one name or another," Levinas writes. "Is it not, however, an essential dimension of the sensible?"[116] What is important for Levinas is that Sartre *exports* the messianic dimension of a Jewish vision of history. Judaism, Levinas thus suggests, could serve as a model for a new thinking of history and politics, one that is accessible to Jew and gentile alike.[117]

Bernard-Henri Lévy makes a similar claim. He concludes his 650-page *Le siècle de Sartre* with an epilogue that evaluates the significance of *Hope Now* for Sartre's legacy. One section in this epilogue is entitled "Jewish Like Sartre," the next "Sartre with Levinas." For Lévy, it is not Cohen who serves as the intermediary for reading these final essays but Levinas.

Levinas was, importantly, the avenue by which Sartre came to phenomenology; otherwise, Sartre makes very few references to Levinas in his work.[118] He mentions Levinas in his *Notebooks for an Ethics* in order to respond to Levinas's critique of his vision of freedom in *Time and the Other*.[119] By and large, however, Levinas does not appear in Sartre's work as one of his interlocutors. Most likely, this is because Levinas did not truly attain his fame and vast readership until after Sartre had himself gone blind.[120] Thus, it is by way of Benny Lévy that Levinas's ideas filter into Sartre's thinking, and, if they appear in *Hope Now*, it is in a diluted form, as vague concepts such as "obligation for the other," "dialogue," and a depiction of Jewish messianism as an ethical modality.[121] While this influence does not, as Bernard-Henri Lévy wants to claim, make

116. Ibid.

117. As will be clear in the next chapter, this argument is consistent with Levinas's larger claims about the significance of Judaism for a post-1945 world. Levinas also associates this possibility with the state of Israel, which seems to be in tension with the claim that the history of the Jews is an alternate history to that of nation-states.

118. In his eulogy of Merleau-Ponty in 1961, Sartre credits Levinas's translation of Husserl as providing the avenue by which he came to phenomenology.

119. Levinas refers to Sartre's philosophy as one that ignores the weight of materiality by assuming an absolute subjective freedom in an "angelic present." See Emmanuel Levinas, *Le temps et l'autre* (Paris: Fata Morgana, 1979), 44, translated by Richard Cohen as *Time and the Other* (Pittsburgh, PA: Duquesne University Press, 1987), 62; and Jean-Paul Sartre, *Cahiers pour une morale* (Paris: Gallimard, 1983), 431, translated by David Pellauer as *Notebooks for an Ethics* (Chicago: University of Chicago Press, 1992), 416.

120. In his introduction to *The Cambridge Companion to Levinas*, ed. Simon Critchley and Robert Bernasconi (Cambridge: Cambridge University Press, 2002), Simon Critchley cites 1982—two years after Sartre's death—as the moment when, with Philip Nemo's broadcast interviews, Levinas appeared as a culturally important figure in France.

121. Bernard-Henri Lévy describes Benny Lévy as a "hyphen made flesh between the two philosophers," shuttling back and forth between them (*Le siècle de Sartre*, 658, and *Sartre: The Philosopher of the Twentieth Century*, 497).

Sartre a Levinasian,[122] it does affect the conversation between Benny Lévy and Sartre, whether or not Sartre is himself fully aware of this dynamic.[123] While Levinas himself backs off from calling a resistance to Hegel's dialectic intrinsically Jewish, it may, nonetheless, be that it is Levinas's philosophy that indirectly makes possible the revalorization of the figure of the Jew in the interviews.[124]

When Bernard-Henri Lévy titles his section "Jewish Like Sartre," it is with Levinas's influence in mind; it is also with his tongue in his cheek. About this he is clear. "A Jewish Sartre?" he asks. "No, but more interesting: Jewish thought at work in Sartre's thinking."[125] By Lévy's logic, it is Jewish thinking that has finally undone the definition of history with which Sartre had been operating. But this for Lévy does not amount to an undoing of Sartre's previous philosophy. For Sartre's thought has, according to Lévy, always held within it something Jewish, defined, that is, according to Hegel's definition as a form of unhappy consciousness. For Lévy, those thinkers who have held a view of particularity as unsurpassable fall into the category of Hegel's Jews. Sartre, at least the Sartre of *Being and Nothingness*, is such a thinker for Lévy. The significance of the final interviews for Lévy, then, is that, by means of the encounter between Sartre and Judaism, the impulse to resist dialectics has finally taken the upper hand in Sartre's thinking.

I would contest that reading Sartre's final words on Judaism as the product of an encounter with Judaism is as untenable as reading Sartre as "finally" a Levinasian. For Sartre has not come into contact with Judaism so much as he has come to appreciate "Hegel's Jews." Read together, Bernard-Henri Lévy, Levinas, and Schwarzchild all point the way toward this conclusion through their shared recognition that the importance of Judaism for Sartre is in helping him conceive of a resistance to the Hegelian vision of history.

Additionally, all three thinkers deal with the relation between *Réflexions sur la question juive* and *Hope Now* by viewing the texts in opposition to one another: the earlier one is a product of Sartre's ignorance, the

---

122. "This last Sartre was a Levinassian. He was a Levinassian obviously, indisputably and profoundly. The imprint is so strong, the community of languages so total, that it's like the two theologians in the story by Borges discovering, at the end of their lives, that they were the same soul in two different bodies" (ibid., 655; 495).

123. Ibid., 654; 494.

124. Bernard-Henri Lévy reports that he went himself to visit Levinas and ask about his influence on Sartre. Levinas, he reports, at first resisted the possibility. "'No, no, you can't think that. . . . I certainly never influenced to such an extent that very honorable and eminent philosopher. . . . I wouldn't have dared. . . . I wouldn't have taken such a risk,'" Lévy reports him having said (ibid., 656; 496). Levinas nonetheless went on to report the history of their contact, as brief and insignificant as it was.

125. Ibid., 650; 492.

later a product of his knowledge. The first is to be excused, overlooked, explained away; the second is to be applauded and developed. *Réflexions* is a product of Sartre's insistence on viewing Judaism as something created from the outside, *Hope Now* his acknowledgment that Judaism has its own internal reality. In my own reading, I have shown what the two texts share: both produce an image of the Jew as the stranger, as the figure whose identity does not derive first from a relation to land or to a political body, from the continual recuperation of the subject's identity to itself, or from its autoaffection. In addition, both texts arise out of an opposition to a dominant ideology. In the case of *Réflexions*, the viewpoint in question is racialist essentialism. In the case of *Hope Now*, it is a totalizing view of history. The trope of the Jew that emerges in both cases functions as a tool of critique, as a means to oppose a dominant discourse.

Interpreters of Sartre have not, however, understood the critical function of Sartre's various treatments of Judaism. Their failure to identify this dynamic in Sartre's work is clearly a consequence of Sartre's own lack of reflexivity with regard to his representation of Jews and Judaism. As will be clear in later chapters, the trope of the Jew can operate critically only if it is not simultaneously functioning descriptively. What is missing from Sartre is a mistrust of his procedures of representation. His own inability to make explicit the distinction between the Jew as a revalorized idea and the Jews as a people with a tradition and a history led to two misreadings: In the case of *Réflexions sur la question juive*, Sartre was received by many as a participant in anti-Semitic rhetoric rather than as a rehabilitator of the notion of estrangement as a morally and politically significant category. In the case of *Hope Now*, he was read to be, if not a near convert, than something like an honorary Jew. Neither of these readings adequately accounts for the fact that, in his descriptions, Sartre engages, not with Judaism, but with its negative representations and, in the process, enacts a revalorization of these representations. The deployment of this revalorization will demand, however, a consideration of the question of what this revalorized notion of the Jew implies for non-Jews. That is to say, it demands that we consider what it means for anyone after 1945 to say, "In speaking about the Jews, I was speaking of myself."

We turn to this question in the following three chapters. Maurice Blanchot's analysis of the May '68 chant "Nous sommes tous des juifs allemands" will explicitly address the possibility that such a claim could represent something other than a usurpation of Jewish identity. But Blanchot himself will come to contemplate what it means to say "I am a Jew" only through his interpretation of the writings of Emmanuel Levinas.

# THREE

# The Ethics of Uprootedness: Emmanuel Levinas's Postwar Project

If Judaism is attached to the here below, it is not because it lacks the imagination to conceive of a supernatural order, or because matter represents some sort of absolute for it; but because the first light of conscience is lit for it on the path that leads from man to his neighbor.

EMMANUEL LEVINAS, *DIFFICILE LIBERTÉ*

His eulogy for Sartre, "A Language Familiar to Us," was not the first praise Levinas offered Sartre for his attention to Judaism. In 1947, long before Levinas had achieved fame, he responded in *Les cahiers de l'Alliance israélite universelle* to *Réflexions sur la question juive* and Sartre's subsequent appearance in June 1947 at the Alliance israélite universelle.[1] In "Existentialism and Anti-Semitism," Levinas concurs with the common judgment that Sartre failed in *Réflexions* to acknowledge the internal meaning and essence of Judaism by describing Jewish destiny as a function of anti-Semitism. He nonetheless lauds him for finding a philosophical path that can address the root causes of

---

*Epigraph*: Levinas, *Difficile liberté*, 144, and *Difficult Freedom*, 100 (translation slightly altered).

1. Sartre's talk was primarily a summary of the book that showed some attention to the demographics of his audience and responded to a few of the early critiques of the book. For more on this appearance, see Judaken, *John-Paul Sartre and the Jewish Question*, 242.

anti-Semitism.[2] Existentialism, Levinas suggests, negotiates between universalizing rationalism and a particularist philosophy of belonging by means of a method that confers on the concrete circumstances of the individual the utmost importance without reasserting a thinking of rootedness.[3]

Levinas's philosophy had itself already set out on a similar road of negotiation. By retooling the methods of Heideggerian phenomenology, Levinas had begun to conceptualize the human being as marked by a call more fundamental than any tug of belonging but no less concrete.[4] In this brief text, commenting on Sartre, he expresses the political exigency of making such a move:

> But because existentialism brings, for the first time, intellectual instruments to understand commitments as other than materiality, it can take opposition to anti-Semitism. Until then, thinkers who contested man's independence with regard to his concrete situation contested human rights and professed anti-Semitism. . . . All those historians of belonging . . . those poets of violence and the native soil, all those epigones of Nietzsche had a great time. A tormented unbalanced world conferred authority on them even when it half-heartedly disavowed them or spilled its blood to silence them.
>
> Until then the persecuted vainly sought protection in Descartes and Spinoza . . . hanging on for dear life to those truths proclaimed as the very essence of humanism.[5]

Levinas would never have described his own philosophy as "existentialist," but, like Sartre, he was motivated by the failures in the philosophical project of the West to offer a description of human existence that could reckon with the constraints of material existence without resorting to determinism.[6] By 1947, the political ramifications of this failure were for Levinas incontrovertible. Enlightenment humanism had shown itself to offer scant protection against doctrines of blood and soil, and the targets of this political vision had been left stranded. Although Sartre's *Réflexions sur*

---

2. Whether Levinas knew at this point that his translation of Husserl had been the impetus pointing Sartre in this direction is unclear. He may have guessed it. Sartre did not acknowledge the role that Levinas's translation played in his development until 1961. See n. 124, chapter 2, above.

3. Emmanuel Levinas, "Existentialisme et antisémitisme," *Les cahiers de l'Alliance israélite universelle* 14–15 (June–July 1947): 2–3, translated in *Unforeseen History*, 73–75.

4. In the same year as this essay, Levinas had published *De l'existence à l'existant*, in which he reconceived Heidegger's phenomenological description of the relation between *Dasein* and being as marked by the burden of an overwhelming positivity rather than finitude. He had at this point also given the series of lectures at Jean Wahl's Collège philosophique that would later constitute the text of *Les temps et l'autre*.

5. Levinas, "Existentialisme et antisémitisme," 2–3, and *Unforeseen History*, 75.

6. As noted in the previous chapter, Levinas criticizes Sartre for conveying the present as "situated above matter" (Levinas, *Le temps et l'autre*, 44, and *Time and the Other*, 62).

*la question juive* does not trace out the conflict between determinism and freedom in strictly philosophical terms, there are clear parallels between the way the problem of anti-Semitism is established in Sartre's text and Levinas's own formulation. In "Existentialism and Anti-Semitism," Levinas reparses the dynamic between the anti-Semite and the republican as a conflict between philosophical determinism and abstract universalism. Where Sartre ends up casting Judaism as an empty reflection of society's biases, Levinas sees an alternative way of being in the world, one that he will ultimately argue must become Europe's guiding light.

For Sartre, in 1946, the Jews were merely the victims of a conflict between deterministic particularism and abstract universalism. According to Levinas in "Être juif," another 1947 response to Sartre published soon after "Existentialism and Anti-Semitism": "The Jew is the entrance itself of the religious event in the world; better yet, it is the impossibility of the world without religion."[7] In calling this essay "Être juif," Levinas was already developing the experience of "being Jewish" as an object for phenomenological study and, thus, differentiating it from a treatment of Judaism as a purely religious category.[8]

Judaism's wisdom, Levinas came to argue, is that it too offers a response to the determinism of the flesh and soil, not through a mere escape to the language of transcendence, which marks for him both Christianity and the tradition of abstract humanism, but rather through Judaism's emphasis on the neighbor, the other man for whom I am responsible to the point of abnegating my own needs. It is attached to the here below, "but not because matter represents some kind of absolute for it."[9] In presenting Judaism's message, Levinas revamps and co-opts the language of transcendence without leaving behind or devaluing materiality. What he presents is a philosophy of uprootedness.[10]

7. Emmanuel Levinas, "Être juif," *Confluences* 7 (1947): 261, reprinted in *Cahiers d'études lévinassiennes* 1 (2002): 104.

8. Benny Lévy, "Commentaire d'"Être juif,'" *Cahiers d'études lévinassiennes* 1 (2002): 107–17.

9. Levinas, *Difficile liberté*, 144, and *Difficult Freedom*, 100.

10. Samuel Moyn (*Origins of the Other: Emmanuel Levinas between Revelation and Tradition* [Ithaca, NY: Cornell University Press, 2005]) argues that Levinas's notion of otherness has its clearest historical source in his reading of Kierkegaard and Barth and, thus, in their notion of transcendence. Levinas thus fails, he argues, to produce an ethics that is secular. According to Moyn, he has merely relocated the site of the transcendent other to the other man. While I find Moyn's book to be astoundingly clear and well researched, I disagree that one can see Levinas's move to locate otherness in the other person as a mere "transposition" and, thus, as theological. No doubt, Levinas relies on a theological analogy. I think, however, that this is a different claim than Moyn's, for an analogical relation does not amount to a logical dependence. Furthermore, the importance of this move is in its resistance to a kind of solitude/escapism that Levinas sees as fundamental to Kierkegaard's theology. See Emmanuel Levinas, *Noms propres* (Paris: Fata Morgana, 1975), 82, translated by Michael B. Smith as *Proper Names* (Stanford, CA: Stanford University Press, 1975), 70.

In a radical move that has left its mark on a generation of think-ers and writers, both Jewish and non-Jewish, Levinas gave deracination an ethical content and assigned to Judaism the privilege of bearing the message of deracination as its most fundamental teaching. In both the first and the second chapters, we saw how the idea of the Jew was con-structed around a notion of deracination by way of the anti-Semitic dis-course that surrounded and followed from the Dreyfus affair. In Levinas's thought, we encounter another source and significance for deracination. While the term is not one that Levinas employs, the notion of deraci-nation pervades the text, appearing alternately as *exile, estrangement,* and *uprooting.* The most significant shift to this set of terms in Levinas's work is their application beyond geography. With Levinas, deracination becomes the condition for ethics.

We can trace this association back to Levinas's renegotiations of Hei-degger's philosophy after 1933. In the process of rethinking the Hei-deggerian analysis of the relation between the existent and existence, Levinas developed an account of Judaism that gained its particular con-notations in opposition to what he referred to as Heidegger's "pagan-ism." His conception of Judaism has distinctly political overtones as it is presented as a countertradition to "a thinking of the West," which he faults for not having adequately guarded itself against the return of paganism. His retooling of uprootedness in ethical terms consequently serves as the primary source for the postmodern trope of the Jew.[11] His presence in this narrative is, thus, absolutely central.

When Blanchot and Derrida speak of being Jewish, they often refer-ence Sartre's *Réflexions sur la question juive,* yet it is not Sartre with whom they primarily engage. While we can have no doubts about the impact of Sartre's book on a generation of thinkers, it is, ultimately, Levinas's own response to Sartre that becomes the blueprint for the postmodern

11. This genealogy is rarely noted by scholars considering the postmodern trope of the Jew. Moyn represents a rare exception to those scholars who have faulted the "essentialism" of postmodern writers on Judaism while refusing to acknowledge its source. Moyn is also rare in tracing Levinas's concern with Judaism back to a reaction to Heidegger's *Being and Time.* I disagree with him, however, in the position he grants to Levinas's "Être juif" in this narrative. He suggests that the modality of "Être juif" offers Levinas a way to conceive of being "riveted" that "left itself open to radically tran-scendent exteriority." What Moyn misses here is the particular importance of deracination as a recla-mation of the diasporic idea that opens up a third path, which can be differentiated from the pagan and the Christian. It is of course the project of this chapter and this book to develop the history of this idea and to locate Levinas's place in that history. See Samuel Moyn, "Judaism against Paganism: Emmanuel Levinas's Response to Heidegger and Nazism in the 1930's," *History and Memory* 10 (March 1998): 25–58.

trope of the Jew. Where Sartre develops the Jew as a figure of human alienation, Levinas refigures that alienation as the essence of ethical subjectivity. In reemploying a set of issues surrounding being Jewish, Blanchot and Derrida do not offer their own analyses of the essence of Judaism; rather, they engage with that of Levinas. Jewish moral exemplarity will represent for both a resource *and* a problem.

The connection that Levinas forges between Judaism and deracination is, ultimately, troubled by the demands that such a connection makes on the definition of Judaism. Levinas's writings on Judaism are dogged by the following questions: If Judaism is to be defined as an ethical modality, does that not make it universally accessible? Does the very association of deracination with Judaism require that Judaism be redefined in universal terms? How can this be done without destroying the very parameters of Jewish community? How can Judaism define itself against a doctrine of roots if it does not define itself universally? While Levinas himself does not contend adequately with these concerns, the postmodern trope of the Jew gains its political cogency through the mobilization of these very tensions. This chapter thus follows the transformation that Levinas engineers in the concept of deracination in its association with Judaism and lays out the tensions that this very association produces. In the following two chapters, I will consider how Maurice Blanchot and Jacques Derrida take up Levinas's concept of deracination and call into question its association with the Jew, without, however, severing this link.

## The Philosophical Roots of Deracination

The preoccupation with deracination in Levinas's work does not originate with his engagement with Judaism, but it culminates with his associating the two. His contention that Judaism could serve as a source for philosophical reflection and his subsequent study of Jewish sources are themselves reactive.[12] It develops out of an engagement with and critique of Heidegger's phenomenology and can be traced back to some of his earliest phenomenological writings of the 1930s.

12. Moyn's *Origins of the Other* makes a strong case for locating the sources of Levinas's ethics in Kierkegaard and Barth rather than Jewish sources such as the Bible or the Talmud. Levinas himself never made it a secret that his interest in Talmud was a late occurrence, commencing in the 1950s with his meeting Chouchani. See François Poirié, *Emmanuel Lévinas: Essai et entretiens* (Arles: Actes sud, 1987), 159–60.

As is well-known, Levinas was largely responsible for introducing Heidegger's philosophy to France.[13] In his earliest writings on phenomenology between 1929 and 1932, he presents Heidegger as a beacon for the future of philosophy. He closes his 1930 *The Theory of Intuition in Husserl's Phenomenology* by describing Heidegger as the only thinker who has thus far dared to consider the way in which Husserl's foregrounding of a "pure, primary, and eminently concrete consciousness" opens the way for an inquiry into the manner in which the constitution of consciousness sheds light on the meaning of existence.[14] He refers to Heidegger thus as an inspiration for his own project. In a 1931 reflection in which he relates the experience of attending Heidegger's lectures in Freiburg in 1928 and 1929, Levinas calls Heidegger, seemingly without irony, "Germany's glory."[15] As late as 1932, in the first article published on Heidegger in France, "Martin Heidegger and Ontology," he makes it his task to introduce France to the radicality of Heidegger's transformation of Idealism's subject-object problem.[16]

It is only after 1933, when Heidegger accepted the position of rector at Freiburg, which made him an administrator of the Nazi Party, that Levinas's responses to his philosophy shifted, most explicitly in the text that Levinas composed for the most part while in captivity in Germany, *Existence and Existents*. The points of contrast that develop in this text do not involve a retreat from the praise expressed in the early 1930s, praise that pointed largely to the method Heidegger had pioneered. Rather, Levinas's critique centers on Heidegger's characterization of being and the situation of tragedy within that characterization. Levinas acknowledged that his own work was "inspired" by the philosophy of Martin Heidegger but also motivated by "a profound need to leave the climate of that philosophy."[17] In response to Heidegger's interpretation of being in terms that suggest a fundamental generosity, a characterization that places evil in the form of limitation or finitude, Levinas replies: "Does

13. Levinas published the first article on Heidegger to appear in France, "Martin Heidegger et l'ontologie," *Revue philosophique de la France et de l'étranger* 113 (May–June 1932): 395–431, reproduced and abridged in *En découvrant l'existence avec Husserl et Heidegger* (Paris: J. Vrin, 1967), 77–110, and translated in "Martin Heidegger and Ontology," *Diacritics* 26, no. 1 (1996): 11–32. For detailed accounts of the part he played in introducing Heidegger to French readers, see Ethan Kleinberg, *Generation Existential: Heidegger's Philosophy in France, 1927–1961* (Ithaca, NY: Cornell University Press, 2005); and Marie-Anne Lescourret, *Emmanuel Levinas* (Paris: Flammarion, 1994).

14. Emmanuel Levinas, *La théorie de l'intuition dans la phénoménologie de Husserl* (Paris: Félix Alcan, 1930), 218, translated by André Orianne as *The Theory of Intuition in Husserl's Phenomenology* (Evanston, IL: Northwestern University Press, 1998), 154–55.

15. Levinas, *Les imprévus de l'histoire*, 91, and *Unforeseen History*, 64.

16. See n. 13 above.

17. Emmanuel Levinas, *De l'existence à l'existant* (Paris: J. Vrin, 1978), 19–20, translated by Alphonso Lingis as *Existence and Existents* (Dordrecht: Kluwer Academic, 1995), 19–20.

Being contain no other vice than its limitation and nothingness?[18] Is there some sort of underlying evil in its very positivity? Is not anxiety over Being—horror of Being—just as primal as anxiety over death? Is not the fear of Being just as originary as the fear for nothingness?"[19] As Samuel Moyn has pointed out, even this rejection of Heidegger's characterization of being has its origins in Heidegger's own analysis of *Dasein*.[20] In *The Theory of Intuition in Husserl's Phenomenology*, Levinas praises Heidegger for recognizing in his analysis of *Geworfenheit* (thrownness) and *Befindlichkeit* (projection) that *Dasein* is riveted (*rivé*) to his possibilities. In *Existence and Existents* and the phenomenological texts leading up to it, that praise becomes the germ cell for reconceiving Heidegger's characterization of being itself.[21]

The notion that the positivity of being is something menacing appears in his analyses as early as the short piece that Levinas wrote for *Esprit* in 1934, "Reflections on the Philosophy of Hitlerism." Many of the themes that are merely hinted at in this occasional piece are then better developed in the 1935 essay "De l'évasion" ("On Escape").[22] Rare among Levinas's writings in the directness with which it uses phenomenology to address a historical-political phenomenon, "Reflections on the Philosophy of Hitlerism," when read with "De l'évasion," reveals that Levinas's philosophical project arose out of a reaction to a political crisis. By placing "Reflections on the Philosophy of Hitlerism" in a primary position in Levinas's corpus, a reading of his philosophy develops that discloses its political concerns.

Unlike "De l'évasion" and *Existence and Existents*, "Reflections on the Philosophy of Hitlerism" is not constructed as a pure phenomenological description. It is, rather, a phenomenological-political history of Western culture's response to the way in which human beings are riveted to being. This problem is presented, as it is in *Time and the Other*, primarily through the categories of temporality. In this brief essay, there are the seeds of a cultural typology that Levinas develops most explicitly in his occasional writings on Judaism from the 1950s and 1960s, a typology that shadows the phenomenological writings.

In "Reflections on the Philosophy of Hitlerism," the intellectual tradition of the West is represented as a series of attempts to escape the

18. This is the language that Heidegger uses to characterize Being in *Was ist Metaphysik?*

19. Levinas, *De l'existence à l'existant*, 19–20, and *Existence and Existents*, 19–20.

20. See Moyn, "Judaism against Paganism"; and Levinas, *La théorie de l'intuition dans la phénoménologie de Husserl*, 219, and *The Theory of Intuition in Husserl's Phenomenology*, 156.

21. Levinas, *De l'existence à l'existant*, 19–20, and *Existence and Existents*, 19–20.

22. I have maintained the French title here because the standard English translation does not seem to capture the nuance of the French.

binding of time. Christianity comes to respond to the Greek tragedy of *Moïra* by offering the cross that sets one free: "[It] promises to reopen the finality brought about by the flow of moments of a past that is forever challenged, forever called into question, to go beyond the absolute contradiction of a past that is subordinate to the present." At the center of this narrative of escape is the notion of the soul. Levinas describes it as that which is capable of purification, as detached, "independent of the material or social conditions of people."[23] Even when in the Enlightenment philosophy distinguishes itself from theology, the notion of the soul, Levinas argues, is maintained. The eighteenth-century conception of freedom proposes the rational mind as that which can transcend the forces of materiality. Levinas thus asserts a kinship between Christian and Enlightenment anthropologies by proposing an analogy between the immateriality of the Christian soul and Kantian autonomy on the basis that both maintain the privilege of transcendence.

Neither Christian nor Enlightenment anthropology is able to respond, however, to the experience of enchainment.[24] Levinas describes enchainment as the fact of being riveted to the body, to materiality, riveted, thus, to being. In the face of certain aspects of material existence, such as the inescapability of pain, the feeling of identity between self and body appears incontestable. The philosophy of Hitlerism, Levinas argues in 1934, begins with this identity and declares rebellion against the view of modern society as "founded on the harmony of free wills." The philosophy of Hitlerism refuses the avenue of escape—the assertion of transcendence. It is a philosophy of enchainment figured positively as a philosophy of roots. It is for Levinas a return to paganism.[25]

Although Levinas does not mention Heidegger explicitly in the essay, he makes it clear in the prefatory note that accompanied the essay's republication in 1990 that he intended the essay to reference the dangers inherent in a philosophical thinking that focuses on the embeddedness

23. Emmanuel Levinas, *Quelques réflexions sur la philosophie de l'hitlérisme* (Paris: Payot & Rivages, 1997), 10, 11, translated by Sean Hand as "Reflections on the Philosophy of Hitlerism," *Critical Inquiry* 17 (Autumn 1990): 65, 66.

24. *Esprit*, the magazine in which the essay was published, was a progressive Catholic publication, founded by Emmanuel Mounier, the leader of personalism and a scholar of Péguy. Some have read this essay as consistent with the position of Mounier's personalism, which offers a Christian philosophy of the person that can speak to political realities, absorbs some of Marx's insights, and strongly resists Idealism. Despite certain overlaps and common concerns, Levinas should be seen as offering a critique of personalism in the essay, for he is subtly suggesting that Christianity does not have the resources to combat Hitlerism. This is most clearly visible in his treatment of the Christian model of transcendence. See John Caputo, "Hyperbolic Justice: Deconstruction, Myth and Politics," *Research in Phenomenology* 21 (1991): 3–20; and Howard Caygill, *Levinas and the Political* (London: Routledge, 2002), 30.

25. Levinas, *Quelques réflexions sur la philosophie de l'hitlérisme*, 17, 19 (quote), and "Reflections on the Philosophy of Hitlerism," 68, 69.

of man in being, "a being, to use the Heideggerian expression, *'dem es in seinem Sein um dieses Sein selbst geht.'*[26] This statement does not amount, however, to a rejection of Heidegger's influence. As many have noted, there is no more essential philosophical resource for Levinas than Heidegger.[27] Levinas will consequently go to great lengths to distinguish his own thought from Heidegger's and to paint his and Heidegger's differences in the starkest of terms, often at the expense of explicitly acknowledging his dependence on Heidegger's thought and the construction of his own modalities of ethical subjectivity on a Heideggerian methodological foundation.[28] From this point forward, Levinas will explicitly associate Heidegger with a category of relation to being that he calls *pagan*—with a philosophy of rootedness. As being comes to be figured in his work, particularly in *Existence and Existents*, as sheltering within it an elemental evil, the endorsement of enchainment comes to appear as an acceptance of evil and bears as its consequence a vision of the world (explicitly associated with Nietzsche in "Reflections on the Philosophy of Hitlerism")[29] in which value is derived from earth and blood, a world of masters and slaves.[30]

26. Ibid., 25; 63. This is most explicitly a reference to sec. 9 of *Being and Time*, though, word for word, the quote comes from sec. 23: "that Being which is an *issue* for its entity in its very Being." See Heidegger, *Sein und Zeit*, 42 (sec. 9), 104 (sec. 23), and *Being and Time*, 67, 137.

27. Rodolphe Calin, *Levinas et l'exception du soi* (Paris: Presses universitaires de France, 2005), 229.

28. Scholars have long noted that the distinctions between Levinas's thought and Heidegger's are not as clear as Levinas represents them to be. Derrida treats this dynamic already in "Violence and Metaphysics" (in *L'écriture et la différence*, 133–37, and *Writing and Difference*, 86–92). Jean-Luc Marion makes the compelling argument that the concept of substitution, so central to *Otherwise Than Being*, has its source in sec. 26 of *Being and Time*. See Jean-Luc Marion, "La substitution et la sollicitude: Comment Levinas reprit Heidegger," in *Emmanuel Levinas et les territoires de la pensée*, ed. Danielle Cohen-Levinas and Bruno Clément (Paris: Presses universitaires de France, 2007). See also François Raffoul, "Being and the Other: Ethics and Ontology in Levinas and Heidegger," in *Addressing Levinas*, ed. Eric Sean Nelson, Antje Kapust, and Kent Still (Evanston, IL: Northwestern University Press, 2005), 138–51. Raffoul argues that Levinas oversimplifies Heidegger's representation of being by conflating "Heideggerian ontology" with classic ontology and, thus, deemphasizing the fact that Heidegger's philosophy is aimed at calling into question "the meaning and truth of *Being* itself" (144). Rodolphe Calin shows how Levinas consistently overdetermines the role of *Jemeinigkeit* in Heidegger, in order to call into question this structure while at the same time transposing it to the ethical plane (*Levinas et l'exception du soi*, 238).

29. Levinas, *Quelques réflexions sur la philosophie de l'hitlérisme*, 23, and "Reflections on the Philosophy of Hitlerism," 71. Levinas's representation of Nietzsche is even more reductive and simplistic than his representation of Heidegger. No doubt his claim that Nietzsche is a source for a thinking of blood and soil is ill conceived. None of Levinas's work attests to a sustained engagement with Nietzsche's philosophy. Of course, the difficulties of differentiating between Nietzsche's writings and his impact is a thorny one. Derrida's *Oreille de l'autre* (*Ear of the Other*) addresses the complexity of how and whether we can disentangle one from the other.

30. Levinas, *Quelques réflexions sur la philosophie de l'hitlérisme*, 23–24, and "Reflections on the Philosophy of Hitlerism," 70–71. It is fascinating that, in this essay, the logic that Levinas is suggesting as the logic of Hitlerism is more explicitly the logic of the fascist movement in France, particularly of Maurice Barrès (discussed in the first chapter), who harangues against the bankruptcy of the abstract

In "De l'évasion," Levinas develops more fully the argument that the thinking of the West has thus far failed to protect itself against a philosophy of rootedness and that perhaps it is time to think differently. He concludes "De l'évasion," in fact, with the declaration that it is the task of philosophy to find a way of "getting out of being by a new path, at the risk of overturning certain notions that to common sense and the wisdom of nations seemed the most evident." The claim here implied by the terms *common sense* and *wisdom of nations* is that the paths that the West has taken in its own attempt to overcome the constraints of finitude fail because they have been consistently founded on a notion of freedom, where freedom is conceptualized as the capacity to overcome the limitation of the material through the transcendence of the mind. Levinas argues that this is a voyage always doomed to failure because it is unable to transcend the limitations of the self. It is an enactment of the present, but the present as solitude where my venture out of my self (a venture that for Levinas never, in fact, makes contact with alterity but remains within the domain of the same) culminates in a return to self. In suggesting that we need to find a new method of self-transcendence "at the risk of overturning certain notions . . . that seem most evident," Levinas is suggesting that we need to locate that which is more originary to the subject than its freedom, that which may even call into question the subject's freedom.[31]

*Existence and Existents* takes up from "De l'évasion" the description of the experience of being as an experience of enchainment. Analysis of the human modalities of fatigue and indolence (*la paresse*) demonstrates our relation to being as one of impotent resistance. In formulating these modalities, Levinas is both following in Heidegger's footsteps and providing a counternarrative to Heidegger's account of *Dasein*. Like Heidegger, he resists treating mood as "contents of the mind" whose substance is a secondary property to thought. Rather, fatigue and indolence are themselves the avenues through which objects are disclosed. These moods do not reflect an act of resistance; they *are* the resistance. Weariness (*la lassitude*) is "the recoil before existence" itself. Just as "vision alone is the apprehension of light and hearing alone the perception of sound," wea-

---

humanism expounded by the Dreyfusards. As Derrida points out, the association of Heidegger with such logic cannot be made by explicitly associating Heidegger's writings with such an ideology of nationalism; rather, it must be made with reference to the "climate" of his philosophy, a climate from which Levinas suggests in *Existence and Existents* his own work is trying to depart. Derrida argues, furthermore, that this climate is, perhaps, that of thinking itself and, thus, inescapable for Levinas. See Derrida, *L'écriture et la différence*, 215, and *Writing and Difference*, 145.

31. Emmanuel Levinas, "De l'évasion," *Recherches philosophiques* 5 (1935–36): 391, translated by Bettina Bergo as *On Escape* (Stanford, CA: Stanford University Press, 2003), 73.

riness is "the very way in which refusal to exist comes about." While the structure of disclosure mirrors the analysis of mood in *Being and Time*, the moods themselves are meant to contrast with Heidegger's. Where Heidegger locates care as "the act of being on the brink of nothingness," Levinas asserts that it arises from the very excess of being, its imposition on the existent.[32]

Building on the work accomplished in "De l'évasion," the project central to *Existence and Existents* is to think through the avenues by which the existent liberates itself from the weight of being. Once again, the self-transcendence of rational consciousness is exposed as a ruse. Subjectivity, Levinas asserts, is not yet freedom, for "the I always has one foot caught in its own existence."[33] The self cannot but be a self. It is riveted to its own being. Levinas's search for the possibility of an encounter with alterity is, thus, first and foremost a search for the possibility of escape from enchainment to the self. In *Existence and Existents* and in *Time and the Other*, this search culminates in sociality.[34] Levinas makes the argument already in *Existence and Existents* that will undergird all his subsequent work—that "social exteriority is an original form of exteriority and takes us beyond the categories of unity and multiplicity that are valid for things."[35] *Existence and Existents* and *Time and the Other* focus primarily on the deficient models of relation. Levinas rehearses potential solution after potential solution to the predicament of the isolated and riveted self, showing first how death presents itself as other, but as an other to which we can have no relation. Eros appears as the relation to what cannot come to presence, what always slips away, but fails to represent an avenue out of solitude as it concludes in "dual solitude, closed society, the supremely non public."[36] This sequence culminates finally in the ethical relation, which finds its mature expression in *Totality and Infinity* (1961). The face-to-face encounter with the other is presented as *the* relation with alterity and, thus, as the solution to the problem that all of Levinas's early work had focused on articulating.

32. Levinas, *De l'existence à l'existant*, 31, 32, 36, and *Existence and Existents*, 24, 25, 27.

33. Ibid., 143; 84.

34. *Time and the Other* was not published under this title until 1979, but its content is a series of lectures given between 1946 and 1947 at Jean Wahl's Collège philosophique. The lectures were first published as a part of a larger volume including the work of Jeanne Hersh, Alphonse de Waelhens, and Jean Wahl entitled *Le choix—le monde—l'existence* (Grenoble and Paris: Arthaud, 1947).

35. Levinas, *De l'existence à l'existant*, 163, and *Existence and Existents*, 95.

36. Emmanuel Levinas, *Totalité et infini: Essai sur l'extériorité* (La Haye: M. Nijhoff, 1961), 297, translated by Alphonso Lingis as *Totality and Infinity: An Essay on Exteriority* (Pittsburgh, PA: Duquesne University Press, 1969), 265.

## *Totality and Infinity*: From Enchainment to Ethics

Just as being Jewish may seem like an unlikely solution to the rootedness of paganism, so the ethical relation may seem like an unlikely solution to the problem of enchainment. Levinas's ethics replaces one encumbrance with another—the burden of the self with the burden of the other. As was clear from his portrait of Judaism, Levinas does not conceive of liberation as the means to overcome enchainment. In the process of constructing his ethics, he has reformulated the Hegelian dialectic of enslavement and freedom into a dichotomy of solitude and sociality, thus making the relation to the other the opposing counterpart to the self's enchainment. In so doing, he maintains transcendence—that cornerstone of both Christianity and the Platonic tradition—as the ideal goal of an isolated self, but he reconceives the structure of desire at its heart. The Platonic/Neoplatonic model of transcendence, which appears as a counterexample to his own model of transcendence throughout *Totality and Infinity*, is presented as inadequate to the very desire for alterity that drives it. "Transcendence is to be distinguished from a union with the transcendent in participation," Levinas writes as a part of the claim that metaphysical desire properly understood, as distinguished from need, "tends toward *something else entirely*, toward *the absolutely other*." The nature of desire is to be inclined toward what cannot be assimilated. It is not modeled on hunger, which culminates in enjoyment, but is nurtured by distance. It is a relation "whose positivity comes from remoteness." In making this argument, Levinas is directly responding to the Neoplatonic and Christian *exitus-reditus* structure, in which transcendence is figured as ascension and ascension is itself a return. There is no real reaching beyond in this cycle, but, rather, the movement of *extasis* remains within a circuit whose principle is participation: "Participation is a way of referring to the other: it is to have and unfold one's own being without at any point losing contact with the other."[37]

Levinas includes Heidegger's philosophy among those that operate on a principle of participation and, consequently, consolidates the two alternatives that dominated "Reflections on the Philosophy of Hitlerism."[38] In place of a dichotomy between the spiritual and the material, he proposes a contrast between rootedness and uprootedness. What Heidegger's "philosophy of existence" and the *exitus-reditus* model of creation and ascension share, according to this analysis, is a vision of

37. Ibid., 75, 21, 22, 55; 77, 33, 34, 61.
38. Ibid., 54–55; 60–61.

the self as constituted by lack. Where *Dasein* is marked by finitude and uncertainty, the Neoplatonic/Christian self is defined by its separation from its source. Desire is, thus, the pull toward fulfillment in both cases. Levinas contends that, insofar as this movement "proceeds from the subject," it is, in fact, need and not desire. Desire is for Levinas the movement to overcome interiority. It is initiated by the object rather than by the subject. Desire is inaugurated by an interruption of the self's interiority, by a revelation. It is this structure of desire that allows Levinas to set up the dichotomy between rootedness and uprootedness: "Enrootedness, a primoridial preconnection, would maintain participation as one of the sovereign categories of being, whereas the notion of truth marks the end of this reign." Truth here is revelation, which initiates desire. The pursuit of truth is the pursuit of the other, and its structure breaks with the circuit, commencing a journey that uproots: "The metaphysical desire does not long for return, for it is desire for a land not of our birth, for a land foreign to every nature, which has been our fatherland and to which we shall not betake ourselves. The metaphysical desire does not rest upon any prior kinship."[39]

Levinas claims the idea of the infinite from the third meditation of Descartes' *Meditations on First Philosophy* as the source for this model of a revelatory truth. In that meditation, Descartes offers a proof for the existence of God by arguing that the idea of God that I have in my mind has an infinite objective reality and, thus, cannot be caused by me, as the source of an idea must have as much formal reality as the cause has objective reality. From Descartes, Levinas receives the idea of the infinite as that idea whose "ideatum surpasses its idea." The very idea of infinity is defined by the impossibility of a coincidence between its "objective" and its "formal" realities: "The distance that separates *ideatum* and idea here constitutes the content of the *ideatum* itself." This model allows Levinas to think through a "relation with a being that maintains its total exteriority with respect to him who thinks it." Descartes' notion of the idea of the infinite is consummated, Levinas argues, in the intersubjective relationship. For the other person at every moment overflows any idea of him I may have, interrupting my idea, introducing alterity where there was none, and disclosing the inadequacy of my ideational powers in the face of his reality. As such, the other uproots me, arouses a desire, not to consume or absorb, but to give: "The infinite in the finite, the more in the less, which is accomplished by the idea of Infinity, is produced as Desire—not a Desire that the possession of the Desirable

39. Ibid., 56, 54–55, 22; 62, 60–61, 33.

slakes, but the Desire for the Infinite which the desirable arouses rather than satisfies. A Desire perfectly disinterested—goodness. But Desire and goodness concretely presuppose a relationship in which the Desirable arrests the 'negativity' of the I that holds sway in the Same—puts an end to power and emprise."[40] The presence of the other person opens up a new avenue of relation by disenabling the power to assimilate that characterizes thought. I cannot approach the other person with the faculties that I use to approach objects. This mode of relation must be replaced by a new mode. I break through my own solitude when I sacrifice my own happiness and independence to the other. Desire thus becomes goodness. The other uproots me from myself. I am affected, and, in turn, I channel my powers into production *for* the other person.

In *Totality and Infinity*, Levinas presents the solution to the problem that had been at the center of all his earliest original work. Not only is *Totality and Infinity* a response to the problem of being as it is worked out in *Existence and Existents* and *Time and the Other*; it is also a response to "Reflections on the Philosophy of Hitlerism," which argues that the resources of Enlightenment philosophy have failed to see the threat inherent in "the philosophy of Hitlerism." Levinas retrospectively responds to that threat. He rewrites the story of being with an eye toward reconceiving the connection between Europe's politics and its philosophy and constructing an alternate solution. Even when his philosophy seems distant from the realm of politics, it is always already political by virtue of its genesis, by virtue of its impetus as a response to a philosophical crisis in the West, which for Levinas was inseparable from a political crisis.[41]

Levinas's philosophy is often described as lacking an avenue of transition into the political. Derrida, for example, opens *Adieu to Emmanuel Levinas* with the operating assumption that Levinas provides "no assured passage . . . between an ethics or a first philosophy of hospitality, on the one hand, and a law or politics of hospitality, on the other."[42] Levinas himself moves in both *Totality and Infinity* and *Otherwise Than Being* toward a conceptualization of the interaction between politics and ethics, but Derrida is right to zero in on the problem of transition.[43] However, to focus on this locus as the site of the political in Levinas's work is to miss that the work is conceived originally and primarily as a response to politics. Levinas himself makes it nearly impossible to forget

40. Ibid., 40, 42; 49, 50.
41. See Caygill, *Levinas and the Political*, 96.
42. Derrida, *Adieu à Emmanuel Levinas*, 45–46, and *Adieu to Emmanuel Levinas*, 20.
43. On this problem and its solutions, see also Simon Critchley, "Five Problems in Levinas's View of Politics and the Sketch of a Solution to Them," *Political Theory* 32, no. 2 (April 2004): 172–85.

this fact. For he begins the work with a description of politics as "the art of foreseeing war and of winning it by every means," a process that the exercise of reason is enjoined to make its primary task.[44]

In these opening lines, Levinas sets up an alliance between politics and philosophy under the guiding principle of totality. Insofar as politics and philosophy operate according to the principle of totality, they are aligned with the act of making war: "The visage of being that shows itself in war is fixed in the concept of totality, which dominates Western philosophy." Totality thus serves as another means to reorient the dichotomy between the material and the spiritual set out in "Reflections on the Philosophy of Hitlerism." Where in "Reflections" the exercise of reason is contrasted with the use of force, in *Totality and Infinity* the history of philosophy is presented as too often operating according to the same principles as war. "Does not the experience of war and totality coincide, for the philosopher, with experience and evidence as such?" Levinas inquires in the preface to *Totality and Infinity*.[45] Recalling Hegel's *Phenomenology of Spirit*, Levinas asks whether the rule of combat is, in fact, the world's operating principle. In "Reflections," the exercise of reason is presented as a means to transcend the material world. The expansion of force, on the contrary, stems from its embrace. In *Totality and Infinity*, these two movements are aligned to the extent that they reduce the other to the same. Insofar as philosophy has been concerned first and foremost with comprehension, it has functioned according to the same rule of expansion that marks war. It has refused to be disturbed by anything other. By reducing all that it encounters to an object for thematization, it allows for the autonomy and isolation of the knowing subject.

The idea of infinity is, thus, as Levinas's title suggests, totality's opposing term. If totality is the governing principle of politics, then infinity is the governing principle of what Levinas refers to as *religion*. *Totality and Infinity* is constructed with a political critique at its center. It aims at exposing the complicity between the West's philosophical tradition and its thirst for political conquest, culminating for Levinas in the Second World War. The category of religion that Levinas constructs as a principle opposed to politics must itself be read politically, for he conceptualizes it as the rupture of the law of politics by the "gleam of exteriority."[46]

Just as the idea of infinity provides the model for the interruption of intentional consciousness, so the eschatological vision of the prophet,

---

44. Levinas, *Totalité et infini*, 5, and *Totality and Infinity*, 21.
45. Ibid., 5, 9; 21, 24.
46. Ibid., 9; 24.

defined as "that which interrupts history, declaring judgment at every and any instant," provides the model for how religion can interrupt politics. Levinas contrasts the prophet's judgment with the Hegelian judgment of history. Where Hegel judges the value of each moment for its relative contribution to the accomplishment of history, the prophet, Levinas asserts, "restores to each instant its full signification in that very instant." The prophet's judgment is the interruption of the exterior, transcendent plane into history. Consequently, it signals the possibility for *"signification without a context"* for the possibility of a superior plane of judgment.[47]

The goal of this paradigm is, not to restore the biblical tradition as a source of moral judgment, but to argue that the piercing of the immanent plane by the light of transcendence is accomplished already in the face-to-face relation. "The idea of infinity" that I confront in the face of the other person "delivers the subjectivity from the judgment of history to declare it ready for judgment at every moment." Not only does the gaze of the other submit me to judgment; it also calls me toward my vocation in my particularity to "go beyond the straight line of judgment."[48]

In this second moment, Levinas introduces another trope with a biblical origin and, with it, cements his emphasis on deracination. In describing the demand the other makes on me in my particularity, Levinas uses the language of election. "The I is a privilege and an election," he states explicitly, comparing the "I" in its confrontation with the other to Abraham, called without knowing where. The goodness demanded of me Levinas compares to a land of exile, which extends "infinite and unexplored."[49] The other thus uproots me just as God uprooted Abraham, taking him from the land of his father in Genesis 12 and into an unknown land, which will make unforeseeable demands on me.

Religion is in *Totality and Infinity* what interrupts and uproots. It is defined by these functions both in relation to the subject's solitary world and in relation to the West's political and philosophical structures. Levinas is careful to delimit it in such a way that it cannot be confused or mistaken with any "positive" tradition. It is no coincidence that the language and the paradigms that characterize religion for Levinas have the Hebrew Bible as their source, which raises the very important question as to whether Levinas's ethics are in some way Jewish.

47. Ibid., 7, 8; 23.
48. Ibid., 11, 245; 25, 274.
49. Ibid., 245; 274.

The debate over whether *Totality and Infinity* should be read as a Jewish book has dominated its reception.[50] In "Violence and Metaphysics," Derrida frames it as a confrontation between "Greek" and "Jew" and asks after the meaning of this distinction and the potential for it to reveal itself in a philosophical work.[51] Adriaan Peperzak, responsible for introducing Levinas to many American readers, speaks of the influence of "Levinas' long mediation on Jewish history as well as on biblical, literary and philosophical texts and commentaries" on his philosophy.[52] More recently, scholars have rightly called into question the influence of Judaism on his philosophy. Against those who see Levinas as a reviver of the Jewish philosophical tradition, Leora Batnitzky argues that he "emerges not as a defender of 'Judaism'" but as a relentless defender of "the need for philosophical activity for social and political purposes."[53] In the process, she suggests, he makes no room, in fact, for the autonomy of Judaism. Levinas himself made numerous statements on the relation of Judaism to his philosophy, arguing that both his philosophy and his writings on Judaism have the same source for their inspiration but speak "as separate languages."[54] Such statements give rise to the metaphor of translation as a means to conceptualize the role of Judaism in his texts. It is often stated that his philosophy is a translation of Hebrew into Greek.[55] This metaphor suggests that Levinas is transmitting ancient biblical wisdom in a philosophical language and accords him the role of transmitter. It is

50. The only other issue that has received close to the attention accorded the Jewish question is the question of the status of the feminine. Most famous is Simone de Beauvoir, *Le deuxième sexe* (Paris: Gallimard, 1949), 15. Other treatments have followed: Catherine Chalier, *Figures du feminine: Lecture d'Emmanuel Levinas* (Paris: Verdier, 1982); Luce Irigaray, "Fécondité de la caresse," *Exercices de la patience* 4 (1983): 119–37; Jacques Derrida, "En ce moment même dans cet ouvrage me voici," in *Textes pour Emmanuel Levinas*, ed. François Laruelle (Paris: Collection surfaces, 1980); Tina Chanter, "Feminism and the Other," in *The Provocation of Levinas*, ed. Robert Bernasconi and David Wood (London: Routledge, 1988); and Claire Elise Katz, *Levinas, Judaism and the Feminine* (Bloomington: Indiana University Press, 2003).

51. Derrida, *L'écriture et la différence*, 117–228, and *Writing and Difference*, 79–153.

52. Adriaan Peperzak, "Emmanuel Levinas: Jewish Experience and Philosophy," *Philosophy Today* 27 (Winter 1983): 305.

53. Leora Batnitzky, *Leo Strauss and Emmanuel Levinas: Philosophy and the Politics of Revelation* (Cambridge: Cambridge University Press, 2006), xx.

54. Emmanuel Levinas, "Emmanuel Levinas and Richard Kearney: Dialogue with Emmanuel Levinas," in *Face to Face with Levinas*, ed. Richard A. Cohen (Albany: State University of New York Press, 1986), 18.

55. See, e.g., Annette Aronowicz, introduction to Emmanuel Levinas, *Nine Talmudic Readings*, trans. Annette Aronowicz (Bloomington: Indiana University Press, 1968), ix; Robert Gibbs, *Correlations in Rosenzweig and Levinas* (Princeton, NJ: Princeton University Press, 1992), 155–75; and Judith Friedlander, *Vilna on the Seine: Jewish Intellectuals in France since 1968* (New Haven, CT: Yale University Press, 1990), 80. Levinas himself uses this metaphor, speaking of philosophy as a Septuagint, which translates Hebrew into Greek. See, e.g., the 1984 interview with Levinas in Salomon Malka, *Lire Levinas* (Paris: Cerf, 1984), 107, translated as *Is It Righteous to Be? Interviews with Emmanuel Levinas*, ed. Jill Robbins (Stanford, CA: Stanford University Press, 2001), 97.

more accurate to suggest that his phenomenological model arises from a confrontation with Heidegger's philosophy and an insight into the connections between the politics of modern Europe and its philosophical tradition. In *Totality and Infinity*, he chronicles the interruption of the self's solitary voyage by the ethical encounter. He mines the Hebrew Bible for tropes that allow him to associate his model with a very old tradition. He is careful in his phenomenological writings to make these associations in such a way that the biblical verses lose both their theological meaning and their historical significance. In his confessional writings, however, he carries out the project of making the association between ethics and Judaism explicit by arguing, not only that Judaism is the historical carrier of an age-old message, but also that it has itself functioned in the West as the prophetic voice of eschatology.

In turning to these writings, it is crucial that we not take Levinas's claims on this matter at face value. By reading *Totality and Infinity* as a work conceived and assembled at the same time and with the same aims as his confessional writings, we can discern that it ought to be read as one part of a larger strategy to construct and present a vision of Judaism formed in opposition to what Levinas conceives of as Heideggerian paganism. In his confessional texts, he builds this opposition by playing off the popular association between Jews and rootlessness. This association, which had served as a touchstone for so much anti-Semitism, he presents as the source of Judaism's greatest virtue.

## Judaism against Paganism and the Thinking of the West

Fourteen years lapsed between the appearance of *Existence and Existents* and that of *Totality and Infinity*. During this time, Levinas published periodic articles that moved him closer to the model presented in *Totality and Infinity*. At the same time, he continued to consider the connections between philosophy and politics. While solving for himself the problem of enchainment that began with an engagement and confrontation with Heidegger's philosophy, he was also writing essays that directly addressed the Jewish question in France. These essays develop a schema already nascent in "Reflections on the Philosophy of Hitlerism." Like that 1934 essay, they often divide Western culture into three categories: the pagan, the Christian, and the Jewish. In working out the themes of rootedness and uprootedness as a means to discussing the relationship between the existent and being and between the self and the other,

Levinas was not unaware of the more political connotations of these terms, of their popular political usage and their links to the history of anti-Semitism. The project of reconfiguring the valence of these terms is broadcast clearly in his confessional essays, in which the very real connection between these notions and the politics of land is made explicit. His typology is often shifting and seems sometimes to take place on a rhetorical rather than a strictly conceptual level. Nonetheless, its two extremes are clearly marked out as paganism and Judaism, with Christianity appearing as a failed alternative to paganism.

Already in 1935 in *Paix et droit*, a journal of the Alliance israélite universelle, Levinas was speaking of Judaism's vocation to fulfill its diasporic destiny in the face of Hitlerism and, thus, to resist the call of nationalism.[56] In the late 1930s, he defined Judaism consistently as "anti-paganism par excellence." Anti-Semitism was cast as the rebellion of paganism against the distrust of the natural world exhibited in both Judaism and Christianity. It is, he wrote, "the revolt of nature against the supernatural, the aspiration of the world toward its proper apotheosis, toward its beautification in nature."[57] For Levinas, the opposition between paganism and Judaism was, not between advocating one god and advocating many, but between two very different ways of inhabiting the world. Taking a page straight out of Barrès, he suggested that Judaism's main contribution to the world was its expression of a feeling of estrangement from the natural world and a "resistance to the cult of power and earthly greatness."[58] He thus forged a connection between Judaism and deracination in many of his occasional essays, making explicit the political nuances of this idea and at the same time presenting Judaism as its embodiment.

Levinas's emphasis on these themes may have arisen as a consequence of his 1935 reading of Rosenzweig's *Star of Redemption*, which seems to have provided him with a source for differentiating Judaism from paganism and Christianity, supplying him both with a revalorized notion of the Jews' estrangement from land and with the idea of the Jews as an eternal and ahistorical people. It is clear, however, particularly after the war, that the contrast between Judaism and paganism develops in an

56. Emmanuel Levinas, "L'inspiration religieuse de l'Alliance," *Paix et droit* 8 (October 1935): 6–7, republished in *Emmanuel Levinas: Cahier de l'Herne*, ed. Catherine Chalier and Miguel Abensour (Paris: L'Herne, 1991), 144–45.

57. Emmanuel Levinas, "L'essence spirituelle de l'antisémitisme (d'après Jacques Maritain)," *Paix et droit* 5 (May 1938): 4, republished in *Emmanuel Levinas: Cahier de l'Herne*, 151.

58. Emmanuel Levinas, "A propos de la mort du pape Pie XI," *Paix et droit* 19 (March 1939): 3, republished in *Emmanuel Levinas: Cahier de l'Herne*, 151–52.

engagement with Heidegger's writings against technology.[59] After the war, Levinas's rhetoric about paganism becomes more clearly directed at Heidegger as Heidegger's own essays in the 1950s elaborate the theme of "dwelling" and come to emphasize poetry and thinking over and against instrumental reason.[60] "For Judaism, the world becomes intelligible in front of a human face and not, as for a great contemporary philosopher who sums up an important aspect of the West, through houses, temples and bridges," Levinas writes in 1957, explicitly connecting paganism to Heidegger's preoccupations in "Building, Dwelling, Thinking" (1951).[61] While it is clear in all Levinas's writings on Judaism that his positive conceptualization of Jewish rootlessness rehabilitates the negative associations among Jews, technology, and cosmopolitanism, nowhere is this clearer than in Levinas's 1961 "Heidegger, Gagarin and Us," written on the occasion of the first manned space flight. Here, the metaphoric notions of rootedness and rootlessness are literalized as the possibility of departure from the earth is actualized by Gagarin's flight. Heidegger's critique of technology is subtly figured as a nostalgia to which the movement of progress is compared. Levinas takes up here the stereotype that the Jew is associated with technology, with the destruction of an existence that is characterized by "the fascination of nature . . . the mystery of things, of a jug, of the worn-down shoes of a peasant girl." He suggests in the process that these images, drawn from Heidegger's "Origin of the Work of Art" (1935–36) and "The Thing" (1950), are images that reveal "the eternal seductiveness of paganism." Thus, in associating Judaism with technology, he is also defining Judaism as "the negation of all that." The claim that underscores the shift in value is that "the mystery of things"—a phrase clearly meant to characterize the relation to being that Heidegger's thought endorses from the 1930s through the 1950s—is "the source of cruelty towards men."[62] The

59. "Yet even before National Socialism, in the mounting peril of the interwar years, the philosopher Franz Rosenzweig, who died in 1929 but exerts a growing influence on contemporary Jewish thought, plans Judaism and Christianity within the common programme of a religious truth that is certainly not pluralist but dualist. Truth in itself would entail a double manifestation in the world; that of the eternal people and that of the mission on the eternal way" (Levinas, *Difficile liberté*, 228–29, and *Difficult Freedom*, 163).

60. See, e.g., Martin Heidegger, *Vorträge und Aufsätze* (Pfullingen: G. Neske, 1985); and Martin Heidegger, *Poetry, Language, Thought*, trans. Albert Hofstader (New York: Harper & Row, 1971).

61. Levinas, *Difficile liberté*, 40–41, and *Difficult Freedom*, 23 (translation altered).

62. Most precisely, Levinas seems to be referencing Heidegger's lecture "The Thing," which begins with a critique of the way in which technology is shrinking time and space, naming flight first among inventions such as the radio and the camera, and moves on to contrast the way in which these inventions obliterate distance with the way in which the jug reveals nearness while preserving farness. See Heidegger, "Das Ding," in *Vorträge und Aufsätze*, 166, translated as "The Thing" in *Poetry, Language, Thought*, 157.

attachment to *place* that this nostalgia signifies, Levinas argues, "is the very splitting of humanity into natives and strangers."[63] Thus, he suggests, the critique of technology that is ever present in Heidegger's works during this period is misguided, for it names as a modern menace the relation to the world that technology embodies. Heidegger fails to see that the far greater danger to humanity is the relation to time and place that founds his own critique. The consequence of such an approach, according to Levinas, is that it prioritizes the relationship of man to being, and, thus, to time, space, and things, over the relationship of one human being to another.[64] Thus, Heidegger groups together the atomic bomb with the airplane and the radio, each of these diagnosed as problematic insofar as each annihilates the mode of being-in-the-world that Heidegger calls *dwelling*.

In opposition to the vision of technology that Heidegger offers in "The Thing," where technology is defined as that which obliterates the distinction between nearness and farness, Levinas suggests that Gagarin represents the possibility for a perspective of true distance, for he "wrenches us out of the Heideggerian world and the superstitions surrounding place," providing an image of the human as free of place. Here, Judaism makes an entrance as that way of thinking that has always been "free with regard to place." Its rootlessness sets it outside the way of being that differentiates native from stranger, for the Bible "knows only a Holy Land, a fabulous land that spews forth the unjust, a land in which one does not put down roots without certain conditions."[65]

Given that the opposition that Levinas forges here opposes Judaism to paganism by contrasting their respective relations to the natural world, it might seem difficult for him to make this argument without acknowledging the emphasis on transcendence in Christianity. Insofar as he is keen to attack what he identifies as the return to paganism in the Nazi threat, he allies Christianity and Judaism on this score, defining anti-Semitism as Christianity's mortal enemy as much as it is the enemy of Judaism.[66] His goal is clearly to summon the church toward taking an active stance against the threat of Nazi Germany. In 1939, he says as much: "In a world that is growing more and more hostile, that is filling up with swastikas, it is toward the straight pure arms of the cross that we so often lift our eyes." In an essay commemorating the death of Pope

---

63. Levinas, *Difficile liberté*, 347–49, and *Difficult Freedom*, 231–32.

64. Raffoul, "Being and the Other."

65. Levinas, *Difficile liberté*, 326, and *Difficult Freedom*, 233.

66. Levinas, "L'essence spirituelle de l'antisémitisme," 3–4, and *Emmanuel Levinas: Cahier de l'Herne*, 150–51.

Pius XI, Levinas differentiates Judaism from Christianity by harnessing a distinction he gathered from Rosenzweig's *Star of Redemption*. Christianity is cast as the historical religion, which has made its pact with the forces of the world through the institution of the church, whose steeples dominate the skylines of Europe's villages as markers of its battle against barbarism. Judaism, on the contrary, is the martyr, "never having known real political power, separating out human dignity from power and success."[67] Within this call for help there is stronger criticism of Christianity than Rosenzweig's own. For Christianity is branded with the charge of syncretism, accused of having absorbed along the way elements of paganism and, thus, some of its valorization of the natural.[68] Christianity therefore lacks the power of critique that Judaism maintains, for it has compromised itself to sustain itself.

The strength of this judgment is greatly amplified in Levinas's essays following the war. What was a stern call to action becomes a condemnation. Looking back at the damages of the war and the destruction of the European Jewish community, Levinas charges Christianity with having failed to make the world better. "Christianity's failure on the political level cannot be denied," he declares in 1950.[69] This failure is two pronged. Returning to the schema laid out in "Reflections on the Philosophy of Hitlerism," he charges Christianity both with being somewhat corrupted by paganism and with having advocated escapism from the world. Christianity, he writes in "Place and Utopia," misapprehends "the weight of the reality that it wants to improve" by either overestimating it or underestimating it. It overestimates when it "hopes for a miraculous intervention on the part of Divinity" that "will transfigure this brutal weight." This overestimation leads to the path of the mystic who uproots herself but does so by denying the place "where it is incumbent on me to do something" for "an anchorite's salvation." Christianity underestimates the weight of being when it gives in to the given order and adopts "the virtues of being warrior-like and putting down roots, of being a man-plant, a humanity-forest whose gnarled joints of root and trunk are magnified by the rugged life of a countryman." Against these two potentialities in Christianity, Judaism is treated as a response to elemental evil that nonetheless maintains a commitment to the here

67. Levinas, "A propos de la mort du pape Pie XI," 3–4, and *Emmanuel Levinas: Cahier de l'Herne*, 150–51.

68. Péguy's glorification of the peasant life as part of the Catholic mystique serves as an ideal representation of such a tendency. Levinas refers to Péguy among others as an example of how the poetry of the pagan is preserved in Christian literature. See Levinas, "Être juif," 101.

69. Levinas, *Difficile liberté*, 143, and *Difficult Freedom*, 99.

below. In contrast to Christianity, where the ethical order is subordinated to the ascension toward divinity, in Judaism, Levinas claims, the ethical order *is* "accession to the Divinity."[70] There is, thus, in Judaism, according to Levinas, no movement of flight from the material world. One's relation to the divine is actualized only by action in that world.

Judaism appears as the possibility of recognizing the brutal force of being without attempting to flee it through either the path of personal salvation (Christianity) or a noumenal freedom (Kant). Judaism acknowledges the individual in his materiality but responds to that materiality, not by embracing a model of the human as *conatus*, but with the command, "Thou shalt not kill," the command that is the beginning of conscience, for it teaches that all life is usurpation.[71] If paganism is the acceptance of the natural order, the acceptance that it is natural to put down roots, and Christianity is that which responds to the material by fleeing, Judaism for Levinas is the resistance to the natural order through care for the other man.

To return to the theme of enchainment that dominated Levinas's early phenomenology, his claim is not that Judaism breaks free of the natural order or even the experience of enchainment. Rather, this experience is reoriented when understood through the lens of Judaism's message. In discussing the experience of being Jewish, Levinas does not discard the language of enchainment. He speaks of the Jew as "riveted to his Judaism," self-consciously transforming the rhetoric of race that marks the ideology of Maurice Barrès as well as Adolf Hitler. By defining Judaism in racial terms, "Hitler has recalled that *one doesn't desert Judaism*," he writes in 1935.[72] Rejecting the rhetoric of race, he nonetheless sees in Hitler the resurfacing of the fact of Jewish existence as persecuted. It is by refusing the logic of race but reappropriating the yoke of Judaism that the Jewish people will surmount the trial of Hitlerism, he counsels. He refers to the Nazi threat here as an *épreuve*, employing the same term that the French translation of the Hebrew Bible uses to translate the Hebrew *nisa* in Genesis 22, which refers to God's "trying" Abraham in the story of the binding of Isaac. The threat of Hitler is, thus, imbued with a religious

---

70. Levinas, *Difficile liberté*, 143, 144, 147. and *Difficult Freedom*, 99, 100, 102.

71. Levinas often refers to the *conatus*, Spinoza's definition of the self as appetitive, to indicate a model of the self that ethics shatters. Spinoza thus represents for Levinas another thinker of immanence, though he comes around in a brief essay, "Have You Reread Baruch," to defending a certain reading of the *Tractatus Theologico-Politico* that sees it as teaching a nondogmatic, ethical interpretation of the scriptures. His truly major failure remains, nonetheless, for Levinas, that he was unable to recognize the grandeur of the thinking of the talmudic masters. See Levinas, *Difficile liberté*, 158–69, and *Difficult Freedom*, 111–18.

72. Levinas, "Être juif," 103.

resonance. Surmounting this trial for Levinas means reclaiming Judaism as religion, reclaiming its irremissibility in religious terms by replacing the destiny of race with the destiny of election. Levinas's thought in the following decades is, subsequently, driven by the task of disentangling the particularism of election from that of race and the ensuing question of whether deracination and election are compatible.

After "Reflections on the Philosophy of Hitlerism" and "De l'évasion," which speak of Western philosophy as the struggle to overcome the experience of being "riveted" to being and to one's self, it is surprising to find that Levinas uses the same language to refer to being Jewish. In his 1947 response to Sartre, he repeats his earlier claim about Hitlerian anti-Semitism: that it recalls the Jew to the irremissibility of his being. There is a truth, he concedes, to the Heideggerian and Sartrean descriptions of "facticity" in terms of "thrownness," yet, he suggests, there is a way of transforming that "supreme engagement" into a "supreme liberty."[73] Judaism does this, he argues, by opening up this principle of the present by means of the past. To find one's self riveted to one's being is within the Jewish context, not merely to find one inescapably attached to one's self, but rather to find one's self inescapably *chosen*, inescapably *commanded*. The difference between *Geworfenheit* and election is the difference between saying, "I find myself in this situation, and these are its parameters," and saying, "I find myself commanded to be here, and this is what I have been commanded to do." Where Heidegger, through the concept of care, speaks of *Dasein* taking up its possibility, Levinas speaks of the yoke of responsibility. The introduction of "creation" and "election" transforms the experience of being riveted into the experience of being responsible, Levinas claims. Samuel Moyn has argued that, in Levinas's essay "Être juif," he "neutralized" what he believed to be the difficulties in Heidegger's presentation of the problem of being "through modification to being Jewish."[74] While Moyn is right to point out that Levinas's formulation of the notion of being Jewish is a consequence of his engagement with Heideggerian ontology, the term *neutralized* does not capture the nature of the transformation. The verb *neutralize* suggests the counterbalancing of something toxic so that it becomes innocuous. Levinas, on the contrary, intensifies the grip of enchainment by reconceiving it as the yoke of election; in the process, he paradoxically transforms it into deracination. Creation and election introduce the element of the past into one's experience of the present so as to revamp

73. Ibid., 103–4.
74. Moyn, "Judaism against Paganism," 25.

being into being-for. Election is, thus, a means of understanding the irremissibility of being and the key to Levinas's notion of uprooting.

In "Place and Utopia," Levinas defines the difference between the Jewish and the pagan relation to being while at the same time recasting the Christian notion of the carnal Jew:

If Judaism is attached to the here below, it is not because it does not have the imagination to conceive of the supernatural order, or because matter represents some sort of absolute for it; but because the first light of conscience is lit for it on the path that leads from man to his neighbor. What is an individual, a solitary individual, if not a tree that grows without regard for everything it suppresses and breaks, grabbing all the nourishment, air, and sun, a being that is fully justified in its nature and its being? What is an individual, if not a usurper? What is signified by the advent of conscience, and even the first spark of spirit, if not the discovery of corpses beside me and my horror of exiting by assassination? Attention to others and, consequently, the possibility of counting myself among them, of judging myself—conscience is justice.[75]

The difference between enchainment in the pagan sense and enchainment in the Jewish sense is, as Levinas makes clear here, the difference between solitude and sociality. That is to say, the relation between enchainment in the pagan sense and enchainment in the Jewish sense mirrors the difference between ontology and ethics as Levinas develops this distinction in both *Totality and Infinity* and *Otherwise Than Being*. The drama that Levinas constructs between Judaism, Christianity, and paganism has its counterpart in his phenomenology. Just as Judaism provides the alternative of election to Christianity's transcendence and paganism's rootedness, so the ethical relation establishes election as the path out of the subject's solitude. By establishing the other person as the site of election both in his discussions of Judaism and in his ethics, Levinas is able to eclipse the very difference between the two. In his

---

75. Levinas, *Difficile liberté*, 144, and *Difficult Freedom*, 100. The notion of the carnal Jew can be traced back to Paul's epistles and his association of Judaism with the material and the literal as against the spiritual: "Behold Israel according to the Flesh" (1 Cor. 10:18). This verse is taken up explicitly as referring to "carnal Israel" by Augustine in his *Tractatus adversus Judeos* (7.9). For more on this notion in Augustine, see Daniel Boyarin, *Carnal Israel: Reading Sex in Talmudic Culture* (Berkeley and Los Angeles: University of California Press, 1993). Péguy explicitly revalorizes this notion in his portrait of Bernard Lazare, referring to the Jews as the "carnal voice and temporal body" bearing the message of prophecy. Péguy thus returns to the Pauline division between spirit and flesh to endorse a notion that the Jews' mission is to be the physical carrier of the seed of prophecy. For Levinas, the carnality of Judaism, its association with the material, is used to refer to what he identifies as its "this-worldliness," its regard for the suffering of the other in this world and at this very moment. In the essay "Simone Weil against the Bible," Levinas addresses this characterization of Judaism directly with the claim that "the advent of the scriptures is not the subordination of the spirit to the letter, but the substitution of the letter to the soil. The spirit is free within the letter, and it is enslaved within the root" (Levinas, *Difficile liberté*, 194–95, and *Difficult Freedom*, 137).

essays on Judaism, Judaism is limited to its ethical dimensions. In his philosophy, the proper name of Judaism is called *ethics*.

Thirty-four years after "Être juif," *Otherwise Than Being* reproduces its model of election almost word for word, but it does so in strictly phenomenological terms. Without referencing Judaism, Levinas opens the section of *Otherwise Than Being* entitled "Substitution" with a near quotation from "Être juif": "It is perhaps here, in this reference to a depth of anarchical passivity, that the thought that names creation differs from ontological thought."[76] In *Otherwise Than Being*, he transfers the structure of creation to the ethical relation, using creation as a paradigm for the subject who, called into subjectivity by the address of the other person, discovers himself "obeying before hearing."[77] Like the subject of the ontological tradition, the ethical subject finds itself in a situation that is inescapable: "I have not done anything and I have always been under accusation—persecuted." Substitution thus serves for Levinas as a means to universalize the structure sketched out in "Être juif." In *Otherwise Than Being*, Levinas shifts his attention from the otherness of the other person to the self who is affected in the moral relation and elaborates a phenomenology of the ethical subject as always already under accusation. To be a subject is to be first the object of a call, to have first been summoned. I am always already for an other. On the one hand, the irremissibility of the call to which I am subject recalls the irremissibility of being that Levinas discusses in his early work, but it also breaks free of it. For, once again, as we saw in "Être juif," we are dealing with the inescapability, not of *being*, but of *being-for*. At the same time that the subject is always already a hostage by virtue of having been called, substitution, which Levinas defines as a responsibility so radical that it is a responsibility for the other's responsibility, by virtue of the structure of election "frees the subject from ennui, that is from the enchainment to itself, where the ego suffocates in itself due to the tautological way of identity." In being-for another, I escape the insularity of solitude by having the very inauguration of my being irrevocably tied to the other who calls me in my singularity. Levinas refers to the responsible self as *paradoxically liberated*, both inspired and exiled from itself. By becoming responsible for all, the ethical subject escapes the self-coinciding of presence. The subjectivity of

76. Emmanuel Levinas, *Autrement qu'être* (La Haye: M. Nijhoff, 1978), 179, translated by Alphonso Lingis as *Otherwise Than Being; or Beyond Essence* (Pittsburgh, PA: Duquesne University Press, 1998), 113. I owe this point to Annabel Herzog, "Benny Levy versus Emmanuel Levinas on 'Being Jewish,'" *Modern Judaism* 26 (2006): 18.

77. Ibid. This phrase subtly references Exod. 19:17, to which Levinas devotes one of his most famous talmudic readings, "The Temptation of Temptation," published in *Quatre lectures talmudiques* (Paris: Minuit, 1968), and translated in *Nine Talmudic Readings*.

the subject is "one absolved from every relationship, every game, literally without situation, without a dwelling place, expelled from everywhere and from itself, one saying to the other . . . 'here I am [*me voici*].'"[78]

The structure of the subject as inaugurated by the call of the other is tied for Levinas to the grammatical form in the response *me voici*. The objective form of the pronoun points to the subject's passivity as foundational. It is also for Levinas always linked to the paradigmatic figure of election, Abraham, who instantiates the tie between election and exile or uprootedness in his response to God in Genesis 12: *Hineni*, which in Hebrew as well retains the objective form of the personal pronoun.

Levinas alludes to this structure in essays throughout his corpus. In "The Trace of the Other," he writes: "To the myth of Ulysses returning to Ithaca we wish to oppose the story of Abraham who leaves his fatherland forever for a yet unknown land, and forbids his servant to even bring back his son to the point of departure."[79] Even when unmentioned, Abraham continues to resonate in allusions to Ulysses, to whom Levinas opposes Abraham, and in the consistent emphasis on the response *me voici*.[80] At the same time, Levinas's invocation of Abraham also points toward the way in which his formulation of his ethics is a manifestation of his reclamation of figures and modes critiqued in the classic formulations of the philosophy of religion.

As chapter 1 established, in the Enlightenment quest to free reason from religion, Judaism often played the foil, providing the paradigmatic example of reason's enslavement under the rule of religion. Levinas makes use of that historical relation in defining the ethical subject against the ideal of autonomy. The ethical subject is heteronomous, subject to another, the biblical Abraham to Homer's Odyseus. Levinas often represents this opposition by way of a critique of Hegel. He reclaims Hegel's Abraham in *The Spirit of Christianity and Its Fate* and, thus, Hegel's representation of Judaism more generally.

In "Hegel and the Jews," Levinas charges that Hegel's own interpretations seem both to inform and to be informed by anti-Semitism.[81]

---

78. Levinas, *Autrement qu'être*, 180, 198, 229, and *Otherwise Than Being*, 114, 124, 146.

79. Emmanuel Levinas, "La trace de l'autre," *Tijdschrift voor filosofie* 25 (September 1963): 605–23, translated as "The Trace of the Other" in *Deconstruction in Context: Literature and Philosophy*, ed. Mark C. Taylor (Chicago: University of Chicago Press, 1986), 345–59.

80. For a sustained discussion of the role of Abraham in Levinas's thought, see Gary D. Mole, *Lévinas, Blanchot, Jabès: Figures of Estrangement* (Gainsville: University Press of Florida, 1997), 100–110.

81. Levinas, *Difficile liberté*, 328–33, and *Difficult Freedom*, 235–39. This essay is written in response to Bernard Bourgeois's study of Hegel's early theological writings, *Hegel à Frankfort au judaïsme, christianisme, hégélianisme* (Paris: J. Vrin, 1970), which treats the representations of Judaism that appear in the essay in a systematic fashion.

Rather than develop this theme, however, he backs away, claiming that the very act of participating in the thematization of Hegel shows us only to be in his debt, for it is Hegel, he suggests, who introduced the notion that philosophy is that which *"speaks the truth* of . . . an art, or a politics, or religion."* Perhaps, Levinas responds, there is another way out of this vision that encompasses the world; perhaps, he suggests, the "so-called 'non-thought' 'representations' of the Bible hold more possibilities than the philosophy that 'rationalizes' them." The question then becomes "whether we should leave the System, even if we do so by moving backwards, through the very door by which Hegel thinks we enter it."[82]

Levinas implies that it is the representation of Abraham "'who founds the Jewish people'" in "'an act of separation, the breaking of all ties with the surroundings,'" that offers us a way out of the Hegelian dialectic.[83] As we saw in chapter 1, Hegel consolidates his condemnation of Judaism in *The Spirit of Christianity and Its Fate* in a diatribe against the figure Abraham. Abraham is the personification of all the traits against which he will define the spirit of Christianity. He is described as estranged from nature, enslaved to God, and responsible for the spirit of alienation that continues to characterize Judaism. Levinas not only reverses the valence of Hegel's critique of Judaism so that Abraham's separation appears as Judaism's virtue; he also argues that the very structure of ethical subjectivity follows an exilic model, commencing with expulsion, an expulsion that is the subject's subjection to the other.

## Toward a Jewish Universalism

The anti-Hegelian thrust of Levinas's philosophy was already apparent in my discussion of the role of prophetic eschatology in *Totality and Infinity*. Prophetic eschatology is defined in the opening pages of that work as a judgment that interrupts the Hegelian interpretation of history. Levinas is, here, employing a biblical model against Hegel, but he is also offering an interpretation of Judaism from within Hegel's own characterization of Judaism. Levinas's own interpretation is consistent with Hegel's claim that Judaism is resistant to the spirit of reconciliation. Judaism's "mean, abject, wretched circumstances" in the late eighteenth century are, Hegel says, "consequences and elaborations" of this "original fate."[84]

82. Levinas, *Difficile liberté*, 333, and *Difficult Freedom*, 238.
83. Ibid., 330; 236.
84. Hegel, *Theologische Jugendschriften*, 256, and *Early Theological Writings*, 199.

By exploiting Hegel's notion that the Jewish people are "the most reprobate and rejected" of peoples, Levinas is able to develop a reading of Judaism such that it appears as a path out of totalizing thought.[85]

What is important here is the notion of Judaism as "exterior" to the interpretation of history wherein history culminates in the nation-state. Building on Rosenzweig's presentation of Judaism in *The Star of Redemption*, Levinas suggest that it is its exclusion from Hegel's model of history that allows Judaism to function as a judgment of the political, a judgment that the Hegelian interpretation of history disallows by its very structure:

Suppose for a moment that political life appears not as a dialectical adjustment which men make toward another, but as an infernal cycle of violence and derision; suppose for a moment that the moral ends which politics prides itself on achieving but amends and limits by virtue of achieving them—that these ends appear steeped in the immorality that claims to sustain them; suppose in other words that you have lost the meaning of the political and the consciousness of grandeur, that the non-sense or non-value of world politics is your first certainty, that you are a people outside peoples (and that is what, in good prose is meant by "a people living apart—or a people not counted among the peoples"); suppose that you are a people capable of disaster, capable of remaining outside alone and abandoned: then you have a totally different vision of universality, one no longer subordinated to confrontation.[86]

In this passage from Levinas's 1961 address to the Colloque des intellectuels juifs de langue française, Judaism is explicitly given the role that Levinas will ascribe to prophetic eschatology in the preface to *Totality and Infinity*. It retains the capacity to judge history where Christianity has abnegated it by allying itself with the state. It is also here presented as the voice for a universalism that is not subordinated to totality. Once again, this interpretation is cultivated by way of a reorientation of one of the charges leveled against the Jews. The notion that the Jews are an exclusive and arrogant people who envision themselves as chosen becomes the very principle of Jewish universalism.

Subverting the debates over Jewish particularism that, as we saw in the first chapter, dominated the arguments for and against Jewish emancipation, Levinas argues that it is Jewish particularism that provides for its

---

85. "Just so, it may be said of the Jewish people that it is precisely because they stand before the portal of salvation that they are the most reprobate and rejected" (Hegel, *Phänomenologie des Geistes*, 198, and *Phenomenology of Spirit*, 206).

86. Levinas, *Difficile liberté*, 135–36, and *Difficult Freedom*, 94.

universalism. The peculiar vocation of the Jew is to be a witness to the universal.[87] Repeatedly in his writing on Judaism, Levinas asserts that the chosenness of the Jews reorients the discourse on universalism that Christianity represents in the West because Jewish universalism is a non-proselytizing universalism. It consists of responsibility: not I am like all others, or all others ought to be like me, but I am *responsible* for all others. This notion is, according to Levinas, both messianic and nondogmatic in that it amounts, not to spreading a teaching, but to claiming a task: as chosen, the Jew "knows [himself] at the center of the world and for him the world is not homogeneous: for I am always alone in being able to answer the call, I am irreplaceable in my assumption of responsibility."[88]

Although Levinas does not reference Hermann Cohen here, he is following his interpretation of Judaism as messianic.[89] For the Jews to be messianic means for Cohen that their very existence outside the structure of nations (outside Hegelian history) provides for the nations a glimpse of a world beyond a politics of divisiveness. Levinas follows Cohen in the way in which he articulates messianism as a noncoercive universalism. Unlike Cohen, however, he presents the Jews as messianic, not by virtue of their exemplarity, but rather as a consequence of their ethics, which "consists in serving the universe."[90]

This is not to say that Levinas has not also produced his vision of Judaism as exemplary. His project to present Judaism as an alternative to paganism and Christianity amounts to charging it with another form of universalism, one that is in some ways proselytizing, despite his claims to the contrary. In many of his postwar essays, he presents Judaism as a model worthy of emulation. The passive and estranged Jewish people, left behind by the march of history, are recast as its moral exemplars by virtue of their alienation. They are called to this role because they were set apart from a world that developed in such a way that it could call for their destruction.

---

87. As Paul Mendes-Flohr notes in "Between Existentialism and Zionism: A Non-Philippic Credo," this is a tactic that has marked liberal Judaism since its inception. Abraham Geiger used similar rhetoric to negotiate the charge of particularism levied at Jews in the Enlightenment, writing that Israel "never lost the awareness that it embraced all of mankind and that its labors were on behalf of humanity as a whole." See Mendes-Flohr, *Divided Passions*, 427 (where Geiger is quoted).

88. Levinas, *Difficile liberté*, 247, and *Difficult Freedom*, 176–77.

89. The influence of Cohen on Levinas may have come by way of Jacob Gordin, who studied with Cohen's disciples in Berlin and became influential in Jewish intellectual circles in Paris after the war by giving seminars on medieval Jewish thought and teaching at Robert Gamzon's École Gilbert Bloch, also known as the École d'Orsay. Gordin was himself deeply influenced by Cohen's messianism and the role he assigned to the Jewish Diaspora. Levinas credits Gordin as an influence on his own thinking. See Friedlander, *Vilna on the Seine*, 120; and Levinas, *Difficile liberté*, 238, and *Difficult Freedom*, 169.

90. Levinas, *Difficile liberté*, 136, and *Difficult Freedom*, 95.

## Judaism as Model

Levinas's presentation of Judaism works with rather than against the anti-Semitic charges levied at Judaism during the nineteenth century and the first half of the twentieth. With the advent of the Nazi Party, Jews who had accepted the critiques of Judaism as "a dead religion"[91] or as a "closed system of morality,"[92] as an intransigence, an obstinancy,[93] and a materialism,[94] found themselves faced in the Second World War with the reality that "the monstrosity of Hitlerism could be produced in an evangelized Europe." The Jews, in response, Levinas reports, "began to believe that their stiff-necks were the most metaphysical part of their anatomy."[95] In other words, the Holocaust provoked the sense that the very reasons for which the Jews were targeted as the enemy might, in fact, be the same reasons why Judaism has something to offer to the modern West. Given that the West's own recourses had failed to avert the catastrophe, Judaism might now finally function as a positive exemplar.

Judaism was, thus, to serve as a model by which a world that had lost its moral compass might reorient itself. This claim was itself a part of a larger movement on the part of the postwar Jewish intellectual community in France and was in many ways an extension of the prewar work of the Alliance israélite universelle. With 75 percent of its population intact, the Jewish community of France was the only Jewish body in Europe in a position to revive Jewish thought and culture there. There was a sense among the Jewish intellectuals in

91. One of the roles of the Wissenschaft des Judentums in Germany was, according to its early pioneers, to give Judaism "a decent burial" since it was already on its way to the grave. For more on the moribund approach of the Wissenschaft movement, see Gerschom Scholem, "The Science of Judaism—Then and Now," in *The Messianic Idea in Judaism*. The phrase "a dead religion" is attributed to Moritz Steinschneider, but similar sentiments are attributed to the movement's founder, Leopold Zunz.

92. Despite Bergson's admiration for the prophets, this is the terminology that he uses to characterize Judaism, contrasting it with Christianity, which he characterizes as open and, thus, spiritual. See Henri Bergson, *Les deux sources de la morale et de la religion* (Paris: F. Alcan, 1937), 256–57, translated by R. Ashley Audra and Cloudesly Brereton as *The Two Sources of Morality and Religion* (Notre Dame, IN: Notre Dame University Press, 1977), 240–41.

93. This is the language characteristic of Bernard Lazare's own depictions of Judaism in *L'antisémitisme*. See particularly the final chapter, "Les destinées de l'antisémitisme" (*L'antisémitisme*, 190–99, and *Antisemitism*, 175–83).

94. "Let us look for the secret of the Jew not in his religion, but let us look for the secret of religion in the actual Jew. What is the secular basis of Judaism? Practical need selfishness. What is the secular cult of the Jew? Haggling. What is his secular God, Money" (Karl Marx, "Zur Judenfrage," in *Werke*, 4 vols. [Berlin: Dietz, 1975], 1:375, translated in *Karl Marx: Selected Writings*, ed. David McLellan [Oxford: Oxford University Press, 2000], 66).

95. Levinas, *Difficile liberté*, 225–26, and *Difficult Freedom*, 161.

the two decades following the war that this was not merely a responsibility they owed to world Jewry but a responsibility they owed to the world.[96]

One center of activity was the École d'Orsay, an institution established by Robert Gamzon, the founder of the Éclaireurs israélite de France after the war to educate young Jews about the history of their culture and to train them to act as ambassadors to the rest of the world.[97] Under the influence of Gamzon and Jacob Gordin, a devoted group gathered to study and revive the Jewish tradition, to reinvest in "the riches of Midrash and Jewish Mysticism," and to develop what Levinas called "an ambitious Judaism."[98] Later, a number of the same intellectuals met at the annual conferences of the Colloque des intellectuels juifs de langue française to synthesize Jewish learning and ideas with the philosophical and literary traditions of modern Europe.[99]

Levinas participated in this movement through his work for the Alliance israélite universelle, as the director of the École normale israélite orientale (ENIO), a position he took up in 1946, as well as through the Talmud readings that he gave at meetings of the Colloque. As a continuation of the prewar mission of the Alliance, those advocating revival continued to speak of Judaism's universal importance and its compatibility with French republicanism. The relationship between these two entities, however, had shifted. Rather than acting as an agent of France, spreading the nation's enlightened values to Jews worldwide, as they had before the war, it was the message of Judaism that was now "called to play an eminent role in the world not only in the countries where the *Alliance* cultivated minds, but everywhere." In his commemoration of the hundredth anniversary of the Alliance, Levinas thus exhorted his own institution to develop a more active sense of mission in the face of a modern civilization still operating according to the principles of aggression and acquisition. Undergirding this claim was criticism of the relativism that Levinas saw emerging in the vacuum that followed from Europe's fall from eminence. "The ancient forms of universality, the French and the Jewish, don't they have any special virtue? . . . Aren't

96. See the remarks of Edmond Fleg and others at the first meeting of the Colloque des intellectuels juifs de langue française in Congrès juif mondial, *La conscience juive* (Paris: Presses universitaires de France, 1963).

97. For the most comprehensive account of the school, see *Pardès: Revue européene d'études et de culture juive*, vol. 23 (1997).

98. Levinas, *Difficile liberté*, 237, and *Difficult Freedom*, 169.

99. See also Shmuel Trigano, "The Jews and the Spirit of Europe: A Morphological Approach," in *Thinking about the Holocaust After Half a Century*, ed. Alvin H. Rosenfeld (Bloomington: Indiana University Press, 1997), 309.

certain civilizations teachers in relation to others? Isn't anything in this world still classic?" he asked.[100]

Levinas invokes Judaism in the address as a civilization whose texts and traditions have lessons to teach the world. But what lessons are these? Is the very possibility of being "a summit" in the history of the world, as Levinas says in the speech, at odds with his characterization of Judaism as "resistant to power"?[101] What would it mean to take up the mantle of this position? By definition can it be taken up? The inconsistencies that mark Levinas's own essays on Judaism attest to the fact that these were questions that haunted and frustrated his effort to argue for the importance of Judaism as a voice on the political scene.

In some texts, *Judaism* seems to refer to a concept rather than a tradition. In "Être juif," Levinas proclaims the human soul "perhaps naturally Jewish."[102] In *Difficult Freedom*, he describes Jewishness as a moral disposition "rather than a historical fact."[103] In a number of his talmudic readings, he insists against a great deal of evidence that the term *Israel* refers, not to a particular people, but to "the humanity of the human."[104] He elaborates elsewhere: "Each time Israel is mentioned in the Talmud one is certainly free to understand by it a particular ethnic group which is probably fulfilling an incomparable destiny. But to interpret in this manner would be to reduce the general principle in the idea enunciated in the Talmud passage, to forget that Israel means a people who have received the law and, as a result, a human nature which has reached the fullness of its responsibility and self-consciousness."[105] Judaism is, thus, presented as a universal idea, a category that would seem to be open to anyone. It would appear to be a universalism, not only in the weak sense that Jewish messianism is a concern for the unity of all people, but also in the strong sense that it is disassociated from a people, a race, an ethnicity.

This definition is consistent with Levinas's claims that Judaism is essentially freedom from the dogma of rootedness that characterizes the determinism of thinkers like Barrès. It is not, of course, consistent with the halachic conception of Judaism, which defines the Jew according to

100. Levinas, "L'École normale israélite orientale: Perspectives d'avenir," in *Les droits de l'homme et l'éducation: Actes du Congrès du centenaire*, ed. Alliance israélite universelle (Paris: Presses universitaires de France, 1961), 75, 79.

101. Ibid., 79.

102. Levinas, "Être juif," 103.

103. Levinas, *Difficile liberté*, 39, and *Difficult Freedom*, 22.

104. Emmanuel Levinas, *A l'heure des nations* (Paris: Minuit, 1988), 97, translated by Michael B. Smith as *In the Time of the Nations* (Bloomington: Indiana University Press, 1994), 84.

105. Emmanuel Levinas, "Judaïsme et revolution," in *Jeunesse et revolution dans la conscience juive: Données et débats*, ed. J. Halpérin et G. Lévitte (Paris: Presses universitaires de France, 1972), 62, translated in *Nine Talmudic Readings*, 98.

matrilineal descent. It departs radically even from Rosenzweig's conception of Judaism as a "community of blood."[106]

The principle that allows Levinas to make such an audacious claim is disclosed in the opening chapter of *Beyond the Verse*:

As a prophetic moment of human reason where every man—and all of man—end up refinding one another, Judaism would not mean simply a nationality, a species in a type and a contingency of History. Judaism, rather, is a rupture of the natural and historical that are constantly reconstituted and thus a Revelation which is always forgotten. It is written and it becomes Bible, but the revelation is also continued; it is produced in the guise of Israel: the destiny of a people that is jostled and jostles through its daily life that which, in this life, is content with its natural or "historical" meaning.[107]

As "a prophetic moment of human reason," Judaism is defined here philosophically as the moment of reason that takes place between men and founds discourse. Israel is, thus, the people who remain faithful to the truth of an interpersonal moment and disclose it to the world through their persistent existence outside the security of political power and its accompanying sedentary life. According to this definition, it would be possible to remain faithful to this revelation without being a part of the people Israel. Could we suppose, then, that, each time the duty to the other man is revealed in its absolute exigency, Judaism appears—appears as the revelation of the other man? In much of his writing, Levinas seems devoted to this possibility.

Judaism is described in this passage from *Beyond the Verse* in terms quite similar to those Levinas uses to present prophetic eschatology in the preface to *Totality and Infinity*. Judaism here, like prophetic eschatology, is playing the role of that which ruptures the natural and the historical. On the basis of this passage, we might, in fact, assume that the terms *Judaism* and *prophetic eschatology* can be used interchangeably. The function of prophetic eschatology in *Totality and Infinity* is, of course, to serve as a metaphor for the face. The face is developed as that which plays the same role phenomenologically as eschatology plays in relation to history: "Without substituting eschatology for philosophy, without philosophically 'demonstrating' eschatological 'truths,' we can proceed from the experience of totality back to the situation where totality breaks

106. Rosenzweig, *Der Stern der Erlösung*, 331, and *The Star of Redemption*, 299.

107. Emmanuel Levinas, *L'au-delà du verset* (Paris: Minuit, 1982), 18, translated by Gary D. Mole as *Beyond the Verse* (Bloomington: Indiana University Press, 1994), 4.

up, a situation that conditions the totality itself. Such a situation is the gleam of exteriority or of transcendence in the face of the Other."[108]

By way of these two passages, we can see that, for Levinas, there is inevitably an analogy between Judaism and the face. Described phenomenologically, both Judaism and the face appear as interruption. This interruption is evoked as the demand for justice, which, more concretely, is the demand that the revelation of the face not be effaced. Levinas represents Judaism as the interruption itself and as the tradition of loyalty to the interruption of the face. But is it possible to remain faithful to "a revelation that is always forgotten," to a rupture in the historical and the natural, to that which by its very nature would seem resistant to appearing?

Insofar as the face is the interruption of intentionality, it is also that which resists thematization, for thematization is the mode of intentionality. As Derrida has argued in "Violence and Metaphysics," the dynamic that Levinas has set up in *Totality and Infinity* between the face and intentional reason—and, by analogy, between Judaism and history— puts him in the position of trying to signify a revelation that is opposed to ontology with the tools of ontology.[109] In using the term *revelation*, he is already returning to the notion that something is uncovered, that it appears. Although Levinas has argued for the face as that which escapes the structures of illumination and manifestation characteristic of philosophy from Plato to Heidegger, he nonetheless cannot avoid the terminology of illumination in his own description of the face. This is evident in the essay "Philosophy and the Idea of Infinity," when he writes: "By its apparition, its epiphany [*son épiphanie*] it opposes all my powers. Its epiphany is not simply the apparition of a form in the light, sensible or intelligible, but already of this *no* cast to powers."[110] The term *epiphany* here signals the struggle within Levinas's own language to escape the language of light while still being indebted to it. As a reference to Epiphany (the festival of Twelfth Night), it refers to a revelation that occurs in darkness, which is fitting given Levinas's schema. Yet, even here, light is symbolic of revelation, as Christ's birth is communicated through the appearance of a star.[111] Furthermore, the term *epiphany*, from the Greek *epiphaneia*, meaning "manifestation" or "showing," exposes Levinas's

---

108. Levinas, *Totalité et infini*, 9, and *Totality and Infinity*, 24.

109. Derrida, *L'écriture et la différence*, 125–37, and *Writing and Difference*, 84–92.

110. Emmanuel Levinas, "La philosophie et l'idée de l'infini," in *En découvrant l'existence avec Husserl et Heidegger*, 240, translated as "Philosophy and the Idea of Infinity" in Adriaan Peperzak, *To the Other* (West Lafayette, IN: Purdue University Press, 1993), 109.

111. Matt. 2:2.

dependence on the language and structures of appearance. Thus, in response to this tension in Levinas's work, Derrida asks: "How . . . will the metaphysics of the face as *epiphany* of the other free itself of light? Light perhaps has no opposite; if it does, it is certainly not night."[112]

While his analysis exposes Levinas as trapped by his own tools of analysis, Derrida also discloses another way of reading his methodology and, thus, another way of understanding what he is pursuing with his definition of Judaism. According to this reading, Levinas would be, not claiming to speak a language untainted by philosophy, but rather attempting to expose what cannot appear to philosophy by revealing in philosophy its rigidity and its resistance to that which threatens it. As Derrida puts it: "The unthinkable truth of living experience, to which Levinas returns ceaselessly, cannot possibly be encompassed by philosophical speech without revealing, by philosophy's own light, that philosophy's surface is severely cracked, and that what was taken for its solidity is its rigidity. It could doubtless be shown that it is in the nature of Levinas's writing, at its decisive moments, to move along these cracks, masterfully progressing by negations, and by negation against negation. Its proper route is not that of an 'either this . . . or that,' but of a 'neither this . . . nor that.'"[113] Following this model, we can understand Levinas's descriptions of Judaism to function similarly. When Judaism is understood as a rupture of history, its meaning can be sought in the very moments when it is denigrated. Levinas says as much when he defines Israel in *Beyond the Verse* as "the destiny of a people that is jostled and jostles through its daily life that which, in this life, is content with its natural or 'historical' meaning."[114] Israel's meaning and purpose are defined here by its relation to the natural and the historical. Judaism would seem to appear in and through the persecution of Israel. If Levinas inaugurates in his writings a return to Judaism conceived as interruption, the manifestation of that return would consist in a repetition of the tropes of its denigration.[115] The way to seek the meaning of Judaism and to uncover its

112. Derrida, *L'écriture et la différence*, 137, and *Writing and Difference*, 92.
113. Ibid., 134; 90.
114. Levinas, *L'au-delà du verset*, 18, and *Beyond the Verse*, 4.
115. Following this model, we can understand Levinas to be pursuing a method of thinking different in aim but similar in method to Heidegger's early phenomenological hermeneutics, where the task is to develop a strategy for confronting, in place of a stable object of cognition, a fundamental existential and temporal "questionableness" (*Fraglichkeit*). This latter strategy is guided, not by a thematized concept of what is in question, but by a provisional "indication" that both prevents predetermined notions from entering into interpretation and opens access to the questionableness being pursued. Is it possible that Levinas's "concept" or "formal indication" of Judaism itself functions according to a similar procedure? As Derrida points out as well, there is also a repetition, on Levinas's part, of Heidegger's operation in *Sein und Zeit*, in the very claim that, in Judaism, we are seeking out

potential to serve as a model would not be through a historical analysis of its positive forms; rather, we would seek the meaning of Judaism in the very places where it appears only as that which "jostles" against that which is "content in its natural or historical meaning."[116]

We must, consequently, ask what happens to the *tradition* of Judaism in this analysis. Has Levinas dispensed with it? Does not his reduction of the term *Judaism* to an "interruption" denigrate the way of life and the set of practices and beliefs that have accompanied the Jewish people? This question points us toward a fundamental tension in Levinas's writings on Judaism. In his philosophical texts, it is clear that his method is phenomenological (even insofar as its aim exceeds phenomenology). Thus, the revelation of the face does not depend on tradition; it is not revealed by way of Judaism. That said, there is the argument in *Totality and Infinity* that the "thinking of the West" records the history of the way in which this revelation has been covered over by a tradition of "egology," a thinking of the same. But there is no explicit claim made, in *Totality and Infinity* at least, that we can locate a parallel tradition that would carry the message of "ethics." We have assumed thus far that the writings on Judaism fulfill this function, however the definition of *religion* in *Totality and Infinity* calls into question the possibility that *any* tradition could by definition be faithful to this message. In *Totality and Infinity*, the revelation of the face is called *religion*, but *religion* here represents, not a lineage, but an encounter. *Religion*, in fact, would seem to represent that which could not be maintained by "tradition," insofar as tradition is, by definition, the reception of an idea in history, its thematization. "The difference between 'to appear in history' . . . and to appear to the Other while attending one's apparition distinguishes again my political being from my religious being," Levinas writes in *Totality and Infinity*.[117] We can read this statement in one of two ways. Either no tradition can claim to constitute religion for Levinas, or only Judaism can make such a claim. Judaism would, thus, by definition be that tradition that does not appear in history. If we assume that Levinas is using the term *history* in its purely Hegelian sense, then we might accept the possibility of Judaism as the ahistorical tradition. However, such a reading sorely complicates our capacity to engage Judaism in its positive form as

---

something originary that has consistently been covered over. If Lyotard's question in *Heidegger and "the jews"* is how Heidegger could have missed what was more originary and radical than the question of being, might not we ask conversely how Levinas could pursue his object by following the very path that he seems so interested in critiquing.

116. Levinas, *L'au-delà du verset*, 18, and *Beyond the Verse*, 4.

117. Levinas, *Totalité et infini*, 283, and *Totality and Infinity*, 253.

a living complex and contingent tradition and still read it as conforming to Levinas's own definition.

Perhaps the ambiguity in Levinas's definition is a product of what it means to be the people Israel. Israel has attested in its history to the possibility of passivity; it has experienced the suffering that arises from its relation to the nations; its very history attests to the possibility of a meaning that is not garnered by victory. But what impact does this historical attestation have on the status of Judaism? It would seem to confine the term to those who had, in fact, experienced the suffering that accompanied being part of the people Israel. Yet, as we have seen, Levinas so often argues for Israel as a name for all people. Some scholars want to hold him to a universalizing definition. Others argue that he did not go far enough toward establishing the exceptional role of election for the Jewish people.[118] Annabel Herzog claims that Levinas moves from a particularizing definition of Judaism in his early work toward embracing universalism in his later work.[119] However, this interpretation ignores the tension inherent even in *Beyond the Verse* (1981), where Levinas is dogged by an inability to clearly differentiate the universal from the particular. Samuel Moyn argues that his definition of Judaism always refers to a universal.[120] In fact, what we find in Levinas's philosophy and confessional writings from the 1940s forward is an oscillation between these two possibilities. Rather than a trend toward one path or another, his writing exhibits an inherent tension between these two tendencies. We can locate in this indecision on the topic of Judaism signs of an instability at the very center of his thought, one that threatens its coherence, endangering most profoundly the idea that Levinas painstakingly began building from the 1930s forward: the claim that Judaism offers the world a teaching of uprooting.

## Judaism as Tradition or Judaism as Idea

In Levinas's talmudic readings, as well as in his occasional pieces, which cover a range of topics from Jewish identity to the politics of the state of Israel and the future of Jewish education, the universalized account is adduced alongside the more traditional notions that the Jews are a people, that to be a Jew is to be born into a tradition, and that with

118. Benny Lévy, *Être juif: Étude lévinassienne* (Paris: Verdier, 2003), 19.
119. See Herzog, "Benny Levy versus Emmanuel Levinas."
120. Moyn, "Judaism against Paganism."

that tradition comes a set of practices involving an adherence to law and study.[121]

In some cases, Levinas seems to want to uphold all these possibilities simultaneously. In the dedication to *Otherwise Than Being*, for example, he writes (in French): "To the memory of those who were closest among the six million assassinated by the National Socialists, and of the millions of all confessions and all nations, victims of the same hatred of the other man, the same anti-Semitism." Here, anti-Semitism is defined universally in such a way that we can also infer that the Jew is defined consequentially as "the other man."[122] However, below this dedication is another one, this one in Hebrew. In it, the book is again devoted to those who were closest to Levinas among the six million, but here he spells out who they are, calling them by name, devoting the book more precisely to his father, mother, brothers, and parents-in-law. In Hebrew, he excludes the addition that universalizes Judaism, opening it up to all confessions and nations. The fact of this doubled dedication reminds us that the text itself is addressed to two different audiences: those from within the Jewish community, who can decode the dedication, and all the others who cannot.

Within the text itself, the terms that phenomenologically mark Jewish identity in Levinas's explicitly Jewish essays are transferred to the ethical subject. While this can clearly be read as a universalization of Judaism, there is also a sense in which this act maintains the doubling of the dedication. Levinas goes to greater lengths in this text to obscure the biblical references and images that so often mark his philosophy, yet they remain submerged, just below the surface, available to the reader who can interpret their significance, especially the reader who recognizes these terms from the confessional writings themselves. Referring to the origin of the subject in an experience of exile, Levinas writes: "There is expulsion in that it assigns me before I show myself, before I set myself up. I am assigned without recourse, without fatherland [*sans patrie*], already sent back to myself but without being able to stay there, compelled before commencing." The use of the term *patrie* recalls the reader to the paradigm of Genesis 12, but Abraham's name is effaced from the model. Elsewhere, what is explicitly referred to as "the Jewish tradition" in the confessional essays is here named merely "the concept of creation *ex nihilo*," which is contrasted with "Western thought."[123] This

121. See Levinas, *Difficile liberté*, 78–85, and *Difficult Freedom*, 50–53.
122. See also Peperzak, "Emmanuel Levinas," 297.
123. Levinas, *Autrement qu'être*, 163, 179–80, and *Otherwise Than Being*, 103, 113–14.

substitution of terms is consistent with the aim of universalizing Jewish structures in order to show that they in fact name universal human modalities; however, read in light of the dedication, the very obscuring of straightforwardly Judaic terminology can also cement the notion that there are two echelons of readers for which the text is intended.

The doubling between the confessional writings and the philosophy is further complicated by a duplicity within the confessional writings themselves where Judaism is at once defined in a way that would make it expansive and as that which can be invoked only by way of what Levinas often referred to as "those square letters." Insofar as he adhered to the second definition, Levinas insisted on the centrality of the Talmud for Jewish life and on the practices of interpretation central to Talmud study, rejecting, thus, the confessional definition of Judaism that become dominant in France after the revolution. Judaism was to be understood, not as a set of beliefs that mark a form of adherence, but as a commitment to a set of practices, foremost of which was the commitment to the reading and interpretation of Jewish texts.

His emphasis on this revival made Levinas key to a movement of Jewish community building in France. He came to the Talmud late in life, despite his Orthodox upbringing and his knowledge of Hebrew; he began reading and studying the Talmud only when he was already in his forties through his relationship with Chouchani, the mysterious teacher whom Levinas credits as the inspiration for much that he wrote on the Talmud.[124] Nonetheless, despite his lack of training with these texts, despite his inexperience, it is safe to say that, for a whole generation of French intellectuals, Levinas served as the interpreter of the rabbinic corpus and, ultimately, of Judaism. In his years as director of the ENIO, he influenced the school's curriculum by introducing into it traditional text study. Saturdays were marked out for what were called *les cours Rachi*: sessions of Talmud and midrash study with the occasional reference

124. "What I myself have written in my *Talmudic Lectures* has been written in the shadow of his shadow. It was this postwar encounter that reactivated my latent—I might even say dormant—interest in the Judaic tradition," Levinas said in an interview of his relationship to Chouchani. See Levinas, "Emmanuel Levinas and Richard Kearney," 18. Levinas's Talmud teacher remains something of an enigma to scholars. He was a prodigy, and a vagabond, who never revealed his true identity and traveled from place to place offering his wisdom. An unparalleled expert in Jewish thought, with a mastery of physics and mathematics as well, he escaped internment, legend has it, during the war by challenging a Nazi officer with a math problem that he could not solve. Levinas mentions him rarely by name, and the facts of his existence are difficult to sort out. Elie Wiesel, who also studied with him, has been more forthcoming about his personality and impact. See Elie Wiesel, *Le chant des morts, nouvelles* (Paris: Seuil, 1966), 119–44; and Elie Wiesel, *Paroles d'étranger* (Paris: Seuil, 1982), 108–13. See also Salomon Malka, *Monsieur Chouchani: L'enigma d'un maître du XXᵉ siècle* (Paris: J. C. Lattès, 1994). For the impact of Chouchani on Levinas, see Shmuel Wygoda, "Le maître et son disciple: Chouchani et Levinas," *Cahiers d'études lévinassiennes* 1 (2002): 149–83.

to Immanuel Kant thrown in for good measure. These lessons became a rite of passage for the Parisian Jewish community, drawing a group of regulars from the community who hung on Levinas's every word.[125] Levinas's more formal Talmud readings were given at yearly meetings of the Colloque des inellectuels juifs de langue française. He used these occasions to encourage France's Jewish intellectuals and Jewish students to return to the Hebrew texts. A return to the reading practices of the rabbis, he argued, could reinvigorate Judaism. "It is through reading," he wrote, "that references take on reality; through reading in a way, we come to inhabit a place. The volume of the book can provide the *espace vital*! In this sense too the people of Israel are the people of the Book, whose relationship to the Revelation is unique."[126]

Judaism, Levinas argued on these occasions, was not about belief but about participating in a tradition of text reading. It is striking in his discussion of the Jew's relation to the text how often he uses the language of homecoming and dwelling. He refers to the text as a "place to inhabit." Given his resistance to the language of homecoming in his ethics, his insistence that ethical subjectivity is fundamentally uprooting, it is surprising to see him thinking of the text as a place of Jewish belonging. It is the rabbinic respect for polysemy and the surplus of meaning engendered by respecting the plurivocity of the biblical text that make it so hospitable. The Bible and the Talmud show themselves to be divinely inspired because they have the power to inspire new responses in their readers. In their polyvalence, they can support multiple interpretations and can be infinitely renewed. They illuminate the present, and the present can illuminate in them possibilities and meanings that burst forth or ignite when reinvigorated by the breath of a new reader.

Levinas aligned his theory concerning scripture's hospitality with his philosophy by suggesting that the Jewish conception of revelation correlated with his own validation of "the saying"—the capacity of language to enact a relationship between people—over the "said," language's discursive meaning. Rabbinic interpretation reinvigorated the spoken word. It emphasized the potential for speech to affirm the face-to-face encounter between two people. This was something that Levinas saw particularly in the yeshiva practice of reading out loud and working as a *havruta*, in pairs.

---

125. Lescourret, *Emmanuel Levinas*, 140; Salomon Malka, *La vie et la trace* (Paris: Albin Michel, 2005), 120–21.

126. Levinas, *L'au-delà du verset*, 159, and *Beyond the Verse*, 130 (translation slightly altered).

That said, Levinas's various statements about hermeneutics also expose the inherent tensions in his vision of Judaism. In his own talmudic readings, he is not able to offer textual interpretations consistent with his argument for plurivocity. One of the ways in which the plurivocity of the talmudic or midrashic text reveals itself is in the move to preserve dissenting opinions. One common midrashic trope is that opinions of Hillel and Shammai, two opposing patriarchs of the Sanhedrin, are both the words of the living God, a statement that amounts to saying that truth is itself plural.[127] While Levinas lauds this vision in theory, his own talmudic readings betray it when they insist on construing Judaism as an idea whose truth is universally accessible.

Levinas ends up making the argument in the talmudic readings that the universal message is, not one possible reading among many, but the *primary* meaning, the philosophical core buried beneath a multifaceted surface. The model that he invokes ends up looking ironically much like Kant's in *Religion within the Limits* or Maimonides' in the *Guide to the Perplexed*, where a hierarchy of meaning prioritizes the philosophical truth. Philosophical meaning is cloaked or buried by an outward mythology. Scripture's truth is arrived at, not by discovering its seventy faces of meaning, but in the location of the text's philosophical core.

This is evident already in the introduction to Levinas's *Four Talmudic Readings*. The claim in the introduction is that the Talmud harbors philosophical arguments but hides them in "apologues" and "adages" that require the philosopher's reformulation: "A Talmudic text does not belong to 'edifying discourse' even though this literary genre is one of the forms that its proper form can take on [*emprunter*] when it degenerates. But one can retrieve the initial design of its force, even when it is enveloped and made more palatable by thoughts that want only to be pious." The truth can be recovered through rubbing and digging, Levinas suggests, in images that recall Heidegger's own metaphors of destruction. The consequence of this mode of reading is that it reduces polyvalence to a vehicle. It makes of the text's opacity a nut to be cracked, an occasion for clarification. Consequently, in readings such as "Judaism and Revolution," a mishnaic passage that discusses whether fair practices of payment should be derived from a general principle or from the custom of the land shows itself to be a text that "reveals that the other man's right is practically an infinite right." In his discussion of Tractate Shabbat 88a 88b, on Exod. 19:17, a midrash that appears to be a commendation of the Israelites for their absolute

127. Babylonian Talmud, Eruvin 13b.

obedience to God's commandments, an obedience that precedes understanding, is reread to reveal a Levinasean lesson: "The Torah is given in the light of a face. The epiphany of an other person is ipso facto my responsibility toward him: seeing the other is already an obligation toward him."[128]

One of the payoffs of this mode of interpretation for Levinas is that, like the sun over a thin layer of clouds, it burns off the particularism of these texts, making visible the underlying universal message. As a consequence of these readings, Judaism appears as a message that can and must speak to every man. Levinas is often at pains to make this point, particularly when the Talmud itself seems to be distinguishing between the rights owed to the people Israel and the rights owed to the stranger. He insists that Israel in fact stands for "every man." The problem is, of course, that his philosophical model of reading Talmud forces him to make statements that are at odds with his own validation of the plurivocity of the scriptural text.

This inconsistency is a consequence of Levinas's attempt to protect his own interpretation as foundational and fundamental, but it reveals the tension between his building up the Jewish community and his impulse to universalize the category of Judaism. When he emphasizes the plurivocity of the text, Levinas consistently speaks of the renewal of the Jewish people. In these passages, there is no mention of the universalization of Judaism. When he universalizes the category, he also deemphasizes the text's plurivocity, prioritizing its philosophical essence. As Moshe Halbertal has shown, the emphasis on rabbinic plurivocity goes hand in hand with other strategies of policing the border of the community. Without a clear demarcation of who has the authority to engage in interpretation, the principle of interpretive openness threatens to disrupt community cohesion.[129] Conversely, Levinas's universalization of Judaism can function meaningfully only if agreement can be established concerning the tradition's core teachings. Otherwise, there can be no clear criteria for association or identification.

Another site where the doubling of Levinas's definitions of Judaism is clearly problematic is in his writings on Zionism. Given his insistence that Judaism's message to the world arises out of its rejection of the pagan attachment to land, its incompatibility with the Hegelian narrative of a history of nation-states, and its general aversion to a politics

128. Levinas, *Quatre lectures talmudiques*, 13, 103–4, and *Nine Talmudic Readings*, 4, 47.

129. Moshe Halbertal, *People of the Book*: *Canon, Meaning and Authority* (Cambridge, MA: Harvard University Press, 1997), 7.

of aggression, it might seem surprising that, after World War II, Levinas developed a position of support for the Zionist project.

The establishment of the Jewish state after the Second World War is first and foremost justified for Levinas as a venture brought about by historical necessity. Such a justification would seem to free the Zionist project from any dogma about the essence of Judaism.[130] Levinas could, consequently, have chosen to separate his support of Israel from his philosophical project.[131] He might equally have claimed that, if the name *Judaism* points toward a universal, if it is detached from the particularism of tradition and ethnicity, then the establishment of the state of Israel is no more problematic than the establishment of any state. The teachings of Judaism would serve as a check equally on Israel and every other nation. But Levinas's approach is, on the contrary, to argue for Judaism as the possibility of the actualization of a prophetic politics in history.[132]

Because of Levinas's definition of Judaism as a demand for justice, for a politics that would be the antithesis of nationalism, he comes to treat the establishment of the state of Israel as *the* possibility for such a politics rather than as a betrayal of Judaism. Given the realities of the structure of the state, its official differentiation between Arab and Jew, the establishment of the right of return, and the forced exile of a native people, this distinction seems empirically difficult to support. Levinas is, of course, aware of the discrepancy between his descriptions of Israel and Israel's reality and often tries to mobilize the gap between the ideal and the very real Israel to demand more of its politics: "At the heart of daily conflicts, the living experience of the government—and even the painful necessities of the occupation—allow lessons as yet untaught to be detected in the ancient Revelation. Is a monotheistic politics a contradiction in terms? Or on the contrary, is this the very culmination of Zionism? Beyond the concern to ensure a refuge for those who are persecuted,

---

130. When asked by François Poiré in 1986 what the existence of the state of Israel meant for him, Levinas replies that, under given circumstances, the state was the only condition under which the people and the culture of Israel could survive. See François Poirié, *Qui êtes-vous?* (Lyons: La manufacture, 1987), 135. This is a surprising response given his frequent and adamant claims that the existence of Israel represents the promise of a truly just state.

131. Levinas's stance toward Zionism clearly shifts as a consequence of World War II. The term *Zionism* does not even appear in his prewar writings, but a position of support for the movement before the war is evidently in conflict with his vision of Judaism as a resistance to politics. His mature position of support for Zionism is, thus, clearly a consequence of his struggle to square his vision of Judaism with the necessary reality of the state of Israel. For a detailed chronology of the development of Levinas's position, see Françoise Mies, "Levinas et le sionisme (1906–1952)," in *Levinas à Jerusalem*, ed. Jöelle Hansel (Paris: Klincksieck, 2007), 207–28.

132. Caygill, *Levinas and the Political*, 170.

is this not the main task?" At the same time, however, the claim that Israel represents a true adventure, the possibility of an ethical politics, leads him often to excuse some of the state's less righteous actions, to twist his own categories so that they apply to Israel. If the Jew represents the persecuted person in many of Levinas's writings, Israel comes to represent the persecuted state: "An armed and dominating State, one of the great military powers of the Mediterranean basin, against the unarmed Palestinian people whose existence Israel doesn't recognize! Is that the real state of affairs? In its very real strength is not Israel also the most fragile, the most vulnerable thing in the world, in the midst of its neighbors, undisputed nations, rich in natural allies, and surrounded by their lands? Lands, lands and lands, as far as the eye can see."[133]

Levinas thus borrows from his representation of Judaism as the persecuted people par excellence in order to imbue the state of Israel with an analogous status. He praises Zionism, writing: "Its inalienable idea is the necessity for the Jewish people, in peace with its neighbors, not to continue being a minority in its political structure . . . in order for the attack and murder of Jews in the world to lose their character of an uncontrollable and unpunished phenomenon."[134] This description from the opening of *Beyond the Verse* (1982) would seem to starkly oppose the definition of Judaism as that which resists the politics of nations, for it suggests that Judaism must, indeed, reshape itself as a nation among nations. We can assume that this represents a shift in Levinas's own political sensibilities, and it may, in fact, represent a shift in the general zeitgeist of French Jews, who became more vocally pro-Zionist and communitarian after the Six-Day War.[135] However, it also points toward the inevitable conflict and hypocrisy that result from Levinas's attempts to hold together the real historical people of Israel with the ideal and universalizable idea of Israel. The definition of Judaism and the people Israel as carriers of a moral message ultimately serves as a justification for unconditional support of a state that has failed to embody the ideals ascribed to it. The way in which Levinas holds together the universal and particular definitions of Israel in his discussions of the state makes it exceptional for him, in both senses of the term. Israel represents the unique promise of prophetic politics. It consequently should be defended and protected even when its actions, if performed by another state, would warrant critique and sanction. In "The State of Israel and

---

133. Levinas, *L'au-delà du verset*, 220, 226, and *Beyond the Verse*, 187, 193.
134. Ibid., 14; xvii.
135. Trigano, "The Jews and the Spirit of Europe," 309.

the Religion of Israel," Levinas states: "The state of Israel will be religious because of the intelligence of its great books which it is not free to forget."[136] Then, in the preface to *Beyond the Verse*, he suggests that defending the state of Israel in its wars against the Arab peoples follows from the ethical teachings of the Bible: "I think that in the responsibility for others prescribed by a non-archaic monotheism, it [the Bible] reminds us that it should not be forgotten that *my* family and *my* people, despite the possessive pronouns, are my 'others,' like strangers, and demand justice and protection. The love of the other—the love of one's neighbor. Those near to me are also my neighbor." He even argues in this essay that, insofar as the burden of the Holocaust falls, not just on the West, but on every man, the Arab nations ought to take up that responsibility by offering their recognition to Israel.[137]

This is not to say that Levinas's vision of Israel cannot serve as a means for a strong and very concrete critique of the state of Israel. In a radio interview with Alain Finkielkraut and Salomon Malka after the revelation of the massacres at Sabra and Chatilla in 1982, Levinas plays it both ways. He insists that his own philosophy supports the defense of one's neighbor against one's enemy, thus defending Israel's actions in Lebanon, at least obliquely. On the other hand, he argues that events like those at Sabra and Chatilla risk putting, not only "our souls" in jeopardy, but also our books—"our books which carry us through history, and which, even more deeply than the earth are our support."[138] The logic here is the same. Because Israel is a Jewish state, it is held to the ethical standards that Levinas sees as instantiated in the Jewish canon. We must grant it an exceptional status for this reason. That status seems both to allow it more leeway and to demand of it more responsibility.

Insofar as Levinas applies his idealized conception of Judaism to the real political dynamics of Israeli politics, he can seem to resemble a religious Zionist, one who subordinates all other considerations to the enactment of a dream foreseen in the Bible.[139] He differentiates himself, however, from groups such as Gush Emunim by clearly distinguishing his dream from theirs. Gush Emunim and groups like it represent for him the danger that the Zionist project could lapse into a mysticism of land or a return to paganism. For Levinas, the Jewish dream is always one that subordinates the holiness of the land to the holiness of the

---

136. Levinas, *Difficile liberté*, 306, and *Difficult Freedom*, 219.

137. Levinas, *L'au-delà du verset*, 14 (quote), 13, and *Beyond the Verse*, xvii, xvi.

138. Emmanuel Levinas and Alain Finkielkraut, "Israël: Éthique et politique," *Les nouveaux cahiers* 18 (1983): 7, translated in *The Levinas Reader*, ed. Sean Hand (New York: Blackwell, 1989), 296.

139. Leora Batnitzky makes this argument in *Leo Strauss and Emmanuel Levinas*, 158.

person.[140] The question is whether the political project of state building can ever remain loyal to that insight.

The risks involved in Levinas's line of interpretation were recognized by some of his most loyal interpreters. Readers of Levinas tend to line up on one side or another of his definitions of Judaism, and, thus, their sense of whether and how he betrayed his own insights depends on which definition they see as primary. By virtue of the doubling in his interpretations of Judaism, Levinas is, in fact, the father of two lines of thought in France, both of which critique him for his duplicity. He is central to a movement within the Jewish community that involved a return to observance and strong support for the state of Israel.[141] He is also central to a philosophical trajectory that adopts his universal definition of Judaism as the principle of deracination and from that concept develops Judaism as a fundamentally anticommunitarian ideal.

When asked about his role as the leader of a movement back to tradition, Levinas demurred, saying that his own lack of training in rabbinic study disqualified him from such a position. He also showed hesitation about the very idea of return, suggesting that a renaissance of Judaism would come, not from repeating old texts, but from opening up new directions in Jewish thought.[142] Benny Lévy was one figure in the renaissance movement who saw Levinas as its spiritual father, but he argued that Levinas had not gone far enough toward reviving the classic forms

140. Levinas does not refer to this group of religious Zionists who began the settlers movement, justifying their action with the warrant that the Hebrew Bible ought to be the source of the boundaries of the nation-state of Israel, but he does conclude his interview with Malka and Finkielkraut with a warning against confusing Zionism with a mystique of "earth as native soil." See Levinas and Finkielkraut, "Israël," 8, and *The Levinas Reader*, 296.

141. Levinas is considered to be one of the key figures in the École juive de Paris (the name was coined by Levinas and Wladimir Rabi), a postwar movement charged with the renaissance of Judaism in Europe whose key figures also include Léon Askénazi, André Neher, and Elaine Amado-Levy-Valensi. Levinas is the only one of these figures who did not ultimately emigrate to Israel. His centrality to this movement of return is attested to by the changes he made to the curriculum of the École normale israélite orientale, where he served as director for thirty-three years. As a school organized under the supervision of the Alliance israélite universelle, it functioned in the second half of the nineteenth century to help train teachers to work with, and, thus, spread French values to, the North African Jewish communities, which were seen as primitive. Thus, it was not in its original function particularly a center for education in Jewish texts and Jewish modes of reading and study; that changed under Levinas. See Ami Bouganim, "Levinas pédagogue," in Alliance israélite universelle, *Emmanuel Levinas: Philosophe et pedagogue* (Paris, 1998). Some who attended those courses continued on in Jewish thought, among them Bouganim and Catherine Chalier. Levinas's influence in this capacity is also attested to by the interpretation of his work that is maintained by some of the contributors to the Institut d'études lévinassiennes, centered in Jerusalem, formerly run by Benny Lévy. At the same time, it is clear that Levinas resisted the return to literalism in French Judaism that accompanied the rise to prominence of the Sephardic Jewish community in France. Marie-Anne Lescourret reports that Levinas ended his participation in the French consistory system in 1989, the same year that it came under the control of that faction. See Lescourret, *Emmanuel Levinas*, 364.

142. Poirié, *Qui êtes-vous?* 136.

of Jewish life. He was inspired by Levinas's conception of being Jewish, but he was also critical of what he saw as Levinas's departure from this concept. According to Lévy's reading, Levinas's original and most profound insights are recorded in the 1947 text "Être juif." In an essay of his own that reprises the same title, Lévy reads Levinas "with Levinas in spite of Levinas."[143] He contends that Levinas's return to Judaism was initiated as a response to Sartre.[144] It arose, he contends, out of a confrontation with philosophy. Philosophy represents the point of entry, providing the initial impulse for *Teshuvah*.[145] Levinas, however, does not stay true to his own antiphilosophical impulse, nor does he complete his voyage of return. He is not faithful enough to Judaism as "science of Torah," as the faith of a historical people, as covenant.[146] Lévy recalls Levinas's own claim that to be Jewish is not to be able to escape from one's Jewishness and argues that Levinas's alteration of this Jewish paradigm into a philosophical model was itself a betrayal of that insight. In his writings on Judaism, Lévy claims, Levinas wrote for Jews, but, in his philosophy, he attempted to universalize the structures of Jewish life. In so doing "he chose the path of the philosophical conversion, the anti-return."[147]

For those of his readers who favor the universalizing impulse in his thought, the danger is that Levinas will raise Judaism up as a kind of exemplary model of justice, a model that in its very insistence on its exemplary status would betray its most basic insight: that justice begins in a movement out of oneself, in the act of being uprooted. The danger is that Levinas's Judaism could, in fact, become what it became for Benny Lévy, that it could become, in the terms of Jean-Luc Nancy and Philippe Lacoue-Labarthe, the antimythic myth, one that reestablishes the irremissibility of identity, revives the discourse of roots by insisting on the relation between Judaism's ideals and Judaism proper. The question for Blanchot and Derrida—whom among postwar thinkers Levinas counts as most influential on his own thought, perhaps because they are his most faithful and exacting readers—is whether Levinas's own thought provides the resources to maintain its attentiveness to its most radical insights. Can Levinas teach us, despite his prevalent statements

143. Lévy, "Commentaire d'"Être juif,'" 19.
144. Lévy is, thus, drawing a parallel between his own experience and Levinas's. For Lévy too claims that it was his exposure to Sartre and his conversations with Sartre about Judaism that turned him back toward Judaism. Thus, in recounting Levinas's return, he downplays Heidegger's influence in order to establish the symmetry between his own situation and Levinas's. See ibid., 33–34.
145. *Teshuvah*, Hebrew for return, connotes both a return to the fold (new Haredim are often called *baalei teshuvah*) and the movement of repentance.
146. Lévy, "Commentaire d'"Être juif,'" 34.
147. Ibid., 55.

to the contrary, how to resist elevating Judaism to the status of the summit, how to resist granting it the status of exception?[148] It is with this question in mind that I turn to Maurice Blanchot. For Blanchot's conception of literature will provide the resources to prove that it is only in the transgression of the proper meaning of *being Jewish* that we find a way to be loyal to its concept.

# FOUR

# Literary Unrest: Maurice Blanchot's Rewriting of Levinas

The fact of Israel, its Scriptures and their interpretations (but also the tortuous line winding its way through history, traced by the passion of Israel, by its permanence, in faithfulness to the inspiration or to the prophetism of its Scriptures) constitute a figure in which a primordial mode of the human is revealed, in which before any theology and outside any mythology, God comes to mind.

EMMANUEL LEVINAS, *A L'HEURE DES NATIONS*

In 1988, *L'arche*, a popular French Jewish monthly, ran the headline: "Maurice Blanchot expresses himself on Judaism for the first time." In the essay itself, published as an open letter to Salomon Malka, Blanchot begins by revealing that this is exactly what he would not do. "In some sense Judaism is so close to me," he writes, "that I do not feel that I possess the dignity to speak of it, except to make known this proximity and the reasons for this proximity (but even that though, can I express it?) Is it not presumptuous to hope one day to be able to speak of it? Will there ever be a day on which to express it? The answer: not in the time to come [*l'avenir*], but perhaps in the future." A note follows. It begins by quoting Levinas: "You will recall what Levinas said during the course of an interview with you [Malka], 'Judaism is an essential modality of every human being.'" Rather than explaining his reticence, these words

Epigraph: Levinas, *A l'heure des nations*, 127–28, and *In the Time of the Nations*, 110.

would seem to provide Blanchot with the capacity to claim and explain his proximity to Judaism. But he supplements the quote with an addition of his own: "an essential modality, but most often unrecognized, buried or worse perverted and finally recused."[1] These conditions recall Levinas's own statement from *Beyond the Verse* that "Judaism is a rupture of the natural and historical, which are constantly reconstituted and thus a Revelation which is always forgotten."[2] Tellingly, Blanchot does not choose to quote these lines; he follows up instead with one of Levinas's unqualified statements on Judaism's universalism. It is as though his own additions to Levinas's universalizing definition are a reminder intended for Levinas himself.

In what follows, I will show that, as innocuous as it appears, particularly in an interview published in a Jewish magazine, Blanchot's note conceals a critique of Levinas's frequent claim that Judaism will provide the way forward for a new universalizing humanism. This is not to say that Blanchot's reply to Levinas discounts Judaism's universality; it discounts only its ability to appear as recognizable. Blanchot suggests that Judaism is universalizable only insofar as it cannot be taken up, claimed, or inhabited as an identity. In Blanchot's comment, there is the implied suggestion that to thematize Judaism is already to bury it. Yet, as we will see, Blanchot does not in his essays refuse to speak of Judaism; rather, he speaks of it in such a way that his speech self-reflexively enacts a betrayal. This betrayal goes by the name *literature*.

Blanchot's literary betrayal is one perpetrated on behalf of Judaism as the antimythic ideal par excellence. Like Nancy and Lacoue-Labarthe, who derive their conception of myth from him, Blanchot represents the Jews as an antimythic people. Although he does not explicitly develop the dichotomy between myth and literature, it is implicit in his theorization of literature as an erring discourse.[3] For Blanchot, the only way to be true to the ideal of Judaism is to approach it by way of literature, understood as antimyth, as the force that disrupts the impulse toward social fusion.

If there is a single strand of contention that runs through the decades of dialogue between Levinas and Blanchot, it is on the question of literature. Where Levinas is suspicious of the seductions of art, literature

---

1. Maurice Blanchot, "N'oubliez pas," *L'arche*, May 1988, 68–71, reprinted in Blanchot, *Écrits politiques*, 165, and *The Blanchot Reader*, 244 (translation altered).

2. Levinas, *L'au-delà du verset*, 18, and *Beyond the Verse*, 4.

3. Lacoue-Labarthe quotes Blanchot as the source of the insight that, in destroying the Jews, what Heidegger was attempting to destroy "was man liberated from myths" (Lacoue-Labarthe, *La fiction du politique*, 139, and *Heidegger, Art and Politics*, 96).

included, Blanchot argues that literature marks out a space of resistance to philosophy, a space that Levinas's own thought has overlooked.[4] For Blanchot, the importance of reading and writing arises from literature's ability to upset the structures of our identity, exiling us from ourselves. Literature becomes a political force when, as a mode of discourse woven out of figurative language, it disenables easy and triumphant identification with a present community and disrupts our allegiances. For Blanchot, this importance is redoubled when thought of in relation to Levinas's retrieved conception of Judaism, for it is Levinas himself who defines Judaism as a teaching of exile. Blanchot thus performs a literary operation on Levinas's thought by repeating it and altering it through commentary. His aim is to signal the difference between Levinas's definition of Judaism and his political deployment of the category, highlighting the tension between Levinas's desire to build up Judaism's presence in the world and his articulation of Judaism as a teaching of deracination. It is the operation that literature performs on the figure of the Jew that inaugurates a new way of thinking about the role of the figure of the Jew in political discourse.

In the *L'arche* interview, Blanchot proceeds, after claiming he is unable to speak on the topic, to approach the issue of his relation to Judaism by way of a description of his sixty-year friendship with Emmanuel Levinas, which began in 1926 at the University of Strasbourg and lasted until Levinas's death in 1995.[5] It is not surprising that Blanchot would proceed to (not) explain his relation to Judaism by way of Levinas, for the descriptions of the Jew that appear in Blanchot's writings from the 1960s on are indelibly marked by this relation and by his closest friend's writings. In his work, it is always in conjunction with Levinas that Blanchot refers to Judaism. Often, it is as though *Judaism* could be used as another name for Levinas's ethics, and vice versa. Not only is Blanchot

4. With the publication of *The Infinite Conversation* (1969), Blanchot replaces the term *literature* (*la littérature*) with *writing* (*l'écriture*).

5. It is tempting at this point to dwell on the details of their friendship, given the oddity of the fact that Blanchot was himself aligned with the far-Right royalist, anti-Semitic faction in France from the late 1920s until at least the end of the 1930s and the fact that Blanchot saved the lives of Levinas's wife and daughter during the war. For the sake of concision, however, I will stick to their intellectual relationship. It should be noted, however, that much has been made of Blanchot's alignment with the far Right and that a number of studies have attempted to read in his work an element of anti-Semitism, not just in his early political writings, but even buried within the philo-Semitism that characterizes his later work. This interpretation does not bear out when either period is examined closely. For more on this issue and his friendship with Levinas, see Lescourret, *Emmanuel Levinas*, 64–65, 113–16. For a summary of the attacks and an explanation and defense of Blanchot's activities in the 1930s, see Leslie Hill, *Blanchot: Extreme Contemporary* (New York: Routledge, 1997), 36–46; and Leslie Hill, "La pensée politique," *Magazine littéraire: L'énigme Blanchot*, October 2003, 35–38. For the case against Blanchot, see Mehlman, *Legacies of Anti-Semitism in France*, chaps. 1 and 7; and Steven Ungar, *Scandal and Aftereffect* (Minneapolis: University of Minnesota Press, 1995), chap. 3.

convinced that Levinas's philosophy instantiates the essence of Judaism; he is also persuaded by this vision of Judaism, drawn to it.

It is that conviction, however, that leads Blanchot ultimately to critique Levinas, though he rarely does so outright. It is only through subtle juxtapositions of points, or hardly tangible displacements, that his essays on Levinas's philosophy expose it as incapable of being true to its own insight. The letter to Malka published in *L'arche*, seemingly one expressing great admiration for Levinas, functions similarly. This is not to say that the letter is not an expression of admiration; rather, Blanchot's own proximity to Levinas is one that he exhibited by insisting that Levinas's own thought provides an insight that his mode of thinking could not fully express. Blanchot thus distorts Levinas's writings in order to nudge them in a direction that Levinas did not himself fully embrace. He coaxes their meaning so as to be able to read them as loyal to the trajectory toward exile, toward uprootedness, that marked Levinas's philosophical project from its beginnings. Levinas himself once referred to Judaism as a "figure"; Blanchot's extensive work on the nature of literary language reveals the powerful implications of such a claim.[6]

### *Il y a* versus *Es Gibt*: An Invitation to Leave the Heideggerian World

It is in reference to Heidegger and to the question of literature that the idea of the Jew came to circulate between Blanchot and Levinas in a conversation that began in the late 1950s and continued through the 1980s. As Levinas's own discourse on Judaism often revolves around his resistance to Heidegger's characterization of being, so the affinities and differences between Levinas and Blanchot turn around their respective characterization of the "climate" of Heidegger's philosophy.

Before Judaism entered their conversation, however, the exchange between the two took place over the issue of being. The conversation in writing between Blanchot and Levinas began in earnest in the 1940s with the description of being that Levinas develops out of and in opposition to Heidegger's *es gibt*: the *il y a*. In *Existence and Existents*, Levinas credits Blanchot as a source for his notion of being as "the presence of absence, the night, the dissolution of the subject in the night, the horror of being, the return of being to the heart of every negative moment, the reality of irreality."[7] He retrieved this characterization, he reports,

---

6. See epigraph to this chapter.
7. Levinas, *De l'existence à l'existant*, 103, and *Existence and Existents*, 63.

from Blanchot's description of the dissolution of objects in the night in *Thomas the Obscure*, in which Blanchot describes the pressing in of existence as the feeling of being suffocated by one's own body.[8]

In "Literature and the Right to Death," published soon after *Existence and Existents* and often considered to be his most programmatic and significant statement concerning the relation between literature and philosophy, Blanchot proceeds to retrieve Levinas's description of existence emptied of existents, but he does so by associating it with literature, particularly with what literature exposes about the nature of being in its inescapability. The essay, published in January 1948, was written first and foremost as a response to Sartre's 1947 *Qu'est-ce que la littérature?* Against Sartre's case for writing as a form of action, a means of engaging in the world on behalf of the collectively, Blanchot argues for literature as a mode of worklessness. "Literature does not act," he counters, "but what it does is plunge into this depth of existence which is neither being nor nothingness and where the hope of doing anything is radically suppressed."[9]

Literature's value arises, not in its capacity to change the world, but in its capacity to expose the relentlessness of being from which we try to escape by means of the world. Literature, Blanchot writes, is a "blind vigilance which in its attempt to escape from itself plunges deeper and deeper into its own obsession, is the only rendering of the obsession of existence, if this itself is the very impossibility of getting out of existence, if it is being which is always flung back into being, that which in the bottomless depth is already at the bottom of the abyss, a recourse against which there is no recourse."[10] Blanchot borrows here from Levinas's *Existence and Existents* for his characterization of being as relentless and inescapable. Literature's value is in exposing us to this reality through its very work of deception. Its power is its expression of powerlessness.

This notion of literature develops primarily from Blanchot's encounter with Hegel's description of comprehension. Drawing from Kojève's seminars, Blanchot begins with the notion that language involves the absence (the annihilation or death) of the object, such that, for one to possess the idea of the cat, one must annihilate the uniquely real cat in its existence. "Therefore," Blanchot writes, "it is accurate to say that

---

8. Maurice Blanchot, *Thomas l'obscur* (Paris: Gallimard, 1950), 14–15, translated by Lydia Davis, Paul Auster, and Robert Lamberton as "Thomas the Obscure" in *The Station Hill Blanchot Reader*, ed. George Quasha (Barrytown, NY: Station Hill, 1998), 59–61.

9. Maurice Blanchot, *La part du feu* (Paris: Gallimard, 1949), 327, translated by Charlotte Mandel as *The Work of Fire* (Stanford, CA: Stanford University Press, 1995), 340 (translation slightly altered).

10. Ibid., 320; 332 (translation slightly altered).

when I speak, death speaks in me. My speech is a warning that at this very moment death is loose in the world, that it has suddenly appeared between me, as I speak and the being I address."[11] What Blanchot calls *common language* recognizes this operation as unproblematic or at least productive. For, in killing the real cat, I have gained something more secure, the idea of the cat, which cannot die.

Literary language differs from common language not in the act itself, for, by the very fact that it is language, literary or poetic language must also enact a negation of the object. "But literary language," Blanchot suggests "is made of uneasiness, it is also made of contradictions." Literary language draws attention to the negativity of the operation, focusing on the fact that the word expresses the nonexistence of the cat and that what it has given us as a replacement is a word. Literature dramatizes the operation of replacement by offering an "endless sliding of 'turns of phrase' which do not lead anywhere. Thus is born the image that does not designate the thing, but rather what the thing is not." The mark of the literary is the mark of the trope: a turn. A figure of speech is a turn that multiplies the absence between the object and the word, for now what we have is a word that refers, not to the object, but to another word: "It speaks of a dog instead of a cat."[12]

Literature additionally dramatizes the absence of the object by emphasizing the materiality of language. In this way, it illustrates a longing for the object itself in its physicality: "Literature wants the cat as it exists . . . Lazarus in the tomb and not Lazarus brought back into the daylight, the one who already smells bad, who is Evil, Lazarus lost and not Lazarus brought back to life."[13] This operation, despite its nostalgic element, actually multiplies the opacity of language, for it presents the word as another material object in place of the object lost. The word in its materiality disrupts the transparency of the operation of referral even as it harks back to the original object.

Consequently, Blanchot argues, what literature communicates is not the world, the thing in itself, but a doubling of that world. It is a game that *plays* at the work of the world, at the nihilation that is action, but it is a game that operates outside the field of action in the world, parodying action. It is worklessness that resists the productivity of Hegelian negativity, the force of transformation in the world. Literature thus dramatizes the negativity beneath death, what Blanchot calls the *impossibility* of dying:

11. Ibid., 313; 323–24.
12. Ibid., 315; 325, 326.
13. Ibid., 316; 327.

Literary language is . . . "*my* consciousness *without me*, the radiant passivity of mineral substances, the lucidity of the depths of torpor. It is not the night; it is its haunting; it is not the night but the consciousness of the night, which lies awake watching for a chance to surprise itself and because of that is constantly being dissipated. It is not the day, it is the side of the day that day has rejected in order to become night. And it is not death either because it manifests existence without being . . . death as the impossibility of dying.[14]

Literature dramatizes the *il y a*, that experience of being that is the rustling of the night, an existence without existents that thus excludes death "because it is still there underneath death," immune to the activity of negation. It dramatizes the *il y a* because it mimics activity and in this doubling creates a space of instability where valences are multiplied; nothing is as it seems. For, even in its gesture back toward the original object, in its turning (which is effected through the multiplication of images and the animation of language's materiality), what is achieved is not greater clarity or another form of possession, the rendering of presence; rather, Blanchot argues, it is instability that creates ambiguity at every level, such that one does not know when language is expressing or representing: "if it is a thing or means that thing, if it is there to be forgotten or if it only makes us forget it, so that we will see it; if it is transparent because what it says has so little meaning or clear because of the exactness with which it says it, obscure because it says too much, opaque because it says nothing."[15]

Literature is, for Blanchot, a form of erring. He does not play on the word *errer*, which communicates both error and wandering, in "Literature and the Right to Death." But it is by way of the characterization of literature that he comes to *associate* literature, and the *il y a*, with the wandering of the Jew. Blanchot first establishes the associations between literature and erring and between literature and Jewishness in *The Space of Literature* (1955). This text develops further the interpretation of literature first articulated in "Literature and the Right to Death" by way of a series of interpretive essays on other writers and poets, including Kafka, Hölderlin, Heidegger, Mallarmé, and Rilke. The association between writing and Judaism, however, puts him at odds with Levinas on two accounts: in its association of the *il y a* with the uprootedness of Judaism and in its characterization of aesthetic activity.

Levinas first signals his distrust of literature as an aesthetic art form in his own response to Sartre's *What Is Literature?* Just months after Blanchot

14. Ibid., 317; 328 (translation slightly altered).
15. Ibid., 317, 329; 328, 341–42.

published "Literature and the Right to Death" in *Critique*, Levinas published "Reality and Its Shadow" in Sartre's journal, *Les temps modernes*.[16] In this essay, Levinas, like Blanchot, resists the notion that literature is action. He offers an account of the relation between representational art and the philosophical concept that is not contrary to Blanchot's but comes at it from a different tack. For Levinas, its relation to truth and to reality is a function of how art arrests time: "The eternal duration of the interval where the statue is immobilized is radically different from the eternity of the concept; it is the *meantime*, never finished, still lasting, inhuman and monstrous."[17] Despite the difference in approach, Blanchot and Levinas share certain features in their characterization of literature. Like Blanchot, Levinas opposes the image or the figure to the concept whose preservation lifts the object into a kind of eternality. He too sees literature (and other representational art) as exposing a dimension of time that is defined by its lack of productivity. He too sees it as occupying a gray zone between the concept and the thing itself. For Levinas, however, all these features signal art's danger rather than its value: "The world to be achieved is replaced by the essential achievement of its shadow. This is not the disinterestedness of contemplation; it is irresponsibility. The poet exiles himself from the city."[18] For Levinas, it is clear, if literature is tied to exile or erring, this is a form of exile distinct from that inaugurated by the call of the other. It is not responsibility but its opposite, the attempt to escape.

While "Reality and Its Shadow" clearly responds to "Literature and the Right to Death," it does not address Blanchot directly. It is not until Blanchot's *The Space of Literature* (1955) appears that Levinas writes as a critic of his aesthetics, approaching in "The Poet's Vision" his interpretation of literature by comparing it to Heidegger's.[19] By a fascinating shift, Levinas analyzes here the reapplication of his own category in the work of his friend. In his reading of Blanchot, he is able to consider the way in which the *il y a* as a reinterpretation of *es gibt* reorients Heidegger's interpretation of being and to associate the contrast between the two

---

16. *Critique* was founded by Georges Bataille in 1946, and Blanchot was a major contributor in its early years.

17. Levinas, *Les imprévus de l'histoire*, 119, and *Unforeseen History*, 85. Levinas uses the statue as a metonym for all representational art: "To say that the image is idol is to assert that all images are, finally, plastic and that all works of art are, finally, statues: an arrest of time, or rather its lateness to itself" (ibid.).

18. Ibid., 125; 90.

19. Some critics have read Levinas's essay as an endorsement of Blanchot because of the way it distinguishes him from Heidegger. However, this interpretation misses the strong rebuke that accompanies the praise. See, e.g., Geoffrey Hartman and Kevin Hart, eds., *The Power of Contestation: Perspectives on Blanchot* (Baltimore: Johns Hopkins University Press, 2004), 6.

representations with the contrast between Judaism and paganism. Thus, within Blanchot's own context, Levinas himself associates the Jew with the description of being of the *il y a*, but he uses this association once again to advocate Judaism as a thinking that offers a rupture with being rather than its acceptance.

One of the elements of *The Space of Literature* that allows for Levinas's comparison in "The Poet's Vision" between *es gibt* as a pagan modality and the *il y a* as a Jewish modality is the inclusion of essays on both Kafka and Heidegger in the collection.[20] Thus, we must consider the content of these essays before we can fully appreciate Levinas's analysis of *The Space of Literature* in "The Poet's Vision."[21]

In "Kafka and the Work's Demand," Blanchot first enunciates the parallel between Judaism and literature by representing each as a discourse of "exteriority." Persistently in this essay, he reads Kafka through the lens of his Jewishness, an operation made possible by Kafka's own references in his diary to his experience of exile, wandering in the desert, and exclusion from Canaan. The comparison is, thus, made, by way of Kafka, between literature as a form of erring and Jewish "nomadic truth."

Describing this nomadic truth as it appears in Kafka's diaries and through a certain interpretation in *The Castle*, Blanchot writes:

> The migration has the desert for a destination and it is his approach to the desert which is now the true promised land. . . . And in this land of error one is never "here," but always "far from here." And yet, in this region where the conditions of a real dwelling are lacking, where one has to live in an incomprehensible separation . . . in this region which is the region of error because in it one does nothing but stray without end, there subsists a tension: the very possibility of erring, of going all the way to the end of error, of nearing its limit, of transforming wayfaring without any goal into the certitude of the goal, without any way there.[22]

Through a subversion of the Jewish figures of exile and the promised land, a subversion that he sees as already enacted by the Judaism of

20. In rendering the dichotomy between Levinas's characterization of Heidegger's description of being as pagan and his characterization of the *il y a* in terms that mark it as Jewish, I mean, not to endorse the oversimplification of this distinction, but rather to show how Levinas's characterization of Heidegger's philosophy is mobilized by his interchange on aesthetics with Blanchot.

21. The last chapter in the work, a set of interrelated essays on art, "Literature and the Original Experience," does not mention Heidegger except in passing but nonetheless seems to be a response to Heidegger's "Origin of the Work of Art," given the number of references and points the two essays share in common. Leslie Hill makes this argument in *Blanchot*, 121-27. Levinas certainly reads the essay as a commentary on Heidegger.

22. Blanchot, *L'espace littéraire* (Paris: Gallimard, 1955), 91-92, translated by Ann Smock as *The Space of Literature* (Lincoln: University of Nebraska Press, 1982), 77 (translation slightly altered).

Lurianic kabbalah, Blanchot interprets Kafka as transforming his own experience of exile into an end in itself, an end to which the land of Canaan—which sometimes literally refers to Israel for Kafka by way of his Zionism—is developed as that from which he is excluded.[23] This relation illustrates the structure of hope in Kafka, about which Kafka, responding to Max Brod's comment, said that there is hope outside the world as we know it: "oh, plenty of hope, an infinite amount of hope—but not for us."[24] For Blanchot, this dynamic is also a dramatization of the relation between art (literature) and the world:

For art is linked, precisely as Kafka is, to what is "outside" the world, and it expresses the profundity of this outside bereft of intimacy and of repose—this outside which appears when even with ourselves, even with our death, we no longer have relations of possibility. Art is the consciousness of "this misfortune." It describes the situation of one who has lost himself, who can no longer say "me," who in the same movement has lost the world, the truth of the world, and belongs to exile, to the *time of distress* when, as Hölderlin says, the gods are no longer and are not yet.[25]

Here, the description of literature that Blanchot gives as a relation of exteriority to the world aligns it with the *il y a*, with the experience of a passivity where the negativity of death signifies as impossibility rather than possibility. Already this is a relation that opposes the Heideggerian description of projection (*Entwurf*). Literature enacts the *il y a*, not through representation, but through the disruption of representation. In its turning, its troping, its materiality, its slippages, literature communicates the detachment of language from agency. It becomes an impersonal force. Words, Blanchot writes in "Literature and the Right to Death," "no longer *signify* shadow, earth, they no longer represent the absence of shadow and earth which is meaning, which is the shadow's light, which is the transparency of the earth: opacity is their answer; the flutter of closing wings is their speech; in them, physical weight is present as the shifting density of an accumulation of syllables that has lost all meaning."[26] Literature, according to Blanchot, strips language of its

23. Blanchot describes Kafka as initiating a new kabbalah: "What he has to win is his own loss, the truth of exile and the way back into the very heart of dispersion. This struggle can be compared to profound Jewish speculations, when, especially after the expulsion from Spain, religious minds tried to overcome exile by pushing it to its limit" (ibid., 82; 70). He bases his analysis on Gerschom Scholem's *Major Trends in Jewish Mysticism* (New York: Schocken, 1954) and quotes Scholem on the belief in metempsychosis.

24. Kafka quoted in Benjamin, *Illuminations*, 116.

25. Blanchot, *L'espace littéraire*, 89, and *The Space of Literature*, 75.

26. Blanchot, *La part du feu*, 319, and *The Work of Fire*, 331.

productivity, replacing it with language that errs or wanders. Thus, for Blanchot, literary language is analogous to the Jew for whom his state of exile becomes ironically the goal in and of itself, a goal that is the impossibility of attaining the goal.

It is not surprising, given Blanchot's characterization of literature in these terms, that Levinas would want to emphasize the way in which Blanchot's interpretation capitalizes on the trope of Jewish exile. Blanchot, however, links this state of erring with Hölderlin and "the *time of distress* when the gods are no longer and are not yet." This connection complicates, and, perhaps, motivates, Levinas's reading, for it would seem to put Blanchot very close to Heidegger, who refers often to Hölderlin's time of distress and suggests with Hölderlin that this is the time when the poets must perform their task of staying on the tracks of the absent gods "and so trace for their kindred mortals the way toward the turning."[27] Thus, it might seem that Blanchot links the erring of literature with what Heidegger calls the *thinking of being* and describes as *errant* in its nature, a path that "refuses to be a path of salvation and brings no new wisdom."[28]

In the final chapter of *The Space of Literature*, Blanchot seems at his most Heideggerian in his oblique response to Heidegger's "Origin of the Work of Art." While he mentions Heidegger only in a note, Blanchot takes up his question of art's *Ursprung*, defines the term in a manner similar to Heidegger's, as a leap, and proceeds to play on a number of his themes: like Heidegger, he takes up Hegel's claim in the *Lectures on Aesthetics* that art is a thing of the past.[29] He returns to the subject of Hölderlin and claims along with the poet that "the gods having disappeared . . . art remains the language in which their absence speaks." He even at one point describes the work of art in Heideggerian terms, as a manifestation of strife, when he defines it as "torn unity, always in struggle, never pacified."[30]

Yet, as Levinas argues in "The Poet's Vision," it is in this seeming proximity that the radical differences between Blanchot and Heidegger appear. Primarily, these differences can be understood to arise from a fundamental divergence between Blanchot's and Heidegger's character-

27. Martin Heidegger, "Wozu Dichter?" in *Holzwege* (Frankfurt a.M.: Vittorio Klostermann, 1950), 250, translated as "What Are Poets For" in *Poetry, Language, Thought*, 94.

28. Heidegger, "Das Ding," in *Vorträge und Aufsätze*, 177–78, translated as "The Thing" in *Poetry, Language, Thought*, 185.

29. Like Heidegger, Blanchot refers to art's beginning as a leap (*un saut*). See Blanchot, *L'espace littéraire*, 328, and *The Space of Literature*, 244. See the analysis of "Literature and the Original Experience" in Hill, *Blanchot*, 121–27.

30. Blanchot, *L'espace littéraire*, 289, 305, and *The Space of Literature*, 218, 229.

izations of being and from the way in which those characterizations reflect back on the relation of art and truth. Like Heidegger, Levinas argues, Blanchot is concerned with showing the relation between art and being. Like Heidegger's world, the world that Blanchot describes is one from which the gods have withdrawn. It is a world where their absence resonates as a being or a nothingness that initiates an impersonal call. But it is at this point, Levinas suggests, that Heidegger and Blanchot part ways.

That art and thinking in Heidegger are expressed as responses to a call that is impersonal, that thought responds to this call "by wandering byways," and that Heidegger characterizes this response as a form of erring, does not change the fundamental fact for Levinas that the relation between art and being in Heidegger is one of disclosure. Art expresses the truth of being, and this relation is one that is figured in terms of illumination. In Blanchot, by contrast, art expresses the *untruth* of being. This difference, Levinas writes, derives first from the description of being in Blanchot as exteriority, outside any structure of economy, a darkness prior to any division between day and night, subject and object. (Without referencing the *il y a* specifically, Levinas describes this "existence without world" in terms drawn from *The Space of Literature*, which mirror his own description of the *il y a* in *Existence and Existents*.) As a consequence of the difference between their characterizations of existence, the relation of art to existence in Blanchot is one, according to Levinas, that is, ultimately, opposed to that in Heidegger. Art (literature) expresses for Blanchot, not the "truth" of being, but "the errancy of being—more external than truth."[31]

This claim, Levinas argues, made in the name of literature, a discourse that in Blanchot threatens philosophy, nonetheless brings to philosophy a "category" and a "new way of knowing." Levinas thus interprets Blanchot to be supplying philosophy with "an invitation to leave the Heideggerian world":

The literary space into which Blanchot leads us has nothing in common with the Heideggerian world that art renders inhabitable. Art according to Blanchot, far from elucidating the world, exposes the desolate, lightless substratum underlying it, and restores to our sojourn its exotic essence—and to the wonders of our architecture, their function of makeshift desert shelters. . . . Art is light. Light from on high in Heidegger, making the world, founding place. In Blanchot it is a black light, a night

31. Emmanuel Levinas, *Sur Maurice Blanchot* (Paris: Fata Morgana, 1975), 21, 19, translated in *Proper Names*, 136, 134.

coming from below—a light that undoes the world, leading it back to its origin, to the over and over again, the murmur, ceaseless lapping of waves, a "deep past, never long enough ago."

Heidegger's world is a sheltering world, one where being illuminates and there is a primary connectedness between sky, earth, mortals, and gods (the fourfold). It is a world, in short, where man is at home. It is a world, Levinas writes, "that flatters our taste as privileged persons and as Europeans. But it implies asserting the impossibility of human wretchedness." If Blanchot's analysis of art offers us an invitation to leave the Heideggerian world, it is because it offers us a vision in which the human is first nomad, "a world in which dwelling is stripped of its architectural wonders" and "not only are the gods absent but the sky itself." For Levinas, this "uprooting [of] the Heideggerian universe" that Blanchot attributes to art preconditions the possibility of justice, allows for the face of man to shine forth. It is a world, Levinas asserts in so many words, that is biblical in its dimensions rather than pagan.[32]

In this interpretation, presented as a review of *The Space of Literature*, Levinas thus suggests to Blanchot that, in the interpretation of being that he and Blanchot have developed in tandem, there is something that by its very contrast with Heidegger harks back to a time "long before the gods, landscapes, and Greek and German mathematics," to a time when perception (i.e., light/illumination) was "abandoned as a system of reference in the revelation of the Invisible God which 'no sky can contain.'"[33] Levinas asserts that there is a question of being that is more primary than that which Heidegger claims the West has forgotten. Blanchot brings us back to that question, a question that is biblical, if not Jewish, in its dimensions.

In this interpretation, however, Levinas also launches a profound criticism of Blanchot, a criticism of the analogy between literature and Jewish exile that Blanchot asserts in his essay on Kafka. We must note that he sees in Blanchot, not a departure from the Heideggerian world, but an *invitation* to depart.

Aside from considering the contrast between Heidegger and Blanchot in *The Space of Literature*, Levinas also considers Blanchot's claim that literature offers us a space that is outside the illumination of the world in which the self is sovereign. He acknowledges that, like his own work, Blanchot's poses the question, "How can the Other appear, that is, be for

32. Ibid., 18, 20, 23, 25; 133, 135, 137, 138, 139.
33. Ibid., 25; 138.

someone without already losing its alterity and exteriority by that way of offering itself to view? How can there be appearing without power?" He sees that Blanchot's consideration of literature as a discourse that disrupts the movement of conceptualization is thus an endeavor, like his own, interested in investigating the possibility of an appearance outside intentionality, outside sovereignty: "Its way of being, its nature, consists in being present without being given, in not delivering itself up to the powers, since negation has been the ultimate human power, in being the domain of the impossible, on which power can get no purchase, in being a perpetual dismissal of the one who discloses it." Levinas acknowledges here, moreover, that, like the face, literature is that which says no to my powers. Nonetheless, he will hint that the path Blanchot has chosen ends where his begins. Blanchot thus has not gone far enough. For Levinas, the importance of the *il y a* is that it demonstrates the immanence of being, outside of which the transcendence of the face appears. His reading of Blanchot shows us that this is a structure to which Levinas remains loyal. For, as he admits, he is less interested in the challenge that literature claims to pose to philosophy than he is in the way in which Blanchot's analysis of art offers philosophy a new category. The importance of this category is then explicated, not as a form of exteriority, but rather as that dimension *out of which* "the face of man shines forth." Levinas thus challenges Blanchot, challenges a characterization that would associate exile or nomadism with literature without illustrating the connection between this modality and justice. "If the authenticity Blanchot speaks of is to mean anything other than a consciousness of the lack of seriousness of edification," Levinas writes, "anything other than derision—the authenticity of art must herald an order of justice, the slave morality that is absent from the Heideggerian city."[34]

To put his critique back into the terms of the biblical idiom that he employs here, Levinas argues that Blanchot has forgotten that the Jews do not merely wander in the desert, that it is in the desert that the Jews receive the covenant. Thus, while the *il y a* may remind us of the weightiness of being, a weightiness that is consistent with a biblical view of existence, as a state of erring, this is significant only as the condition for the possibility of a more profound deracination, the deracination that is for Levinas the revelation of the face, a deracination that is also an election. Without ever articulating his aim, Levinas has, thus, through the consideration of the *il y a* as it appears in Blanchot's work, managed to articulate once again the difference between his own thought and

34. Ibid., 14, 25, 24; 130, 131, 139, 137.

Heidegger's as a difference between Judaism and paganism. In the process, moreover, he has insisted on ethics as the only path to exteriority.

## Writing and the Relation to the Other

The impact of Levinas's interpretation and critique of Blanchot can be felt through much of Blanchot's subsequent writings. This impact is evident particularly in the collection *The Infinite Conversation* (1969), which even in its title references Levinas's claim that it is through the voice of the other that we are called away from the Heideggerian world.[35] In *The Infinite Conversation*, of which a substantial part is devoted to Levinas's *Totality and Infinity*, Blanchot reconfirms that his work shares with Levinas's a concern for exteriority, a concern for a writing that would break with unity, with the "system," and with "totality." The essays in the collection are concerned, Blanchot asserts, to locate a speech that would leave "dialectics, but also ontology." With this last claim, he affirms clearly what is only oblique in *The Space of Literature*—that, like Levinas's, his writings are concerned to leave the climate of Heidegger's philosophy. This will involve, he admits, not only a characterization of being different from Heidegger's, but also a path of departure from being.[36] This concern with identifying a mode of departure explains Blanchot's emphasis on speech and on the intersubjective in *The Infinite Conversation*. He is following Levinas's lead here, accepting intersubjective relations as that path. Thus, this text replies to Levinas not only by reaffirming a commitment to an exteriority that would have to imply a break with being; it also replies by its very structure. The essays, which were written over a span of twelve years, are periodically interrupted by a conversation between two interlocutors who remain nameless. This is a gesture in the direction of Levinas, through the acknowledgment that language is first language spoken to another. It is also, however, a gesture in the direction of literature. With this text, Blanchot inaugurates a new style, one that merges the literary and the critical. He subsequently makes

35. See ibid., 26; 139. For a discussion of the word *entretien* in Blanchot's work, see Joseph Libertson, *Proximity: Levinas, Blanchot, Bataille and Communication* (The Hague: Martinus Nihjoff, 1982); and Jill Robbins, "Blanchot Reading Levinas in *L'entretien infini*," in Hartman and Hart, eds., *The Power of Contestation*, 72–73.

36. Maurice Blanchot, *L'entretien infini* (Paris: Gallimard, 1969), 11, translated by Susan Hanson as *The Infinite Conversation* (Minneapolis: University of Minnesota Press, 1993), 10. Both Blanchot and Levinas treat Heidegger's work as an ontology. They consequently ignore the fact that, for Heidegger, even in the work following his "turn," being still remains a question, that which remains to be thought. On this issue, see Reginald Lilly, "Levinas's Heideggerian Fantasm," in *French Interpretations of Heidegger: An Exceptional Reception*, ed. David Pettigrew and François Raffoul (Albany: State University of New York Press, 2008).

a demand on his readers that they approach even his critical discourse as a form of literature, with all literature's unsettling properties.

However, in this text, the term *literature* is superseded by the term *writing*. As Blanchot announces in the note to the reader that opens the text, the project of writing that he undertakes in this collection is one that is meant to challenge even "the principles and truths that are sheltered by literature:"

Writing, the exigency of writing: no longer the writing that has always (through a necessity in no way unavoidable) been in the service of the speech or thought that is called idealist (that is to say moralizing), but rather the writing that through its own slowly liberated force (the aleatory force of absence) seems to devote itself solely to itself as something that remains without identity and little by little brings forth possibilities that are entirely other: an anonymous, distracted, deferred, and dispersed way of being in relation, by which everything is brought into question—and first of all the idea of God, of the self, of the subject, then of truth and the One, then finally the idea of the Book and the Work—so that this writing (understood in its enigmatic rigor), far from having the book as its goal rather signals its end, a writing that could be said to be outside discourse, outside language.[37]

Insofar as Blanchot insists on the challenge that writing poses to the idea of God, the self, the One, the Book, *The Infinite Conversation* functions also as a response to Levinas in his dismissal of art and literature as idol and escape.

This challenge is posed directly in the essays that consider *Totality and Infinity*. Here, Blanchot first aligns himself with Levinas against Heidegger by acknowledging with Levinas that illumination and sight belong to the province of ontology and participate in the reduction of all otherness to the same. What Levinas's philosophy provides through its consideration of the relationship with *autrui* (the other person) is the possibility that otherness could signify outside light. For Blanchot, it is Levinas's turn to speech that best leads us to this thought: "The revelation of autrui that does not come about in the lighted space of forms belongs wholly to the domain of speech. *Autrui* expresses himself, and in this speaking, proposes himself as other. If there is a relation wherein the other and the same, even while holding themselves in relation *absolve themselves* of it (being terms that thus remain *absolute* within the relation itself, as Levinas firmly states), this relation is language."[38]

37. Blanchot, *L'entretien infini*, vi, vii, and *The Infinite Conversation*, xi, xii.
38. Ibid., 79; 55.

Speech, Blanchot affirms, is the avenue out of dialectics as well as ontology. The relation speech affirms is one that cannot be reduced to unity; the other in speech remains absolutely other. Blanchot maintains that Levinas's ethics, his philosophy of *autrui*, provides us a path toward plurality and exteriority, toward a thinking that would be a thinking, not of power or of possibility, but rather of impossibility. What interests Blanchot in Levinas's philosophy is less its emphasis on responsibility and more the structure of a relation founded on difference, a structure that Blanchot now embraces in place of the *il y a* as a thinking of exteriority, impossibility, and plurality.[39] Blanchot nonetheless contends, this time taking the part of critic, that perhaps Levinas himself has not been as faithful to the radicality of this thought as he might have been. His criticisms, a number of which Derrida will echo in "Violence and Metaphysics," are first directed toward Levinas's insistence on aligning the transcendence of the other with God, his invocation of what Blanchot refers to as a *theological context*.[40] While Blanchot admits that this is a term to which Levinas would object, he uses it nonetheless to highlight a tendency in Levinas's thought that tilts it toward the theological. As one of Blanchot's interlocutors states: "Now and then in listening to you, I wonder whether *autrui* were not simply the locus of some truth necessary to our relation with the true transcendence that would be the divine one."[41] This claim amounts to the assertion that Levinas's invocation of God threatens to return the relation to the other to the sphere of ontology, a sphere of representation. The concern is to highlight the relation to the other as one with exteriority. Consequently, Blanchot insists on breaking down Levinas's description of transcendence, seeing in Levinas's insistence on height a reliance on a notion of space that the relation with *autrui* should dismantle as it destabilizes fixed relations.[42] Such metaphors threaten to reestablish the other within a horizon, like an object whose meaning is mediated by its horizon. Thus,

---

39. Jill Robbins points out that Blanchot's "translation" of Levinas in *L'entretien infini* subordinates ethics ultimately to the experience of impossibility. See Jill Robbins, "Blanchot Reading Levinas," 78.

40. Blanchot's first version of "Knowledge and the Unknown" appeared in 1961 in *La nouvelle revue française*. Derrida subsequently quotes it in "Violence and Metaphysics" (see *L'écriture et la différence*, 152, and *Writing and Difference*, 103). In the final version of the essay, appearing in *The Infinite Conversation*, Blanchot references Derrida's critique that Levinas would object to the notion that he was invoking a "theological context."

41. Blanchot, *L'entretien infini*, 82, and *The Infinite Conversation*, 57.

42. Leslie Hill points out that Blanchot changes Levinas's language of asymmetry to dissymmetry, a movement that also opens up the ethical space to become a communal space by doubling the relation. See Hill, *Blanchot*, 176.

Blanchot refers to *autrui* as speaking to me from "no site," for he is without horizon.[43]

The second critique is of Levinas's suspicion of writing. Blanchot ties this suspicion to the tradition, going back to Plato, who treats writing as a secondary and corrupt form of communication and speech as primary, as supporting presence. In speech, my interlocutor maintains the capacity to support his statements. Speech is, thus, "a privilege attributed to the vigilance of the self who speaks in the first person, that is, with the privilege attributed to all subjectivity and no longer to the incommensurable presence of the visage." Such an interpretation would seem to return the quality of equal exchange to the interpersonal relation and would, thus, reinvoke language as a mere *medium* of representation. It would obviously not be consistent with Levinas's description of the role of speech in the ethical relation. For Blanchot, then, insofar as the relation to the other is one of infinite distance between myself and him, insofar as it must undo even the relations of space implied by "immanence and transcendence," insofar as it is a relation that says *no* to the subject of power, inaugurating "a relation of impossibility and strangeness," the language that invokes this relation must be one unsupported by presence; that is, it must be writing.[44] Blanchot specifies writing as the mode of language that leads us to sense the relation with the other, a mode that would unravel speech as a means of self-presencing: "To write is to renounce being in command of oneself or having any proper name, and at the same time it is not to renounce, but to announce, welcoming without recognition of the absent. Or it is to be in relation, through words in their absence, with what one cannot remember."[45]

Blanchot goes even further in his insistence on the importance of writing to a thinking of the relation to the other, suggesting that, as a mode of communication, philosophy itself fails to be faithful to this relation because it requires a language that prioritizes clarity. "How can one say inequality by means of what tends to equalize?" he asks. "The language we are using at this moment can only send us back to speech as dialectics—

---

43. Kevin Hart argues that this move on the part of Blanchot is, ultimately, conceptually unstable, for it refuses the theological dimension without a criteria for differentiation: "If the other person is infinitely other and thereby cannot be assimilated to me, by what right can I reduce the alterity in question to the scale of the human? The immemorial past of the other person can always call God to mind" (Kevin Hart, *The Dark Gaze: Maurice Blanchot and the Sacred* [Chicago: University of Chicago Press, 2004], 214). As this quotation makes clear, Blanchot thinks, on the contrary, that such a move to "call God to mind" is exactly what would reinscribe the other person within a horizon, by allowing a theological mode of thought to circumscribe the relation with alterity.

44. Blanchot, *L'entretien infini*, 81, 101, and *The Infinite Conversation*, 57, 71.

45. Maurice Blanchot, *L'écriture du désastre* (Paris: Gallimard, 1980), 186, translated by Ann Smock as *The Writing of the Disaster* (Lincoln: University of Nebraska Press, 1980), 121.

the only 'legitimate' speech, let us not forget. Yet what we are seeking to express in affirming the inordinate relation beyond measure of *'autrui'* to 'the self' is a non-dialectical experience of speech. The inequality in question signifies perhaps nothing other than a speech that would speak without leveling, without identifying, that is, without tending toward the identity implied by satisfaction and full meaning."[46] This mode of speech is, as Blanchot discloses, literary. He invokes literature (or writing) as a form of speech that can signal difference without grasping it or capturing it, for, even when it represents its relation toward a referent, it is characterized, as we saw above, by what Blanchot characterizes as "a turn."

In *The Infinite Conversation*, the essays on Levinas appear at the end of a section entitled "Plural Speech (the Speech of Writing)." In the preceding essays, the primary topic is the turn of speech, writing understood as detour. Here, Blanchot returns to the theme first announced in "Literature and the Right to Death" and works out the dynamics of literary language as it differs from philosophical language. For him, the turn is what marks literary language, as is evident already in the word *verse* (*vers*). Once again, the significance here is the way in which literary language complicates the movement of reference. In the literary image, for example: "The image is image by means of this duplicity, being not the object's double, but the initial division [*dédoublement*] that then permits the thing to be figured; still further back than this doubling it is a folding, a turn of the turning, the 'version' that is always in the process of inverting itself and that in itself bears the back and forth of a divergence."[47]

Thus, even in the literary image, what is announced is a likeness or a comparison, but one that emphasizes divergence. In this literary play, language proceeds by erring: "To err is to turn and to return, to give oneself up to the magic of the detour." Even when it appears to grasp through the act of representation, the doubling of figuration twists language away from its object. What appears, is not a better vision of the intended object, but the difference between the image and the referent. This is language, Blanchot argues, of the outside, once again likening it in its wandering (in a trope of his own) to the biblical exile. As a form of erring, literary language is opposed to language that names. It is figured instead as response, a response to impossibility, to that which says no to my powers. "Such is the secret lot, the secret decision of every essential speech in us: *naming* the possible, *responding* to the impossible," Blanchot writes, concluding the section that precedes his discussion of Levinas.[48]

46. Blanchot, *L'entretien infini*, 90, and *The Infinite Conversation*, 63.
47. Ibid., 42; 30.
48. Ibid., 36, 68; 26, 48.

As the relation to the other is characterized by impossibility, we can conclude, on the basis of the placement of the essays on Levinas within the section "Plural Speech" and the emphasis on Levinas's critique of writing, that the purpose in this section is to suggest that writing, as Blanchot has conceived it, would be more faithful to the relation with the other, a relation "of infinity and strangeness," than would a philosophical discourse. With this claim we must also consider the status of Blanchot's own discourse in relation to Levinas's.

In the prefatory note to *The Infinite Conversation*, Blanchot suggests that the book should itself be understood as participating in the *désoeuvrement* (unworking) that characterizes writing.[49] This is a writing that "is called upon to undo the discourse, in which, however unhappy we believe ourselves to be, we who have it at our disposal remain comfortably installed." Insofar as Blanchot's essays on Levinas also participate in the activity of writing, they deform his thought by doubling it through commentary. Commentary, as Blanchot understands it, participates in literature by repeating the work "on the basis of the distance within the work that is its reserve—not obstructing it, but, on the contrary, leaving it empty, designating it by circumscribing it from afar, or translating it in its ambiguity through an interrogation henceforth still more ambiguous since it bears this ambiguity, bears upon it, and ends by becoming dissipated in it."[50] By focusing on the elements in Levinas's thinking that make it a thought of exteriority, by characterizing the ethical relation as a relation of impossibility, by describing it in terms that insist on the capacity of this thought to dismantle subjectivity, Blanchot reads Levinas in such a way that Levinas's concerns come to appear very close to his own. As most readers of Levinas would have to admit, there is something of a disharmony between this reading and most straightforward interpretations of his texts. Even Derrida, who tends to read texts against the grain, doubts the claims of similarity that Blanchot's reading seems to assert, arguing that, between Levinas's thought and Blanchot's, affinities arise only in relation to the critical and negative moments in Levinas's texts.[51]

Blanchot's interpretation is, thus, a doubling that unworks Levinas's thought and pushes it to its extremes, to such an extreme that Blanchot is able to say much later—by way of his own reading—that Levinas's thought "gives us a presentiment that . . . the infinite transcendence, the transcendence of the infinite, to which we try to subject God, will

49. This term derives from Kojève's lectures on Hegel and is utilized by both Blanchot and Bataille.

50. Ibid., viii, 571; xii, 390.

51. Derrida, *L'écriture et la différence*, 152, and *Writing and Difference*, 103.

always be ready to veer off 'to the point of possible confusion with the bustle of the *there is.*'"[52] It is Blanchot's *writing* on Levinas that performs this veering off, this erring. This operation, Blanchot suggests in *The Infinite Conversation*, is, indeed, what the relation with *autrui* demands: "Such then would be my task: to respond to this speech that surpasses my hearing, to respond to it without having really understood it, and to respond to it, in making it speak."[53]

Blanchot continues this project in later texts such as "Discours sur la patience (en marge des livres d'Emmanuel Levinas)" (1975) and *The Writing of the Disaster* (1980).[54] The former text signals by its very title the procedure that he intends to perform on Levinas's writing. It reminds us that his work is a form of commentary, while it also suggests that his engagement with Levinas's thought will push it to its margins, directing it toward the theme of exteriority. The later text reproduces with few alterations the former but embeds the forty-seven fragments of "Discours" within the larger context of meditations on the theme of disaster. *The Writing of the Disaster*, most often treated as a piece of Holocaust literature despite its relatively infrequent invocations of Auschwitz, is itself made up of a series of fragments devoted to the notion of the disaster. *Le désastre*, Blanchot opens the text, "ruins everything, all the while leaving everything intact."[55] The notion of disaster is defined by its resistance to philosophical thought, a nonconcept, impenetrable to experience.[56] It is what undoes the agency of the subject, disallowing disclosure by the "I," consequently passing "me" by. "'I' am not threatened by it, but spared," Blanchot writes. Blanchot uses this nonconcept in surprisingly versatile ways. It seems to apply to everything and nothing. It describes the *désoeuvrement* of writing, the event, provides us with a way to think about the Holocaust, yet remains the unknowable: "But the disaster is unknown; it is the unknown name for that in thought itself which dissuades us from thinking of it, leaving us through its proximity alone."[57]

52. Maurice Blanchot, "Notre compagne clandestine," in Laruelle, ed., *Textes pour Emmanuel Levinas*, 86, translated as "Our Clandestine Companion" in Cohen, ed., *Face to Face with Levinas*, 49.

53. Blanchot, *L'entretien infini*, 92, and *The Infinite Conversation*, 65.

54. Maurice Blanchot, "Discours sur la patience (en marge des livres d'Emmanuel Levinas)," *Le nouveau commerce* 30–31 (Spring 1975): 30–31.

55. Blanchot, *L'écriture du désastre*, 7, and *The Writing of the Disaster*, 1.

56. The book treats extensively the effects of Auschwitz on subsequent thought, but the term *disaster* is not another name for the Holocaust, nor is the Holocaust a species of the Holocaust. Gerald Bruns clarifies the relation between the two nicely when he writes: "The disaster clarifies the question of how we stand with respect to the Holocaust—clarifies, one might say, the *exigency* of the Holocaust" (Gerald L. Bruns, *Maurice Blanchot: The Refusal of Philosophy* [Baltimore: Johns Hopkins University Press, 1997], 215).

57. Blanchot, *L'écriture du désastre*, 7, 14, and *The Writing of the Disaster*, 1, 5.

Recontextualizing Levinas's thought and vocabulary within the framework of the disaster skews its emphasis.[58] Blanchot's reading of *Otherwise Than Being* in these texts makes of Levinas's treatment of ethical subjectivity a thinking that would dismantle subjectivity of any sort, transforming the inauguration of the ethical subject through the call of the other into an operation of *depersonalization*: "The other if he calls upon me, calls upon someone who is not I: the first [to] come or the least of men; by no means the unique being I would like to be."[59] To be called by the other is, thus, to be put under erasure; it is one form of disaster.

This reading strongly conflicts with Levinas's own analysis of election in *Otherwise Than Being*. For Levinas, the ethical relation inaugurates subjectivity; for Blanchot, it ruins it. The effect of this move is to call into question the structure of election that is at the heart of *Otherwise Than Being* and at the heart of Levinas's description of being Jewish. As we will see in the next chapter, Derrida follows Blanchot's lead in signaling the tension between uprooting and election. Blanchot only subtly puts this tension in relief by reading Levinas against the grain, offering us a version of persecution that results in anonymity rather than singular subjectivity. At the same time that this reading recontextualizes Levinas's philosophy under the theme of disaster, it also performs the disaster of writing on Levinas's text: "Writing is per se already (it is still) violence: the rupture there is in each fragment, the break, the splitting, the tearing of the shred—acute singularity, steely point."[60] Blanchot's own repetition of Levinas's text is a "writing" of it, the fragmentation and shredding of it.

## Being Jewish

Thus far I have been able to isolate how Blanchot differentiates writing from philosophy and to see both the relation to this procedure in and its impact on Levinas's thought. I have also considered the way in which Blanchot and Levinas share a concern to develop a notion of the Jew as a figure of exile or rootlessness, which contrasts with what Levinas identifies as Heideggerian paganism. Thus far, this later movement has been shown only by way of Levinas's reading of Blanchot. In turning to

58. Paul Davies offers a helpful analysis of Blanchot's appropriation of Levinas's vocabulary in *The Writing of the Disaster*. See Paul Davies, "A Fine Risk: Reading Blanchot Reading Levinas," in *Re-Reading Levinas.*, ed. Robert Bernasconi and Simon Critchley (Bloomington: Indiana University Press, 1991), 212–13.

59. Blanchot, *L'écriture du désastre*, 35, and *The Writing of the Disaster*, 18.

60. Ibid., 78; 46.

the writings specifically on Judaism and Jewishness, I want, not only to further highlight the way in which Blanchot, by way of Levinas, draws attention to the affinities between Judaism and his own thinking of exteriority, but also to consider the status of his discourse on Judaism, given his insistence on the procedure of writing.

In his discussions of Judaism, Blanchot often approaches the subject by way of authors other than Levinas. His earliest references to the nomadic truth of Judaism address Kafka. He quotes Martin Buber, Rosenzweig, Cohen, and Scholem as well as André Neher and Albert Memmi.[61] He returns often to the poet Edmond Jabès, whom he quotes as making the claim that "Judaism and writing are but the same hope, the same wait and the same wearing away," a claim that leads Blanchot to say that Jabès's *Book of Questions* is always written twice.[62]

It is, nonetheless, clear that, in all his interpretations of Judaism, Blanchot commences from the starting point of his friendship with Levinas. In his interpretations of Judaism, Levinas's philosophy provides the touchstone for framing any subsequent portraits of either the Jews or Judaism. In 1968, he marked his allegiance to this hermeneutic by dedicating a text devoted to Höderlin to Levinas and to their friendship, which he described as "in an invisible relation with Judaism."[63]

One way in which Blanchot echoes Levinas's characterization of Judaism is by adopting the schema that appears in Levinas's writings on Judaism, such that paganism is represented as a thinking of the proper, Christianity as a form of escapism, and Judaism as the prophetic interruption of history. In adopting this schema, however, he shifts the place-

61. For references to Kafka and Judaism, see "The Wooden Bridge" (in *The Infinite Conversation*) and "Kafka and Brod" (in Maurice Blanchot, *L'amitié* [Paris: Gallimard, 1971], translated by Elizabeth Rottenberg as *Friendship* [Stanford, CA: Stanford University Press, 1997]). Blanchot refers to Buber in "Gog and Magog" (also in *Friendship*) and in "N'oubliez pas" (in *Écrits politiques*). In "Being Jewish" (in *The Infinite Conversation*), he refers to both Rosenzweig and Cohen. Scholem is referenced as a source for discussions of messianism in *The Writing of the Disaster* and "The Work's Space and Its Demand" (in *The Space of Literature*). André Neher's *L'existence juive: Solitude et affrontements* (Paris: Seuil, 1962) is obviously a source for "Being Jewish." In "Prophetic Speech" (collected in Maurice Blanchot, *Le livre à venir* [Paris: Gallimard, 1959], translated by Charlotte Mandell as *The Book to Come* [Stanford, CA: Stanford University Press, 2003]), he leans heavily on André Neher's *L'essence du prophétisme* (Paris: Presses universitaires de France, 1955). He quotes Memmi in "Being Jewish."

62. Blanchot, *L'amitié*, 253, and *Friendship*, 223. Blanchot refers to Jabès throughout but specifically in "Traces" (in *Friendship*).

63. Maurice Blanchot, "Parole de fragment," in *L'endurance de la pensée* (Paris: Plon, 1968), cited in Leslie Hill, *Blanchot*, 174. The essay was published in a festschrift for Jean Beaufret. Blanchot added the dedication to Levinas after Robert LaPorte, another contributor to the volume, reported that Beaufret had admitted to his denial of the concentration camps and dismissed Levinas on anti-Semitic grounds. Blanchot, Laporte, and Derrida thus considered pulling out of the volume. When LaPorte confronted Beaufret on these charges in Derrida's office, Beaufret denied them. The volume appeared as expected, but with the added dedication by Blanchot. See Geert Lernout, *The Poet as Thinker: Hölderlin in France* (Columbia, SC: Camden House, 1994), 38.

ment of the structures so that what is presented in Levinas's essays as cultural commentary appears now as a series of tropes, metaphors for human tendencies that can be disengaged from their proper referent. Once again, we see Blanchot writing in Levinas's margins and reorienting his thought so that, even when it appears to be a repetition, the significance has somehow shifted. One site where this shift is particularly clear is in Blanchot's own response to Yuri Gagarin's flight.

Published in the same year as Levinas's "Heidegger, Gagarin and Us," Blanchot's "The Conquest of Space" is a subtle commentary on Levinas's essay, paraphrasing it in places almost word for word. The only mention of Levinas, however, is in the note where Blanchot credits him as a major source for his reflections. In Blanchot's text, Levinas's subtle references to Heidegger are further effaced and transposed so that what Levinas references as Heideggerian/pagan thinking now appears more generally as human thought: "Man does not want to leave his own place. He says that technology is dangerous, that it detracts from our relationship with the world, that true civilizations are those of a stable nature, that the nomad is incapable of acquisition. Who is this man? It is each one of us, at the times we give in to lethargy."[64]

The mode that is attributed to the Jew in Levinas's text is here called merely *nomadic*. Blanchot has, thus, doubly displaced Levinas's terminology, eliding even the reference to exile, a mode historically associated with Judaism and characterized by an attachment to a particular place.[65] It is, nevertheless, clear that the relationship between man and the nomad mirrors the relation between the anti-Semite and the Jew as the nomad is presented as tied to technology and, as such, represents a threat to man. At the same time that it generalizes Levinas's text, the opening of Blanchot's essay nonetheless manages to parallel the first paragraph of Levinas's, even alluding obliquely to Heidegger's critique of flight in "The Thing." Within the body of the essay, Blanchot does explicitly take up the category of the pagan (and the Christian), declaring that Gagarin's space flight is a threat to the pagan in all of us: he who is tied to rootedness, to tradition, to his biological race, he who consoles himself among the trees over the evil of mankind. The Jew, however, is not mentioned. Even when Blanchot paraphrases Levinas, he does so without specific citation; he refers to Levinas, not as someone who speaks in the name of Judaism, but as "the man with no fixed abode,"

64. Maurice Blanchot, "La conquista dello spazio," *Il menabò* 7 (1964): 13, translated as "The Conquest of Space," in *The Blanchot Reader*, 269.
65. Thanks to Clark Gilpin for helping me see this double displacement.

as a representative of the nomads.[66] In repeating Levinas's text, Blanchot insistently resists the move back to the proper name of Judaism. Levinas uses Gagarin's flight to lead to the truth of Judaism, concluding his own essay with the claim that, like technology, Judaism "has demystified the universe" and, moreover, "discovered man in the nudity of the face."[67] Blanchot employs Levinas's text in order to suggest that Gagarin calls into question *every* form of belonging. His omission of both Levinas's name and Judaism underscores the point that deracination as a moral concept would prohibit reappropriation of any kind. The message of Gagarin's speech from space is for no one to claim and for no one to own, "for in the unceasing word, which, accompanied by hissing and conflicting with all the harmony of the spheres, says, to whoever is unable to understand it, only some insignificant commonplace, but also says this to him who listens more carefully: that truth is nomadic."[68]

Given this text, and given what seems to be its radical move—to reject in the name of a nomadic truth reappropriation of that truth by any particular people—it is puzzling that Blanchot publishes "Être juif," one of his clearest statements about Judaism, only a year after "The Conquest of Space" appears.[69] In this essay, he repeats Levinas's gesture of returning nomadic truth to a space of belonging when he describes nomadic truth as Judaism's fundamental teaching.[70]

The essay does not present itself as a commentary on Levinas; rather, it claims to respond directly to Sartre's *Réflexions sur la question juive* and to challenge Sartre's assertion that the Jew is constituted by the anti-Semite. Nonetheless, the title "Être juif" clearly references Levinas's own essay by the same name, published fifteen years earlier.[71] Once again, Blanchot writes in the margins of Levinas's texts; once again, Levinas is hardly mentioned. In its themes, "Être juif" closely follows a number of the strands of Levinas's philosophy and writings on Judaism, functioning on the surface almost like a summary of those writings, although without attribution. At the same time, it serves as a critique. Of all Levinas's texts on Judaism, his "Être juif" is probably the least conducive to a reading sympathetic to Blanchot's concerns. If there is any text in which

66. Blanchot, "La conquista dello spazio," 10, and "The Conquest of Space," 269.
67. Levinas, *Difficile liberté*, 350, and *Difficult Freedom*, 233.
68. Blanchot, "La conquista dello spazio," 10, and "The Conquest of Space," 269.
69. "Être juif," published in two parts in *La nouvelle revue française* 116 (August 1962): 279–85, 117 (September 1962): 471–76, is republished in *L'entretien infini* as the second part the essay "L'indestructible."
70. Blanchot, *L'entretien infini*, 183, and *The Infinite Conversation*, 125.
71. The essay then proceeds by taking up André Neher's classification of "l'homme juif," in *L'existence juive*, a title that is clearly referenced in Blanchot's naming the section "Être juif."

Levinas insists on Judaism as a proper name, it is "Être juif." This is the essay that Benny Lévy claimed Levinas had betrayed in his universalization of Judaism. It is, thus, the essay that most allows for a particularist reading of Judaism. Blanchot's choice of title cannot be accidental. This very choice highlights the tension in Levinas's philosophy between election and deracination. The essay implicitly plays these two strands off one another. In his own essay, Blanchot offers a different vision of Judaism, one that derives equally from Levinas's writing.

Once again, Blanchot employs the classification of pagan, Christian, and Jew, referring to all three by name: "If Judaism is destined to take on meaning for us, it is indeed by showing that, at whatever time, one must be ready to set out, because to go out (to step outside) is the exigency from which one cannot escape if one wants to maintain the possibility of a just relation. The exigency of uprooting; the affirmation of nomadic truth." Judaism is, then, contrasted with paganism. Judaism exists, Blanchot says, to teach us to forgo paganism's temptation: "Nomadism answers to a relation that possession cannot satisfy." It summons us to movement. But this too must be distinguished from a Christian rejection of the here below, which Blanchot describes in terms stronger than Levinas's own as "an abasement of life, a scorn for presence."[72]

Blanchot also follows Levinas in a revalorization of Hegel's claim that Judaism is a form of separation that excludes union. He goes further than Levinas by arguing that Judaism's value is, not in its relation to the one God who remains separate, but in the understanding of speech as a relation of separation. Here, even more than Levinas, Blanchot seems to claim that Judaism's message is identical with the teaching of Levinas's own philosophy: "To speak, in a word, is to seek the source of meaning in the prefix that the words *exile, exodus, existence, exteriority* and *estrangement* are committed to unfolding in various modes of experience; a prefix that for us designates distance and separation as the origin of all 'positive value.'"[73]

Again, this is not quite Levinas's own philosophy as Levinas represents it but Levinas's philosophy as Blanchot has interpreted it, with the emphasis, not on ethics, but on exteriority. In a double reinterpretation, Blanchot's appropriation of Levinas's teaching is attributed to Judaism, which is consequently figured as the teaching of the outside. The importance of this for Blanchot, as it is to some extent for Levinas as well, is, thus, that Judaism would seem to be that which challenges the value of

---

72. Blanchot, *L'entretien infini*, 183, 186, and *The Infinite Conversation*, 125, 127.
73. Ibid., 187; 128.

belonging in all its forms; it would thus be *that* teaching that is defined as an antidote to fascism: "There is a truth of exile and there is a vocation of exile; and being Jewish is being destined to dispersion—just as it is a call to a sojourn without place, just as it ruins every fixed relation of force with *one* individual, *one* group, or *one* state—it is because dispersion faced with the exigency of the whole, also clears the way for a different exigency and finally forbids the temptation of Unity-Identity."[74]

Once again, Judaism's diaspora is its message. But, in Blanchot's version, this is not merely a diaspora in relation to space. Blanchot, moving to the metaphoric level, interprets Judaism as the ruination of all claims of allegiance, all claims of possession. It is a political ideal whose function is to disrupt the temptation toward community fusion, what Blanchot calls here *Unity-Identity* and Nancy and Lacoue-Labarthe will rename *myth*. Judaism is something like the possibility of the relation to the other brought to the level of the political, where relation is thought of, not in terms of allegiance, but in terms of separation. In his readings of Levinas, Blanchot suggests that the question "'Who is *autrui*'" needs to be replaced by the question "'What of human "community?"'" Thus, in a gloss on Levinas's writings on Judaism, he locates that possibility in the idea of Judaism. Judaism would, thus, signify as the community that testifies "to the exigency of strangeness."[75]

Interestingly, this definition of Judaism would ally it with what Blanchot calls a "communism without heritage," the notion of which he formulated as a consequence of the May '68 student protests, defining it as "that which excludes (and is itself excluded from) any already constituted community." The formulation of this definition is key to its importance. It is formulated as the *negation* of traditional forms of community. For Blanchot, communism would be the rejection of everything that binds one into a group identity:

We must repeat those simple things that we constantly forget: patriotism, chauvinism, nationalism have nothing that distinguishes them from each other except that nationalism is the coherent ideology to which patriotism gives sentimental expression (as illustrated still by such lamentable declarations as "I am wedded to France"). Everything that roots men by values, by sentiments, in one time, in one history, in one language, is the principle of alienation that constitutes man as privileged insofar as he is what he is (French, of precious French blood), imprisoning him in contentment with his own reality and encouraging him to offer it as an example or impose it as a conquering

74. Ibid., 184; 126.
75. Ibid., 101, 189; 71, 129.

assertion. Marx said with tranquil force: the end of alienation only begins if man agrees to go out from himself, out from religion, from family, from the state. The call to go out, into an outside that is neither another world nor what lies behind the world, there is no other movement to oppose all forms of patriotism whatever they might be.[76]

The similarity between these two exigencies—that of a "communism without heritage" and that of being Jewish—is, at least on the surface, quite surprising. A comparison, however, between Blanchot's description of both modalities provides insight into his strategy in the essay "The Indestructible." Let us consider the claims that appear in each of these passages. In one we find the argument that Judaism disrupts the "fixed relation of force with *one* individual, *one* group, or *one* state," in the other the claim that Marx, and, thus, communism, reminds us of the dangers of allegiances of any sort. In both cases, there seems to be a certain tension between the message and the name in which this message is offered. It seems ironic that Blanchot would argue for the rejection of allegiances in the name of communism, a thinking that carries in its very name the notion of community and the common. But this is for Blanchot exactly the point. In *The Unavowable Community* (1983) he further elaborates the notion that the importance of community is that it produces its own impossibility: "Left on its own, a being closes itself, falls asleep and calms down. A being is either alone or knows itself to be alone only when it is not."[77] According to this text, the truest moment of community for Blanchot is in the community's dissolution, in the realization that what community in fact means is the impossibility of communion, the impossibility of fusion.[78]

Given what Blanchot says in "The Conquest of Space," we might consider the possibility that Judaism would function for him in a similar

---

76. Blanchot, *Écrits politiques*, 113, and *The Blanchot Reader*, 202 (second translation slightly altered).

77. Maurice Blanchot, *La communauté inavouable* (Paris: Minuit, 1983), 16, translated by Pierre Joris as *The Unavowable Community* (Barrytown, NY: Station Hill, 1988), 5.

78. The sections of *The Unavowable Community* from which I have quoted are a commentary on Jean-Luc Nancy's *The Inoperative Community* (*La communauté désoeuvrée*), which is itself commenting on Georges Bataille. As Lars Iyer (*Blanchot's Communism: Art, Philosophy and the Political* [New York: Palgrave, 2004] 2) suggests, Nancy's text can be read as a further development of the notion of communism implicit in Blanchot's text, for Nancy describes Blanchot's notion as an attempt that went unrecognized. Like many of Blanchot's commentaries, this text proceeds by echoing the text on which it is commenting and adding corrective interpretations of Bataille along the way. In the process, however, it is clear that Blanchot is also attempting to highlight the political elements of his own work and to illustrate the conception of community pregnant therein. He quotes his own texts, even quotes Derrida quoting his text, in the process illustrating that the present text is an attempt to "take up a reflection, never in fact interrupted, although surfacing only at long intervals, concerning the communist exigency" (Blanchot, *La communauté inavouable*, 9, and *The Unavowable Community*, 1).

way. Once Judaism is understood as a form of deracination, it would have to prohibit the very structure of belonging. But this interpretation raises the question of how Blanchot can consistently say that the teaching of deracination somehow *belongs* to Judaism, is *its* truth. For, if Judaism's message is, indeed, parallel to the message of a "communism without heritage," then we would have to assume that Judaism itself would have to break with the claim that it has a unique message or a recognizable identity. The very assertion that it proffers a unique message would seem to reimpose the structure of exemplarity that Blanchot claims a "communism without heritage" must call into question.[79]

It seems nearly impossible to imagine a Judaism that is not tied to values, language, history—one that would not present itself as exemplary. Does not Levinas himself craft a vision of Judaism as exemplary through his association of Judaism and ethical subjectivity? Blanchot's statement that Judaism teaches the truth of exile would, then, repeat that very gesture.

Unless, that is, we understand being Jewish for Blanchot as already a trope. To say that being Jewish functions for Blanchot as a trope is to suggest that it would be the reinscription of a philosophical notion into writing. The path of that reinscription takes place through a repetition.

As we've seen, repetition is one of the paths by which writing deforms philosophical notions introducing ambiguity and contradiction into concepts. Theorizing the *désoeuvrement* of writing in *The Writing of the Disaster*, Blanchot describes repetition as "unpower." He calls for it as a kind of practice. "Let us remember," he writes. "Repetition: nonreligious repetition, neither mournful nor nostalgic, the undesired return. Repetition: the ultimate over and over, general collapse, destruction of the present."[80] It is the means by which a concept comes to function as an image, pointing, thus, to absence rather than presence. Blanchot's path of repetition passes most importantly through Levinas's representation of Judaism. But, as we saw in the last chapter, Levinas's conception of Judaism is already a repetition constructed through a revalorization of the terms of anti-Semitism and other portraits such as Hegel's that constitute Judaism as a form of separation or alienation. In his own recasting of Levinas's ideas, Blanchot passes through these stages as well by revalorizing the notions of affliction and estrangement. What differentiates his description from Levinas's, however, is his attention to the con-

79. As we will see in the next chapter, Derrida makes this claim explicitly through an examination of the structure of exemplarity.

80. Blanchot, *Écriture du désastre*, 20, 72, and *The Writing of the Disaster*, 9, 42.

traditctions that arise with this concept and his subsequent desire, not to repress them, but, in fact, to exploit them.

By playing Levinas's essay "Être juif" against the theme of dispersion harvested from Levinas's own writings, Blanchot harnesses the tension within Levinas's thought merely by repeating its terms. Being Jewish thus operates for Blanchot in the same manner as the word *silence*.[81] Like the word *silence*, of which Blanchot says its evocation elicits the difference between the thing and the name, the trope of being Jewish has a similar "torsion," for, in forbidding the possibility that it can be enacted, it forbids "the temptation of Unity-Identity." This trope disallows the possibility that one could take it up as an identity, by the very fact that it has been defined as that which disallows identification.[82]

This is not to say that Blanchot rejects the fact that there is a community of Jews—individuals who identify as Jews and have the right to that identification. For, here, Blanchot, unlike Levinas, clearly distinguishes between "the exigency of being Jewish" and the future of the Jewish people. The question that being Jewish poses is, Blanchot suggests, "a universal question." In the difference between the definition of *being Jewish* and the facts of political life a question appears—a challenge, moreover, to the very demands of the political, to the demands, that is, of power. This is a question, Blanchot suggests, posed by this trope to the society that is being tried in Palestine as it is posed to any society. The difference is only that, in those societies that have at their heart a claim such as Judaism or communism, there is a claim to justice that might, in fact, show itself, if only negatively, as the dissonance between the demand of "safeguarding" that identity and what that identity demands.[83]

Blanchot makes this distinction in a note that accompanies the essay "Être juif." Within the body of the text, he pursues a different strategy of disclosing the ambiguities and dissonances in the claim that there is such a thing as being Jewish. In an uncharacteristic manner, he actually pursues here a language that is explicitly ontological in nature.

81. Blanchot, *L'entretien infini*, 44, and *The Infinite Conversation*, 32.
82. The way in which Blanchot's essay "Being Jewish" functions as a commentary on Levinas seems to have been missed by most scholars of Blanchot. Consequently, the essay is read as a mere simplification and allegorization of Judaism. Kevin Hart, e.g., suggests that Blanchot's description of Judaism is "Hegelian": "Judaism belongs to a dialectical movement: things happen *so that* other things might be generated by them." He even gives Hegel more credit as a philosopher of religion, adding: "Hegel would pay a little more attention to the specifics of religious practice." Blanchot exposes himself to this misreading by not *always* being explicit about his method of commentary. It is, nonetheless, surprising that his practice of repetition and distortion is so often missed by critiques, given his own frequent statements about the practice of commentary and repetition as a mode of writing. See Hart, *The Dark Gaze*, 187.
83. Blanchot, *L'entretien infini*, 190, and *The Infinite Conversation*, 448.

He speaks of the truth of being Jewish as that which "it is essential to bring to light [*mettre au jour*]," employing the language of both essence and light, when these are explicitly the two elements of Western thought that, he claims, *The Infinite Conversation* aims to disrupt. He emphasizes these metaphors in his own speech even as he contrasts Judaism with "Greek truth," which "proposes to us truth as light, light as measure."[84]

Understood as another tactic of repetition, the juxtaposition reminds the reader, not only that Blanchot is himself pursuing a discourse that deforms his object, but also that the very operation of disclosing the exigency of being Jewish is one that consistently buries it within the only language that would be capable of bringing it to light. Blanchot makes this move explicit in a note to *The Writing of the Disaster* when he says: "There is in Levinas no spectacular break with the language called 'Greek,' wherein the principle of universality is preserved." Judaism, he continues, can be announced only as that which "*waits* to keep on being thought."[85] Once again, we see a contrast between Levinas's writings on Judaism and Blanchot's repetition of Levinas's formulations of Judaism. Where Levinas acknowledges the risks of thematizing the nature of Jewish identity while nonetheless pursuing his theme, Blanchot animates his own discourse so that the cracks within it appear as a dissonance between his own activity and that which he discusses. One ought to deal with this dissonance, his own discourse suggests, not by trying to solve it, but by allowing it to be seen in the very violence it commits.

It is in this spirit as well that Blanchot responds, twenty years after having written "The Indestructable," to Jean-François Lyotard's *Heidegger and "the jews."* He quotes Lyotard's statement that it is our lot, the lot of Jews and non-Jews called by Lyotard "the jews," of which "its being together arrives not from any original root, but from a singular debt of anamnesis."[86] He consents to Lyotard's interpretation of what it would mean to reconstitute community in the wake of the Shoah in every way but one. Lyotard's explanation of his use of quotation marks, he claims, is unconvincing.[87] He does not explain why, but we need only look at what he says about the moment in May '68 when protestors took up the cry, "Nous sommes tous des juifs allemands" in order to understand what is at stake for Blanchot in this gesture of identification.

---

84. Ibid., 182, 186; 125, 127.

85. Blanchot, *L'écriture du désastre*, 45, and *The Writing of the Disaster*, 149.

86. Lyotard, *Heidegger et "les juifs,"* 152, and *Heidegger and "the jews,"* 93. For more on Lyotard's controversial book, see the introduction to this volume.

87. Blanchot, *Écrits politiques*, 174, and *The Blanchot Reader*, 249.

## Opening and Overthrowing the Future

Even before the students took up the chant "Nous sommes tous des juifs allemands," Blanchot spotted in the May events the political instantiation of ideas he had been writing and thinking about for decades. "Outside of any programmatic project, indeed of any project," Blanchot saw the events of May as representing the possibility of maintaining *"a refusal that affirms . . .* an affirmation that does not arrive at an arrangement, but rather that disrupts and undoes itself [*déranger et se déranger*].[88] Blanchot's devotion to a concept of negativity that remained exterior to work was mirrored back to him in the actions of the students. The May protests were not being pursued in the name of a new cause, a new group, or a leader. The movement was antiauthoritarian; the committees that met during the protests were themselves without purpose or goals, their own lack of direction a message of its own, an affirmation of nonpower. They conducted political acts that folded back on themselves, undoing their own work, performing their own *désoeuvrement*.

The involvement of Blanchot in one such committee, the Comité d'action étudiants-écrivains, is well-known. He contributed to statements that were published in *Le monde* on May 9 and June 18 and wrote essays that appeared in *Comité*, a "semi-clandestine magazine," the following October. In these writings, he insists on the right of citizens to resist a government that was governing by force. In the name of the committee, he calls on the students to maintain "a power of refusal capable of bursting open the future."[89] For Blanchot, that refusal was best actualized by the slogan "Nous sommes tous des juifs allemands."

Undoubtedly, it was remarkable for Blanchot when the student protestors of Paris took up this chant. At this moment, the figure of the Jew appeared on the streets, in politics, clothed in an entirely new aura. The Jew appeared as a metaphor for the margins and for a new political valorization of these margins. The event itself, Blanchot wrote, was a moment of infinite violence, a moment that was also paradoxically nonviolent: "Never had this been said anywhere, never at any moment, an inaugural speech-event, opening and overturning borders, opening

88. Ibid.
89. The Comité d'action étudiants-écrivains was one of a number of antiauthoritarian action committees that formed in the spring of 1968. A group of student writers that met between May and October of that year, it produced *Comité*, a journal commenting on the events. (The journal appeared in only one issue, dated October 1, 1968.) Dionys Mascolo, with whom Blanchot collaborated politically from the late 1950s through the 1960s, attributed half the articles published in *Comité* to Blanchot, though they were unsigned. See Hill, *Blanchot*, 17 ("semi-clandestine magazine"), 229. The essays from *Comité* are reprinted in Blanchot, *Écrits politiques*, 97–147.

and overthrowing the future."[90] This was, he suggested, a glimpse of true community, of "communism without heritage."

To fully appreciate the importance of the event for Blanchot, it is helpful to once again consider Alain Finkielkraut's contrary response to May '68. Finkielkraut, the Jewish son of two war refugees, describes in *The Imaginary Jew* his sense of disgust at the protestors, his feeling that "the protestors' generosity" was "too facile and flashy." The slogan "Nous sommes tous des juifs allemands," he writes, "despoiled me and sullied my treasure, as if the demonstrators, while assuring me of their complete support, had picked my pocket of my special status."[91]

This disgust, which evolved into a sense of self-incrimination as well, emerged from the feeling that the protestors in this moment evacuated Judaism of its content, making it merely a symbol for the outsider. Judaism thus became a sign that anyone could try on, like a yellow star that could be taken on and off at will. The protestors, Finkielkraut claimed, were, thus, usurping the position of the victim without having ever been victims themselves. Like Blanchot, he also saw the chant as marking a site at which borders were crossed and barriers opened, but, for him, this was exactly what made the chant so problematic.

Does Blanchot's response, then, indicate a blindness to the fact that, when the protestors took up the call "Nous sommes tous des juifs allemands," they were, indeed, usurping the identity of those Jews who had suffered through the Holocaust? Or can we perhaps read that transgression as part of the demonstration's force? We must keep in mind here Blanchot's conception of communism—his conception, moreover, of community—as an encounter with the impossibility of communion. If this was a moment of true community, it was such by signaling a rupture with the very possibility of identification. In asserting their solidarity with the Jews, the protestors were, indeed, making visible their own transgression, calling attention to the procedure of identification and signaling its failure in the moment. When the students themselves claimed to be Jewish, they did not redefine Judaism so that the category included them. What could have been more obvious in this moment than the fact that they were adopting a label of identity that did not fit? The inappropriate quality of this gesture was made even more evident by their implicit reference to the Holocaust. What appeared then was the gap between who they were and what they claimed to be. It was their apparent audacity that was on display, an audacity that called into

90. Blanchot, *Écrits politiques*, 125.
91. Finkielkraut, *Le juif imaginaire*, 26, and *The Imaginary Jew*, 17–18.

question the very politics of identity. Nowhere is this clearer than in Finkielkraut's response—a sense of infringement that was transformed into self-incrimination. The protest initiated two stages of response: first, What right do they have? then, What right do I have? Whether or not the students had this intention, by dramatizing their own transgression they produced a different form of political speech, one that operates according to the rules of metaphor as Blanchot understands them. Read this way, Finkielkraut's discomfort with the protest would be part of its point. The fact that Finkielkraut was himself led to feel inadequate in the face of the demands of being Jewish, the fact that he himself felt incriminated by the slogan, driven to declare even "that the only thing [he] could hold against these ephemeral German Jews was their caricature of my own Jewishness," was a sign of the protest's political force.[92]

To return, then, to Lyotard, his gesture of claiming that we are all "jews" can maintain its impact, according to Blanchot's logic, only if it allows itself to be transgressive. The quotation marks would, thus, divest the identification of its transgressive sting. Blanchot's own language in the essay "Être juif" dramatizes the relation between the discourse of the West and the exigency of being Jewish by repeating philosophy's operation, an operation that is destined to elide the very demand that being Jewish makes on us. Similarly, the protestors' claim of solidarity with the victims of the Shoah dramatized the risk of forgetting that the wish of all in the camps was both "know what happened, do not forget," and "at the same time never will you know."[93] As such, it was a moment when this risk was revealed and, thus, a moment whose importance resided in the way in which it exposed social dissonance.

What we see in this moment is the repetition of dissonance on multiple levels. Not only are the students claiming something they can never legitimately claim, a solidarity with the victims; they are claiming it in the name of Judaism, which for Blanchot represents the demand

92. Ibid., 27; 18. While there is a site of crossover for these two thinkers in the fact that both Blanchot and Finkielkraut use the slogan to critique the politics of identity, they are doing so from opposite perspectives. For Blanchot, the critique is of the politics of group identification, the move toward fusion and the drive toward allegiance. For Finkielkraut, the critique is of the ease by which identity is assumed. He criticizes the lack of respect such easy assumptions show toward the complexity of heritage and the value the past has to teach us. Thus, where Blanchot opposes the value placed on allegiance, Finkielkraut ultimately argues that we do not place enough value on our allegiances. He advocates a vision of Judaism as a cultural heritage to which Jews ought to claim their attachment, not as a form of property and privilege, but as an unassumable past to which they owe a debt. Recounting the shift in himself from one understanding of Judaism to another, he writes: "Today I love Judaism because I receive it from without, because it brings me more than I contain within. . . . Judaism is no longer for me so much an identity, as a form of transcendence. Not something that defines me, but a culture that can't be embraced, a grace I cannot claim as mine" (ibid., 176 [translation slightly altered]; 212).
93. Blanchot, L'écriture du désastre, 131, and The Writing of the Disaster, 82.

for a politics that would itself be the dissolution of the political, such that any claim to enact or inhabit it would be impossible. For Blanchot, the enactment of this paradox *is* revolutionary politics. In it we glimpse the impossible. The appearance of the impossible as a moment of dissonance is the very rupture of possibility and, thus, for Blanchot, the rupture of time: "At that moment there is a stop, a suspension. In this stop, society falls apart completely. The law collapses: for an instant there is innocence, history is interrupted." He quotes Benjamin in *Theses on the Philosophy of History* to this effect, recalling the notion that the ultimate revolutionary act of the July revolution was the moment when "simultaneously but as a result of separate initiatives, in several places people fired on the clocks in the towers of Paris."[94] Such moments for Benjamin represented a present "shot through with chips of messianic time."[95] It is clear that the very disruptive force of the students' chant initiated for Blanchot a moment similarly messianic in its dimensions. For as he says of the messianic in *The Writing of the Disaster*: "It is not the end of history, the suppression of time . . . it announces a time more future . . . than any prophecy could ever foretell."[96] Thus, in its doubling of solidarity and transgression, hope and impossibility, the moment in May '68 when the students chanted "Nous sommes tous des juifs allemands" might be read as something like the enactment of the call for a future that could never be present. The future that Blanchot speaks of in his open letter to Salomon Malka is to be differentiated from *l'avenir*, "a time to come." This moment does not allow us to glimpse what will arrive by giving us a preview of it; rather, it enacts a call for that future by showing us what *cannot* appear. It is instantiated in Blanchot's *Le pas au-delà*, in his plea "Come, come, come [*viens, viens, venez*] you whom the injunction, the prayer, the wait could not suit."[97] Jacques Derrida, whom we turn to in the next chapter, replicates this plea in "Of an Apocalyptic Tone." He describes it as the only pure relation with the future, pure because it cannot be appropriated by any ontology, theology, rhetoric, or grammar, pure in its gesture toward community—by being a gesture that "is not addressed to any identity determinable in advance."[98]

94. Blanchot, *Écrits politiques*, 127, and *The Blanchot Reader*, 205.

95. Benjamin, *Illuminationen*, 261, and *Illuminations*, 263.

96. Blanchot, *L'écriture du désastre*, 215, and *The Writing of the Disaster*, 142.

97. Maurice Blanchot, *Le pas au-delà* (Paris: Gallimard, 1973), 185, translated by Lycette Nelson as *The Step Not Beyond* (Albany: State University of New York Press, 1992), 135.

98. Jacques Derrida, *D'un ton apocalyptique adopté naguère en philosophie* (Paris: Galilée, 1982), 95, translated by John P. Leavey as "Of an Apocalyptic Tone Recently Adopted in Philosophy," *Oxford Literary Review* 6 (1984): 34.

# FIVE

# "The Last of the Jews": Jacques Derrida and the Case of the Figure

What have I in common with Jews? I have hardly anything in common with myself.

FRANZ KAFKA, *TAGEBÜCHER*

The Jew's identification with himself does not exist.

JACQUES DERRIDA, *WRITING AND DIFFERENCE*

In thinking about Judaism, Jacques Derrida once said: "I always find *myself* once again confronted with a problem of figure, a *cas de figure* as we say in French."[1] Derrida called himself by a handful of names that attest to this confrontation. He referred to himself as "Reb Rida" (in a play on *ride*, the French for "wrinkle" or "fold"), "Reb Derrissa" (in a play on *je ris*, "I laugh"), "the last and the least of the Jews," and "the Marrano."[2] In 1990, four years after he published

---

Epigraphs: Franz Kafka, *Tagebücher in der Fassung der Handschrift*, ed. Jost Schillemeit (Frankfurt: Fischer, 1992), 622, translated as *The Diaries of Franz Kafka, 1910–1913*, ed. Max Brod, trans. Joseph Kresh and Martin Greenberg, 2 vols. (New York: Schocken, 1954), 2:11; Derrida, *L'écriture et la différence*, 112, and *Writing and Difference*, 75.

1. Derrida in Weber, *Questions au judaïsme*, 75, and *Questioning Judaism*, 40.

2. For "Reb Rida," see Derrida, *L'écriture et la différence*, 116, and *Writing and Difference*, 78. For "Reb Derrissa," see ibid., 436; 300. For "the last and least of the Jews," see Derrida, "Circonfession," 145, and "Circumfession," 154. For "the Marrano," see ibid., 160; 170. On the relation between the Marrano and the case of the figure, see Jacques Derrida, *Apories* (Paris: Galilée, 1996), 140, translated by Thomas Dutoit as *Aporias* (Stanford, CA: Stanford University Press, 1993), 81.

a collection of writings devoted to Maurice Blanchot, Blanchot suggested that we might add to this list the name of Moses.

In "*Grâce (soit rendue)* à Jacques Derrida," Blanchot hardly speaks of Derrida but rather of Moses. Yet, by the very fact of its title, the essay begs to be read as recognition on Blanchot's part of the game that Derrida had already begun playing. In its opening lines, it acknowledges as much: "After such a long silence (perhaps hundreds and hundreds of years) I shall begin to write again, not on Derrida (how pretentious!), but with his help, and convinced that I shall betray him immediately."[3] The reference to betrayal conveys Blanchot's acknowledgment of Derrida's strategy of deconstructive reading, a method that functions by performing a betrayal of the text it analyzes, revealing, thus, the way in which the text betrays itself. Blanchot's own homage to Derrida is to offer him the same treatment and, at the same time, to add another Jewish name to Derrida's list of aliases.[4]

Blanchot's essay does not make the analogy between Derrida and Moses explicit. Instead of pursuing the nature of Blanchot's relation to Derrida, it offers a gloss on the story of Moses and the giving of the law. On one level, the relation of this story to Derrida's own work is not difficult to discover; it responds to a comment that Derrida makes in his first essay on the poet Edmond Jabès, namely, that, within the book of Exodus, "writing is . . . originally hermetic and secondary."[5] Following an implicit suggestion in this claim, Blanchot argues that the division between orality and writing is not itself well maintained within the Jewish tradition.[6] There is, he asserts, a certain undecidability to this question: the oral Torah is given priority by the rabbis "to the extent that it makes readable the unreadable," but it arises (like deconstruction) from within the text, as a commentary on the text itself, a text from which nothing can be added or taken away.[7]

3. Maurice Blanchot, "*Grâce (soit rendue)* à Jacques Derrida," *Revue philosophique* 2 (1990): 167, translated as "*Grâce (soit rendue)* à Jacques Derrida," in *The Blanchot Reader*, 317.

4. The 1990 essay has a prescient quality. Derrida had already used the aliases of Reb Rida and Reb Derissa in *Writing and Difference*. He had already given a great deal of thought to the practices of troping and the possibilities for his own performances, but "Circumfession," the most explicit demonstration of this practice, was not published until 1991.

5. Derrida, *L'écriture et la différence*, 103, and *Writing and Difference*, 67.

6. Derrida's claim that writing is *originally* hermetic and secondary points to the claims that he develops more fully in *Of Grammatology* in his analysis of Rousseau and Lévi-Strauss that writing is simultaneously represented as secondary yet reveals itself to be original or primary insofar as an *archewriting* secures the very possibility of meaning.

7. Derrida, *L'écriture et la différence*, 169, and *Writing and Difference*, 319. This rabbinic reading could be intended to remind Derrida that he may be closer to Judaism than he would expect; it would also be relevant to Blanchot's and Derrida's respective relationships to Levinas, who clearly prioritizes the value of the spoken word in his own scriptural hermeneutics.

This brief discussion makes up only a tiny fraction of the essay's content, which finally seems more concerned with filling out a portrait of Moses as man and intermediary than it does with discussing Derrida's ideas. The very discrepancy between the title and the content of the piece thus calls for further interpretation. It demands that we ask after the relation proposed here between Moses and Derrida.

The temptation is to read the essay as somehow *about* Derrida, precisely because Blanchot has told us that the text is not about Derrida, while at the same time proceeding to drop clues that would suggest that he is formulating an analogy between Derrida and Moses. Moses is figured, not only as redoubling every message he receives, but also as opposing Plato's teaching that writing is both bad and secondary.[8] Either Moses would seem to be a deconstructionist *avant la lettre*, or Derrida would seem to be a second Moses.[9]

Even as the temptation of this reading is rendered, however, it is already taken away. For the analogy between Moses and Derrida produces far more dissonance than assonance. First of all, it would place Blanchot in the position of Aaron, who is destined to betray Moses the moment he begins speaking for or with him. If one were to examine the relationship between Derrida and Blanchot, this relationship would have to be reversed as it is Derrida who has more often played the role of Blanchot's interpreter, rather than vice versa. Second, and more important, reading this essay as if the figure of Moses referred to Derrida leads us to envision Derrida as the shaper of a people, as its lawgiver and governor, whereas it is exactly the tendency to situate justice within these founding operations that Derrida's work consistently renders suspect.[10]

8. This description would also seem to accurately portray Blanchot as well. Reading the essay this way allows for the possibility that he was formulating an analogy between Derrida and Aaron. The analogy thus also signals the proximity of these two thinkers and the debt that Derrida owed to Blanchot, one of which Blanchot could not have been unaware.

9. Geoffrey Bennington makes a similar claim: "Derrida would thus be in the position of Moses, proposing an unintelligible liberation in so abstract and forced a rhetoric, a writing so artificial and full of ruses that one would have to say it was a foreign language" (Bennington, *Jacques Derrida* [French], 274, and *Jacques Derrida* [English], 297). Bennington is citing here a passage from *Glas* in which Derrida is paraphrasing Hegel on Moses. There is, perhaps, an argument to be made that Blanchot himself had the following passage from *Glas* in mind when he wrote this text: "When Moses proposes to the Jews to set themselves free, his rhetoric is forcefully cold and artificial. He resorts to artifices, to ruses [*Künsten*] of eloquence. He dazzles more than touches or convinces. A stranger to the symbol, to the concrete and felt union between the infinite and the finite, the Jew has access only to an abstract and empty rhetoric. That is why he writes very badly, as if in a foreign language. The split between the infinite and the finite blinds him, deprives him of all power to represent to himself the infinite concretely" (Jacques Derrida, *Glas* [Paris: Galilée, 1974], 58A, translated by John P. Leavey Jr. and Richard Rand as *Glas* [Lincoln: University of Nebraska Press, 1986], 48A).

10. See, in particular, "Force of Law," in which Derrida situates deconstruction "in the interval that separates the undeconstructibility of Justice from the deconstructibility of Law." Derrida situates

Nevertheless, the temptation of this reading has its function, for it places us, as readers, into the position that Blanchot himself occupies at the opening of the essay. That is, it makes us his betrayers, given that he has *told* us that the essay is not about Derrida. What is clear is that the kind of ambivalence and irony resulting from a comparison of Derrida and Moses recalls Derrida's own strategy of naming himself according to tropes from the Jewish tradition in such a way that the very application of these names indicates his betrayal of the tradition. At the same time, the strategy recalls Blanchot's own theories on the nature of literature. The Jewish names Derrida dons function according to the same principle that Blanchot works out concerning the literary figure: they expose the distance between the term (the Jewish name) and its referent (Derrida) as much as, if not more than, they reveal a similarity.[11]

Blanchot's essay thus establishes an exchange between Blanchot and Derrida on the trope of the Jew, one that indicates that they are both aware of the game being played. The trope of the Jew is volleyed between them in a match between two masters. For both thinkers, Levinas is a key element—if not the ball, then the racquet—as is already evident in one of Derrida's earliest essays, "Violence and Metaphysics." Derrida, however, brings to this endeavor an important additional factor: his ambivalent relation to his own Judaism. Blanchot's analysis of Levinas focuses on the tension between the demands of deracination and the impossibility of inhabiting that ideal: one cannot simultaneously claim that Judaism exemplifies the possibility of deracination and claim to be the one who instantiates that ideal. Derrida echoes this argument: "Everyone would like to be the best example of identity as nonself identity and so an exemplary Jew. From this point of view, Jews—I won't say 'actual' Jews because that no longer means anything—Jews who base their Jewishness on an actual circumcision, a Jewish name, a Jewish birth, a land, a Jewish soil, etc.—they would by definition be no better placed than others for speaking in the name of Judaism. Who can speak in the name of Judaism?"[12]

What separates Derrida from Blanchot is the way in which his relation to his own Jewish past colors how he handles those marks that

---

justice, not in the establishment of a "just" program, but in the deconstructive act that uncovers the injustice inherent in the establishment of any program, at the heart of any decision made, every law given. See Jacques Derrida, *Force de loi* (Paris: Galilée 1994), 52–53, translated as "Force of Law: The 'Mystical Foundation of Authority'" in *Acts of Religion*, ed. Gil Andijar (Routledge: New York, 2002), 252–53.

11. See my discussion of "Literature and the Right to Death" and "Plural Speech (the Speech of Writing)" in chapter 4.

12. Weber, *Questions au judaïsme*, 71, and *Questioning Judaism*, 41.

allow "actual" Jews to claim insider status. In his engagement with the trope of the Jew, Derrida thus approaches it from two different directions. Like Blanchot and Levinas before him, he considers the means by which Judaism is announced as universal discourse, representing a figure for humanity. Additionally, he approaches Judaism by analyzing the means by which it announces its own particularism, its own exclusivity. Neither of these discourses remains uncontaminated. Ultimately, Derrida's interest is in showing how they trouble each other. Thus, the question becomes how to make this contamination productive. Derrida, I contend, uses the category of literature as a technique to exploit this contamination in such a way that it gains its critical political import.

As the themes of Judaism appear in Derrida's work, they do so almost always in the service of illustrating undecidability. There are certainly other themes that function similarly for Derrida, such as the gift and the trace. Judaism, as it signifies in modernity, develops a particular political and ethical importance in his thought: it appears as one of the key sites through which he highlights his concerns with the problems of negotiating between political/philosophical claims to universality and structures of exclusivity. As he discloses late in life, in the essay "Abraham, l'autre" (2000), written for a conference on the theme of Derrida's relation to Judaism, being Jewish becomes the site at which the *very possibility* of such an opposition can be deconstructed. Moreover, he sees being Jewish as a key site and the source for deconstruction itself: "Being-Jewish would be more than and other than the simple strategic or methodological lever of a general deconstruction, it would be the experience of deconstruction itself, its chance, its menace, its destiny, its earthquake."[13]

Considered in relationship to the argument I have been developing, my concern is to show how Derrida deploys the tensions within discourses of or about being Jewish with the purpose of calling into question both a particularist politics of identity and a discourse of political universalism or humanism. What motivates this strategy is, not only that discourses concerning being Jewish would appear to fit neither of these extremes, but also that, by deploying both extremes, the discourses in question function to undermine the fundamental distinction between them. By mapping these two possibilities in modern theoretical, political, and literary discourse, Derrida reveals the duplicity inherent in these

---

13. Jacques Derrida, "Abraham, l'autre," in *Judéités: Questions pour Jacques Derrida*, ed. Bettina Bergo, Joseph Cohen, and Raphael Zagury-Orly (Paris: Galilée, 2003), 37, translated as "Abraham, the Other," in *Judeities: Questions for Jacques Derrida*, ed. Bettina Bergo, Joseph Cohen, and Raphael Zagury-Orly, trans. Bettina Bergo and Michael B. Smith (New York: Fordham University Press, 2007), 29 (translation slightly altered).

discussions. Consequently, being Jewish becomes for him the exemplary case of both the problems and the virtues of exemplarity as such. This dynamic, ironic in its own right, gives rise within his own corpus to a specific procedure of troping the Jew. In turn, he uses his own problematic relationship to Judaism to cultivate a discourse of being Jewish that capitalizes on its ambiguities and contradictions in the service of a political end.

## I. The Cut

*Circumcision*

After 1967, with Jewish identity in France largely reconfigured in particularist or communitarian terms,[14] Derrida's own descriptions of Judaism's exclusivity read as a reminder that even minority identities define themselves by means of a certain violence, what Derrida refers to as the violence of the cut.[15] *The cut (la coupure)* is a term that he introduces

14. For more on this issue, see Pierre Birnbaum, *Destins juifs: De la Révolution française à Carpentras* (Paris: Calmann-Lévy, 1995), translated by Arthur Goldhammer as *Jewish Destinies: Citizenship, State and Community in Modern France* (New York: Hill & Wang, 2000). Birnbaum describes the reconfiguration of Jewish identity from 1789 to the desecration of the Carpentras cemetery in 1990. The turn toward communitarianism within the French Jewish community in the 1960s and after can be read clearly as a reaction to what came to be seen as a betrayal of the French state under the Petain government. Usually, the turning point in this movement is dated by de Gaulle's 1967 statement about the Jews, which was prompted by the Israeli-Arab war of that year. They were, he said during a November 22, 1967 news conference, "un people d'élite, sûr de lui-même et dominateur" (cited in Abd er Rachman Leonev, *De Gaulle devant ses juges: Réquisitoire* [Paris: Debresse, 1970], 218). This statement was taken by many in the Jewish community as confirmation that they were, indeed, singled out by their religious affiliation despite the rhetoric of equality that accompanied their citizenship. As Birnbaum puts it, this incident, along with the growing support of France for the Arab nations opposed to Israel, "appeared to be a symbol of the end of the dream of 'des fous de la République' the position of which, since the 19th century was occupied by the 'state Jews'" (*Destins juifs*, 222, and *Jewish Destinies*, 220). One saw this shift in identity both in a lay and in a religious context. It was marked in the lay context by movements such as Le cercle Gaston Crémieux for the development of a Jewish diasporic identity modeled on the regional identities of groups such as the Bretons. In the religious context, it was marked by a growing religiosity among France's Jews. Birnbaum notes that, after 1975, there were five hundred Talmud study circles and, among them, ten thousand regular students (ibid., 206; 204).

15. Derrida does address the contemporary situation of Jews in many of his writings that broach the topic of being Jewish. Generally, these comments consist of two types: the first type is critiques of Israel for its morally ambivalent status and nationalist politics; the second is comments that address Jewish communitarianism more generally and often concern the question of who is entitled to speak for the Jew. He writes, for example: "One cannot *do* without truth but it's not the one they think they're confessing, they still haven't understood anything about it, especially those I see queuing up, *too late*, to get themselves circumcised and authorize themselves to speak for the 'Jews'" ("Circonfession," 114, and "Circumfession," 109). While there is a certain ambivalence here as to whom he is, in fact, referring, I assume that this addresses those French Jews who have rediscovered their Jewish identity in a post-1967 context. This is only speculation, however, given the vagueness of the comment.

in *Glas* by way of his reading of Hegel's *Spirit of Christianity*: "The Jew effects (on) himself a simulacrum of castration in order to mark his own-ness, his proper-ness, his property, his name; to found the law he will suffer in order to impose it on others and to constitute himself as the favorite slave of the infinite power. By first incising his glans, he defends himself in advance against the infinite threat, castrates in his turn the enemy, elaborates a kind of apotropaic without measure. He exhibits his castration as an erection that defies the order."[16] *The cut* becomes a term Derrida uses to refer to the literal mark that attempts to elude universal-ization. He refers to the cut of circumcision as *apotropaic*, indicating the way in which it is both a protective measure against outside influence and a measure meant to avoid the transferability of a sign (although it is, according to him, already a figure for castration). Circumcision marks the Jews as the particular people who resist assimilation and universal-ization. It thus becomes a theme in his work to which he repeatedly returns. Most notably, it appears as an element in the title of his 1991 autobiographical essay "Circumfession."

Getting to the heart of the matter, Derrida writes: "The circumcised is the proper."[17] The term *propre* is key here because of its multiple mean-ings. It applies to what belongs to me: *Il a son propre voiture* (He has his own car); that which is appropriate or suitable (*kasher* in Hebrew): *Ca n'est pas un lieu propre à la conversation* (This is not the proper place for conversation); that which is literal: *au propre* (in the literal sense); and that which is clean: *Leurs enfants sont très propre* (Their children are always neat and tidy).[18] In saying that circumcision is the proper, Der-rida points to the interconnection between these meanings, between the way in which what is designated as "appropriate" helps ensure a clear sense of what "belongs," between the literal sense of a term or a name and the fact of belonging. The multivalence of the *proper* thus also reveals how moving from the use of a term in its literal sense to its use in a metaphoric sense disrupts the dynamics of inscription, the rules of belonging. This connection thus also establishes the possibility for procedures that could both underscore and disrupt the relation of the proper to property and the possibility of being proprietary.

"Circumfession" includes within it a series of entries from a note-book started in 1976 as a preparatory exercise for a projected book on circumcision. In the following passage from this notebook, Derrida

16. Derrida, *Glas* (French), 56, and *Glas* (English), 46.
17. Ibid., 154; 145.
18. *Le Robert et Collins super senior français-anglais grand dictionnaire* (Paris: Le Robert, 1995).

plays with metaphor as a means of appropriation, disappropriation, and reappropriation:

> Circumcision, that's all I've ever talked about, consider the discourse on the limit, the margins, marks, marches, etc., the closure, the ring, the sacrifice, the writing of the body, the pharmakos excluded or cut off, the cutting/sewing of Glas, the blow and the sewing back up, whence the hypothesis according to which it's that, circumcision, that without knowing it, never talking about it or talking about it in passing, as though it were an example, that I was always speaking or having spoken, unless another hypothesis, circumcision itself were merely an example of the thing I was talking about, yes that I have been, I am and always will be, me and not another, and there's a region that is no longer that of an example, that's the one that interests me and tells me how I am a case but where I am no longer a case, when the word first of all, at least, CIRCUMCISED, across so many relays, multiplied by my "culture," Latin, philosophy, etc., as it imprinted itself on my language circumcised in its turn, could not have not worked on me, pulling me backward, in all directions . . . in my family and among Algerian Jews, one scarcely ever said "circumcision" but "baptism," not Bar Mitzvah but "communion," with the consequences of softening, dulling, through fearful acculturation, that I've always suffered from more or less consciously, of unavowable events, felt as such, not "Catholic," violent, barbarous, hard, "Arab," circumcised circumcision, interiorized, secretly assumed accusation of ritual murder.[19]

Here, Derrida draws the term *circumcision* into circulation. He deploys it to disrupt the distinction between the particular and the universal. Circumcision is glossed as something like a trope for *the cut*, a mark that is felt on the body proper. Paradoxically, this makes it a trope for inscription, for the various marks that bind us to any community through language or culture. He simultaneously shows the way in which his own family attempted to erase the particularity and cultural specificity of this mark by referring to it with a Christian term, *baptism*, which, in turn, becomes a trope for circumcision. Yet, even as Derrida uses the term figuratively, he reminds us that circumcision *is* literal and that it cannot appear as merely an example among others because, as a cut on the body, the mark itself is not transferable or universalizable.

Derrida relates to his own circumcision as that which has already taken place on *his* body. By virtue of his circumcision, he has been marked. He has been inscribed into Judaism—if not against his will, then without his will—for he finds himself always already circumcised, scarred in such a way that it can never be undone. Circumcision is, thus,

19. Derrida, "Circonfession," 70–72, and "Circumfession," 70–73.

what marks him as distinctly *not* Catholic in both senses of the term: it is that which would exclude him from a particular group no less than from the universal.

In personal terms, Derrida recounts the impact of this mark in his own life. It is the mark of circumcision that cut him off from the community of France when, in 1942, he was expelled from school as a consequence of a newly instituted Jewish quota system, an effect of the 1940 revocation of the 1870 Crémieux decree, which had granted Algerian Jews French citizenship.[20] It is the same mark that inscribed him in the Jewish community when he studied for exams and for bar mitzvah a year later at "the other school, the jewish one," on the rue Émile Maupas, of which he writes, "I used to flee that place," unable to tolerate the way it folded him into an "alliance" with other Jews.[21]

For Derrida, as he demonstrates in *Mal d'archive* (1995), the structure of exclusivity can be signaled in numerous ways, and the logic of the circumcision can be repeated by various methods that do not necessarily make their ties to religious themes overt.[22] In this text, circumcision is treated as a case of the *archive*, a term that for Derrida refers here and elsewhere to the singular and the unrepeatable, to the event as it affects or marks a system. This text considers the status of the archive in Freud's writings, not as driving the function of repression, but rather as that *in* Freud's own discourse of psychoanalysis that shows itself as marked or affected by the proper. It is here that the question of circumcision arises both in its literal and in its figural sense:

I want to speak of the impression left by Freud by the event which carries his family name [refers to circumcision which is also a naming ceremony], the impression that is quasi-unforgettable and irrecusable, undeniable (even by those who deny it) that Freud will have made on whoever after him speaks of him, speaks of him or to him and must thus, accepting it or not, knowing it or not, leave a mark: in his culture in his discipline, whatever that would be, and particularly philosophy, medicine, psychiatry . . . the history of texts and discourse, the political history, the history of duty, the history of ideas or of culture, the history of religion and religion itself, the history of this institutional and scientific project which is called psychoanalysis.

20. Jacques Derrida, *La carte postale* (Paris: Flammarion, 1980), 97, translated by Alan Bass as *The Post Card* (Chicago: University of Chicago Press, 1987), 87–88.

21. Derrida, "Circonfession," 175, and "Circumfession," 164. Derrida plays here with the notion of the *alliance*, which was also a term for the Alliance israélite universelle, which ran Jewish schools in Algeria. This is also the organization for which Levinas worked as director of the École normale israélite orientale.

22. I refer to this text and others by Derrida with their French titles when they are not strictly translatable.

The question of circumcision for Derrida shows itself to be the question more generally of how the proper makes its mark on those discourses that demand a universal status, those that claim by their "objective" status to have no ties to the particular: "We well know that in diverse and complicated ways, proper names and signatures count. But the structure of the theoretical, philosophical scientific utterance, even those concerning history, do not have, must not have in principle an intrinsic and essential need of the archive, and of that which ties the archive under all its forms to the proper name or the body proper, to filiation (familial or national), alliances, secrets."[23]

The relationship highlighted here between the universal and the particular resurfaces in much, if not all, of Derrida's work from *The Origin of Geometry* forward. But it takes on a further complexity in the case of Freud, not only because of the importance that Freud made of such scars in speech, but also, and more important, because of the accusation that dogged psychoanalysis that it is a "Jewish science."[24] This is an accusation that was first made in order to discredit psychoanalysis and, thus, as a part of an anti-Semitic discourse that called into question the potential for Jews to speak objectively in the name of science. It resurfaces as a revalorization in a postwar Zionist context.[25] Anna Freud herself raised the possibility of this revalorization when she spoke on behalf of her father at the occasion of the naming of the Sigmund Freud Professorship at Hebrew University in Jerusalem in 1977 by calling this formerly derogatory comment "a title of honor" "under present circumstances."[26] In his work on Freud's relation to his Jewish origins, *Freud's Moses*, Yosef Hayim Yerushalmi pursues this issue further, asking in a style of apostrophe that resurfaces throughout the book: "But what did she mean by 'under present circumstances'? Was her statement merely a rhetorical flourish? . . . Professor Freud, at this point I find it futile to ask whether, genetically or structurally, psychoanalysis is really a Jewish science. . . . I want only to know whether *you* ultimately came to believe it to be so."[27]

23. Derrida, *Mal d'archive*, 53, 73, and *Archive Fever*, 30, 45.

24. It is important to note that this problem complex is already an inheritance of phenomenology, present, as we saw in the last chapter, in both Heidegger's and Levinas's thinking as an issue of origins, the supposedly Greek origins of philosophy, and the supposedly Jewish origins of a certain ethics. For Derrida, this relation is one that he problematizes yet accepts.

25. See Yosef Hayim Yerushalmi, *Freud's Moses: Judaism Terminable and Interminable* (New Haven, CT: Yale University Press, 1991), 46–50, 96–100.

26. Yerushalmi points out that the honor had been refused by the International Association of Psychoanalysis ten years earlier. Additionally, Anna herself did not accept the honor in person but sent a paper to be read on her behalf. See Yerushalmi, *Freud's Moses*, 99.

27. Ibid., 100.

It is to these questions of Yerushalmi's that Derrida turns in *Mal d'archive*, not to discuss merely the way in which Freud's Jewish background affects his work, but to discuss the way in which the signs of one's particularity that appear in a text can be used to *reinscribe* a text, a discourse, or a subject into its proper context. As is clear from his other writings on this question, Derrida has no interest in denying that the cut scars every discourse with ambitions to present itself as universal, nor is he concerned merely to reaffirm along with Yerushalmi the signs of Freud's Judaism that appear in his texts.[28] Rather, he uses the occasion of Yerushalmi's analysis of Freud to demonstrate how the cut can resurface as an instrument of reinscription. Just as Derrida is recalled to the alliance of Judaism by the Jewish school on the rue Émile Maupas as a young boy of thirteen, so is Freud reeled back into the Jewish fold by Yerushalmi's discovery of signs of his Judaism in his texts and in artifacts from the Freud Museum, documents from his archive.

The possibility for this reinscription appears in Yerushalmi's text first through his description of a piece of evidence that he found in his analysis of the Freud archive in London; it appears once more in what Derrida calls *les coups de théâtre* that Yerushalmi performs on Freud.[29] The piece of evidence in question is a Bible that was apparently Freud's as a child but was re-presented to Freud with a new binding (in "a new skin") and a new inscription on his thirty-fifth birthday by his father, Jakob Freud.[30] The first coup de théâtre is Yerushalmi's use of this Bible to recall Freud to an origin he had attempted to deny. The second is the rhetorical gesture that Yerushalmi makes in the conclusion to the book, which is presented as a "monologue with Freud." The use of apostrophe in this section not only allows Yerushalmi to address Freud in the second person; it also sets the stage for his reclamation of Freud's Jewishness. It is here that Yerushalmi takes the liberty of assuming the conclusion of his argument, which is that Freud *is* in some sense Jewish, despite his insistence that he had distanced himself from the religion. Here, Yerushalmi speaks to Freud in the collective first person. Recalling the predominant style of *Moses and Monotheism*, in which Freud uses the third-person plural rather than the first-person plural to refer to the Jews, Yerushalmi writes: "In speaking

28. This concern marks almost all the texts considered in this chapter, but most specifically *Monolingualism of the Other*. Thus, the question of how Judaism, and, more specifically, circumcision, serves as a means to articulate this dynamic will be examined below.
29. Derrida, *Mal d'archive*, 61, and *Archive Fever*, 37.
30. Yerushalmi, *Freud's Moses*, 71.

of the Jews, I shall not say 'they.' I shall say 'we.' The distinction is familiar to you."[31]

For Derrida, these gestures—the one on the part of the father and the others on the part of the scholar who positions himself, according to Derrida, in the place of the son (with all the psychoanalytic implications that follow)—are linked by the fact that, in both cases, they are attempts to return Freud to the fold of Judaism. Thus, Jakob Freud's gift of the Bible in "a new skin," itself a figure for circumcision, becomes a trope for Yerushalmi's reinscription of Freud.

Not only is the re-presentation of the Bible a gesture that would seem intended to recall to Sigmund Freud the fact of his belonging to Judaism, but the inscription in the Bible itself that Jakob Freud adds on the occasion of the re-presentation doubles this gesture. For the inscription is, as Yerushalmi makes clear, both in content and in form a reminder to Freud of his position *within* the Jewish community. The inscription begins by literally recalling Freud's circumcision: "In the seventh of the days of your life the Spirit of the Lord began to move you." It goes on to describe the book itself as something of an archive that had been stored "like the fragments of the Tables in an ark with me" and was now being presented as "a memorial and as a reminder of love from your father."[32]

The inscription itself thus highlights one of Derrida's main points in *Mal d'archive*: the archive is never merely of the past but also a figure of the future by the very fact that it recalls one to the promise itself inscribed by the cut. (I will come back to the relevance of this promise for Derrida.) Additionally, the inscription is written in Hebrew and presented as a *melitzah*, a traditional rabbinic form created by weaving together citations from the Torah in order to make a new occasional composition. It is in order to repeat the gesture already repeated by Jakob Freud that Yerushalmi harnesses his actions, which already serve to reassert the structure of circumcision. Freud is, thus, circumcised thrice, once literally and twice figuratively: first as a baby, then when his father re-presents his Bible "in a new skin," and then a third time through Yerushalmi's reading. Yerushalmi employs the fact that the inscription was written in Hebrew and in the form of the *melitzah* as evidence that Freud's own claims to have left the world of Judaism behind were false. It is important here that Yerushalmi has himself renegotiated the terms

---

31. Ibid., 81, 82. Freud refers to himself as belonging to the Jewish people in the first sentence of the book but then refers to the Jews throughout the text in the third person. See Sigmund Freud, *Der Mann Moses und die monotheistische Religion* (Amsterdam: A. de Lange, 1939), 9, translated by Katherine Jones as *Moses and Monotheism* (New York: Knopf, 1939), 3.

32. Yerushalmi, *Freud's Moses*, 82.

of such a departure by reconfiguring the terms of belonging to Judaism. Freud claimed his distance from Judaism on account of his own break with Jewish practice and tradition.[33] But, for Yerushalmi, Freud's own boundaries are no longer clear enough to establish a separation. As Derrida points out, the subtitle of Yerushalmi's text, *Judaism Terminable and Interminable*, reminds us that one element of Yerushalmi's project is also a rethinking of the category of Judaism, which is a prerequisite, in fact, for his project: Yerushalmi expands the category of Judaism by introducing the term *Jewishness* (*judéité*): "If Judaism is terminable, Jewishness is interminable. It can survive Judaism."[34] The notion of Jewishness provides Yerushalmi with a means to understand how the cultural characteristics of Judaism can outlive the religion's demise. Derrida interprets it as another means of closing the circle, corralling Freud like a sheep that has wandered from the fold.[35] For Yerushalmi, the very fact of the Hebrew inscription and its traditional form reveals that Freud's own Jewishness has outlived his Judaism. Freud must have understood Hebrew, and the *melitzah* form must have had meaning for him, Yerushalmi reasons, if his father intended the gift to be received with understanding. According to this logic, Freud belongs to the Jewish community by virtue of his ability to understand its terms. This is a knowledge that cannot be effaced and will be recalled to him as counterevidence against his own denials. What interests Derrida most about these performances on the part of the father and the scholar is the way in which they highlight the heteronymous nature of belonging.[36] It is clear that the sense of belonging that is imposed both precedes and follows Freud's own disavowal.

For Derrida, the violence of this gesture is best demonstrated by Yerushalmi's movement to the "we" within his "monologue with Freud." Freud is present here only as a specter, spoken to only as he who is not present, and, thus, Yerushalmi's address to Freud in the form of the "we" once again recalls the "dissymmetry and the absolute heteronomy in which a son is found when circumcised after the seventh day" when he could not respond, sign, or countersign.[37]

33. As Yerushalmi himself recounts, during his engagement, "Freud virtually bludgeons Martha into abandoning the Jewish rituals of her upbringing if she is to be his wife" (Yerushalmi, *Freud's Moses*, 11).

34. Derrida, *Mal d'archive*, 115, and *Archive Fever*, 72.

35. Interestingly, "Judéitiés" was the title of a 2000 conference on the Jewish resonances in Derrida's work. *Judéitiés* is a term that Derrida will himself take up, clearly with an awareness of its double edge. See Derrida, "Abraham, l'autre," 39, and "Abraham, the Other," 32.

36. Derrida emphasizes the word *scholar* in order to indicate the way in which Yerushalmi departs from a position of objectivity in his monologue with Freud.

37. Derrida, *Mal d'archive*, 67, and *Archive Fever*, 41.

Here, the "we" plays a double function. Derrida highlights the way in which it works within its given context as a substitute for Freud's circumcision; by means of it, Yerushalmi recalls Freud to his relation, and, thus, psychoanalysis's relation, to a particular people. It is also by way of this connection that Derrida is able to make a further rhetorical move. Just as the "we" is a metonym for circumcision in this case, so it can be read as a figure for circumcision in every case. Structurally, it performs the same operation in any community, even if there is no *literal* circumcision founding the community. Derrida adds regarding Yerushalmi's use of the "we": "(Let's note at least within parentheses: the violence of this communitarian dissymmetry remains at the same time extraordinary and *common*. Origin of the common, it shows up each time that we address someone, that we call them *supposing*, that is to say *imposing* a 'we' and thus inscribing the other in this situation, which is simultaneously that of the spectral infant and the spectral patriarch.)"[38]

Derrida reminds us here that the "we" imposed by Yerushalmi on Freud is both extraordinary in its relation to Freud's circumcision and common in the sense that it seems to stand in for every and any communal inscription. Derrida has, thus, used the cut of particularity, which marks out a space of the proper, precisely in order to signal paradoxically to a universal. It is the structure of community that is at issue here. While not every community may have at its foundation a ritual of inscription that is performed on the body, every community, insofar as it is constitutive of community to be shaped by the possibility of saying "we," repeats the archive even if that archive is merely spectral since the "we" itself recalls the one to whom it is addressed to some commonality, to a relation with the past that affects the future. Every "we" recalls the particularity that remains at the foundation of every community as the basis for distinguishing between those who fall within the "we" and those who fall outside it. Judaism and its foundational act thus figure the very act of a founding inscription.

This lends to circumcision an irreducibly double significance within Derrida's work, for it functions both as that mechanism that prohibits one from breaking all ties with the particular while simultaneously coming to represent a structure of universality. Derrida says as much in an interview with Elisabeth Weber that preceded the publication of *Mal d'archive* by several years: "For me 'circumcision' could mean on the one hand the singular alliance of the Jewish people with their God, but just

38. Ibid., 68; 41.

as well on the other hand, it could figure as a sort of universal that we find not only in men but also in women and in all peoples of the world, whether or not they have thought of themselves as chosen or singular."[39] The condition of finding oneself already within a particularizing context is not itself unique to the Jews; it would seem to mark every person, particularly, Derrida will point out, insofar as he speaks a language.

It is important to recognize, however, that Derrida does not want to disregard the importance of circumcision in its singularity, that is, as an event that is unrepeatable, *except* by a figure. The gestures of both Jakob Freud and Yerushalmi toward Freud function only insofar as they *recall* an originary act; they re-present it. The act of circumcision, by its nature unrepeatable, thus gains its force and meaning by being put into circulation, by becoming figural in its re-presentation.

Here, we must recall the nature of the figure. Figural language would, by definition, present itself as a substitute for an original. It presents itself already as a copy and announces its distance from the literal. In announcing itself as such, it also abdicates univocity and the authority of meaning that accompanies the claim to univocity. This distance opens the space of interpretation, and, thus, the possibility for multiple readings, as well as new applications. Just as Yerushalmi is able to argue with Freud over his interpretation of Moses because neither can access the original event (in this case, the supposed murder of Moses) but can only interpret it through signs that would themselves be figures of the original event, so Freud's own Jewishness cannot, ultimately, be reestablished by Yerushalmi's activation of its signs: "By incorporating the knowledge that one deploys toward one's subject, the archive augments itself; engrosses itself; it gains in *auctoritas*. But in the same stroke it loses the absolute and meta-textual authority it might claim to have. One will never be able to objectify it without remainder. The archivist produces the archive and for that reason the archive will never be shut. It is open toward the future."[40]

It is in the nature of the archive, Derrida (along with Freud) suggests, that it makes an appearance only by way of its figural repetition. In that sense, the archivist himself *produces* the archive. Both Jakob Freud and Yerushalmi perform the operation of making the archive of Freud's circumcision appear by way of a repetition, but, as this repetition is itself

39. Weber, *Questions au judaïsme*, 75, and *Questioning Judaism*, 40. The interview with Weber took place in 1991. Although it was conducted in French, it first appeared in 1994 in *Jüdisches Denken in Frankreich* (Frankfurt a.M.: Jüdischer/Suhrkamp, 1994). *Mal d'archive* was published in 1995.

40. Derrida, *Mal d'archive*, 109, and *Archive Fever*, 68.

tropological—it turns around the cut—its reactivation can appear only as the reactivation of a promise, which would remain to be actualized. Like a memento, which activates a futural relation to the past, these signs must be borne out by their ability to affect the future. Yerushalmi, Derrida suggests, concedes as much when he concludes his monologue with Freud: "I find it futile to ask, whether genetically or structurally, if psychoanalysis is really a Jewish science; that we shall know, if it is at all knowable, only when much future work has been done. Much will depend, of course, on how the very terms *Jewish* and *Science* are to be defined."[41]

As we shall see, Derrida's ultimate argument with regard to *Freud's Moses* is that Yerushalmi has not been faithful enough to what is entailed by the futurity that makes its impact felt in this final moment, opened by the structure of the promise that he inaugurates. What is significant for the moment is that, even in his attempt to enclose Freud within the context of Judaism, there remains an opening toward the future. Thus, Yerushalmi's repetition of Freud's circumcision in fact discloses another potential function for repetition and figuration. For, although the repetition and figuration in this text seem aimed at reinscription, there is, Derrida reminds us, a way in which repetition and figuration can serve, if not to annul the fact of the cut (it will always already have taken place in the past), then to direct us toward a future. This gesture serves as an invitation, a beckoning to those excluded by the alliance.

As we saw above, Derrida has already pointed in *Mal d'archive* to the potential for circumcision to open toward the other through his own representation of the term. He himself has put it into circulation by using it as a figure for the very process of inscription. He has allowed for the possibility that all people can say that they are circumcised insofar as they are marked by some feature that reinscribes them into an alliance. While this does not annul the literal mark of circumcision as a mark of exclusivity, it raises the question of the mark to the level of the universal by showing us that, even without an archive, the dynamic of circumcision is already in play in every attempt to carve out the parameters of a community, a community that is recalled each and every time one of us performs a gesture that includes some and excludes others. Moreover, it is already in effect the moment one begins to speak. It is, thus, not only as a *figure* of speech, but also as a *feature* of speech that circumcision has the valence of a universal.

41. Yerushalmi, *Freud's Moses*, 100.

## "All poets are Jews"

For Derrida, the remark by Marina Tsvétayeva that "all poets are Jews," most famously used as an epigram by Paul Celan in the volume *Die Nie-mandsrose*, communicates the universality of the cut "in all languages":

The straightforward fact of speaking establishes us from the outset in the alliance of circumcision, in general. It's the paradox of "All poets are Jews." The poetic relation-ship to language is the experience of what makes us born into language, to language's already-being-there, to the fact that language precedes us, governs our thought, gives us the names of things, etc. This poetical experience of language is from the outset an experience of circumcision (cutting and belonging, originary entrance into the space of law, non-symmetrical alliance between the finite and the infinite). And so in quotation marks and with all the necessary rhetorical precautions, a "Jewish experience." Just as one finds oneself already circumcised, already within the alliance of Judaism, so one finds oneself always already within a language.[42]

The analogy that Derrida pursues in this excerpt from his interview with Elisabeth Weber is that which guides his readings of the poets Edmond Jabès and Paul Celan. But it is first and foremost an analogy already pursued within the writings of the poets themselves. In "Edmond Jabès and the Question of the Book," Derrida points out that the analogy that Jabès himself asserts between the poet and the Jew is made on the basis of a similarity between the Jew's relationship to God or to the alliance of Judaism and the relation of the poet to his language. What they share, Derrida suggests, is the structure of their attachment: "The exchange between the Jew and writing as a pure and founding exchange, an exchange without prerogatives in which the original appeal is, in another sense of the word, a *convocation*—this is the most persistent affirmation of *Le Livre des questions*."[43] One might even say, borrowing another term from Judaism, that what the poet and the Jew share is the structure of election, in the sense that each gives himself over to the alliance in which he finds himself. In both cases, the relationship exemplified can be read as an intensification of a universal case, for it is not only the Jew and the poet who find themselves already inscribed in an alliance. This would be the case for any speaker of a language.

42. Weber, *Questions au judaïsme*, 80, and *Questioning Judaism*, 43. The full line from Tsvétayeva's poem is "In this most Christian of worlds, all poets are Jews." Only the second half is quoted by Celan in Russian as the epigraph to "Und mit dem Buch aus Tarussa."

43. Derrida, *L'écriture et la différence*, 100, and *Writing and Difference*, 65.

The function of the poet is, for Derrida, to articulate the structure of this alliance, to draw attention to its dynamics. For Celan and Jabès, their own relation to Judaism becomes one of the means by which the linguistic dynamic is articulated. Conversely, it is also the poetic use of language that can disclose a way of relating to the event of circumcision within Judaism so that, without annulling the alliance, a route is opened toward the other.

Language is, thus, clearly double-edged for Derrida, and he oscillates between emphasizing the untranslatable nature of language and emphasizing the capacity for language to serve as a site in which meanings are constellated and relations opened up. Literature is key in the way in which it emphasizes both these features without eliding either.

To understand the similarity in the relationship between the Jew and the poet, and to understand how writing might offer a means of transcending the exclusivity of alliance, we must consider Derrida's conception of literature. By comparing it to Blanchot's, we can begin to see why circumcision is such a key figure for Derrida.

To briefly recall the discussion from the last chapter, the difference between literary and philosophical language is, for Blanchot, tied to the way in which each negotiates the pathway between the particular and the universal that language itself supplies. For Blanchot, this distinction arises out of Hegel's interpretation of comprehension as involving the annihilation of the object in its particularity by the word/concept. This is already a move from the particular to the universal. One must efface *this woman*, in her particularity, in order to refer to her *as* a woman. Literary language differs from philosophical language, according to Blanchot, by the way in which it turns back toward the particular object. It cannot resuscitate the particular object, but, by drawing our attention to the materiality of language or by using figurative language to signal the dissonance between the original object and its sign, language can draw attention to the negativity inherent in its referential operation.

Derrida shares with Blanchot the concern to think through the relationship between literary and philosophical language. More precisely, he shares Blanchot's interest in exposing the way in which the attention to particularity illustrated by literary language allows us to better reflect on the universalizing operation of conceptualization constitutive of philosophy.

Derrida differs from Blanchot, however, in that one of his main concerns is to complicate any attempt clearly to differentiate one mode of thinking/writing from the other. It would seem that an easy way to distinguish literature from philosophy would be on account of their respective relationships to the transcendent quality in language, or language's ability to direct us past the signifier and toward meaning. Literary texts would, thus, be those texts that are concerned with the nontranscendent qualities in language, those texts that draw one's attention to the sign rather than directing one past it. They might, thus, be said to be less translatable, for they call attention to that in language which overflows its function as sign.[44] But, as Derrida has consistently shown, one can recognize the literary elements in any text by altering one's intentional relationship to the text. As was evident in *Mal d'archive*, one of Derrida's persistent tasks is to illustrate the way in which texts with pretensions to exceed the particular contextual conditions of their writing will continue to bear within them traces of the untranslatable, of the idiomatic, of that which in language still inhibits access to some pure ideal of universality.[45] Conversely, just as no philosophical text is free of idiom, no literary text is, as Derrida emphasizes, disengaged from the process of making meaning: "A text cannot by itself avoid lending itself to a 'transcendental' reading. A literature which forbade transcendence would annul itself." What distinguishes the self-consciously literary text from the philosophical text is the *way* in which it relates to the thetic act. It is not that literary texts suspend the thetic act itself but that they suspend a "naïve belief in meaning or referent."[46]

Derrida recognizes in literary language the potential for reflecting on the process of signification itself: "Poetry and literature provide or facilitate 'phenomenological' access to what makes of a thesis *a thesis as such*.[47] Before having a philosophical content, before being or bearing such and such a 'thesis,' literary experience, writing or reading, is a 'philosophical' experience."[48] Literary language calls attention to the way in which language comes to mean by complicating this process, by

44. In an interview on the subject of literature, Derrida specifies that the nontranscendent qualities of language are not intrinsic to the text itself but appear as a consequence of the reader's intentional relation to the text, "an intentional relation which integrates in itself, as a component or an intentional layer, the more or less implicit consciousness of rules which are conventional or institutional—social in any case" ("'This Strange Institution Called Literature': An Interview with Jacques Derrida," in Jacques Derrida, *Acts of Literature*, ed. Derek Attridge [New York: Routledge, 1992], 44).

45. See, e.g., the discussion of the untranslatability of the term *religio* in Jacques Derrida, *Foi et savoir* (Paris: Seuil, 1996), 13, translated as "Faith and Knowledge: The Two Sources of 'Religion' at the Limits of Reason Alone" in *Acts of Religion*, 45.

46. Derrida, "'This Strange Institution Called Literature,'" 45.

47. Derrida distinguishes here between poetry and literature, as he does also in "Before the Law" (in *Acts of Literature*), his essay on Kafka. For our purposes, however, I think that it is consistent with Derrida's thinking to treat these terms as indistinguishable insofar as one compares and contrasts them with philosophy. For more on the distinction, see Derrida, "'This Strange Institution Called Literature,'" where these lines are quoted.

48. Derrida, "'This Strange Institution Called Literature,'" 46.

turning around it. Thus, even while emphasizing a certain lack of distinction between literature and philosophy, Derrida suggests that literature relates to philosophy by undoing the easy assumptions that allow one to assume that a text can supply unencumbered access to ideas.

Between Derrida and Blanchot, another difference, at least in emphasis, is apparent in the way in which each relates Judaism to the literary process. For Blanchot, let us recall, literature is a form of erring. Rather than aiming right toward its object, setting out to grasp it, literature turns, makes a detour; it is the speech "in which 'error' speaks."[49] It is, thus, by virtue of literature's status as a wandering language that the analogy is made between poets and Jews. And it is on this basis that Blanchot would likely read the phrase "all poets are Jews." As we saw above, Derrida maintains the analogy on somewhat different grounds. What he shares with Blanchot is a concern for the turn and the fold, for literature's tropism. The turn that concerns Derrida is, in some sense, indistinguishable from Blanchot's, yet his characterization of it is different. He describes the trope, not as form of erring, but as an obsession. He emphasizes the way in which literary language turns or folds, but he also emphasizes the way in which that turn is a turn *around* an event. Like the Jew, the poet maintains an allegiance to that which happens only once, and it is in turning around it that he both preserves the event and annihilates it.

This brings us back to Derrida's reading of Celan and, moreover, to the connection made between literature and circumcision. In an essay on Celan, *Schibboleth*, Derrida opens with a consideration of this relationship:

One time alone: circumcision takes place but once.

Such at least is the appearance we receive, and the tradition of appearance, we do not say of the semblance.

We will have to circle around this appearance. Not so much in order to circumscribe or circumvent some *truth* of circumcision—that must be given up for essential reasons. But rather to let ourselves be approached by the resistance which "once" may offer thought. And it is a question of offering, and of that which such resistance *gives* one to think. As for resistance this will be our theme as well, calling up the last war, all wars, clandestine activity, demarcation lines, discrimination, passports and passwords.[50]

Here once again, circumcision stands in as a figure for that which happens, for the singular. Derrida suggests that he himself will be "turning

49. Blanchot, *L'entretien infini*, 40, and *The Infinite Conversation*, 29.
50. Derrida, *Schibboleth pour Paul Celan*, 11, and "Shibboleth for Paul Celan," 1.

around" this event. It is also the way of poetry to perform such an operation, allowing the singular to be seen as that which resists thought. Once the singular enters language, it enters as the repeatable. The poem can be reproduced at will. Yet the poet reminds us of the scar that remains in language. Just as the circumcision gives itself up to be thought, the event remains only as a figure for that which took place once. In Derrida's text, the very notion of the turn multiplies in meaning. First, it signifies the structure of the circumcision, which is performed by a cut around the head of the penis. Next, it signifies the action of the poem, its obsessive attention to what will not be given over to thought, whose turning around the event allows us to glimpse the event's resistance to thought. Finally, it is a reference to the activity of circulation, the reproducibility of the poem itself. In "Ellipses," the second essay in *Writing and Difference* on Jabès, Derrida writes: "Once the circle turns, once the volume rolls itself up, once the book is repeated, its identification gathers an imperceptible difference which permits us efficaciously, rigorously, that is, discreetly to exit from closure."[51] The turning of the poem is, both in its mode of presentation and in its circulation, a kind of opening that is enacted through the distance that it creates between the event and its commemoration.

If there is a similarity between Derrida's readings of Celan and Jabès, it is in the way in which he sees each poet dealing with Judaism tropologically. If every poem simultaneously commemorates what cannot be put into circulation and makes possible a relation between the reader and the event, thus opening up the space of communication, then, in representing the structures of Judaism in poetry, the poet is able to open Judaism to and for the other. These poets do so, however, only through a repetition that marks their difference, their distance from the alliance of Judaism. Jabès's repetition of the rabbinic context, his use of kabbalistic metaphors, all these repeat the tradition but also assert their distance from it. Through the repetition of these traditional elements, Jabès decenters them and offers them as a gesture toward the reader, even he who is not Jewish. This gesture is not made, however, as a pure transgression of Jewish particularism, for even Jabès, of whom Derrida says "the Jew is but the suffering allegory," includes the resistance to such a move that those within the tradition would have to voice by including among his fantastic rabbis the articulation of this argument:

"You are Jewish for the others and so little Jewish for us."
    "Addressing himself to me, the most contemplative of my blood brothers said:

51. Derrida, *L'écriture et la différence*, 430, and *Writing and Difference*, 295.

"'To make no difference between a Jew and him who is not a Jew, is this not already to cease being a Jew?'" And they added: 'Brotherhood is to give, give, give, and you will never be able to give what you are.'"[52]

Derrida reads Celan as using the Jewish tradition in a similar manner, repeating and displacing elements of Judaism that arise from within the tradition, but without effacing their differential function—that is, the role these elements play in distinguishing between an "us" and a "them," their role as shibboleth. This duality is particularly evident in the only poem in which Celan uses the word *beschneiden* (to circumcise):

| | |
|---|---|
| **Einem, der vor der Tür Stand, eines** | *To one who stood before the Door,* **one** |
| Abends: | evening: |
| ihm | to him |
| tat ich mein Wort auf—: . . . | I opened my word—: . . . |
| Rabbi, knirschte ich, Rabbi | Rabbi, I gnashed, Rabbi |
| Löw: | Löw: |
| Diesem | For this one |
| beschneide das Wort, | circumcise the word, |
| diesem | for this one |
| schreib das lebendige | write the living |
| Nichts ins Gemüt, | Nothing in the heart, |
| diesem | for this one |
| spreize die zwei | spread the two |
| Krüppelfinger zum heil- | cripple-fingers in hal- |
| bringenden Spruch. | lowing sentence. |
| Diesem. | For this one. |
| . . . . . . . | . . . . . . . . . . |
| Wirf auch die Abendtür zu, Rabbi. | Slam shut the eveningdoor, Rabbi. |
| . . . . . . . . . . . . . . . . . . . . . . . . . | . . . . . . . . . . . . . . . . . . . . . . . . . |
| Reiß die Morgentür auf, Ra—[53] | Fling the morning door open, Ra— |

In this poem, circumcision is itself displaced onto the word—"beschneide das Wort." It is already figurative and, thus, at least open to other significations. This displacement of the action of circumcision onto language at the same time recalls the fact that languages carry within themselves the function of circumcision, the power to mark our differences. For Der-

52. Ibid., 112; 75.
53. I have reproduced here the lines that Derrida quotes from the poem. See Derrida, *Schibboleth pour Paul Celan*, 102, 104, 107, and "Shibboleth for Paul Celan," 56, 57, 58, 60 (translation altered). This excludes nine lines after "tat ich mein Wort auf."

rida, this is most clearly communicated by the term *shibboleth*. This term arising out of the Hebrew Bible appears in Celan's poems and as the title of Derrida's essay on Celan. In its biblical context, the word *shibboleth*, which means "rushing stream" in Hebrew, is employed differentially by the army of Jephtah in the book of Judges. At a crossing point on the river Jordan, the men of Gilead use it to distinguish between their own people and fugitive Ephraïmites, who, when asked to pronounce the word, say *sibboleth* because of their inability to form the *sh* sound. Those who cannot pronounce the word correctly are then seized and killed.[54]

Celan uses the term to evoke the borders between languages where translation cannot take place.[55] Derrida recalls this term in relation to "Einem, dem vor der Tür stand" as a reminder that language can also appear as a mark on the body, in a lisp or an accent, an involuntary mark that distinguishes those on the inside from those on the outside. Understood as such, the imperative in this poem, "beschneide das Wort," can ironically be read as a plea to Rabbi Löw to give the word of passage, the password, to open the door to the other.[56] Thus, the term *beschneide* is reversed in its significance by its figurative usage. As an action to be performed on the word, it becomes that which would make the word welcoming rather than a site of difference.

Derrida's complex reading can be summed up this way: On the one hand, language, as something we are born into, an alliance that marks us physically and mentally, can function like the cut of circumcision to recall us back to our alliances. At the same time, it is the means by which we turn the cut into a figure, a means by which access is offered to the other person who stands outside our alliance. Celan, according to Derrida, conveys this double edge of language by ironically calling for the circumcision of the word. In this moment, the power of the figure to open an event to the other is signaled by the use of *beschneiden* as a metaphor for an action to be performed on the word, a word that needs to be "circumcised" because it blocks our access to the other person as much as it can grant it. This plea additionally recalls all the metaphoric

---

54. Judg. 12:5–6.
55. See chap. 3 of *Schibboleth pour Paul Celan*, in which Derrida discusses the poem of that title, and "In Eins" (also in *Schibboleth*), which also employs the word both as image and as device to prohibit translation.
56. Derrida notes that it is important that the rabbi here is Rabbi Löw, the rabbi of Prague who created a golem. Derrida suggests that it is significant that he was the creator of a monster. But it seems more significant, in my opinion, that he brought the golem to life by means of an incantation, an inscription on his forehead, *aleph, mem, tav*, meaning truth. Thus, to ask Rabbi Löw to circumcise the word is also to pray that the word become act. It is also worth noting that, in order to destroy the golem, Rabbi Löw had to "cut" the word on the golem's forehead. He erased the *aleph*, turning the word *Emet* (truth) into the Hebrew verb *mut* (to die), from the root *mem, vav, tav*.

usages of circumcision in both the Hebrew and the Christian Bibles, the "circumcision of the lips" mentioned already in Exod. 6.12, the "circumcision of the ears" in Jer. 6:12, and the "circumcision of the heart" mentioned throughout the Torah and the prophets and then picked up by Paul as a figure for the spiritualization of Judaism accomplished by Christianity: "Real circumcision is a matter of the heart: spiritual and not literal" (Rom. 2:29).

It is important to note, however, that the poem itself does not claim to perform the circumcision on the word, for *beschneiden* is, here, not in the indicative, but in the imperative. The circumcision is pleaded for, prayed for. It does not annul the literal nature of the cut even as it displaces it; rather, it is the prayer to be able to do so. It is oriented toward the future, welcoming the possibility of an opening without asserting the power to enact it.

We see here more precisely the analogy between the Jew and the poet and why these figures are so important for Derrida, particularly in their analogical relationship to one another. For, as I noted above, what distinguishes literary language from philosophical language is the way in which literary language resists the naive movement between the particular and the universal that philosophical language would seem to presuppose. It draws attention to the complications of this passage, functions itself as something of a border guard by maintaining a stance at the border and drawing attention to what gets lost in the passage.

In the poem, it is Rabbi Löw who serves this function. The rabbi is, here, the figure with the power to circumcise and the power to open the door. Like the poet, he complicates an easy passage from the particular to the universal by reminding us of the way in which we are always already inscribed in an alliance. At the same time, he is credited with the capacity to welcome. One might say, then, that it is the very affirmation of the cut or of the shibboleth that opens the possibility that there can even be a welcoming of the other, for an acknowledgment of the shibboleth would be an acknowledgment of the fact of otherness. As such, it is a "watchword or password in a battle against oppression, exclusion, fascism, and racism."[57] To borrow terminology from Jean-François Lyotard, it would be the acknowledgment of the *différend*, of the differences that a discourse of rational humanism would claim to overlook.[58]

57. Derrida, *Schibboleth pour Paul Celan*, 56, and "Shibboleth for Paul Celan," 30.

58. Derrida borrows the metaphor of the sentinal or night watchman from Jean-François Lyotard's *The Differend: Phrases in Dispute* (trans. Georges Van Den Abbeele [Minneapolis: University of Minnesota Press, 1988]) to refer to the point of view that results from the acknowledgment of the shibboleth.

Nonetheless, as has already been demonstrated, Derrida is clear that a valorization of the cut has its dangers. Judaism represents those as well. The acknowledgment that the shibboleth can also function as a path toward reinscription, discrimination, and social control was evident in *Mal d'archive* and is made even clearer in this text by way of a reference to Israel: "And I will add as well that in its horrifying political ambiguity, *shibboleth* today could be another name for the state of Israel, the present state of the state of Israel." Derrida's intention is, not to condemn Israel, or even to signal some particularity of the Jewish state in this regard, but rather to point to the ambivalence in any gesture that prioritizes the acknowledgment of difference: "The value of the shibboleth can always tragically be inverted. Tragically because the inversion exceeds the initiative of subjects, the goodwill of men . . . it can . . . corrupt its differential value, which is the condition of the alliance, and of the poem, making of it a discriminatory limit, a technique of exclusion, or surveillance."[59] The question then becomes, How does one assure that these differential structures, the circumcision and the shibboleth, serve as a means of welcoming the other? Inversely, how does one welcome the other without at least claiming to annul the cut?

This is a power that literature harbors, and, ultimately, as we will see, it is the source of its great political potential. It provides a space of encounter that allows the reader to relate to an event but offers itself merely as a copy that would, by its nature, deny access to the original. In the case of Celan's use of the term *beschneiden*, the poem raises circumcision to the level of metaphor, providing a site in which anyone can relate to this event, without annulling the inaccessibility of the event itself. This is also the effect of Marina Tsvétayeva's comment that all poets are Jews. This metaphor, developed in both Celan and Jabès, opens the possibility that the reader can identify and relate to the idea of the Jew through figuration. Simultaneously, this representation reminds the reader of the fact that what is offered is *figural*. Thus, the distance between the universalized notion and the original cut is made visible even through the act of the offering. What is proffered is, not a sharing of the originary event, but its repetition and figuration. The offering is made in such a way that it is also a reminder of how the reader is excluded from the originary event of circumcision. Furthermore, if the analogy between the poet and the Jew is made on the basis of the cut, then what is communicated on one level is a commonality, a shared structure (i.e., we are all a product of the cut). However, the content of what is communicated is the fact

---

59. Derrida, *Schibboleth pour Paul Celan*, 56, and "Shibboleth for Paul Celan," 30.

of boundaries: the way in which the structure of community excludes, and the way in which the structure of language constrains, us from ever having a pure translation either from one category to another or from one language to another.[60] The question then becomes whether Judaism requires a literary rendering in order for it to open toward the other. Is it destined to be a particularism unless treated metaphorically? Or does it not already assert its own stance as a universalism; does it not itself already claim to be a witness to the universal?

*The Open Door*

Let us recall one of Levinas's statements on the meaning of Jewish election, a portion of which was considered in chapter 3: "The idea of an elect people does not have to be taken for an arrogance. It is not a consciousness of exceptional rights, but of exceptional obligations. It is the prerogative of moral consciousness itself. It knows itself at the center of the world and for it the world is not homogeneous: for I am always alone in being able to answer the call, I am irreplaceable in my assumption of responsibility."[61] Here, Levinas asserts a vision of the Jew that manages to illustrate the possibility that particularism and universalism could, in fact, be coextensive. It is insofar as the Jew is chosen or elected that he asserts a universalism. A Jewish universalism, Levinas suggests, would hinge on an awareness that the world is not homogeneous. It is, thus, my particularity that makes me responsible for the entire universe and, thus, a witness to the universal.

Derrida pays heed to this notion in his reading of Celan's poem "Einem, der vor der Tür Stand." The very notion of the open door can be read as a motif recalling this structure. The open door on Pesach is simultaneously a gesture signifying that anyone who is hungry will have a place at the table and a gesture intended to welcome the prophet Elijah. As Derrida reminds us in his reading of the poem, Elijah is both the prophet who "must be present at each circumcision" and the prophet whose return announces the coming of the Messiah. Derrida does not develop within *Schibboleth* the potential for reading the open door as an opening for the Messiah, except to note the potential reference to Elijah in the poem and to remind us that the poem instantiates the structure of a messianic awaiting; for Derrida, this means that it main-

60. Derrida discusses this issue at length in numerous places. See, in particular, Jacques Derrida, *Le monolinguisme de l'autre; ou, La prothèse d'origine* (Paris: Galilée, 1996), translated by Patrick Mensah as *Monolingualism of the Other; or, The Prosthesis of Origin* (Stanford, CA: Stanford University Press, 1998).

61. Levinas, *Difficile liberté*, 266–67, and *Difficult Freedom*, 176–77 (translation slightly altered).

tains the purity of the future, it is an awaiting for that which cannot be anticipated: "The other remains indeterminate—unnamed in the poem. He doesn't have an identifiable face, he has only a face insofar as he must see the door or receive the word, even if this face remains invisible. Nothing allows it to be seen in the poem, the poem is meant for him, the addressee, it inspires him toward his proper pole in absolute dissymmetry."[62] Here, Derrida's dependence on Levinas and Blanchot in his reading of Celan is unmistakable. Transformed by that reading, the reference to flinging open the morning door becomes a reference to the relation with the other in *dissymmetry*, a term that unmistakably recalls Levinas's description of the face-to-face relation. Read as a description of the way in which the poem calls for the reader, as its addressee, the reading also recalls Blanchot and his claims that writing better enacts the dissymmetrical relation. In Derrida's recuperation, this dynamic is reread according to its messianic potential.

The poem awaits the one who is at the door, and that awaiting preserves the purity of its stance by maintaining an absolute openness to that which is at the door whether it be Elijah or Rabbi Löw's golem: "Here the monster or Eli, the host/guest [*l'hôte*] or the other stands before the door, at the first step [*pas*] of the poem, on the threshold of the text."[63] Derrida thus aligns here, as he does elsewhere, the possibility of welcoming the other as other with a stance of messianic awaiting. As he says in "Faith and Knowledge": "The messianic, or messianicity without messianism. This would be the opening to the future or the coming of the other as the advent of justice. . . . The messianic exposes itself to absolute surprise and, even if it always takes the phenomenal form of peace or of justice, it ought, exposing itself so abstractly, be prepared (waiting without awaiting itself) for the best or the worst, the one never coming without opening the possibility of the other."[64] But Derrida is careful in his recollection of a messianic dynamic to limit its connection to Judaism. His expression of the structure of messianicity recalls certain versions of Jewish messianism, but he insists on a distinction between the structure and any Jewish (or Christian for that matter) content. Yet he will not deny the fact that this structure has a privileged relation with the tradition from which it derives;[65] rather, he will describe it as a

62. Derrida, *Schibboleth pour Paul Celan*, 107, and "Shibboleth for Paul Celan," 60.

63. Ibid., 103; 57.

64. Derrida, *Foi et savoir*, 30, and "Faith and Knowledge," 56.

65. "It belongs properly to no religion (even if I am obliged here 'among ourselves' for essential reasons of language and of place, of culture, of a provisional rhetoric and a historical strategy of which I will speak later, to continue giving it names marked by the Abrahamic religions)" (ibid., 31; 56).

concept that is "stripped [*dépouillée*]" of its dogmatic content, stripped of its relation to a tradition.[66] To understand why Derrida makes this move, we must consider his analysis of exemplarity.

Thus far in this chapter, we have seen how Derrida approaches Judaism as a particularist discourse through his analysis of circumcision and how he then complicates this point by revealing that the structure of the alliance announced by circumcision is a universal feature of culture. I have illustrated how a tropological employment of circumcision can disrupt the closure that circumcision seems to institute. To this end, I analyzed the ways in which a literary approach both to the Jew and to circumcision served as a means of welcoming the other. The very language of welcoming the other recalls Levinas, who, as we have seen, would claim that the cut of Judaism is the very avenue by which it welcomes the other. Its particularism would be, not at odds with universalism, but rather the very source of its universalism. Derrida himself would seem to draw on Levinas's reading of Judaism as he constructs a notion of messianicity. Yet he argues that, even as Judaism announces itself as a universalism, it is troubled by the very structure of this announcement: exemplarity.

## II. The Exemplar

*Trembling before the One*

In her recent *Exemplarity and Chosenness*, Dana Hollander has effectively shown how Derrida's concern for the structure of exemplarity, evident in his work from his introduction to *The Origin of Geometry* forward, leads both implicitly and explicity to the political concerns that guide his later philosophy and, furthermore, how it plays into his representation of Judaism.[67] Hollander's concern is to expose the impact of exemplarity on philosophy as it becomes attentive to the ineradicable particularity

---

66. Ibid., 31; 57.

67. Hollander's concern is to show how this structure is, ultimately, tied for Derrida to the notion of an abstract messianicity. For her, this opens up a rereading of Rosenzweig's *Star of Redemption*, particularly of the seemingly problematic description of the Jewish people in this text, in such a way that it becomes an exemplar of the relation between election and messianicity, understood as a radical openness toward the future. While I do not contest Hollander's reading, I would suggest that, rather than seeing a complementarity between Rosenzweig and Derrida, we must see the way in which the concern for metaphor in Derrida, which Hollander notes, requires a critique of Rosenzweig's text and, thus, the performance of a similar operation to the one I see Derrida performing on Levinas. See Dana Hollander, *Exemplarity and Chosenness: Rosenzweig and Derrida on the Nation of Philosophy* (Stanford, CA: Stanford University Press, 2008), 50–54.

that marks its discourse. My concern in examining the role of exemplarity in Derrida's approach to Judaism is to show the way in which it necessitates a move *beyond* philosophy and into literature so as to mobilize the tensions between particularity and universality that constitute the structure of exemplarity. In the first half of the chapter, I showed how Derrida's critiques of discourses or rituals that claim exclusivity lead to his embrace of literature as a discourse that opens the cut to the other. In what follows, I will illustrate the way in which his critique of exemplarity as a structure that claims universality while guarding the interests of the particular leads to his interest in literature as a discourse that neither disavows particularity nor protects it but rather puts it into play while at the same time annulling alliances through the modes of fiction and figuration. In the process, I will expose how Derrida's own articulations of his relation to Judaism demonstrate this dynamic.

As an issue for phenomenology, the structure of exemplarity arises with Husserl's claim that the categories are themselves given to the intentional subject through the intuition of a particular object.[68] Already in his introduction to *The Origin of Geometry*, when Derrida speaks of exemplarity, he distinguishes it from the example. It is as a *model example* that it functions, not only eidetically, but also teleologically to guide and orient.[69] This structure becomes increasingly important to him as a political paradigm when, in the 1980s, he engages in what he calls the question of *philosophical nationality*. His concern with this issue is dominated by two claims: First, even philosophical discourse cannot be considered to be free of the idiom in which it is expressed, and, thus, it can never make a claim to pure universality. Second, nationalism, which is generally presumed to be a particularist discourse, always presents itself through universals, that is, through the structure of exemplarity:

The self-positing or self-identification of the nation always has the form of a *philosophy*, which, although better represented by such and such a nation, is nonetheless a certain relation to the universality of the philosophical. . . . What I am saying concerns the structure of national consciousness, feeling and demand which means that a nation posits itself not only a bearer of a philosophy but of an exemplary philosophy, i.e. one that is both particular and potentially universal—and which is philosophical by that very fact. Not only does nationalism not happen like an accident or evil to a

68. Edmund Husserl, *Logische Untersuchungen*, 2 vols. (Halle a.d.S.: Max Niemeyer, 1922), 1:14–17 (sec. 6), translated by J. N. Findlay as *Logical Investigations* (New York: Humanities, 1970), 60–63.
69. Jacques Derrida, introduction to *L'origine de la géométrie*, by Edmund Husserl (Paris: Presses universitaire de France, 1962), 46–47, translated by John P. Leavey Jr. as *Edmund Husserl's Origin of Geometry: An Introduction* (Lincoln: University of Nebraska Press, 1989), 58.

philosophy supposedly a stranger to it and which would, by essential vocation, be cosmopolitan and universalist, it is a philosophy, a discourse which is, structurally, philosophical. And it is universalist or cosmopolitan.[70]

The appearance of exemplarity in the political sphere is not by definition nationalism; rather, nationalism represents a way in which the structure of exemplarity, while used as a means to articulate a universalism, is also a means to exalt the priority of that particular entity that instantiates the universal. Like the cut, then, the structure of exemplarity is ambivalent, for it is necessary and universal: "it holds from people to people, from sex to sex, from nation to nation," but it is also insidious.[71]

In the "Onto-Theology of National Humanism," which opened his seminar cycle on philosophical nationality, Derrida uses Fichte's *Addresses to the German Nation* to expose the ways in which nationalist discourse avails itself of the language of universalism and, alternately, how the philosophical idiom "pose[s] itself, claim[s] its rights, appear[s] to itself, attempt[s] to impose itself as national idiom." While this argument might seem to defuse claims that nationalism is inherently violent or bigoted, such is not the case. Rather, Derrida contends that, even "in its worst and most sinister manifestations, those that are the most imperialistic and the most vulgarly violent," nationalism necessarily avails itself of universal language or "philosophy."[72]

Derrida strategically begins his seminar cycle with Fichte, confirming suspicions that the discourse of German nationalism would be the best exemplar of a dangerous nationalism. What he exposes, however, is that this discourse is formed, not through appeals to genealogy, but rather through appeals to universal ideals. He quotes from Fichte's *Discourses to the German Nation*: "The principle (*Grundsatz*) according to which it [the German nation] has to close its circle is laid before it: whoever (*was*) believes in spirituality and the freedom of this spirituality . . . who wills the eternal development (*ewige Fortbildung*) of this spirituality by freedom, wherever he may have been born and whatever language he speaks is of our blood (*ist unser Geslecht . . . es gehort uns an und es wird sich zu uns thun*), he is one of us and will come to our side."[73]

70. Jacques Derrida, "Onto-Theology of National Humanism (Prolegomena to a Hypothesis)," *Oxford Literary Review* 14, nos. 1–2 (1992): 10–11.

71. Weber, *Questions au judaïsme*, 76, and *Questioning Judaism*, 40.

72. Fichte's *Seventh Discourse* from *Discourses to the German Nation* quoted in Derrida, "Onto-Theology of National Humanism," 11.

73. Ibid.

Fichte's *Discourses* reveal, not the uniqueness of the German articulation of nationalism, but the ubiquity of its form: the appeal to freedom and spirit. In analyzing this structure, Derrida argues that such an appeal to universal values engenders violence: "It becomes merged with the evaluating, hierarchising evaluation of the best, true philosophy."[74] Where one sees the "freedom of this spirituality," one sees Germanness. Conversely, where one does not see Germanness, one does not see "freedom" or "Geist." Insofar as a nation establishes itself as *the* instantiation of a particular value, it must, Derrida argues, derail any attempt by others to take up that position: "As soon as there is One, there is murder, wounding traumatism. *The one guards itself from the other.*"[75] To preserve this status as unique once it is articulated through a universal structure requires effacing all others who might make the same assertion since the very status of the claim as a universal opens the possibility that others can, indeed, make the same proclamation.[76] In order for those who assert exemplarity to guard their status as unique, they must deny the claims of others; thus, one has already a war of sorts, a battle over contested territory.

While Derrida opens his seminar cycle on the topic of philosophical nationalism with a discussion of Fichte and German nationalism, his publications arising out of the seminars come to focus on the exemplarity at work in Judaism, on Judaism as exemplary of exemplarity. For Derrida, what creates this status for Judaism is, among other things, the notion of election: "To say 'I am Jewish' . . . means: I am testifying to the humanity of human beings, to universality, to responsibility for universality. 'We are the chosen people' means: we are par excellence, and in an exemplary way, witnesses to what a people can be."[77]

One of the effects of the analysis of Fichte in "The Onto-Theology of National Humanism," particularly as it fits into the larger seminar cycle on philosophical nationalism, is that it exposes the similarity between Jewish claims to election and other discourses of nationalism. Derrida is able to make this point most cogently in his analysis of Hermann Cohen's "Deutschtum und Judentum" in "Interpretations at War: Kant, the Jew,

74. Ibid., 13.
75. Derrida, *Mal d'archive*, 124, and *Archive Fever*, 78.
76. "The other peoples could say the same thing—in another way" (ibid.).
77. Weber, *Questions au judaïsme*, 76, and *Questioning Judaism*, 41. Hollander reports one explanation that Derrida gives for why Judaism appears as exemplary of exemplarity: "Approaching the axiomatic of national affirmations requires paying special attention to concepts such as promise, mission, vocation, covenant, and election. This is a conceptual field which, though it is characteristic of many discourses of national affirmation, also makes reference to the Biblical story of the people Israel and its God" (Hollander, *Exemplarity and Chosenness*, 159, citing session 2 of 1984–85 Seminar Box A.16, folder s64, University of California, Irvine, Derrida Archive).

the German." Cohen's essay, written just prior to World War I, argues that Germany is something like the "spiritual homeland of the Jews" because of the fundamental similarity between Germany's ethos and the foundational message of the Jewish prophets. It is the fact that both these cultures instantiate universal values that makes them so well suited to one another. Derrida does not need to dig deep in order to expose the historical irony of this assertion. It is an irony that reflects back on the whole project of German-Jewish symbiosis, but it is also one that reflects forward on the claims to Jewish exemplarity that have followed since the war. Derrida's analysis might seem even to reflect on Levinas's claims concerning Jewish universalism, particularly given the similarity between Levinas and Cohen on Jewish election. Cohen, like Levinas, understands the Jews as having a specific vocation in relation to the rest of humanity, which is to testify to the oneness of humanity. For Cohen, Jews fulfill their vocation by living in Diaspora, without a nation to call their own. Derrida is explicitly damning of Cohen, confirming the text as "maudit," but he never straightforwardly criticizes Levinas for his use of the structure of exemplarity in his descriptions of Judaism.[78] Nonetheless, his references to Levinas are evident in many of his comments about the nature of exemplarity. Levinas's influence is already clear in the choice of terms Derrida uses to describe the nature of Jewish exemplarity in his interview with Weber. His claim that to say "I am Jewish" amounts to attestation of "responsibility for universality" clearly recalls the language that Levinas uses in *Difficult Freedom*, particularly in the essay "Israel and Universalism," in which Levinas defines Jewish chosenness as a matter, not of exceptional rights, but of "exceptional duties." Derrida argues that this distinction is not enough to annul the sense of privilege that the concept of election implies. To suggest that one people bears this burden is also to suggest that one people claims to represent a morally superior vision of the world. Thus, even as this articulation of election offers a way to open Judaism to the other, it might also serve to shut it down by implying that the Jews would have something like a prior or higher claim to the universalism thus expressed. It is clearly evident from many of Levinas's essays on the mission of Judaism in the twentieth century that his more politicized work runs that risk. Doubtless, we have already seen how claims to Judaism's exceptionality inflect Levinas's essays on Israel and, furthermore, how Blanchot's subtle rereadings of Levinas arise out of a concern for the role of exemplarity and its relation to election in

---

78. Jacques Derrida, *Psyché: Inventions de l'autre II* (Paris: Galilée, 2003), 259, translated in *Acts of Religion*, 146.

Levinas's philosophy. It is, thus, doubly surprising that Levinas does not appear at the center of Derrida's critique of Jewish claims to exemplarity. Along with Cohen, it is Yerushalmi who is most specifically the object of Derrida's critique, which is not to say that Levinas is not an ever-present figure in the background for Derrida in his engagement with both Cohen and Yerushalmi. Ultimately, to understand the role that Levinas plays in Derrida's construction of exemplarity, we must begin with the site of his more explicit critiques.

As we have already seen, Derrida does not pull his punches when approaching Yosef Yerushalmi. And it is in *Mal d'archive* that we find both the clearest expression of his stance on the dangers of Jewish claims to exemplarity and the development of the relation of those dangers to the constitution of messianicity without messianism.

Derrida reads Yerushalmi in *Freud's Moses* as reinscribing Freud into Judaism but, nonetheless, recognizes that Yerushalmi leaves an opening for interpretations that would conclude otherwise. Even as Yerushalmi enacts a reinscription of Freud into the fold of Judaism, he resists closing the circle of this reinscription insofar as his text holds out what Derrida will refer to as three doors to the future or three avenues by which he acknowledges a commitment to the openness of interpretation, to allowing for what has yet to be determined.

This openness to the future that Derrida sees affirmed in Yerushalmi's writing provides what he presents as a space of commonality between the two thinkers. This commonality, he contends, arises from remarks Yerushalmi makes about the future in both *Freud's Moses* and *Marranes*. In *Marranes*, Yerushalmi writes: "The future despite appearances remains always open. The task of the historian, luckily, consists in trying to understand the past." In *Freud's Moses*, he says that what is "uniquely, exclusively Jewish, proper to Jewishness if not to Judaism, is an experience of the future or of hope." He distinguishes *Jewishness* from *Judaism* as a term for the remnants of the tradition that outlive its rightful observance. *Jewishness*, according to this definition, would be defined by a commitment to the possibility that meaning must always be understood as futural, as always yet to come. Derrida recognizes in this commitment to futurity a notion that shares territory with his own concept of messianicity. But his messianicity is a commitment to a welcoming of what cannot be known and is not knowable as such: "Its determination should no longer come under the order of knowledge of the horizon of pre-knowledge but of a coming or of an event which one *allows* or *incites* (without seeing anything come) in an experience heterogeneous to any report or to any horizon of waiting as such, that is to say to any stabilizing theorem as such. It is a question of this performative *to come* whose archive no longer has any relation to the report of that which is, of the presence of that which is or will have been *actually* present."[79] Derrida thus suggests that, when approached rigorously, what Yerushalmi sees as most fundamental to Jewishness requires an overcoming of the very terms of Jewishness. True openness to the future would require a total break with the past and the present; it would require that one not predetermine the shape and form of what is to come, not tie it to a particular doctrine or tradition. Such a stance would be defined by its openness to that which is free from determination.

The question then becomes whether Jewishness can accommodate such a stance. Here is where the structure of exemplarity is crucial and, moreover, where Jewish exemplarity becomes crucial to thinking through both the politically negative and the politically positive potentials of this structure. What troubles Derrida about the attribution to Judaism of an orientation toward the future is the way in which Yerushalmi uses it to outline the territory that would constitute Jewishness. In making the distinction between Judaism and Jewishness, Yerushalmi presents an orientation toward the openness of the future as one of the key attributes that allows him to define Jewishness as that which outlives the practices of and the commitment to Judaism. In order to make this claim, in order to establish the features of Jewishness as recognizable, he emphasizes the uniqueness of this orientation to Judaism. Jewishness could be located as a mode of being distinct from others when there is evidence of this stance. His association of this view with Judaism and its legacy is such that where one sees this orientation toward the future one sees that legacy, where one sees either Judaism or Jewishness one sees an orientation toward the future. Although Yerushalmi's reduction of the Jewish belief in the Messiah to "an orientation toward the future" is clearly an attempt to detheologize the notion, Derrida's point is that, as long as this orientation is definitively tied to Judaism and its cultural outgrowths, it has not, in fact, been stripped of its religious content. It preserves a predetermination by way of the fact that it *defines* Jewishness for Yerushalmi, making Judaism/Jewishness the exemplary case of futurity. Before this exemplarity, Derrida writes: "I tremble . . . [and,] when I say that *I* tremble, I mean that the *one* trembles . . . any*one* [*quiconque*] trembles."[80] This trembling has three significances.

79. Derrida, *Mal d'archive*, 109 (on the space of commonality), 111 (first quote), 115 (second quote), 114 (third quote), and *Archive Fever*, 68, 70 (italicized in the text and quoted from Fréderic Brenner and Yosef Hayim Yerushalmi, *Marranes* [Paris: La différence, 1992], 44), 72, 72.

80. Derrida, *Mal d'archive*, 123, and *Archive Fever*, 77.

The first arises from the political dangers of exemplarity as such and is a trembling before the potential for a community's claim to exemplarity to become violent when it translates into the necessity of defending the position of privilege that exemplarity entails. The second arises specifically with Yerushalmi's claim, insofar as it concerns the future. The "one" trembles before the claim that the orientation toward the future would be definitive of Israel. At the center of Derrida's claims about the indeterminancy of messianicity is the argument that the very structure of *l'à-venir* demands the abandonment of what Derrida calls a *loyalty to the authority of the archive*. As he writes in *Specters of Marx*, a true faithfulness to the future requires "awaiting without horizon of expectation, awaiting what one does not expect yet or any longer, hospitality without reserve, welcoming salutation accorded in advance to the absolute surprise of the *arrivant* from whom or from which one will not ask anything in return and who or which will not be asked to commit to the domestic contracts of any welcoming power (family, State, nation, territory, native soil or blood, language, culture in general, even humanity), *just* opening which renounces any right to property, any right in general, messianic opening to what is coming."[81] Thus, the trembling in this case might be understood as an actual shaking of this structure itself, the shaking of the "one" that cannot hold together simultaneously an orientation toward the future with a claim to propriety, for the welcoming of the other requires the openness to that which undoes the authority of the archive. The conjunction of messianicity with exemplarity thus would seem to create an opposition of imperatives that might, in fact, make the "one" tremble.

This tension, however, also provides the means by which exemplarity can overcome the drive to secure its own uniqueness and, thus, become a productive political structure. It becomes a means, not only to salvage exemplarity, but also to make of it an opening toward otherness. For, as Derrida makes clear in "Onto-Theology of National Humanism," his concern to illustrate the way in which nationalism presents itself as a universalism or a cosmopolitanism is, not merely to illustrate the way in which nationalism expresses itself by way of universalism, but rather to show that the structure of exemplarity is, in fact, the structure of philosophy itself. Nationalist discourse makes manifest what philosophical discourse has historically attempted to overcome or to renounce: its particularity: "Philosophy ought not to *suffer* difference of idiom: it ought not to tolerate it, and ought not to suffer from it. So any affirmation of

---

81. Derrida, *Spectres de Marx*, 111, and *Specters of Marx*, 65 (translation slightly altered).

the idiom or of the irreducibility of the idiom would be an aggression or a profanation with regard to the philosophical as such." Derrida uses the term *idiom* to signal the fact that philosophy does not have access to a metalanguage, that it must be articulated in a language that is marked literally by its own idioms in such a way that it is not fully translatable. He also employs the notion of idiom here in a broader sense. He recovers its original Greek meaning as a term for the: "singular feature, in principle inimitable and inexpropriable."[82] To say that philosophy renounces its idiomatic nature is to say that it claims to be universal. By virtue of the language in which it is expressed (not to mention its cultural roots), this claim is always a falsification.

Derrida's aim, thus, will not be to overcome exemplarity. Even to claim to do so would risk returning to a falsified vision of philosophical universalism. One would take "the risk of reducing or effacing linguistic difference or the force of the idiom . . . instrumentalising language," treating it once again as "a medium which is neutral, indifferent and external to the philosophical act of thought." His aim, rather, is to ask whether "there [is] a thought of the idiom that escapes this alternative?" Here is where messianicity enters, for he concludes: "It does not belong to the past, but is a question of the future. And here I am not just talking about the future of this seminar."[83]

Derrida does not specify in "Onto-Theology of National Humanism" what the role of the future might be in articulating a thought of the idiom that escapes the alternative between nationalism and instrumentalization of language, but it is clear that the future provides a path that manages neither to deny the structure of exemplarity nor to close it in on itself in such a way that it becomes a violent particularism. There is no denying the link between messianism and its archive, no denying that the source for this idea is itself the product of a Jewish idiom, no denying even that Judaism might be the exemplary case of messianism. Yet the very idea of messianism, Derrida claims, is the demand for an effacement of the link. What we have here is a case of exemplarity whose content undermines the possibility that one could assert the claim of priority implied by the structure of exemplarity. Messianicity would, in fact, be the exemplary case of such an exemplarity, for it opens up a direction by which the knot at its center can be expressed.

We have already seen the way in which a gesture toward the future might function; it is, for Derrida, clearly tied to the plea that Celan makes

82. Derrida, "Onto-Theology of National Humanism," 3, 4.
83. Ibid., 23.

in "Einem, der vor der Tür Stand": "beschneide das Wort." Moreover, it is tied to the structure of the *plea*, to a performative mode of language that operates to reinforce the fact of the idiom while directing us toward the other. Messianicity, he says, *is* a plea "beyond all 'messianisms' [for] . . . a universalizable culture of singularities, a culture in which the abstract possibility of the impossible translation could nevertheless be announced."[84]

This messianic potential is best understood in grammatical terms as preserving those speech acts that resist the constative. We might be tempted to say that they are performative insofar as they *enact* a relation with the future. However, Derrida insists: "Performativity is necessary but not sufficient. In the strict sense, a performative still presupposes too much conventional institution to break the mirror."[85] A performative statement still depends on the constative. "I now declare you husband and wife" involves the constative statement "To be married is to be husband and wife in the traditional sense of the term." Derrida argues that the performative thus puts too many limits on the event, neutralizing the unexpected through the conventions that necessarily accompany conventional performative statements in order to make them recognizable and, thus, effective.[86] He thus refers to his own relation to the performative as *perver-formative*, as a perversion of the performative or as *destinerrance*, indicating the wandering destination of the messianic speech act or prayer, addressed to "I don't know whom." This mode of speech would, without announcing a *vision* of that future, welcome the future, let it come while preserving it *as* future. "This justice," Derrida writes, "inscribes itself in advance in the promise, in the act of faith or the appeal to faith that inhabits every act of language and every address to the other."[87] However, the messianicity that Derrida seeks to invoke here would, insofar as it passes beyond the performative, also pass "beyond the possible." It would be "without law, without a horizon of reappropriation, programming, institutional legitimation."[88]

84. Derrida, *Foi et savoir*, 31, and "Faith and Knowledge," 56. Derrida is clearly referencing as a model here the theory of translation put forward by Benjamin in "The Task of the Translator," which he addresses directly in "Les Tours de Babel," calling the act of translation anticipatory and redemptive. Translation both marks the fact "that there are languages" and announces the vision of reconciliation, even if that reconciliation is announced only as a promise and must be announced only as a promise.

85. Jacques Derrida, *Psyché: Inventions de l'autre* (Paris: Galilée, 1987), 60, translated as *Psyche: Inventions of the Other I*, ed. Peggy Kamuf and Elizabeth Rottenberg (Stanford, CA: Stanford University Press, 2007), 46.

86. John D. Caputo, ed., *Augustine and Postmodernism: Confession and Circumfession* (Bloomington: Indiana University Press, 2004), 20.

87. Derrida, *Foi et savoir*, 31, and "Faith and Knowledge," 56.

88. Derrida, *Psyché*, 61, and *Psyché I*, 46.

There is, finally, a third sense in which we can read Derrida's assertion that the "one" trembles before the univocity of the claim to Jewish exemplarity. In the first instance, the trembling is a trembling of fear before a possibility; in the second, it is the very structure of exemplarity that trembles. In this third case, it is the way in which the subject, the unity of the subject, trembles or cracks in the face of the claim to exemplarity, cracks in the face of the claim to *represent* a universal while instantiating a particularity, a claim that would seem to divide the subject against itself. Insofar as the structure of exemplarity is the means by which Jewish particularity relates to the universal, Jewishness would be defined by a self-alienation. It is announced as witness to the humanity of the human being but at the same time as its own particular being, as Jew. As Derrida puts it, Jewishness announces itself as "not being identical to myself, in being foreign, the non-self-coincident one."[89] In making this claim, Derrida is drawing on exemplarity as his source, claiming that the very structure of exemplarity inaugurates non-self-coincidence.

As we saw above in the discussion of "Onto-Theology of National Humanism," exemplarity is, for Derrida, always a product of the claim to be what he calls elsewhere *l'avant-garde*.[90] That is to say, the claim to exemplarity on the part of a nation, for example, is always both that nation claiming to instantiate a universal ideal and that nation claiming that universal as *first and foremost* a definitive of said nation. Thus, in the Declaration of the Rights of Man, we have a case where France claimed to be speaking in the name of humanity, but, by virtue of being *the nation*, to speak thus, France was itself claiming to instantiate this ideal in a unique way. In so doing, it took up the role of what Derrida refers to as *the avant-garde*. Consequently, to be French according to this notion was to be at the same time both French and the universal.[91] I raise this example to point out that the dynamic that seems to mark Judaism for Derrida already characterizes the structure of exemplarity. What makes Judaism exemplary, then, of this dynamic? The Jew is twice over a figure of self-alienation.

89. Weber, *Questions au judaïsme*, 76, and *Questioning Judaism*, 41.
90. Derrida notes the application of this term to the Jews in his response to Daniel Liebeskind on the Jewish Museum of Berlin: "When you said that Jewish culture was the avant-garde, you immediately afterward said that, of course you were speaking metaphorically or metonymically, for it is not as an empirical group that we can use Jewish culture as an example. My anxiety has something to do with this exemplarist logic, and this could well lead me to the question of the void" (Jacques Derrida, "Response to Daniel Liebeskind," *Research in Phenomenology* 22 [1992]: 91).
91. One can see by virtue of this case also the way Jewishness gets defined as a kind of supplement, more and less than human, by virtue of the statement by Christian Wilhelm Dohm that "the Jew is even more man than Jew" (see n. 122, chapter 1, above).

In a certain sense, Derrida's claim that exemplarity leads to non-self-coincidence is structurally reminiscent of Barrès's definition of *deracination*: it is the consequence of being alienated from one's roots by means of the claim to represent the abstract. For Barrès, this condition is constitutive of Jews because they are uprooted from their proper land, because they are foreigners. For Derrida, this condition of self-alienation is not the consequence of a contingent erring. It is a condition constitutive of the inescapable law of exemplarity.[92] That said, Derrida is well aware of the historical claim that the Jews have a particular historical relation to estrangement. Insofar as deracination is conceived of as a symptom of Jewishness, it raises the specter of all the definitions of the Jew that we have encountered thus far: from Hegel's definition of the Jew as unhappy consciousness, to Sartre's claim that Jewishness is an intensification of being-for-others, to Levinas's and Blanchot's claims that Jewishness is a valorization of exile.

Derrida's claim, then, already recalls a history of representation, of which he is well aware. As he puts it in "Abraham, l'autre," Judaism has come to be synonymous on some level with "a deracinating and universalist rupture with place, the local, the familial, the communitarian, the national."[93] We can begin to see, then, the way in which Jewishness redoubles the alienation of the subject, for, not only does the definition of Judaism as estrangement arise for Derrida out of the structure of exemplarity that makes it possible to say, "I am a Jew, witness to the universal," but Jewishness also already carries with it this notion as a consequence of the way it has come to be defined in modernity. Derrida draws on these lines of thought throughout his writings, sometimes more explicitly than others.

For example, in *Glas*, Derrida repeats (sometimes almost word for word) Hegel's rendering of Judaism in *The Spirit of Christianity* as a religion of self-alienation. Elsewhere, he describes his method in this text as a form of writing through citation and, thus, repetition and displacement.[94] In light of this comment, one can, in fact, read all Derrida's descriptions of Judaism as a continuation of the project that began in *Glas*—that is, as a citation and decentering of Hegel's representation of

---

92. Of course, Derrida would invariably see Barrès's traditionalism as a reactionary response to the fact of exemplarity. As he says in *Monolingualism of the Other*, there are multiple responses to the deracination that is, ultimately, part of the law of exemplarity. One is the route of hyperrecuperation that accompanies a nostalgic traditionalism: "the madness of a hyperamnesia, a supplement of loyalty, a surfeit, or even excrescence of memory" (Derrida, *Le monolinguisme de l'autre*, 116, and *Monolingualism of the Other*, 60).

93. Derrida, "Abraham, l'autre," 21, and "Abraham, the Other," 13 (translation slightly altered).

94. Weber, *Questioning Judaism*, 39, 41; Derrida, "Abraham, the Other," 25.

the Jew, for his own renderings of Judaism are never far off from those of Hegel, even when he shifts the valence.[95]

As Derrida reads Hegel's *Spirit of Christianity*, the Jew is defined by the tension between the universal and the particular. The Jew can neither claim what is proper to him, though he has enacted a relation to the proper by way of circumcision, nor accept sublation. Rather, all that remains proper to him is his alienation, for he has projected what is closest to him onto what is farthest: "The Jew bears everything as a gift, rather a loan: garment, livery, name. The Jewish people identifying itself with one of the tribes from which it received its appellation was God's classed property the manager or servant of that domain. . . . Their own-ness, their property remains foreign to them, their secret secret: separate, cut, infinitely distant, terrifying."[96] This same notion of the Jew as con-stitutively a figure of disappropriation is echoed, not only in Derrida's citation of Hegel, but also in his citation of others' citations of Hegel. Derrida picks up on echoes of this dynamic in "Edmond Jabès et la Ques-tion du livre," writing: "The Jewish consciousness is indeed the unhappy consciousness and *Le Livre des Questions* is its poem."[97] In *Schibboleth*, he once again assumes this definition of the Jew when he writes that Celan recalls to us in "Gesprach ins Gebirge" that there is no Jewish property. He quotes these lines from Celan's text: "For the Jew, you know it well, what does he possess, that truly belongs to him, which is not on loan, borrowed, never to be returned."[98]

Thus, as we saw with Sartre, the Jew represents an intensification of a universal structure. Not only is Jewishness a product of the self-estrangement that is constitutive of any claim to exemplarity, but the Jew is also already the bearer of a history that marks him as the figure of estrangement.[99]

Consequently, the very structure of Jewish exemplarity troubles what it means to say, "I am a Jew." Once being Jewish is constituted by an experience of estrangement,

95. Derrida, *Glas* (French), 1A, and *Glas* (English), 1A.

96. Ibid., 60A; 50A.

97. Derrida, *L'écriture et la différence*, 104, and *Writing and Difference*, 68.

98. Derrida, *Schibboleth pour Paul Celan*, 100, and "Shibboleth for Paul Celan," 55. Of course, Celan draws on a host of sources beyond Hegel, including the notions of the Jew as parasite and stranger that were common to the discourse of anti-Semitism, which echoes throughout the poem.

99. In "Abraham, l'autre," Derrida broaches to some extent the similarity between his own discus-sion of Jewishness and Sartre's. One difference between them (among others) is that, while Sartre's definition of the Jew troubles any clear distinction between authenticity and inauthenticity, Sartre himself seemed not to see this. Nor does he see the consequence of this trouble. Derrida sees himself as taking up this trouble, which, to some, might seem disastrous and making of it a resource. See Derrida, "Abraham, l'autre," 36, and "Abraham, the Other," 28.

the attribute "Jewish," the qualities of "Jewish" and "Judaism" are caught up in a bidding war. It makes it possible to say that the less you are what you are, the more you are Jewish and, as a result, the less you are Jewish, the more you are Jewish. . . . The logical proposition "I am Jewish" then loses all certainty; it is carried off into an ambition, a claim, a bidding-up of value with no basis! Everyone would like to be the best example of identity as non-identity and so an exemplary Jew. From this point of view, Jews—I don't want to say "actual" Jews, because that no longer means anything—Jews who base their Jewishness on an actual circumcision, a Jewish name, a Jewish birth, a land, a Jewish soil, etc.—they would by definition be no better placed than others for speaking in the name of Judaism.[100]

At first, Derrida's tone here seems ambivalent. He speaks of "a bidding-up of value with no basis!" and of how saying "'actual' Jews . . . no longer means anything." One might think that, in this discussion of the troping of the Jew, the history of which he does not discuss, Derrida might appear to be in the camp of those commentators who deplore the fact that the Jew has become a metaphor. We can even assume that his comment, "Everyone would like to be the best example of identity as non-identity," references Lyotard's *Heidegger and "the jews,"* given the timing of the interview and the context of the project in which it appears.[101] However, in relation to what Derrida suggested is dangerous about the structure of exemplarity, we can see the way in which the disappropriation that constitutes a Jewish exemplarity might function, if not productively, then at least deconstructively, for a Jewishness defined by nonidentity undoes the very structure of exemplarity. If the political claim to exemplarity is a claim to *instantiate* the universal, how can the logic of exemplarity accommodate the claim that what is truest of said people is that there is nothing proper to them? This results, as Derrida says, in a paradoxical logic, which, even if it is thought through, can never be mastered. This paradox denies one the position of mastery: how can one claim to be the one called if one's calling is not to make claims?

*Le dernier des juifs*

In examining the relation between Judaism and exemplarity, we have so far revealed the way in which Derrida's concept of messianicity arises out of the structure of Jewish messianism while functioning at the same

---

100. Weber, *Questions au judaïsme*, 76, and *Questioning Judaism*, 41.
101. Weber's *Questioning Judaism* was first published in German less than eight years after the publication of Lyotard's text but around the time that it was getting the bulk of its attention from American and British scholars, and it appears in the same volume as an interview with Lyotard on Judaism.

time to undo any claim that the messianic could, in fact, retain ties to its proper origin. In turning back to Derrida's assertions of his own Jewish identity with which the chapter began, a similar dynamic at play can be located. Drawing on the aporetic logic of Jewish exemplarity outlined above, Derrida deploys irony and doublespeak in order to make of the example of his own Jewish identity a challenge, not only to those who assert their own Jewishness with a good conscience, but also to those who claim with a good conscience exemplary status of *any* sort.

Already in Derrida's signatures to the Jabès essays the ambivalence and play that mark his later articulations of Jewish identity are in evidence. *Reb Derrissa* and *Reb Rida* appear at the end of the essays within quotation marks. Derrida simultaneously claims and disavows them as citations and signatures. Both share an association to his name in that his proper name still appears, although reworked by puns. These signatures assert a claim to the tradition while also mocking it. This ambivalence and wordplay can be understood as a continuation of the rabbinic tradition as the rabbis of Judaism's midrashic tradition were themselves players and punners, altering the voweling of a word in order to multiply the significances carried by a biblical verse, often outdoing each other in the exorbitance of their claims.[102] Derrida does not, however, perform his acrobatics *within* or in relation to texts that belong to the tradition. His own commentary is on Jabès's poetry, a poetry that is already a heretical and playful rendering of rabbinic interpretation. Filled with make-believe rabbis and statements about the relation between God and writing, that commentary describes Jabès's *Le livre des questions* as itself "a long metonymy" in which "the Jewish situation becomes exemplary of the situation of the poet, the man of speech and of writing."[103] In signing his own essays on Jabès with a rabbinic pseudonym, Derrida participates in Jabès's game and reminds us that his own relation to the tradition is one of laughter (Reb Derrissa) by way of the figural turn or fold (Reb Rida).

---

102. It is on this basis that Susan Handelman makes the argument in *Slayers of Moses: The Emergence of Rabbinic Interpretation in Modern Literary Theory* (Albany: State University of New York Press, 1982) that Derrida is something like a heretical rabbi. However, this is exactly the kind of claim that Derrida himself protests in *Mal d'archive*, for Handelman is interested in finding a means to reabsorb Derrida into the tradition; thus, she is, as Derrida would say, *reinscribing* him into Judaism, recalling him to his own circumcision. The same can be said for other attempts to read Derrida as a Jewish thinker. John D. Caputo (*The Tears and Prayers of Jacques Derrida: Religion without Religion* [Bloomington: Indiana University Press, 1997]) attempts to read him as a "prophetic" thinker, and, more recently, Gérard Bensussan ("The Last, the Remnant . . . [Derrida and Rosenzweig]," in Bergo, Cohen, and Zagury-Orly, eds., *Judeities*) claims affinities between Derrida and Rosenzweig that disclose the Jewishness of Derrida's language.

103. Derrida, *L'écriture et la différence*, 100, and *Writing and Difference*, 65.

Twenty-four years after the publication of *Writing and Difference*, when in "Circumfession" Derrida describes himself as "the last of the Jews," we can read him as returning to a similar dynamic. Here too his avowal of Jewishness is accompanied by a series of disavowals: "Alliance broken in every aspect (Karet), with perhaps a gluttinous interiorization, and in heterogeneous modes: last of the Jews, what am I . . . the circumcised is the proper." In another passage, he writes: "I am the end of Judaism . . . of a certain Judaism, they will understand it as they like, the fire I'm here playing with is playing with me again." And then: "I am a sort of *marrane* of French Catholic culture. . . . I am one of those marranos who no longer say they are Jews even in the secret of their own hearts." And finally:

For I am perhaps not what remains of Judaism, and I would have no trouble agreeing with that, if at least people really wanted to prove it, and we'll have to get up early, at dawn on this day with no evening, but after all but after all what else am I in truth, who am I if I am not what I inhabit and where I take place, *Ich bleibe also Jude*, i.e. today in what remains of Judaism to this world, Europe and the other, and in this remainder I am only someone to whom there remains so little that at bottom, already dead as son with the widow, I expect the resurrection of Elijah, and to sort out the interminably preliminary question of knowing how they, the Jews and the others, can interpret circumfession, i.e. that I here am inhabiting what remains of Judaism, there are so few of us and we are so divided.[104]

The series of ironies and contradictions in these phrases are not difficult to discern. In the first case, Derrida opens his statement by asserting that he has broken his alliance with Judaism in every respect, only then to state that he is, indeed, "the last of the Jews," which he follows with an affirmation of the power of the alliance. Furthermore, there is an ambivalence to the phrase *last of the Jews*, for it suggests simultaneously that he is something like the worst Jew, and perhaps the only remaining Jew, and, thus, the best Jew.[105] The claim that he is the end of Judaism

104. Derrida, "Circonfession," 145, 117, 160, 279, and "Circumfession," 154, 122–23, 170, 302–3. Dana Hollander points out that the phrase *Ich bleibe also Jude* is a citation of the letter that Franz Rosenzweig wrote to Rudolf Ehrenberg reporting that he had at last decided to remain a Jew rather than convert to Christianity as he had planned. See Hollander, *Exemplarity and Chosenness*, 177. What is significant about this move for my project is the way in which even his avowals of his own Jewishness take place by way of a citation, one in which the original sense of the phrase is deformed. For, in making this statement originally, Rosenzweig was announcing a decision consequent to an experience of great fellow feeling that occurred to him on witnessing a Kol Nidre service, while Derrida seems to be suggesting, in contrast, that his Jewishness is something that he finds himself unable to efface.

105. For more on the significance of these acrobatics, see Hélène Cixous, *Portrait de Jacques Derrida en jeune saint juif* (Paris: Galilée, 2001), translated by Beverly Bie Brahic as *Portrait of Jacques Derrida as a Young Jewish Saint* (New York: Columbia University Press, 2003).

further underscores this ambivalence and adds to it a notion that he will pursue at length in *L'autre cap*, the notion of the end or the tip that becomes for him a figure for exemplarity, for the notion of the avant-garde.[106] To say that he is a *marrane* takes the joke to a new level. For the Marrano would, of course, be one who practiced his Judaism in secret and, thus, could not reveal his identity as a Marrano. To do so would be to admit that one is, in fact, practicing as a Jew.

Derrida himself returns to all these statements in *Monolingualism of the Other* and "Abraham, l'autre," glossing them and interpreting them as citations of the tradition (even when they are not) intended to ironize the very exemplarity of Judaism. On one level, as he suggests in these texts and in his interview with Weber, these phrases illustrate the law of exemplarity; that is to say, they claim for their speaker an exemplary status while at the same time incorporating into their articulation the way in which being the best Jew requires being the least Jewish:

When I say in a particular way—and of course it is all in the tone of the thing—"I am the last of the Jews," that can have more than one meaning (and actually I do mean it in various ways)—both "I am a bad Jew," as we say in French "the ultimate such and such"—that is the last Jew to deserve to be called a Jew, he really is a traitor and a bad Jew; but also, "I am the end of Judaism," and so the death of Judaism, but also its one chance of survival, I am the last one to be able to say that, the others don't even deserve to say it, they've lost the right to, because in order to say "I am Jewish," you perhaps have to say how difficult it is to say "I am Jewish." There is also a painfully ironic way of giving a "final" lesson . . . of giving a lesson in Jewishness to all those who accuse me of not being Jewish enough and calmly think they are themselves.[107]

Derrida is, thus, performing the logic of Jewish exemplarity on multiple levels, first by claiming his own exemplary status, then by illustrating the way in which that status in fact implies a disappropriation of Jewishness. Furthermore, he is showing the way in which any expression to that effect replays the very paradox of exemplarity through a claim to be the best, if only by way of a claim to be the worst. Furthermore, the structure of this irony returns one to the tradition. As Derrida points out, it participates in the tradition of Jewish stories such as those Yid-

---

106. It also, of course, recalls circumcision as the cut performed on the end or tip of the penis. The fact that the image of the end or the tip could serve as a figure both for exemplarity and for circumcision underscores the way in which Derrida's writings on Judaism build up the distinction between exemplarity (as a universalizing discourse) and the cut (as the gesture of reinscription) only to undermine their differences.

107. Weber, *Questions au judaïsme*, 78, and *Questioning Judaism*, 42.

dish folktales about the Chelmites in which belief and skepticism are so closely intertwined that they are almost impossible to distinguish from one another, irony itself appearing as a religious stance.[108]

All this can seem very much like an endlessly self-reflexive play in which irony upon irony pile up, making it finally impossible for one to take a position of any sort, dismantling even the potential for real action or real critique. How might these performances, then, be shown to have political or ethical significance? How might they illustrate a way in which the very procedure of troping the Jew could register as a serious political or ethical action?

To answer this question, let us return to the figure of the Marrano. In every context in which Derrida pursues the issue of Judaism, his analysis comes back to the dynamics of an interlocking set of notions: the proper or propriety, appropriation or reappropriation, and disappropriation. We saw this with circumcision, the way in which it represents the proper and the way in which that representation provokes the possibility for communal reappropriation or a literary or poetic disappropriation. In his analysis of the structure of the Jewish claim to be witness to the universal, Derrida attempts to show how the logic of this claim can dangerously veer into a jealous guarding of that status and, thus, can engender nationalism. But he also shows how the logic of this operation should involve a disappropriation of Jewishness as the most faithful assertion of Jewishness. This possibility is best represented for Derrida by the figure of the Marrano, for the Marrano represents the possibility of responding to election in such a way that the *claim* to election is undone by its disavowal. To be a Marrano is, for Derrida, an intensification of what it is to be a Jew, or at least it is as an intensification of the dynamic of deracination, appearing as a form of betrayal or breech of contract (*parjure*). As he writes in "Abraham, l'autre," the figure of the Marrano is also tied to the literary, to the audacity and duplicity of performance, enacting like literature the "as if" claim—neither an avowal of fiction nor an honest testimony. The Marrano performs for him the logic of Jewish exemplarity

---

108. "But it's perhaps also the irony of the Jew speaking of himself, listening to himself speaking about himself, telling Jewish stories" (ibid., 102; 57). To illustrate this point, though Derrida does not, I have included here a story about the people from Chelm:

> It was once rumored that the Messiah was about to appear. So the Chelmites, fearing that he might bypass their town, engaged a watchman, who was to be on the lookout for the divine guest and welcome him if he should happen along.
>
> The watchmen in the meantime thought to himself that his weekly salary of ten gulden was mighty little with which to support a wife and children, and so he applied to the town elders for an increase.
>
> The rabbi turned down his request. "True enough," he argued, "that ten gulden a week is an inadequate salary. But one must take into account that this is a permanent job." (Irving Howe and Eliezer Greenberg, ed., *A Treasury of Yiddish Stories* [New York: Schoken, 1973], 626)

in such a way that it is "as if it were the one who disavowed the most, and who seemed to betray the dogmas of communitarian or religious belonging, that of the people, the nation, the state, etc., *as if* it were this person who represented the last exigency, the hyperbolic demand of that which he seemed to betray through perjury." The Marrano's avowed betrayal of Judaism represents the strictest of loyalties. This is the law of the Marrano: "The less you show that you are Jewish the more and better you will be Jewish."[109] This law is inextricably bound to the moral claim of election. It is a way, not only of being Jewish by being true to the deracination and estrangement at the heart of Jewishness, but also of being open to the call of responsibility that Judaism represents in such a way that you are never the one who *claims* to be called. How can this dynamic be enacted but by a kind of treason, by a responsibility that breaks with the structure of allegiance, of belonging, and of authenticity?

What is, ultimately, at issue here for Derrida is the possibility of an ethics or a politics that never claims a good conscience for itself. Ironically, it is the figure of election that best encapsulates both the danger of the good conscience and, perhaps by way of that danger, the only escape. One cannot appreciate the importance of such thinking without considering what is at stake in a politics of good conscience.

We have already seen how exemplarity is tied for Derrida to nationalism. We must also consider the way in which the structure of election leads to the rhetoric of mission, to the *higher* calling. This, of course, is already implied by the notion of election, and it becomes for Derrida the foundation, not only of nationalism, but also of totalitarianism—if, that is, this calling becomes the mandate for a program, a plan of action that cannot be checked by other sources because its authority exceeds checks. This structure for Derrida inaugurates a politics of the good conscience. One does not need to look far into political history to see its consequences. All that is necessary to set this possibility in motion is the assertion of a responsibility without the countermechanism of a contradictory law or claim that would question that responsibility: "When a responsibility is exercised in the order of the possible, it simply follows a direction and elaborates a program. It makes of the action the applied consequence, the simple application of a knowledge or a know-how; it makes morality and politics a technology. No longer of the order of practical reason or decision, it begins to be irresponsible."[110] Ironically, then,

---

109. Derrida, "Abraham, l'autre," 22, and "Abraham, the Other," 13 (translation slightly altered).
110. Derrida, *L'autre cap* (Paris: Minuit, 1991), 46, translated by Pascale-Anne Brault and Michael B. Naas as *The Other Heading* (Bloomington: Indiana University Press, 1992), 45.

Derrida claims that the source for a just politics is not a clear and logical metaphysics that would secure a system of law.[111] Rather, as he claims in "Force of Law," the only ground for justice is to recognize that such a grounding can always be upturned, overturned, deconstructed, shown to be the product of a repression of a certain undecidability:

> One often associates the theme of undecideablity with deconstruction. Yet, the undecidable is not merely the oscillation between two significations or two contradictory and very determinable rules, each equally imperative. . . . The undecidable is not merely the oscillation or the tension between two decisions. Undecidable—this is the experience of that which, though foreign and heterogeneous to the order of the calculable and the rule must [*doit*] nonetheless—it is of *duty* [*devoir*] that one must speak. . . . A decision that would not go through the test and ordeal of the undecidable would not be a free decision; it would only be the programmable application or the continuous unfolding of a calculable process. It might perhaps be legal; it would not be just.[112]

Derrida develops here a deconstructive political thinking that would not seek justice on the basis of a rule of internal consistency but would, rather, locate the possibility for just action at the sites where contradictions or tensions in a principle allow themselves to be seen. Ironically, then, the Levinasian principle of election becomes politically productive when the tensions that animate it are put into play.

As already noted, Levinas's own language seems to haunt Derrida's descriptions of Jewish exemplarity, yet Derrida has a tendency to approach Levinas with a certain delicacy that is absent from his engagement with others who express similar themes. Levinas's philosophy would seem glaringly guilty of the problems of exemplarity that Derrida seems keen on exposing, yet Levinas is rarely, if ever, the object

111. Derrida has been harshly criticized for this position by those who claim that his antifoundational politics lead him to an untenable position. Seyla Benhabib argues, e.g., "that he can't have it both ways." His critique of universalism undermines his ability to critique xenophobia, racism, and sexism. See Seyla Benhabib, "Democracy and Difference: Reflections on the Metapolitics of Lyotard and Derrida," *Journal of Political Philosophy* 2 (1994): 1–23. This kind of argument misrepresents the way in which Derrida's political thinking functions. One does not need to retain an uncritical stance toward the assumptions that undergird a doctrine of universal human rights in order to argue for these rights. Derrida's point is that attention to the assumptions that underlie our laws, the act of putting them to the test, is, in fact, the only way to be faithful to their principles. There should be a rigor to this process that allows us to see when we act in an ungrounded fashion, and, as a consequence of that knowledge, we should gain sensitivity and attentiveness to others' claims. To see the risks and dangers is not to be unable to act; it is to prevent us from acting blindly. On the debates over the political utility of Derrida's thought, see Alex Thomson, *Deconstruction and Democracy* (London: Continuum, 2005).
112. Derrida, *Force de loi*, 53, and "Force of Law," 252.

of Derrida's harshest critical gaze. In approaching Levinas, Derrida follows a slightly different strategy. He constructs a reading of Levinas that emphasizes the relation between election and responsibility and argues that the tension between these two principles disrupts any self-assurance on the part of he who is elected. This would seem to make Levinas's philosophy particularly problematic, but, for Derrida, it is by way of this aporia that the figure of the Jew can become a source for a political thinking whose justice rests on its *lack* of self-assurance.

The closest Derrida comes to addressing the tension between election and deracination in Levinas's work is in *Adieu to Emmanuel Levinas* (1997). Here, he takes up the question of the passage from the ethical to the political in Levinas's thought. He begins from the starting point that Levinas's thought in fact offers no plan, no program, no means of passage between the ethical and the political orders. For this very reason, his work demands that we think through the space between these two orders, requires us to "think law and politics otherwise," to consider the transition from the ethical to the political "without the assurance of an ontological foundation."[113]

The name of this site that offers no fixed ground is Sinai. Sinai represents an overlap of discourses both in Levinas's own thought and in discussions of religion and politics more generally. In Levinas's thought, it can stand for the very phenomena of revelation, revelation of the face, but also revelation of the Torah. Levinas recalls Exodus 33 as a metaphor for the trace in the ethical encounter, for the "someone has already passed."[114] But Sinai is also evoked as the site of the particularly Jewish covenant when the Israelites said: "We will do and we will hear."[115] It is, further, a place denoting political contestation and a symbol in Zionist national discourse:

Today Sinai is also, still in relation to the singular history of Israel, a name from modernity. Sinai, the Sinai, a metonymy for the border or frontier between Israel and the other nations, a front and a frontier between war and peace, a provocation to think the passage between the ethical, the messianic, eschatology, *and* the political, at the moment in the history of humanity and the Nation-State when the persecution of all

113. Derrida, *Adieu à Emmanuel Levinas*, 45–46, and *Adieu to Emmanuel Levinas*, 20–21.

114. Emmanuel Levinas, "La trace," in *Humanisme de l'autre homme* (Montpellier: Fata Morgana, 1972), 63, translated as "Meaning and Sense" in *Basic Philosophical Writings*, ed. Adriaan T. Peperzak (Bloomington: Indiana University Press, 1996), 64, quoted in Derrida, *Adieu à Emmanuel Levinas*, 115, and *Adieu to Emmanuel Levinas*, 62.

115. See Levinas, *Quatre lectures talmudiques*, 92, and *Nine Talmudic Readings*, 42.

these hostages—the foreigner, the immigrant (with or without papers), the exile, the refugee, those without a country, or a State, the displaced person or population (so many distinctions that call for careful analysis)—seems, on every continent, open to a cruelty without precedent. Levinas never turned his eyes away from this violence and this distress, whether he spoke of it directly or not, in one way or another.[116]

In Derrida's reading of Levinas, Sinai marks a site of contestation, a territory that requires protection, and a no-man's-land between territories. The name *Sinai* signals the tension in Levinas's writing among his insistence on the ethical relation as a purely philosophical structure, his repeated claims that Judaism is the historical bearer of its message, and his insistence that, as the capital of the very real state of Israel, the earthly Jerusalem is that place "which will have to incarnate the prophetic moral code and the idea of its peace."[117]

The dynamic inaugurated by this tension would seem, as we saw in chapter 3, to point to the dangers of exemplarity. Once Levinas locates Judaism as the site of election, as the historical bearer of the ethical tradition, then it appears that Israel would have to be singled out as the privileged site of its enactment. Israel, according to Levinas, has a vocation to enact a prophetic politics. On the one hand, this vocation requires that we judge Israel by a more stringent standard, one that demands that Israel transcend the status of being "a state like any other." On the other hand, this claim rearticulates the messianic rhetoric of Isa. 42:6, which declares that Jerusalem shall be "a light to the nations." Israel, Levinas suggests, is "impregnated" with a mission necessary for our world, to create the city envisioned in Psalm 48, "the joy of the whole earth," "the city of our God."[118]

It would seem that Levinas's writings on Zionism repeat exactly the dynamic that Derrida condemns in Cohen and Fichte; it would seem that the danger of claiming that Judaism instantiates the humanity of the human would be writ large in the political claims Levinas makes concerning the prophetic status and future of the state of Israel. Thus, the reader of *Adieu* awaits exactly this critique. Derrida hints that such a critique is lurking under the surface of his reading, but he never actually makes it.

In *Adieu* and elsewhere, Derrida signals his political differences from Levinas, objecting to the romanticism that Levinas brings to the Zionist

116. Derrida, *Adieu à Emmanuel Levinas*, 117–18, and *Adieu to Emmanuel Levinas*, 64.
117. Levinas, *L'au-delà du verset*, 228, and *Beyond the Verse*, 194, quoted in Derrida, *Adieu à Emmanuel Levinas*, 151, and *Adieu to Emmanuel Levinas*, 84.
118. Levinas, *L'au-delà du verset*, 14, and *Beyond the Verse*, xvii.

project.[119] Responding to Levinas's claim that the project of Israel creates "the concrete conditions for political invention," he responds:

Has this *political invention* in Israel ever come to pass? Ever come to pass in Israel? This is perhaps not the place to pose this question, certainly not to answer it; we would not have the time, and indeed not just the time, for all the requisite analyses—but does one have the right here to silence the anxiety of such an interrogation, before these words of Levinas, and in the spirit that inspires them? Would such a silence be worthy of the responsibilities that we have been assigned? First of all before Emmanuel Levinas himself?[120]

Derrida's tactic, as is clear from this passage, is, not to criticize Levinas's politics, but to claim that Levinas's philosophy *demands* a questioning of any claim for the election of any one political group, any one nation. Rather than seeing the tension in Levinas between the assertion of exemplarity and that for which Judaism is exemplary, Derrida claims that Levinas offers us the mechanism by which to untether election from a claim to uniqueness. This, for Derrida, would be the true test of hospitality. It would be the true test of responsibility understood as a welcoming of the other. For him, that possibility is built into a rigorous thinking of the very notion of Sinai (and even into the structure of exemplarity). He credits Levinas for having "made us dream in more than one sense of this word, of a revelation of the Torah before Sinai. Or more precisely of a *recognition* of the Torah before this revelation."[121] In other words, the nexus of associations that marks the site of Sinai in Levinas's own texts calls for openness to the other and, thus, a renunciation of the claim that the revelation of Sinai belongs to the Jews. Part of the ethical demand of Sinai is humility and hospitality to the equivalent claims of any and all others.

Derrida finds the resources for this argument in a talmudic lesson that Levinas gave in the mid-1980s. The reading, entitled "The Nations and the Presence of Israel," considers the question of whether the nations will have a part in the messianic future. Derrida focuses on one brief, almost

---

119. See also Jacques Derrida, "Avouer—l'impossible: 'Retours,' repentir et réconciliation," in *Comment vivre ensemble? Actes du XXXVIIIᵉ Colloque des intellectuels juifs de langue française* (Paris: Albin Michel, 2001), 197. Here, Derrida comments on Levinas's claim in the talmudic reading "Toward the Other" that, in Judaism, "the respect of the stranger and the sanctification of the name of the Eternal form a strange equivalence. And all the rest is the dead letter." Derrida argues that the communitarianism of Judaism and of Zionism risk corrupting this demand. See Levinas, *Quatre lectures talmudiques*, 61, and *Nine Talmudic Readings*, 27.

120. Derrida, *Adieu à Emmanuel Levinas*, 147, and *Adieu to Emmanuel Levinas*, 81.

121. Ibid., 204; 119.

parenthetical comment of Levinas's, which appears in the following context: "The nations are determined to take part in the Messianic age! It is a recognition of the ultimate value of the human message borne by Judaism, a recognition reflected in or called for by the verses of *Psalm* 117: Has not the history of the nations already been in a sense that glorification of the Eternal in Israel, a participation in the history of Israel, which can be assessed by the degree to which their national solidarity is open to the other, the stranger? A recognition of the Torah before Sinai?"[122]

The key, for Derrida, is in these final words: "a recognition of the Torah before Sinai." Despite the fact that the first lines of this paragraph would seem to reconfirm Judaism as the bearer of the universal message, the message of which Judaism is designated as the bearer—hospitality to the stranger—necessarily, according to Derrida, undoes the claim that Judaism is, in fact, the proprietor of the message. Levinas himself points out that the passage from the Talmud that he is analyzing tacitly depends on Deut. 23:8: "You shall not abhor an Edomite, for he is your brother; you shall not abhor an Egyptian, because you were a stranger in his land." The revelation of the Torah before Sinai to which Levinas refers here is the hospitality of the Egyptian to Joseph and his family. Before they were slaves in Egypt, the Israelites were guests there.

The significance for Derrida of Levinas's brief comment, "a recognition of the Torah before Sinai," is that it marks a moment within Levinas's writings on Judaism when he seems to acknowledge "that election is inseparable from what always seems to contest it: substitution."[123] For Judaism to serve as the bearer of the message of hospitality to the stranger, a hospitality that, as Levinas himself says, "is the very opposite of a root," it must also include the questioning of its own elect status.[124] "What announces itself here," within this dynamic, Derrida writes, "might be called a structural or *a priori* messianicity. Not an ahistorical messianicity but one that belongs to a historicity without a particular and empirically determinable incarnation." This is not Levinas's thesis, Derrida admits, but it is Levinas "who will have made us dream, in more than one sense of this word, of a revelation of the Torah before Sinai."[125]

How do we then dream of a revelation of the Torah before Sinai, and how can such a dream offer us the transition between the face-to-face and the third of politics? The answer to this question lies with

122. Levinas, *A l'heure des nations*, 112, and *In the Time of the Nations*, 97.

123. Derrida, *Adieu à Emmanuel Levinas*, 128, and *Adieu to Emmanuel Levinas*, 70.

124. Levinas, *Totalité et infini*, 147, and *Totality and Infinity*, 172, quoted in Derrida, *Adieu à Emmanuel Levinas*, 164, and *Adieu to Emmanuel Levinas*, 93.

125. Derrida, *Adieu à Emmanuel Levinas*, 121, 204, and *Adieu to Emmanuel Levinas*, 67, 119.

literature. It is literature, Derrida argues, that teaches us the way toward a just politics, literature that represents a path toward "the democracy to come." Derrida makes this claim most clearly in the essay "La littéra-ture au secret: Une filiation impossible." Here, he argues that there is an "elective affinity" between modern literature and the "elective alliance" between God and Abraham.[126] It is by way of this "elective affinity" that Derrida discloses the impossible path between the face-to-face relation and the third. Literature is that path.

*Abraham, l'autre*

As noted in chapter 3, Abraham is one of Levinas's sources for repre-senting both the Jewish and the ethical subject as deracinated. It is not surprising, then, that it is to Abraham that Derrida turns in order to negotiate the transition between ethics and politics and, ultimately, to explain the significance of his own Judaism. As Gil Andijar notes, "the Abrahamic" in Derrida's work marks "the occasion for an interrogation of the empirico-transcendental distinction," a point of contamination that has both personal and philosophical implications for Derrida.[127] The constellation between Abraham and election has a long history in Derrida's thinking and is present already in both *Glas* and *The Gift of Death*. In *Glas*, as we've seen, the Abraham we encounter is Hegel's Abra-ham. In *The Gift of Death*, the Abraham we meet is Kierkegaard's, the knight of faith who, responding to God's call, illustrates the paradox of duty. As in *Adieu*, the relevant issue is how to extract a politics from Levinas's ethics, through a consideration of the role of the third, or ille-ity: "I cannot respond to the call, the request, the obligation, or even the love of another without sacrificing the other other, the other others. *Every other (one) is every (bit) other* [*tout autre est tout autre*] every one else is completely or wholly other." It is Kierkegaard who allows us to see that the demand of the other always involves "paradox, scandal and aporia," a betrayal of the order of the universal, but also a betrayal of "the other other," every other and any other.[128] But it is Kafka, finally, who provides Derrida with another Abraham, an Abraham who offers a path beyond the scandal of election and toward a politics that can be attentive to the scandal yet make room for the third.

126. Derrida, *Donner le mort* (Paris: Galilée, 1999), 163, translated by David Wills in *The Gift of Death and Literature in Secret* (Chicago: University of Chicago Press, 2008), 121.
127. Gil Andijar, *The Jew, the Arab: A History of the Enemy* (Stanford, CA: Stanford University Press, 2003), 41.
128. Derrida, *Donner le mort*, 98, and *The Gift of Death*, 69.

Kafka himself retells the Abraham story in a parable, and it is this parable that becomes the source for Derrida to imagine how the very structure of election might contain within it the recipe for its own undoing. Before Derrida enlists Kafka's parable in this project, however, he must work out the relation between such a parable and the Abraham story itself. It is the essay "Literature in Secret" that does that work.

In "Literature in Secret," included in the 1999 volume of *Gift of Death*, Derrida argues that literature offers a model for how to move from the alliance of election that characterizes ethics to a politics that does not efface the scandal of the transition. It is literature's relation to secrecy that is instructive here. The alliance between God and Abraham in the story of the *Akedah* discloses to us the role that secrecy plays in the ethical relation. The significance of the secret held between God and Abraham has less to do with its content—what God asks of Abraham—and more to do with the demand that what has been asked of Abraham remain between him and God. Abraham's test (Gen. 22:1) is, thus, a test of secrecy, a test of the alliance. What this story exposes is the secrecy in any relation between two, the fact that the relation between two is a relation of the secret. Fidelity to the alliance forged whenever I respond to the call of the other requires that I not include the third. I include the third when I expose the secret, when I make of it a statement to be revealed: "The request for secrecy begins in this instant: I pronounce your name, you sense yourself being called by me, you say, 'Here I am,' and you are bound by this response to not speak of us, of this word exchanged, of this word given, to no one else, to respond to me alone, in a tête-à-tête, without a third; you are already sworn, already bound to guard between us the secret of our alliance, of this call, of this co-responsibility. The first breaking of an oath [*parjure*, 'perjury,' 'foreswearing'] consists in betraying this secret."[129] It might seem, thus, that literature would be quite contrary to this alliance. And it is, in fact, the negative image of the face-to-face relation. Instead of prizing the direct address that binds me to the other—the "saying," to use Levinassian terminology—literature prizes the "said," the discursive content of the word. For this reason, Levinas clearly resisted literature and saw it as an escape from the realm of ethics.[130] Derrida, however, will argue that the way in which literature betrays the secret, the way in which it moves from the saying to the said, teaches us how to move toward a just politics.

129. Ibid., 164; 122 (translation somewhat altered).
130. See the discussion of "Reality and Its Shadow" in chapter 4.

In speaking of literature here, Derrida is very close to the argument he makes in *Schibboleth*. In *Schibboleth*, he exposed the way in which the alliance of circumcision could be opened to the other, to the reader of the poem, without annulling the singularity of the cut. Here, he argues similarly that literature (and, here, he speaks particularly of fiction) is able to guard the secret while simultaneously betraying it. Literature is a mode of representation and, thus, always involves the third. When I tell a story, I tell *about* what happened. I recount to a third, an observer. I re-present. I betray the secret of what happened in the face-to-face relation. The telling of the story of Abraham's sacrifice of Isaac in the Bible is already a betrayal of the pact between Abraham and God, for it is the recounting of what Abraham could not himself tell, what he could not tell Sarah or Isaac. Modern fiction is the inheritor of this biblical betrayal. But it includes in its mode of representation, according to Derrida, a request of pardon for the betrayal. By treating what it represents as a fiction, it refuses to offer up the secret as something revealed. In that sense, it exposes as betrayal what the Bible conceals. Where, then, lies the elective affinity between the pact of Abraham's alliance with God and literature? It arises from the relation of each to the phrase (not entirely translatable into English) *pardon de ne pas vouloir dire*.[131] The issue of the pardon for the secret is already encoded into the relation between Abraham and God. When God sends an angel, a third, into the scene on Mount Moriah, he has already inscribed a pardon into the tradition, a *pardon de ne pas vouloir dire*. He is not interested in the sacrifice of Isaac; that action has no meaning, except insofar as it is the vehicle to enact the relation of secrecy, the sealing of the alliance between two. Thus, when he intervenes and retracts the demand of the sacrifice by replacing the child with the ram, there is already a kind of pardon demanded, a pardon for not *meaning* anything but the secret. Literature too is intertwined with this phrase, this pardon. *Pardon de ne pas vouloir dire*, Derrida contends in this essay, is the formula of modern literature. This is the case on two accounts. First, fiction is marked by the suspension of a *vouloir dire* insofar as it disrupts any transparent relation between what is represented and reality. When I read the Chekhov story "The Lady and the Lapdog," I enter into a contract as a reader, and I suspend the relation between this story and any real woman who had a real affair. I agree to treat the story as a fiction, and it is this implicit agreement that makes it fiction. A fictional story recounts; it moves the

131. The English translation renders this phrase as "Pardon for not meaning (to say)," but it cannot fully convey the multiple registers on which *pardon* and *vouloir-dire* communicate in French.

secret of the love relationship between this man and this woman to the plane of representation, where it becomes a relationship *for* a third. At the same time, it suspends the status of the relationship. It inherits the biblical task of revealing the secret, but it alters it by presenting its material under the auspices of fiction. Even as fiction might seem to forge a new relationship between two, between an I and a thou, between the writer and the reader, it leaves this relationship undetermined, for, even when I know the author of a story or a novel, I recognize that there is a disguise in play. I do not know from whence the story comes. I do not know from whom arrives the request, *Pardon de ne pas vouloir dire.* Furthermore, she who sends out this pardon does not know to whom it is destined. The circulation of literature opens up the relationship between two to anyone who can pick up and read. "Literature," Derrida writes, "would begin there where one does not know any more who writes and who signs the receipt of the call and of the '*me voici*' between Father and son."[132] It is by suspending these two modes—the status of the content and the identity of the speaker and respondent—that literature guards the secret while at the same time betraying it. Literature is the inheritor of the biblical tradition that betrays the tradition by suspending the truth status of the testament. In this sense, it is itself the request for a pardon, for the betrayal already committed by the tradition.

There is, perhaps, no better demonstration of this possibility than Kafka's own retelling of the Abraham story. It is not surprising that it is to this story that Derrida turns when he finally agrees to settle the question of his relation to his Jewish heritage. "Literature in Secret" has already demonstrated the relation between Derrida and the biblical tradition. He is to his Jewish heritage as modern literature is to the Bible. His explication of Kafka's parable makes explicit that relation by offering the story of another Abraham. This other Abraham, Derrida suggests, is both a different Abraham from Levinas's Abraham and the same Abraham. Kafka's Abraham is one who is able to make us see the tension between election and deracination in Levinas's Abraham. Levinas's Abraham, whom we encountered in chapter 3, is most distinctly the Abraham of Gen. 12:1, who goes forth from his father's house. Levinas's own repeated references to this verse emphasize the call as that which uproots, exiling me from what is properly my own. Yet he is also an Abraham who is clearly called. It is his election that initiates his uprooting. Kafka's Abraham introduces a glitch in this model by asking, How does Abraham know it was he who was called?

132. Derrida, *Donner le mort*, 179, and *The Gift of Death*, 134.

Kafka imagines an Abraham who is ready to respond to God in the right way yet cannot believe that he, an old man, and his "schmutzige Junge [scrubby youngster]" were the ones called. This is an Abraham who would come unsummoned, who would rise to be recognized, like the student in the back of the class, the worst student, at the moment when the best student was about to receive a prize. He would rise because for a moment he thought the teacher was summoning him; he would rise because of a "Hörfehler," a mistake in hearing.[133]

By way of this parable, Derrida once again returns to the relation of secrecy between God and Abraham. He returns to the issue of the third, but, here, the third is not the one who comes after but the one who may have come before. In his reading of Kafka's parable, Derrida asks whether the claiming of the call does not involve an element of presumption. As Derrida writes in the opening pages of the essay: "A call of the name worthy of this name must not make room for any certitude, on the side of the destined one. Without which it would not be a call." The nature of the call is such that one cannot but be the one called, yet Derrida inquires, Is not there a certain danger in the presumption of election? "Whoever is certain—as was not, precisely, the other, the second other Abraham of Kafka—whoever thinks he has the certitude of having been him, him alone, he first, called as the best of the class, corrupts and transforms the terrible and indecisive experience of the responsibility of election into a dogmatic caricature, with the most fearsome consequences, political consequences in particular."[134]

The paradox is that one must respond to the call. Responsibility begins, not in the moment of hearing the call, but in responding. It is, for Levinas, the *response* that inaugurates the uprooting of the subject. The response initiates Abraham's journey of no return. In responding, I divest myself of what is properly my own. Yet to answer the call is already to claim it as my own. As Derrida writes, one cannot but respond to a call: "It is necessary to respond, and to respond yes." Even in responding no, one responds yes: "Even if in the course of the response, in the determined content of the reply, I were to say, 'no . . . I am not here, I will not come, I'm leaving . . . I am here to refuse, to disavow, to deny.'" One must nonetheless claim the call. This is Jonah's plight. Even in denial, we own the fact of having been called. Responsibility demands a rein-

133. Franz Kafka, *Parables and Paradoxes*, bilingual ed. (New York: Schocken, 1961), 44.
134. Derrida, "Abraham, l'autre," 17, 38, and "Abraham, the Other," 7, 31 (translation slightly altered).

voking of what is proper to us. The "yes" at the heart of every response is "the heritage of a place that cannot be uprooted."[135]

Although Derrida evokes a paradox inherent in ethical subjectivity, his aim here is not to make us question the ethics of uprootedness or to suggest that invoking uprootedness leads to the same arrogance and/or boastfulness of any claim to moral righteousness. In fact, he goes further than Levinas by insisting that uprootedness is at the heart of responsibility. Moreover, he insists that activating the tension in Levinas's thought between the dynamic of deracination and the structure of election is key to bringing that thought into the political sphere and, thus, to imagining a just claim to political identity.

We can read Derrida, by way of his own interpretation of Kafka's parable, as setting out the rigor that a philosophy of deracination requires. Going further than Levinas, he suggests that we must return to the source of the call, to the figure of the prophet who is willing to break his connection to land and to home; we must rethink the way in which even this moment reestablishes the structure of belonging. It is not enough to take up the call, nor is it enough to deny it as Jonah did. Rather, deracination begins, he suggests, when one considers the possibility that, in taking up the call, one has perhaps already transgressed, one has already looked past the other for whom, perhaps, the call was intended. It is, thus, a primary questioning of the call, and, thus, a primary risk, he suggests, that inaugurates responsibility, not by founding it, but by calling its ground into question. This does not mean that one does not take up responsibility, that one does not answer the call. Rather, Derrida suggests:

That anyone responding to the call must continue to doubt, to ask himself whether he has heard right, whether there is no original misunderstanding, whether it was in fact his name that was heard, whether he is the only one or the first addressee of the call, whether he is not in the process of substituting himself violently for another, whether the law of substitution, which is also the law of responsibility, does not call for an infinite increase of vigilance and anxiety. It is possible that I have not been called, me, and further, it is not impossible that no One, nobody, ever called any One, any unique one, anybody. *The possibility of an original misunderstanding in the destination is not an evil, it is the structure, maybe of the vocation itself of every call worthy of the name, of all nomination, of every response and of all responsibility.*

It is this law of undecidability that ought to undergird any claim to election, particularly the Jewish one. This, Derrida suggests in his response

135. Ibid., 13; 3.

to the summons to finally own up about his own relation to Judaism, is exactly what is at stake in his ambivalent statements on the topic. Even in claiming Judaism to be his, he disappropriates it through a logic that incriminates the very act of appropriation, an act that is, he admits and illustrates through his own appropriation, unavoidable, ineluctable: "Why do I hold onto it, even as I am not sure of the call to which I respond, not sure that it is addressed to me, not sure of what I mean, of what I want to mean here, be it authentic, inauthentic or quasi-authentic, beyond all identity, all unity or all community? Well, I know that I do not know that, and I suspect all those who believe they know of not knowing, even if, in truth, they do know more—I know—much more than I."[136]

Thus, Derrida makes the performance of his relation to Judaism meaningful and productive by making it a literary performance that dramatizes its paradoxes. In the process, the performance itself develops a political valence. What differentiates his position from Levinas's is his use of the *as if* (*comme si*). In a move that owes much to Maurice Blanchot, Derrida introduces into the formulation of Jewish identity the function of literature. Through literary language, he activates an additional procedure of deracination. While he performs this operation most clearly in "Circumfession," it is in "Abraham, l'autre" that he makes explicit the political function of this *comme si*: "I believe that a certain may-be of the *comme si*, the poetic or the literary, in sum, is at the heart of that which I would like to confide to you here. . . . *As if* the one disavowed the most, and who appeared to betray the dogmas of belonging, be it a belonging to the community, the religion, even to the people, the nation and the state, etc., *as if* this individual alone represented the last demand, the hyperbolic request of the very thing he appears to betray by perjuring himself."[137]

Derrida introduces literary language into the political sphere here because literary language can itself be understood to perjure. Figurative language calls attention to the procedure of representation itself, thus dislodging language from its certainties.[138] The *comme si* that Derrida speaks of here exemplifies this aspect of literature by announcing a discontinuity between language and referent.[139] As Derrida said in an interview con-

136. Ibid., 41, 38; 34 (emphasis added; translation slightly altered), 30.
137. Ibid., 22; 13 (translation slightly altered).
138. Derrida, "'This Strange Institution Called Literature,'" 46.
139. Gil Andijar has also commented on the role of figuration in Derrida's assertions of identity: "Derrida's word, if it is one, will therefore be complicated . . . by figuration (*comme*) and by the lack, precisely, of a precise identity (*cette sorte*). Derrida will not assert, he will not assert (himself), or identify (himself) not simply, (*comme*, as) 'I' nor (as) 'African.' . . . One ought not to lose sight of the rhetoricity of the 'comme' which also separates at the moment it appear to join" (Andijar, *The Jew, the Arab*, 44).

ducted shortly before his death, the ambivalence that is deployed by way of this act menaces the constative structure of its statements. It becomes, thus, not a statement of a fact, but a prayer that is itself something of a protest: "I will always say, in certain situations, 'we the Jews.' This 'we,' which is so tormented [*tourmenté*], is at the heart of that which is most uneasy in my thought, that of which I named, scarcely smiling [*souriant à peine*], 'le dernier des juifs.' It would be in my thinking that which Aristotle profoundly called the plea [*la prière*] (eukhè): it is neither true nor false. It is moreover literally a prayer [*une prière*]. In certain situations thus, I will not hesitate to say 'we the Jews.'"[140]

Derrida thus reads his own iteration of Jewishness as a gesture similar to the one that he interprets Celan to be making in "Einem, der vor der Tür Stand," that is, as a per(ver)formative gesture that by virtue of its indetermination enacts a relation to a future, of which Derrida is not the master. It is, for Derrida, thus, an element in his broader messianic strategy, which aims at justice by suspending the claim that justice has been established. Literature provides a model for the "democracy to come," Derrida writes in "Literature in Secret," because it opens the alliance to the third, but it does not make the move to the third by denying or effacing the violence of the relation between two. It makes the move to the third while exposing this move as a betrayal of the ethical relation between two. Conversely, it is also able, as in the Kafka parable, to expose the fact that every alliance between two is already a betrayal of some "other other." If the status quo of politics effaces both these betrayals, denies the founding gesture, then the mark of the democracy to come would be its setting in place the *pardon de ne pas vouloir dire*. It would be the political equivalent of the literary act, betraying the alliance while at the same time acknowledging its power.[141]

Derrida models this possibility through his own expression of his relation to his Jewish identity. In writing, "I am the last of the Jews,"

140. Jacques Derrida, "Jacques Derrida: 'Je suis en geurre contre moi-meme,'" *Le monde*, October 9, 2004. The interview was published along with his obituary.

141. The phrase *democracy to come* is most thoroughly explored in *The Politics of Friendship*. In some ways, we can see this term as a contribution to the discourses of "community without community" in Blanchot and Nancy. See Jacques Derrida, *Politiques de l'amitié* (Paris: Galilée, 1994), 98–99, translated by George Collins as *Politics of Friendship* (London: Verso, 1997), 82–83. Derrida justifies holding on to the term *democracy* in the name of what he recognizes as democracy's internal drive toward deconstruction, which arises out of the dualing and irreconcilable principles of equality and respect for singularity at its heart (ibid., 126–27; 104). These ideals give rise to the notion of a "democracy to come" that provides "a principle against which any state which claims to be democratic may be judged. . . . Democracy and perhaps politics itself can be nothing other than the negotiation within countable categories, in the name of an undeconstructable limit which is nicknamed justice or 'democracy to come'" (Thomson, *Deconstruction and Democracy*, 26).

or in calling himself Reb Rida or Reb Rissa, he declares himself faithful to Judaism in such a way that the only way to be faithful is to betray it. In so doing, he introduces a new procedure into the political sphere. Although its significance is not as the founding principle of a new sort of polis or as a theory of justice, it is political in the sense that it performs the undoing of two of the most prominent political discourses of our moment. It critiques the claims of a political particularism, whether expressed as a clear ethnocentrism or merely as an assertion of cultural uniqueness. And it critiques the claim to any pure universalism untainted by particularism, by reminding us that even these claims repeat the structure of exemplarity. Ultimately, and most simply (like any good Jewish thinking), it demands of us that we interrogate ourselves for the inevitable traces of a good conscience.

Of course, we must, ultimately, confirm, with and against Blanchot, that Derrida is certainly no Moses, no lawgiver, and that surely he would not claim to be one. Unless, that is, we are speaking of *another* Moses— perhaps the Moses who in the Babylonian Talmud *Menachot* tractate, 29b, sits in the back of the Bet Midrash and listens to Rabbi Akiva expounding the Torah. Though he does not understand his arguments, he recognizes Akiva's greatness and asks The Holy One Blessed Be He how he could have given the Torah to him, Moses, when he had before him Akiva, a man of such greatness? Of course, in the parable, God responds and says, "Be silent, such is my decree." Let us, thus, imagine another other Moses who not only questioned whether it was to him that the Torah should be given but also knows, even as he climbs slowly down the mountain, that God will not assuage his insecurity. This would be a Moses who remembers that the Torah may not be his to claim. For, as Celan reminds us, the Jew is he to whom nothing belongs that was not already borrowed or lent.

# Conclusion

In 2005, Alain Badiou, who at the present moment proclaims himself to be the most translated and widely read living French thinker,[1] published a volume entitled *Circonstances, 3: Portées du mot "juif."* He includes in this volume an excerpt from his 1997 novel *Calme bloc ici-bas*. In this passage, Fulmer, a Jewish mathematician, recounts to Aazami, his Arab interlocutor, the true meaning of the "authentic Jew": "Let's call 'Jew' the one who says in the name of all others that there is no law separating them. He is the one who takes hold of his own proper being in order to break the divisive law and devote humanity to the universal." Assembled with the other excerpts in the volume, the passage is clearly intended to communicate Badiou's universalist political vision and to situate the figure of the Jew at its center. The archetypal "authentic Jew," according to this model, is, thus, St. Paul, who has been followed by other paragons of universalism—Spinoza, Marx, and Freud—all of whom, according to Badiou, advocated the sacrifice of Jewish singularity and election for the sake of the universal. These "authentic Jews," Badiou explains, are inevitably disowned, despised, and denigrated by the "virtual" Jews, those Jews who set themselves apart as a people and want to guard their identity against its possible usurpation.[2] Along with the series of passages from other places in his corpus that address "the word Jew" in *Circonstances, 3: Portées du mot "juif,"* Badiou includes in the English translation a new

---

1. Alain Badiou, *Polemics*, trans. Steve Corcoran (London: Verso, 2006), 234.
2. *Circonstances, 3*, 49, 50, and *Polemics*, 184, 185.

diatribe against what he calls the "S.I.T." complex, standing for "Shoah," "Israel," "Tradition."[3] By constituting Jewish identity according to these three markers, Badiou argues, virtual Jews have erected an identitarian hedge in the postwar era to jealously protect the sacrality of the name of the Jew and to elevate it to the status of exception.[4]

It would appear that Badiou's interest in *Circonstances, 3* is in interrogating the notion of Jewish election. He is critical of the fetishization of Jewish victimhood and reasonably suspicious of postwar Jewish communitarianism, especially as it is manifested in the effort to shield Zionism from political critique. Thus, it may seem that, on some level, his own version of the authentic Jew approximates the sketch of the figural Jew that emerges from my own analysis of the history of the Jew as trope.

In fact, the two are radically divergent. I would like to suggest that the figural Jew is entirely opposed to Badiou's universalism, the model for which is the authentic Jew *Saint Paul*. For what Badiou has done with *Circonstances, 3*, as well as with his *Ethics* and *Saint Paul: The Foundation of Universalism*, is merely to replay the match between particularism and universalism as a confrontation between the carnal Jew and spiritualized Judaism, otherwise known as Pauline Christianity, in such a way that the later triumphs *again* and the "real Jews" are represented as obstinate, backward relics of a dead faith.[5]

My aim in this book has been to expose the way in which the figure of the Jew has actually come to complicate this narrative in the post–World War II era and to provide a political alternative to the universalist and particularist poles of political identity. For the figure of the Jew as it emerged already as the foil to nationalist ideologies emphasizing rootedness in blood and soil in Maurice Barrès and others of his era represents neither of these poles; rather, it is aligned with exile, uprootedness, and alienation. While it began as the essentialized and accidental simplification of a very real historical people, this figure became a trope with a history in its own right, one that was first employed self-consciously by Sartre and Levinas in order to transform the plane of political value in the postwar landscape.

For each of the figures treated in this volume, the trope of the Jew has provided a means to engage in the debate over political particular-

3. Badiou, *Polemics*, 230.
4. Badiou, *Circonstances, 3*, 9; Badiou, *Polemics*, 158.
5. See Alain Badiou, *L'éthique: Essai sur la conscience du mal* (Paris: Hatier, 1993), translated by Peter Hallward as *Ethics: An Essay on the Understanding of Evil* (London: Verso, 2002); and Alain Badiou, *Saint Paul: La fondation de l'universalisme* (Paris: Presses universitaires de France, 1997), translated by Ray Brassier as *Saint Paul: The Foundation of Universalism* (Stanford, CA: Stanford University Press, 2003).

ism and universalism. Even for Barrès, the cogency of the figure of the Jew arose from the ability of this figure to reveal a growing tension in France between those who advocated a pure republican universalism and those who disputed this vision as a corruption of the true essence of the individual formed and shaped by blood, culture, and territory. Sartre harnessed this same tension again to develop the outsider as a political ideal, representing the possibility of a form of political identity under neither the illusion of the discourse of roots nor the naive vision of transcending one's situation. Levinas went even further by suggesting that the reasons for which Jews had been denigrated ought to become the reasons that Judaism should be venerated. In the process, he transformed deracination into a moral ideal. It is his influence that thus dominates the representation of Judaism in the work of both Blanchot and Derrida, and it is these two thinkers that cultivate the figurative nature of the postwar representation of the Jew in order to develop a political strategy that offers a real alternative to the universalism-particularism dichotomy. It is, thus, in the work of Blanchot and Derrida that we find the resources for a new mode of political engagement.

First appearing in Blanchot's texts, and later developed in various directions by Derrida, Jean-François Lyotard, Jean-Luc Nancy, Philippe Lacoue-Labarthe, and Georgio Agamben are visions of community that refuse both the universalizing and the particularizing options.[6] What all these figures have inherited from Blanchot is a resistance to and suspicion of communal fusion, a suspicion, that is, of the modes of identification that bind people to a group, whether through territory, language, culture, or ethnicity. In reaction to previous models of identification, they develop a vision of the "unavowable community" (Blanchot), "the inoperative community" (Nancy and Lacoue-Labarthe), "the democracy to come" (Derrida), or "the coming community" (Agamben).[7] Despite the differences among these visions, in each the principle of identification with the larger polis is replaced by an ideal of disappropriation, a rejection of the ideal of belonging as such. As Blanchot writes in *The Unavowable Community*, the ideal of a community defined by its resistance to the mythic model of fusion would be one "which is bound to its

6. Blanchot will himself credit Bataille as the source of the notion of "community of those who do not have a community" (Blanchot, *La communauté inavouable*, 9, and *The Unavowable Community*, 1). For a sophisticated and sustained reading of how Blanchot's mystical practices amount to a politics, see Amy Hollywood, *Sensible Ecstasy: Mysticism, Sexual Difference, and the Demands of History* (Chicago: University of Chicago Press, 2002), 25–110.

7. See Georgio Agamben, *The Coming Community*, trans. Michael Hardt (Minneapolis: University of Minnesota Press, 2007).

own refusal or rejection."[8] Its absence would be, then, not a "failure of community," but a moment of community in which it is exposed to the ordeal of its necessary disappearance. Such would be a community of those who have nothing in common.[9] As extreme and, perhaps, impractical as such models are as guides to building real political structures, their critical significance is undeniable. They respond to the dichotomy between universalism and particularism, two modes of constituting belonging based on differing criteria, with paradigms that confront and accept plurality without making it a means of creating smaller exclusivist communities. They raise to an ideal the possibility of living in common without the necessary presupposition that to do so requires that we indeed have something in common. This ideal, Derrida argues in *L'autre cap*, can become the principle behind a politics of hospitality. Writing of Europe and the challenges it faces, he argues that it is under a double injunction to embrace "neither monopoly, nor dispersion." Like Badiou, he rejects the possibility that Europe would fracture into a "myriad of provinces, into a multiplicity of self-enclosed idioms or petty little nationalism, each one jealous and untranslatable," but he resists Badiou's alternative, which treats ethnic and cultural difference as an obstacle to be transcended, or at the very least ignored, in the name of an overarching truth.[10] Derrida does not deny that refusing either the particularist or the universalist option leads to an aporia. He suggests, rather, that "ethics, politics and responsibility, *if there are any*, will only ever have begun with the experience and experiment of the aporia."[11]

The danger with Derrida's claim would seem to be that it would lead to political indecision, quietude, and inaction. It is in response to this critique that the history of the figural Jew can be instructive. The gesture of disidentification that emerges from this history illustrates a means of intervention into the status quo, a check on the impulses that tug us toward either the universalist or the particularist models of belonging. As a figure for both deracination and election, the Jew becomes the symbol of an uninhabitable identity. In May '68, when the student protestors took up the chant "Nous sommes tous des juifs allemands," they demonstrated a method for inserting into the political sphere a gesture that communicated resistance to the dynamics of group identification.

8. Blanchot, *The Unavowable Community*, 13.

9. Alphonso Lingis, *The Community of Those Who Have Nothing in Common* (Bloomington: Indiana University Press, 1994).

10. Derrida, *L'autre cap*, 41–43, and *The Other Heading*, 39–41; Badiou, *Saint Paul* (French), 15, and *Saint Paul* (English), 14.

11. Derrida, *L'autre cap*, 43, and *The Other Heading*, 41.

The force of this gesture was, in many ways, the consequence of history—the difficult history of Judaism and the terrible history of anti-Semitism—which is largely responsible for the creation of the trope. The effects of this history continue to resonate and can lead, as Badiou rightly points out, to the reification of communitarianism, even as they enable its dismantling. According to Badiou, however, the danger of communitarianism ought to motivate the depoliticization of "the name 'Jew'" by way of its sacrifice through universalization.[12]

His response shows Badiou to be insensitive to the potential that emerges for the resignification of Judaism in the postwar era, particularly as Levinas figures into this narrative. He offers instead a reading of Levinas that aligns him with identitarian politics as a form of fetishized difference, even as he recognizes that such a politicization of Levinas's notion of otherness constitutes a misreading. Badiou's own narrative of what the word *Jew* has come to signify centers around the effect that the Holocaust has had on this term, but it oversimplifies even this relation. Badiou claims that, as a consequence of the Holocaust, the word *Jew* carries with it the stipulation of a good conscience. The Jew, according to him, is relieved of guilt by virtue of modern history. Certainly, this characterization would seem very far from Levinas's characterization, even as Levinas seems to occupy for Badiou the position of the quintessential Jew, against which his Pauline version is modeled.

The only relation, then, that Badiou's authentic Jew has to the trajectory traced out in this book is as a misreading of Levinas and a recuperation of the model of supersession. Nothing makes this clearer than Badiou's notion of militancy, which he defines as fidelity to an event that serves as the arbitrator of truth. The authentic Jew would, thus, be one who stakes his identity on an allegiance and declares the position of the virtual Jew to be null and void. Critics such as the Boyarins, Michael Weingrad, and Susan Shapiro who first attacked the postmodern French interest in the trope of the Jew have found a true target in Badiou.[13] For Badiou's professed interest in "reviving" "the word Jew" in the name of "political emancipation" is nothing but a ruse.[14] The only Jew left standing is the militant crusader against difference who calls himself the "New Israel."

What Badiou misses in *Circonstances, 3* is that the word *juif* also carries with it—as consequence of its political and philosophical history—the

---

12. Badiou, *Circonstances, 3*, 18, and *Polemics*, 164.
13. See my discussion of critics' response to Jean-Francois Lyotard in the introduction.
14. Badiou, *Polemics*, 232–33.

value of deracination, a value that serves to dismantle the communitarianism of which he is so critical. This dismantling takes place, I have argued, not through a mere reengagement with a diasporic tradition within Judaism, for that would only reconstruct Jewish communitarianism around this value. Rather, it is performed when we engage with being Jewish as a literary figure, when we treat it as a trope. This literary procedure allows for deracination to signify as an idea whose moral valence arises out of the tradition of Judaism and the discourses surrounding it. It resists, however, the move to reappropriation that might seem to follow from the claim that deracination or diaspora is somehow *intrinsically* Jewish. Literature, understood as the modality of language that dramatizes the difficulties of thematization, offers us a path toward a political form of self-articulation that would function analogously. It offers us the model for conceiving of modes of political speech that do not aim toward transparency but, rather, cultivate irony and ambiguity in order to point to the limits of a politics conceived around the structure of identity. It enables speech acts that remind us, not of who we are, but of who we are not, allowing the gaps between people, the impossibility of union, to function meaningfully. Thus, both in Derrida's statement that he is "the last of the Jews" and in Blanchot's analysis of the slogan "Nous sommes tous des juifs allemands," we encounter a mode of testimony whose force lies, not in the content of the assertion, but in the way in which the assertion, in its constative and performative function, unravels under the paradoxical conditions of its deployment. In exposing the ambivalences and ambiguities that are expressed when *anyone* asserts his or her Jewishness, we call into question the very terms by which all of us have learned to express our sense of belonging to our ethnicities, to our communities, and to our nations, and we recall the stakes involved in each of these ventures.

Undoubtedly, the history of republican France deeply inflects the way in which the Jew has been figured in post-1945 French thought. France has its own peculiar relation to the contestation between universalism and particularism, a relation that continues to play out today in the nation's attempt to discern the limits of *laïcité* in the face of a growing Muslim minority. At the same time, however, the conflict over political identity made manifest by this history is no less relevant to the United States. In our universities, and in the larger sphere of our national politics, Americans are attempting to redefine the discourses that developed in the 1980s and 1990s around ethnicity and gender. We are attempting to move beyond the debates over multiculturalism and to find new ways of defining and understanding pluralism. We must do so, however, without claiming, as Badiou does, that we can overlook difference, a move that merely denigrates those who position themselves on the cultural margins. Certainly, we must do so without offering as our alternative a mere pendulum swing back toward homogeny and universalism. The history of the trope of the Jew has, thus, been offered as one narrative of how the history of bigoted speech could be redeployed, not only to revalorize what had formerly been denigrated, but furthermore to disengage the associations of this speech from its proper referent, making it available to all, not as a sign of universal identity, but as a signifier that communicates the aporias involved in group identification and mobilizes those aporias in the public sphere, creating the possibility for a new politics of disidentification.

No doubt, the last step in this procedure must be to perform one final deracination of the trope of the Jew. One must, indeed, show that the history of the trope of the Jew is not *the* privileged case for such a possibility. One must resist the exemplarity of this particular case and expose it to the claims of others. I thus conclude this book with the call for multiplication of this model and with the hope that other histories can equally or better provide us with the means to "fling the morning door open" and develop a hospitable politics that does not depend on the homogenizing rhetoric of humanism.[15]

15. Paul Celan, "Einem, der vor der Tür Stand," in *Gesammelte Werke*, 1:242

# Selected Bibliography

Agamben, Georgio. *Remnants of Auschwitz: The Witness and the Archive*. Translated by Daniel Heller-Roazen. New York: Zone, 1999.

Alter, Robert. *Necessary Angels: Tradition and Modernity in Kafka, Benjamin and Scholem*. Cambridge, MA: Harvard University Press, 1991.

———. *Walter Benjamin and the Bible*. New York: Continuum, 1996.

Anderson, George K. *The Legend of the Wandering Jew*. Providence, RI: Brown University Press, 1965.

Andijar, Gil. *The Jew, the Arab: A History of the Enemy*. Stanford, CA: Stanford University Press, 2003.

Arendt, Hannah. *Antisemitism: The Origins of Totalitarianism*. New York: Harcourt Brace, 1951.

———. "The Jew as Pariah: A Hidden Tradition." *Jewish Social Studies* 4 (April 1944): 99–122.

Aron, Raymond. *The Elusive Revolution: Anatomy of a Student Revolt*. Translated by Gordon Clough. New York: Praeger, 1969.

Aronowicz, Annette. *Jews and Christians on Time and Eternity*. Stanford, CA: Stanford University Press, 1998.

Auron, Yair. *Les juifs d'extrême gauche en Mai 68: Une génération révolutionnaire marquée par la Shoah*. Translated by Katherine Werchowski. Paris: Albin Michel, 1998.

Badiou, Alain. *Circonstances, 3: Portées du mot "juif."* Paris: Lignes & Manifestes, 2005.

———. *Ethics: An Essay on the Understanding of Evil*. Translated by Peter Hallward. London: Verso, 2002.

———. *L'éthique: Essai sur la conscience du mal*. Paris: Hatier, 1993.

———. *Polemics*. Translated by Steve Corcoran. London: Verso, 2006.

———. *Saint Paul: La fondation de l'universalisme*. Paris: Presses universitaires de France, 1997.

———. *Saint Paul: The Foundation of Universalism.* Translated by Ray Brassier. Stanford, CA: Stanford University Press, 2003.

Barrès, Maurice. *Mes cahiers.* 11 vols. Plon: Paris, 1929–57.

———. *Scènes et doctrines du nationalisme.* Paris: Emile-Paul, 1902.

———. *Sous l'oeil des barbares.* Paris: Plotin, 1952.

Batnitzky, Leora. *Leo Strauss and Emmanuel Levinas: Philosophy and the Politics of Revelation.* Cambridge: Cambridge University Press, 2006.

Baugh, Bruce. *French Hegel.* New York: Routledge, 2003.

Bauman, Zygmunt. *Intimations of Postmodernity.* London: Routledge, 1992.

Beauvoir, Simone de. *Adieux: A Farewell to Sartre.* Translated by Patrick O'Brian. New York: Pantheon, 1984.

———. *La cérémonie des adieux.* Paris: Gallimard, 1981.

Benbassa, Esther. *The Jews of France: A History from Antiquity to the Present.* Translated by M. B. DeBevoise. Princeton, NJ: Princeton University Press, 1999.

Benda, Julien. *La jeunesse d'un clerc.* Paris: Gallimard, 1936.

———. *La trahison des clercs.* Paris: B. Grasset, 1927.

Benhabib, Seyla. "Democracy and Difference: Reflections on the Metapolitics of Lyotard and Derrida." *Journal of Political Philosophy* 2 (1994).

Benjamin, Walter. *Illuminationen: Ausgewählte Shriften 1.* Frankfurt a.M.: Suhrkamp, 1977.

———. *Illuminations.* Edited and with an introduction by Hannah Arendt. Translated by Harry Zohn. New York: Schocken, 1977.

Bennington, Geoffrey. *Jacques Derrida.* Chicago: University of Chicago Press, 1993.

———. "Lyotard and 'the Jews.'" In *Modernity, Culture and "the Jew."* Edited by Bryan Cheyette and Laura Marcus. Cambridge: Polity, 1998.

Bergoffen, Debra. "Interrupting Lyotard: Wither the We?" In *Lyotard: Philosophy, Politics, and the Sublime,* ed. Hugh J. Silverman. London: Routledge, 2002.

Bergson, Henri. *The Two Sources of Morality and Religion.* Translated by R. Ashley Audra and Cloudesly Brereton. Notre Dame, IN: Notre Dame Press, 1977.

Berkovitz, Jay. *The Shaping of Jewish Identity in Nineteenth-Century France.* Detroit: Wayne State University Press, 1989.

Birnbaum, Pierre. *The Antisemitic Moment.* Translated by Jane Marie Todd. New York: Hill & Wang, 2003.

———. *Destins juifs: De la Révolution française à Carpentras.* Paris: Calmann-Lévy, 1995.

———. *Les fous de la République.* Paris: Fayard, 1992.

———. *La France imaginée: Déclin des rêves unitaires?* Paris: Fayard, 1998.

———. "Grégoire, Dreyfus, Drancy and the Rue Copernic: Jews at the Heart of French History." In *Realms of Memory,* ed. Pierre Nora, vol. 3. New York: Columbia University Press, 1996.

———. *Jewish Destinies: Citizenship, State and Community in Modern France.* Translated by Arthur Goldhammer. New York: Hill & Wang, 2000.

———. "Sorry Afterthoughts on *Anti-Semite and Jew.*" Translated by Carol Marks. *October,* no. 87 (Winter 1999): 89–107.

Blanchot, Maurice. *L'amitié*. Paris: Gallimard, 1971.

———. *The Blanchot Reader*. Translated by Christopher C. Stevens. Edited by Michael Holland. Cambridge: Blackwell, 1995.

———. *The Book to Come*. Translated by Charlotte Mandell. Stanford, CA: Stanford University Press, 2003.

———. *La communauté inavouable*. Paris: Minuit, 1983.

———. "La conquista dello spazio." *Il menabò* 7 (1964): 10–13.

———. *Écrits politiques, 1958–1993*. Paris: Lignes, 2003.

———. *L'écriture du désastre*. Paris: Gallimard, 1980.

———. *L'espace littéraire*. Paris: Gallimard, 1955.

———. "Grâce (*soit rendue*) à Jacques Derrida." *Revue philosophique* 2 (1990): 167–73.

———. *The Infinite Conversation*. Translated by Susan Hanson. Minneapolis: University of Minnesota Press, 1993.

———. *The Instant of My Death*. Translated by Elizabeth Rottenberg. Stanford, CA: Stanford University Press, 1998.

———. *Le livre à venir*. Paris: Gallimard, 1959.

———. "Notre compagne clandestine." In *Textes pour Emmanuel Levinas*., ed. François Laruelle. Paris: Collection Surfaces, 1980.

———. "Our Clandestine Companion." In *Face to Face with Emmanuel Levinas*, ed. Richard A. Cohen. Albany: State University of New York Press, 1986.

———. *La part du feu*. Paris: Gallimard, 1949.

———. *Le pas au-delà*. Paris: Gallimard, 1973.

———. *The Space of Literature*. Translated by Ann Smock. Lincoln: University of Nebraska Press, 1982.

———. *The Station Hill Blanchot Reader*. Translated by Lydia Davis, Paul Auster, and Robert Lamberton. Edited by George Quasha. Barrytown, NY: Station Hill, 1998.

———. *The Step Not Beyond*. Translated and with an introduction by Lycette Nelson. Albany: State University of New York Press, 1992.

———. *The Unavowable Community*. Translated by Pierre Joris. Barrytown, NY: Station Hill, 1988.

———. *The Work of Fire*. Translated by Charlotte Mandel. Stanford, CA: Stanford University Press, 1995.

———. *The Writing of the Disaster*. Translated by Ann Smock. Lincoln: University of Nebraska Press, 1980.

Bourgeois, Bernard. *Hegel à Francfort au judaïsme, christianisme, hégélianisme*. Paris: J. Vrin, 1970.

Bowen, John R. *Why the French Don't Like Headscarves: Islam, the State and Public Space*. Princeton, NJ: Princeton University Press 2007.

Boyarin, Daniel. *Carnal Israel: Reading Sex in Talmudic Culture*. Berkeley and Los Angeles: University of California Press, 1993.

———. *A Radical Jew: Paul and the Politics of Identity*. Berkeley and Los Angeles: University of California University Press, 1994.

Boyarin, Daniel, and Jonathan Boyarin. "Diaspora: Generation and the Ground of Jewish Identity." *Critical Inquiry* 19, no. 4 (Summer 1993): 693–725.

Boyarin, Jonathan. *Thinking in Jewish*. Chicago: University of Chicago Press, 1996.

Boyarin, Jonathan, and Daniel Boyarin. *Powers of Diaspora: On the Relevance of Jewish Culture*. Minneapolis: University of Minnesota, 2002.

Brenner, Fréderic, and Yosef Hayim Yerushalmi. *Marranes*. Paris: La différence, 1992.

Brinker, Menachem. "Sartre on the Jewish Question: Thirty Years Later." *Jerusalem Quarterly* 10 (Winter 1979): 117–32.

Bronner, Stephen Eric. *A Rumor about the Jews: Reflections on Antisemitism and the Protocols of the Learned Elders of Zion*. New York: St. Martin's, 2000.

Butler, Judith. *Subjects of Desire: Hegelian Reflections in Twentieth Century France*. New York: Columbia University Press, 1987.

Calin, Rodolphe. *Levinas et l'exception du soi*. Paris: Presses universitaires de France, 2005.

Caputo, John, ed. *Augustine and Postmodernism: Confession and Circumfession*. Bloomington: Indiana University Press, 2004.

———. *The Prayers and Tears of Jacques Derrida: Religion without Religion*. Bloomington: Indiana University Press, 1997.

Carroll, David. *French Literary Fascism: Nationalism, Anti-Semitism, and the ideology of Culture*. Princeton, NJ: Princeton University Press, 1994.

Celan, Paul. *Gesammelte Werke*. 5 vols. Frankfurt a.M.: Suhrkamp, 1983.

———. *Le méridien et autres proses (édition bilingue)*. Translated by Jean Launay. Paris: Seuil, 2002.

Chalier, Catherine. *Judaïsme et altérité*. Lagrasse: Verdier, 1982.

———. "Singularité juive et philosophie." In *Emmanuel Levinas: Les cahiers de la nuit surveillée*. Lagrasse: Verdier, 1984.

Charmé, Stuart. "Sartre's Jewish Daughter: An Interview with Arlette Elkaim-Sartre." *Midstream* 32, no. 8 (October 1986): 24–28.

———. *Vulgarity and Authenticity: Dimensions of Otherness in the World of Jean-Paul Sartre*. Amherst: University of Massachussetts Press, 1991.

Chaumont, Jean-Michel. *La concurrence des victimes: Génocide, identité, reconnaissance*. Paris: La découverte, 1997.

Chouraqui, André. *L'Alliance israélite universelle et la renaissance juive contemporaine, 1860–1960*. Paris: Presses universitaires de France, 1965.

Cixous, Hélène. *Portrait de Jacques Derrida en jeune saint juif*. Paris: Galilée, 2001.

———. *Portrait of Jacques Derrida as a Young Jewish Saint*. Translated by Beverley Bie Brahic. New York: Columbia University Press, 2004.

Cohen, Hermann. *Jüdische Shriften*. Berlin: C. A. Schwetschke, 1924.

———. *Reason and Hope: Selections from the Jewish Writings of Hermann Cohen*. Translated by Eva Jospe. New York: Norton, 1971.

———. *Die Religion der Vernunft aus den Quellen des Judentums*. Leipzig: Gustav Fock, 1919.

———. *Religion of Reason Out of the Sources of Judaism*. Translated by Simon Kaplan. Atlanta: Scholar's, 1995.

Cohen-Solal, Annie. *Reason and Hope: Selections from the Jewish Writings of Hermann Cohen*. Cincinatti: Hebrew Union College Press, 1993.

———. *Sartre: A Life*. Translated by Anna Cancogni. New York: Pantheon, 1987.

Critchley, Simon. "Five Problems in Levinas's View of Politics and the Sketch of a Solution to Them." *Political Theory* 32, no. 2 (April 2004): 172–85.

Critchley, Simon, and Robert Bernasconi, eds. *The Cambridge Companion to Levinas*. Cambridge: Cambridge University Press, 2002.

Datta, Venita. *Birth of a National Icon: The Literary Avant-Garde and the Origins of the Intellectual in France*. Albany: State University of New York Press, 1989.

Deleuze, Gilles, and Félix Guattari. *Kafka: Pour une littérature mineure*. Paris: Minuit, 1975.

———. *Kafka: Toward a Minor Literature*. Translated by Dana Polan. Minneapolis: University of Minnesota Press, 1986.

———. *A Thousand Plateaus: Capitalism and Schizophrenia*. Translated by Brian Massumi. Minneapolis: University of Minnesota Press, 1987.

de Man, Paul. *Allegories of Reading: Figural Language in Rousseau, Nietzsche, Rilke and Proust*. New Haven, CT: Yale University Press, 1979.

Derrida, Jacques. "Abraham, l'autre." In *Judéités: Questions pour Jacques Derrida*, ed. Joseph Cohen and Raphael Zagury-Orly. Paris: Galilée, 2003.

———. "Abraham, the Other." In *Judeities: Questions for Jacques Derrida*, ed. Bettina Bergo, Joseph Cohen, and Raphael Zagury-Orly, trans. Bettina Bergo and Michael B. Smith. New York: Fordham University Press, 2007.

———. *Acts of Literature*. Edited by Derek Attridge. New York: Routledge, 1992.

———. *Acts of Religion*. Edited by Gil Andijar. New York: Routledge, 2002.

———. *Adieu à Emmanuel Levinas*. Paris: Galilée, 1997.

———. *Adieu to Emmanuel Levinas*. Translated by Pascale-Anne Brault and Michael Nass. Stanford, CA: Stanford University Press, 1999.

———. *Aporias*. Translated by Thomas Dutoit. Stanford, CA: Stanford University Press, 1993.

———. *Apories*. Paris: Galilée, 1996.

———. *Archive Fever*. Translated by Eric Prenowitz. Chicago: University of Chicago Press, 1998.

———. *L'autre cap*. Paris: Minuit, 1991.

———. "Avouer—l'impossible: 'Retours,' repentir et réconciliation." In *Comment vivre ensemble? Actes du XXXVIII<sup>e</sup> Colloque des intellectuels juifs de langue française*. Paris: Albin Michel, 2001.

———. *La carte postale: De Socrate à Freud et au-delà*. Paris: Flammarion, 1980.

———. "Circonfession." In *Jacques Derrida*, by Geoffrey Bennington. Paris: Seuil, 1991.

———. "Circumfession." In *Jacques Derrida*, by Geoffrey Bennington. Chicago: University of Chicago Press, 1993.

———. *De l'esprit: Heidegger et la question*. Paris: Galilée, 1987.

———. *Demeure: Fiction and Testimony*. Translated by Elizabeth Rottenberg. Stanford, CA: Stanford University Press, 1998.

———. *Donner la mort*. Paris: Galilée, 1999.

———. *D'un ton apocalyptique adopté naguère en philosophie*. Paris: Galilée, 1981.

———. *L'écriture et la différence*. Paris: Seuil, 1967.

———. *Edmund Husserl's Origin of Geometry: An Introduction*. Translated by John P. Leavey Jr. Lincoln: University of Nebraska Press, 1989.

———. *Feu la cendre*. Paris: Des femmes, 1987.

———. *Foi et savoir*. Paris: Seuil, 1996.

———. *Force de loi*. Paris: Galilée, 1994.

———. *Glas*. Paris: Galilée, 1974.

———. *Glas*. Translated by John P. Leavey Jr. and Richard Rand. Lincoln: University of Nebraska Press, 1986.

———. "An Interview with Derrida." In *Derrida and Différance*, ed. David Wood and Robert Bernasconi. Evanston, IL: Northwestern University Press, 1988.

———. Introduction to *L'origine de la géométrie*, by Edmund Husserl. Paris: Presses universitaires de France, 1962.

———. "Jacques Derrida: 'Je suis en geurre contre moi-même." *Le monde*, October 9, 2004.

———. *Mal d'archive: Une impression freudienne*. Paris: Galillée, 1995.

———. *Marges de la philosophie*. Paris: Minuit, 1972.

———. *Margins of Philosophy*. Translated by Alan Bass. Chicago: University of Chicago Press, 1982.

———. *Le monolinguisme de l'autre; ou, La prothèse d'origine*. Paris: Galilée, 1996.

———. *Monolingualism of the Other; or, The Prosthesis of Origin*. Translated by Patrick Mensah. Stanford, CA: Stanford University Press, 1998.

———. "Of an Apocalyptic Tone Recently Adopted in Philosophy." Translated by John P. Leavey *Oxford Literary Review* 6 (1984): 3–37.

———. *Of Grammatology*. Translated by Gayatri Chakravorty Spivak. Baltimore: Johns Hopkins University Press, 1976.

———. "Onto-Theology of National Humanism (Prolegomena to a Hypothesis)." *Oxford Literary Review* 14, nos. 1–2 (1992): 3–24.

———. *Politics of Friendship*. Translated by George Collins. London: Verso, 1997.

———. *Politiques de l'amitié*. Paris: Galilée, 1994.

———. *The Post Card*. Translated by Alan Bass. Chicago: University of Chicago Press, 1987.

———. *Psyché: Inventions de l'autre*. Paris: Galilée, 1987.

———. *Psyché: Inventions de l'autre II*. Paris: Galilée, 2003.

———. *Psyche: Inventions of the Other I*. Edited by Peggy Kamuf and Elizabeth Rottenberg. Stanford, CA: Stanford University Press, 2007.

———. "Response to Daniel Liebeskind." *Research in Phenomenology* 22 (1992): 88–95.

———. *Schibboleth pour Paul Celan*. Paris: Galilee, 1986.

———. *Sovereignties in Question: The Poetics of Paul Celan.* Edited by Thomas Dutoit and Outi Pasanen. New York: Fordham University Press, 2005.

———. *Specters of Marx: The State of Debt, the Work of Mourning and the New International.* Translated by Peggy Kamuf. New York: Routledge, 1994.

———. *Spectres de Marx.* Paris: Galilée, 1993.

———. *Writing and Difference.* Translated by Alan Bass. Chicago: University of Chicago Press, 1978.

Drumont, Édouard. *La France juive.* 200th ed. 2 vols. Paris: Flammarion, ca. 1880s.

Dumont, Louis. *German Ideology: From France to Germany and Back.* Chicago: University of Chicago Press, 1997.

Fackenheim, Emil L. *Encounters between Judaism and Modern Philosophy: A Preface to Future Jewish Thought.* New York: Basic, 1973.

Feenberg, Andrew, and Jim Freedman. *When Poetry Ruled the Streets: The French May Events of 1968.* Albany: State University of New York Press, 2001.

Finkielkraut, Alain. *Au nom de l'autre: Réflexions sur l'antisémitisme qui vient.* Paris: Gallimard, 2003.

———. *La défaite de la pensée.* Paris: Gallimard, 1987.

———. *Le juif imaginaire.* Paris: Seuil, 1980.

———. "Les juifs face à la religion de l'humanité." *Le débat* 131 (2004): 13–19.

———. *Le mécontemporain.* Paris: Gallimard, 1991.

———. *La sagesse de l'amour.* Paris: Gallimard, 1988.

Fontenay, Élisabeth de. *Une tout autre histoire: Questions à Jean-François Lyotard.* Paris: Fayard, 2006.

Freud, Sigmund. *Der Mann Moses und die monotheistische Religion.* Amsterdam: A. de Lange, 1939.

———. *Moses and Monotheism.* Translated by Katherine Jones. New York: Knopf, 1939.

Friedlander, Judith. *Vilna on the Seine: Jewish Intellectuals in France since 1968.* New Haven, CT: Yale University Press, 1990.

Greenberg, Eliezer, ed. *A Treasury of Yiddish Stories.* New York: Schocken, 1973.

Grégoire, Henri. *Essai sur la régénération physique, morale et politique des juifs.* Paris: Flammarion, 1989.

Guillemin, Henri. *Charles Péguy.* Paris: Seuil, 1981.

Gutting, Gary. *French Philosophy in the Twentieth Century.* Cambridge: Cambridge University Press, 2001.

Habermas, Jürgen. *Philosophical-Political Profiles.* Translated by Frederick G. Lawrence. Cambridge, MA: MIT Press, 1983.

Halbertal, Moshe. *People of the Book: Canon, Meaning and Authority.* Cambridge, MA: Harvard University Press, 1997.

Ha-Levi, Judah. *Kuzari.* Translated by Henry Slonimsky. New York: Schocken, 1964.

Handelman, Susan A. *Fragments of Redemption: Jewish Thought and Literary Theory in Benjamin, Scholem and Levinas.* Bloomington: Indiana University Press, 1991.

————. *The Slayers of Moses: The Emergence of Rabbinic Interpretation in Modern Literary Theory*. Albany: State University of New York Press, 1982.

Harrowitz, Nancy, ed. *Tainted Greatness: Antisemitism and Cultural Heroes*. Philadelphia: Temple University Press, 1994.

Hart, Kevin. *The Dark Gaze: Maurice Blanchot and the Sacred*. Chicago: University of Chicago Press, 2004.

Hartman, Geoffrey, and Kevin Hart, eds. *The Power of Contestation: Perspectives on Blanchot*. Baltimore: Johns Hopkins University Press, 2004.

Hasan-Rokem, Galit, and Alan Dundes, eds. *The Wandering Jew: Essays in the Interpretation of a Christian Legend*. Bloomington: Indiana University Press, 1986.

Hegel, G. W. F. *Lectures on Philosophy of Religion*. Edited by Peter C. Hodgson. Translated by R. F. Brown, P. C. Hodgson, and J. M. Stewart. 3 vols. Berkeley and Los Angeles: University of California Press, 1984–87.

————. *Phänomenologie des Geistes*. Banberg and Würzburg, 1807.

————. *Phenomenology of Spirit*. Translated by A. V. Miller. Oxford: Oxford University Press, 1977.

————. "Spirit of Christianity and Its Fate." In *Early Theological Writings*, trans. T. M. Knox. Philadelphia: University of Pennsylvania Press, 1971.

————. *Theologische Jugendschriften*. Tubingen: Mohr, 1907.

————. *Vorlesungen über die Philosophie der Geschichte*. Vol. 12 of *Werke*. 20 vols. Frankfurt a.M.: Suhrkamp, 1969–72.

Heidegger, Martin. *Being and Time*. Translated by John Macquarrie and Edward Robinson. New York: Harper & Row, 1962.

————. *Holzwege*. Frankfurt a.M.: Vittorio Klostermann, 1950.

————. *Poetry, Language, Thought*. Translated by Albert Hofstader. New York: Harper & Row, 1971.

————. *Die Selbstbehauptung der deutschen Universität*. Frankfurt a.M.: Vittorio Klostermann, 1983.

————. *Sein und Zeit*. 11th ed. Tübingen: Max Niemeyer, 1967.

————. *Vorträge und Aufsätze*. Pfullingen: G. Neske, 1985.

————. *Was Ist Metaphysik?* Frankfurt a.M.: Klostermann, 1969.

Herder, Johannes Gottfried. *Auch eine Philosophie der Geschichte zur Bildung der Menschheit*. Frankfurt a.M.: Suhrkamp, 1967.

————. *Ideen zur philosophie der Geschichte der Menschheit*. 4 vols. Riga and Leipzig: J. F. Hartknoch, 1784–91.

————. *J. G. Herder on Social and Political Culture*. Edited by F. M. Barnard. Cambridge: Cambridge University Press, 1969.

————. *Reflections on the Philosophy of the History of Mankind*. Chicago: University of Chicago Press, 1968.

Hertzberg, Arthur. *The French Enlightenment and the Jews*. New York: Columbia University Press, 1968.

Herzog, Annabel. "Benny Levy versus Emmanuel Levinas on 'Being Jewish.'" *Modern Judaism* 26 (2006): 15–30.

Hewitt, Nicholas. "'Portrait de l'antisémite' dans son contexte: Antisémitisme et judéocide." *Etudes sartriennes* 1 (1984): 111–22.

Hill, Leslie. *Blanchot: Extreme Contemporary*. New York: Routledge, 1997.

———. "La pensée politique," *Magazine littéraire: L'enigme Blanchot*, October 2003, 35–38.

Hollander, Dana. "Exemplarity and Chosenness: Rosenzweig and Derrida on the Nation of Philosophy." Ph.D. diss., Johns Hopkins University, 2001.

———. *Exemplarity and Chosenness: Rosenzweig and Derrida on the Nation of Philosophy*. Stanford, CA: Stanford University Press, 2008.

Hollywood, Amy. *Sensible Ecstasy: Mysticism, Sexual Difference, and the Demands of History*. Chicago: University of Chicago Press, 2002.

Hourwitz, Zalkind. *Apologie des juifs*. Paris: Sylepse, 2002.

Husserl, Edmund. *Logical Investigations*. Translated by J. N. Findlay. New York: Humanities, 1970.

———. *Edmund Husserl's Origin of Geometry: An Introduction*. Translated by John P. Leavey Jr. With an introduction by Jacques Derrida. Lincoln: University of Nebraska Press, 1989.

———. *Logische Untersuchungen*. 2 vols. Halle a.d.S.: Max Niemeyer, 1922.

———. *L'origine de la géométrie*. Paris: Presses universitaires de France, 1962.

Hyman, Paula E. *From Dreyfus to Vichy: The Remaking of French Jewry, 1906–1939*. New York: Columbia University Press, 1979.

———. *The Jews of Modern France*. Berkeley and Los Angeles: University of California Press, 1998.

Hyppolite, Jean. *Genèse et structure de la phénoménologie de l'esprit*. Paris: Aubier, 1946.

———. *Genesis and Structure of Hegel's Phenomenology of Spirit*. Translated by Samuel Cherniak and John Heckman. Evanston, IL: Northwestern University Press, 1974.

Isaac, Jules. *Expériences de ma vie, Péguy*. Paris: Calmann-Lévy, 1959.

Iyer, Lars. *Blanchot's Communism: Art, Philosophy and the Political*. New York: Palgrave, 2004.

Jennings, Jeremy. "Citizenship, Republicanism and Multiculturalism in Contemporary France." *British Journal of Political Science* 30 (2000): 575–98.

———, ed. *Intellectuals in Twentieth-Century France: Mandarins and Samurais*. New York: St. Martin's, 1993.

———. "Of Treason, Blindness and Silence: Dilemmas of the Intellectual in Modern France." In *Intellectuals in Politics: From the Dreyfus Affair to Salman Rushdie*, ed. Jeremy Jennings and Anthony Kemp-Welch. New York: Routledge, 1997.

Joffrin, Laurent. *Mai 68: Histoire des événements*. Paris: Seuil, 1988.

Johnson, Douglas. *France and the Dreyfus Affair*. London: Blandford, 1966.

Judaken, Jonathan. *Jean-Paul Sartre and the Jewish Question: Anti-Antisemitism and the Politics of the French Intellectual*. Lincoln: University of Nebraska Press, 2006.

————. "Jean-Paul Sartre and 'the Jewish Question': The Politics of Engagement and the Image of 'the Jew' in Sartre's Thought." Ph.D. diss., University of California, Irvine, 1997.

Judt, Tony. *Past Imperfect: French Intellectuals, 1944–1956*. Berkeley and Los Angeles: University of California Press, 1992.

Kafka, Franz. *Parables and Paradoxes*. Bilingual ed. New York: Schocken, 1961.

————. *Tagebücher in der Fassung der Handschrift*. Edited by Jost Schillemeit. Frankfurt a.M.: Fischer, 1992.

Kant, Immanuel. *Critique of Judgment*. Translated by J. H. Bernard. New York: Prometheus, 2000.

————. *Critique of Practical Reason*. Translated by Louis White Beck. Upper Saddle River, NJ: Prentice-Hall, 1993.

————. *Critique of Pure Reason*. Translated by Norman Kemp Smith. New York: St. Martin's, 1965.

————. *Religion within the Limits of Reason Alone*. Translated by Theodore M. Greene and Hoyt H. Hudson. New York: Harper & Row, 1960.

Kaplan, Alice Yaeger. *Reproductions of Banality, Fascism, Literature and French Intellectual Life*. Minneapolis: University of Minnesota Press, 1986.

Katz, Jacob. *Jews and Freemasons in Europe, 1723–1939*. Translated by Leonard Oshry. Cambridge, MA: Harvard University Press, 1970.

Kleeblatt, Norman L., ed. *The Dreyfus Affair: Art, Truth and Justice*. Berkeley and Los Angeles: University of California Press, 1987.

Kleinberg, Ethan. *Generation Existential: Heidegger's Philosophy in France, 1927–1961*. Ithaca, NY: Cornell University Press, 2005.

Lacoue-Labarthe, Philippe. *La fiction du politique: Heidegger, l'art et la politique*. Paris: Christian Bourgois, 1987.

————. *Heidegger, Art and Politics: The Fiction of the Political*. Translated by Chris Turner. London: Blackwell, 1990.

Lazare, Bernard. *Anti-Semitism: Its History and Its Causes*. With an introduction by Robert S. Wistrich. Lincoln: University of Nebraska Press, 1995.

————. *L'antisémitisme: Son histoire et ses causes*. Paris: Albin Michel, 1982.

————. *Le fumier de Job*. Paris: Circé, 1990.

————. *Job's Dungheap: Essays on Jewish Nationalism and Social Revolution*. Translated by Harry Lorin Binsse. New York: Schocken, 1948.

————. *Le miroir des légendes*. Paris: A. Lemerre, 1892.

Lernout, Geert. *The Poet as Thinker: Hölderlin in France*. Columbia, SC: Camden House, 1994.

Lescourret, Marie-Anne. *Emmanuel Levinas*. Paris: Flammarion, 1994.

Levi, Primo. *The Drowned and the Saved*. Translated by Raymond Rosenthal. New York: Summit, 1988.

Levinas, Emmanuel. *A l'heure des nations*. Paris: Minuit, 1988.

————. *L'au-delà du verset*. Paris: Minuit, 1982.

————. *Autrement qu'être ou au-delà de l'essence*. La Haye: M. Nijhoff, 1978.

———. *Beyond the Verse*. Translated by Gary D. Mole. Bloomington: Indiana University Press, 1994.

———. "De l'évasion." *Recherches philosophiques* 5 (1935–36): 373–92.

———. *De l'existence à l'existant*. Paris: J. Vrin, 1978.

———. *Difficile liberté*. Paris: Albin Michel, 1963.

———. *Difficult Freedom*. Translated by Sean Hand. Baltimore: Johns Hopkins University Press, 1990.

———. "L'École normale israélite orientale: Perspectives d'avenir." In *Les droits de l'homme et l'education: Actes du Congrès du centenaire*, ed. Alliance israélite universelle. Paris: Presses universitaires de France, 1961.

———. *Emmanuel Levinas: Basic Philosophical Writing*. Edited by Adriaan T. Peperzak, Simon Critchley, and Robert Bernasconi. Bloomington: Indiana University Press, 1996.

———. *Emmanuel Levinas: Cahier de l'Herne*. Edited by Catherine Chalier and Miguel Abensour. Paris: L'Herne, 1991.

———. "Emmanuel Levinas and Richard Kearney: Dialogue with Emmanuel Levinas." In *Face to Face with Levinas*, ed. Richard A. Cohen. Albany: State University of New York Press, 1986.

———. *En découvrant l'existence avec Husserl et Heidegger*. Paris: J. Vrin, 1967.

———. "Être juif." *Confluences*, nos. 15–17 (1947): 253–64.

———. *Existence and Existents*. Translated by Alphonso Lingis. Dordrecht: Kluwer Academic, 1995.

———. "Existentialisme et antisémitisme." *Les cahiers de l'Alliance israélite universelle* 14–15 (June–July 1947): 2–3.

———. *Humanism of the Other*. Translated by Nidra Poller. Urbana: University of Illinois Press, 2003.

———. *Les imprévus de l'histoire*. Paris: Fata Morgana, 1994.

———. *In the Time of the Nations*. Translated by Michael B. Smith. Bloomington: Indiana University Press, 1994.

———. "Judaïsme et revolution." In *Jeunesse et revolution dans la conscience juive: Données et débats*, ed. J. Halpérin and G. Lévitte. Paris: Presses universitaires de France, 1972.

———. *Nine Talmudic Readings*. Translated by Annette Aronowicz. Bloomington: Indiana University Press, 1990.

———. *Noms propres*. Paris: Fata Morgana, 1975.

———. *On Escape*. Translated by Bettina Bergo. Stanford, CA: Stanford University Press, 2003.

———. *Otherwise Than Being; or Beyond Essence*. Translated by Alphonso Lingis. Pittsburgh, PA: Duquesne University Press, 1998.

———. "Philosophy and the Idea of Infinity." In *To the Other: An Introduction to the Philosophy of Emmanuel Levinas*, by Adriaan Peperzak. West Lafayette, IN: Purdue University Press, 1993.

———. *Proper Names*. Translated by Michael B. Smith. Stanford, CA: Stanford University Press, 1996.

———. *Quatre lectures talmudiques*. Paris: Minuit, 1968.

———. "Quelques réflexions sur la philosophie de l'hitlérisme." *Esprit* 26 (November 1934): 199–208.

———. "Reflections on the Philosophy of Hitlerism." Translated by Sean Hand. *Critical Inquiry* 17 (Autumn 1990): 62–71.

———. *Le temps et l'autre*. Paris: Fata Morgana, 1979.

———. *La théorie de l'intuition dans la phénoménologie de Husserl*. Paris: Félix Alcan, 1930.

———. *The Theory of Intuition in Husserl's Phenomenology*. Translated by André Orianne. Evanston, IL: Northwestern University Press, 1998.

———. *Time and the Other*. Translated by Richard Cohen. Pittsburgh, PA: Duquesne University Press, 1987.

———. *Totalité et infini: Essai sur l'extériorité*. La Haye: M. Nijhoff, 1961.

———. *Totality and Infinity: An Essay on Exteriority*. Translated by Alphonso Lingis. Pittsburgh, PA: Duquesne University Press, 1969.

———. "La trace de l'autre." *Tijdschrift voor filosofie* 25 (September 1963): 605–23.

———. *Unforeseen History*. Translated by Nidra Poller. Urbana: University of Illinois Press, 2004.

Lévy, Benny. *Être juif: Étude lévinassienne*. Paris: Verdier, 2003.

———. "Commentaire d'"Être juif.'" *Cahiers d'études lévinassiennes* 1 (2002): 107–17.

———. *Le nom de l'homme*. Paris: Verdier, 1984.

———. "Sartre et judéité." *Etudes sartriennes* 2–3 (1986): 139–50.

Lévy, Bernard-Henri. *L'idéologie française*. Paris: Grasset, 1981.

———. *Le siècle de Sartre*. Paris: Grasset, 2000.

Levy, Ze'ev. *Spinoza's Interpretation of Judaism: A Concept and Its Influence on Jewish Thought* (in Hebrew). Tel-Aviv: Safreet Poalim, 1972.

Libertson, Joseph. *Proximity: Levinas, Blanchot, Bataille and Communication*. The Hague: Martinus Nijhoff, 1982.

Lingis, Alphonso. *The Community of Those Who Have Nothing in Common*. Bloomington: Indiana University Press, 1994.

Locke, John. *An Essay Concerning Human Understanding*. Edited by Peter H. Nidditch. Oxford: Oxford University Press, 1975.

Löwy, Michael. *Redemption and Utopia: Jewish Libertarian Thought in Central Europe*. London: Athlone, 1992.

Lyotard, Jean-François. *The Differend: Phrases in Dispute*. Translated by Georges Van Den Abbeele. Minneapolis: University of Minnesota Press, 1988.

———. "Discussions or Phrasing After Auschwitz." In *The Lyotard Reader*, ed. Andrew Benjamin. Oxford: Blackwell, 1989.

———. *Heidegger and "the jews."* Translated by Andreas Michel and Mark Roberts. Minneapolis: University of Minnesota Press, 1990.

———. *Heidegger et "les juifs."* Paris: Galilée, 1988.

———. *Political Writings/Jean François Lyotard*. Translated by Kevin Geiman and Bill Readings. Minneapolis: University of Minnesota Press, 1993.

Malino, Frances, and Bernard Wasserstein, eds. *The Jews in Modern France.* Hanover, NH: University Press of New England, for Brandeis University Press, 1985.

Malka, Salomon. *Lire Lévinas.* Paris: Cerf, 1984.

———. *La vie et la trace.* Paris: Albin Michel, 2005.

———. *Monsieur Chouchani: L'enigma d'un maître du XX<sup>e</sup> siècle.* Paris: J. C. Lattès, 1994.

Marion, Jean-Luc. "La substitution et la sollicitude: Comment Levinas reprit Heidegger." In *Emmanuel Levinas et les territoires de la pensée,* ed. Danielle Cohen-Levinas and Bruno Clément. Paris: Presses universitaires de France, 2007.

Marks, Elaine. "The Limits of Ideology and Sensibility: J-P Sartre's *Réflexions sur la question juive." French Review* 45, no. 4 (March 1972): 779–88.

Marrus, Michael R. *The Politics of Assimilation: A Study of the French Jewish Community at the Time of the Dreyfus Affair.* Oxford: Clarendon, 1971.

Marrus, Michael R., and Robert O. Paxton. *Vichy France and the Jews.* Stanford, CA: Stanford University Press, 1995.

Marx, Karl. *Karl Marx: Selected Writings.* Edited by David McLellan. Oxford: Oxford University Press, 2000.

Maurras, Charles. *Romantisme et révolution.* Paris, 1922.

McClelland, J. S. *The French Right: From De Maistre to Maurras.* New York: Harper & Row, 1970.

Mehlman, Jeffrey. *Legacies of Anti-Semitism in France.* Minneapolis: University of Minnesota Press, 1983.

Meltzer, Françoise. *Hot Property: The Stakes and Claims of Literary Originality.* Chicago: University of Chicago Press, 1994.

Mendes-Flohr, Paul. *Divided Passions: Jewish Intellectuals and the Experience of Modernity.* Detroit: Wayne State University Press, 1991.

Mendes-Flohr, Paul, and Jehuda Reinharz, eds. *The Jew in the Modern World: A Documentary History.* New York: Oxford University Press, 1995.

Misrahi, Robert. "Sartre and the Jews: A Felicitous Misunderstanding," *October,* no. 87 (Winter 1999): 63–72.

Mole, Gary D. *Lévinas, Blanchot, Jabès: Figures of Estrangement.* Gainesville: University Press of Florida, 1997.

Mosès, Stéphane. *L'ange de l'histoire: Rosenzweig, Benjamin, Scholem.* Paris: Seuil, 1992.

Mosse, George. *The Crisis of German Ideology: Intellectual Origins of the Third Reich.* New York: Schocken, 1981.

Moyn, Samuel. "Judaism against Paganism: Emmanuel Levinas's Response to Heidegger and Nazism in the 1930's." *History and Memory* 10 (March 1998): 25–58.

———. *Origins of the Other: Emmanuel Levinas between Revelation and Tradition.* Ithaca, NY: Cornell University Press, 2005.

Nancy, Jean-Luc. *The Ground of the Image.* Translated by Jeff Fort. New York: Fordham University Press, 2005.

———. *The Inoperative Community.* Translated by Peter Connor, Lisa Garbus, Michael Holland, and Simona Sawhney. Minneapolis: University of Minnesota Press, 1991.

Nancy, Jean-Luc, and Philippe Lacoue-Labarthe. *Le mythe Nazi.* Paris: L'aube, 1991.

———. *Retreating the Political.* Edited by Simon Sparks. London: Routledge, 1997.

Neher, André. *L'existence juive: Solitude et affrontements.* Paris: Seuil, 1962.

Newton, Adam Zachary. *L'essence du prophétisme.* Paris: Presses universitaires de France, 1955.

———. *The Fence and the Neighbor: Emmanuel Levinas, Yeshayahu Leibowitz, and Israel among the Nations.* Albany: State University of New York Press, 2001.

Nietzsche, Friedrich. *The Portable Nietzsche.* Edited by Walter Kaufmann. New York: Viking, 1959.

———. *Werke.* 15 vols. Leipzig: C. G. Naumann, 1899–1905.

Oriol, Philippe, ed. *Bernard Lazare: Anarchiste et nationaliste juif.* Paris: Honoré Champion, 1999.

Ory, Pascal, and Jean-François Sirinelli. *Les intellectuels en France: De l'affaire Dreyfus à nos jours.* Paris: Armand Colin, 1986.

Otto, Rudolph. *Das Heilige: Über des Irrationale in der Idee des Göttlichen und sein Verhältnis zum Rationalen.* Gotha: F. A. Perthes, 1924.

———. *The Idea of the Holy.* Translated by John W. Harvey. London: Oxford University Press, 1924.

Ouston, Phillip. *The Imagination of Maurice Barrès.* Toronto: University of Toronto Press, 1974.

Péguy, Charles. *Notes politiques et sociales.* Paris: Cahiers de l'Amitié Charles Péguy, 1957.

———. *Notre jeunesse.* Paris: Gallimard, 1933.

———. *Oeuvres en prose, 1909–1914.* Paris: Pleiade, 1957.

———. *Un poète l'a dit.* Paris: Gallimard, 1953.

Peperzak, Adriaan. "Emmanuel Levinas: Jewish Experience and Philosophy." *Philosophy Today* 27 (1983): 297–305.

Plato. *The Republic.* Translated by Richard W. Sterling and William C. Scott. New York: Norton, 1985.

Poirié, François. *Emmanuel Lévinas: Essai et entretiens.* Arles: Actes sud, 1996.

Poliakov, Leon. *The History of Anti-Semitism.* 4 vols. New York: Vanguard, 1965–85.

Poster, Mark. *Existential Marxism in Postwar France: From Sartre to Althusser.* Princeton, NJ: Princeton University Press, 1975.

Prajs, Lazare. *Péguy et Israël.* Paris: Nizet, 1970.

Raffoul, François. "Being and the Other: Ethics and Ontology in Levinas and Heidegger." In *Addressing Levinas*, ed. Eric Sean Nelson, Antje Kapust, and Kent Still. Evanston, IL: Northwestern University Press, 2005.

Rancière, Jacques. *Disagreement: Politics and Philosophy.* Translated by Julie Rose. Minneapolis: University of Minnesota Press, 1999.

———. *La mésentente*. Paris: Galilée, 1995.

Renan, Ernest. "What Is a Nation?" In *Discours et conferences*. Paris: C. Levy, 1887.

*La Révolution française et le rabbinat*. Avignon: Imprimerie spéciale de la cara-
vane, 1890.

Ricoeur, Paul. *La métaphore vive*. Paris: Seuil, 1975.

———. *The Rule of Metaphor*. Translated by Robert Czerny. Toronto: University
of Toronto Press, 1977.

Robbins, Jill. *Altered Readings*. Chicago: University of Chicago Press, 1999.

Rolland, Jacques, ed. *Emmanuel Levinas*. *Les Cahiers de La nuit surveillée*, no. 3.
Paris: Verdier, 1984.

Rosenberg, Alfred. *The Myth of the Twentieth Century*. Torrance: Noontide, 1982.

Rosenzweig, Franz. *The Star of Redemption*. Translated by William W. Hallo.
Boston: Beacon, 1972.

———. *Der Stern der Erlösung*. Frankfurt a.M.: Suhrkamp, 1993.

Rotenstreich, Nathan. *Jews and German Philosophy: The Polemics of Emancipation*.
New York: Schocken, 1984.

Rybalka, Michel. "Publication and Reception of *Anti-Semite and Jew*." *October*,
no. 87 (Winter 1999): 161–83.

Sartre, Jean-Paul. *Anti-Semite and Jew*. Translated by George J. Becker. New York:
Schocken, 1965.

———. *Being and Nothingness*. Translated by Hazel E. Barnes. New York: Washington Square, 1992.

———. *Between Existentialism and Marxism*. Translated by John Mathews. New
York: Morrow Quill, 1979.

———. *Cahiers pour une morale*. Paris: Gallimard, 1983.

———. *Critique de la raison dialectique*. Paris: Gallimard, 1960.

———. *Critique of Dialectical Reason*. Vol. 1. Translated by Alan Sheridan-Smith.
London: Verso, 2004.

———. *L'espoir maintenant: Les entretiens de 1980*. Paris: Verdier, 1991.

———. *L'être et le néant*. Paris: Gallimard, 1943.

———. *Hope Now: The 1980 Interviews*. Translated by Adrian can den Hoven.
With an introduction by Ronald Aronson. Chicago: University of Chicago
Press, 1996.

———. *Literary and Philosophical Essays*. Translated by Annette Michaelson. New
York: Criterion, 1955.

———. *Le mur*. Paris: Gallimard, 1939.

———. "New Writing in France: The Resistance 'Taught That Literature Is No
Fancy Activity Independent of Politics.'" *Vogue*, July 1945, 84–85.

———. *Notebooks for an Ethics*. Translated by David Pellauer. Chicago, University
of Chicago Press, 1992.

———. *Plaidoyer pour les intellectuels*. Paris: Gallimard, 1972.

———. "Présentation." *Les temps modernes*, October 1, 1945, 1–21.

———. *The Problem of Method*. Translated by Hazel E. Barnes. London: Methuen,
1961.

———. *Réflexions sur la question juive*. Paris: Paul Morihien, 1946.

———. *Qu'est-ce que la littérature?* Paris: Gallimard, 1948.

———. *Questions de méthode*. Paris: Gallimard, 1960.

———. *The Wall*. Translated by Lloyd Alexander. New York: New Directions, 1948.

———. *What Is Literature? and Other Essays*. Cambridge, MA: Harvard University Press, 1988.

———. *The Words*. Translated by Bernard Frechtman. New York: George Braziller, 1964.

Scholem, Gershom. *The Correspondence of Walter Benjamin and Gershom Scholem, 1932–1940*. Translated by Gary Smith and Andre Lefevre. Cambridge, MA: Harvard University Press, 1992.

———. *The Messianic Idea in Judaism*. Translated by Michael Meyer. New York: Schocken, 1971.

———. *On Jews and Judaism in Crisis*. Edited by Werner A. Danhauser. New York: Schocken, 1976.

Schor, Naomi. "Anti-Semitism, Jews and the Universal." *October*, no. 87 (Winter 1999): 107–17.

Schwarzschild, Steven. *The Pursuit of the Ideal: Jewish Writings of Steven Schwarzschild*. Albany: State University of New York Press, 1990.

Seale, Patrick, and Maureen McConville. *Red Flag/Black Flag: French Revolution 1968*. New York: Putnam's, 1968.

Segel, Benjamin W. *A Lie and a Libel: The History of the Protocols of the Elders of Zion*. Translated and with an introduction by Richard S. Levy. Lincoln: University of Nebraska Press, 1995.

Shapiro, Susan E. "'Écriture judaïque': Where Are the Jews in Western Discourse?" In *Displacements: Cultural Identities in Question*, ed. Angelika Bammer. Bloomington: Indiana University Press, 1994.

Soucy, Robert. *Facism in France: The Case of Maurice Barrès*. Berkeley: University of California Press, 1972.

Steiner, George. *No Passion Spent*. London: Faber & Faber, 1996.

Sternhell, Zeev. *The Birth of Fascist Ideology: From Cultural Rebellion to Political Revolution*. Princeton, NJ: Princeton University Press, 1994.

———. *La droite révolutionnaire, 1885–1914*. Paris: Seuil, 1978.

———. *Maurice Barrès et le nationalisme français*. Paris: Armand Colin, 1972.

Suleiman, Susan. "Sartre's *Réflexions sur la question juive*." In *The Jew in the Text*, ed. Linda Nochlin and Tamar Garb. London: Thames & Hudson, 1995.

Surya, Michael. *Georges Bataille: An Intellectual Biography*. Translated by Krysztof Fijalkowski and Michael Richardson. London: Verso, 2002.

Szafran, Maurice. *Les juifs dans la politique française: De 1945 à nos jours*. Paris: Flammarion, 1990.

Taylor, Charles. "The Politics of Recognition." In *Multiculturalism and the Politics of Recognition*, ed. Amy Guttman. Princeton, NJ: Princeton University Press, 1992.

Thomson, Alex. *Deconstruction and Democracy*. London: Continuum, 2005.

Touraine, Alain. *The May Movement: Revolt and Reform*. Translated by Leonard F. X. Mayhew. New York: Random House, 1971.

Trigano, Shmuel. "The Jews and the Spirit of Europe: A Morphological Approach." In *Thinking about the Holocaust After Half a Century*, ed. Alvin H. Rosenfeld. Bloomington: Indiana University Press, 1997.

———. "Lévinas et le projet de la philosophie-juive." *Rue Descartes: Emmanuel Levinas* 19 (February 1998): 141–64.

Ungar, Steven. *Scandal and Aftereffect*. Minneapolis: University of Minnesota Press, 1995.

Vidal-Naquet, Pierre. *The Jews*. Translated by David Ames Curtis. New York: Columbia University Press, 1995.

———. *Les juifs: La mémoire et present, II*. Paris: La découverte, 1991.

Viswanathan, Gauri, ed. *Power, Politics, and Culture: Interviews with Edward Said*. New York: Pantheon, 2001.

Voltaire. *Dictionnaire philosophique*. Paris: Cluny, 1930.

———. *Philosophical Dictionary*. Translated by Peter Gay. New York: Basic, 1962.

Weber, Elisabeth. *Questioning Judaism*. Translated by Rachel Bowlby. Stanford, CA: Standford University Press, 2004.

———. *Questions au judaïsme*. Paris: Desclée de Brouwer, 1996.

Weingrad, Michael. "Jews (in Theory): Representations of Judaism, Anti-Semitism, and the Holocaust in Postmodern French Thought." *Judaism* 45, no. 1 (Winter 1996): 79–98.

Willett, Cynthia, ed. *Theorizing Multiculturalism: A Guide to the Current Debate*. London: Blackwell, 1998.

Wilson, Nelly. *Bernard-Lazare*. Cambridge: Cambridge University Press, 1978.

Wohlfarth, Irving. *The Problems of Modernity: Adorno and Benjamin*. London: Routledge, 1989.

Wolitz, Seth. "Imagining the Jew in France: From 1945 to the Present." *Yale French Studies* 85 (1994): 119–34.

Wood, David, and Robert Bernasconi, eds. *Derrida and Différance*. Evanston, IL: Northwestern University Press, 1988.

Yerushalmi, Yosef Hayim. *Freud's Moses: Judaism Terminable and Interminable*. New Haven, CT: Yale University Press, 1991.

Yovel, Yirmiyahu. *Dark Riddle: Hegel, Nietzsche, and the Jews*. Cambridge: Polity, 1998.

# Index